Advanced
Lotus® 1-2-3®

Advanced Lotus® 1-2-3®

With Applications

Hossein Bidgoli
Professor and Coordinator
Management Information Systems
California State University, Bakersfield

West Publishing Company
St. Paul   New York   Los Angeles   San Francisco

• Release 2.01

Copy Editor: Sheryl Rose
Composition: green apple graphics
Cover Photograph: David Bishop

Printed in the United States of America
Library of Congress Cataloging-in-Publication Data

Bidgoli, Hossein.
    Advanced Lotus 1-2-3 with applications
    Includes index.
    1. Lotus 1-2-3 (Computer program) 2. Business — Data processing. I. Title.
HF5548.4.L67B528 1989 005.36'9   88-27726
ISBN 0-314-47211-8

To my sisters Azam and Akram for buoying my
spirits throughout the years.

About The Author

Dr. Hossein Bidgoli is Professor and Coordinator of Management Information Systems at California State University, Bakersfield. He holds a Ph.D. degree in systems science from Portland State University with a specialization in design and implementation of MIS. His master's degree is in MIS from Colorado State University. Dr. Bidgoli's background includes experience as a systems analyst, EDP consultant, and financial analyst. He was director of the Microcomputer Center at Portland State University and has done computer-related consulting for numerous organizations including Tektronix, Inc. in Oregon.

Dr. Bidgoli has authored four texts and numerous professional papers and articles presented and published throughout the United States on the topics of computers and MIS. For the past nine years, he has been conducting executive seminars on all aspects of computers and MIS.

Table of Contents-in-Brief

Table of Contents

Lotus Command Menu

Preface

Lotus 1-2-3, one of the microcomputer industry's best-selling software packages, set the standard for electronic spreadsheets. Because Lotus has many complex and powerful features, it is important that students learn all facets of the program. Often, however, introductory courses leave students on their own to discover the advanced features of this powerful software.

There are several books and manuals about Lotus; some are brief and do not cover the entire programs. Others are detailed and teach Lotus commands, but do not tell readers how to utilize them. This book, which uses Release 2.01, covers the entire Lotus package in an easy-to-understand, step-by-step manner. The text, written for advanced Lotus courses, first provides students with a quick overview of the program's elementary materials. After refreshing readers' knowledge, the text focuses on advanced topics.

For Release 1A users, comprehensive coverage in Appendix E highlights the differences between Release 2.01 and Release 1A. Chapter 1 deals with information regarding the most recent version of Lotus, Release 3.0.

All programs and screens in the book also are on three disks and are available from the publisher. The disks will be helpful to both computer sophisticates and students learning about advanced Lotus features. Because the disks make it unnecessary to type files from scratch, students and professors will save time and avoid the frustration of busy work.

The programs related to macros, also available on the disk, can be accessed and modified by readers to enhance their understanding of macro design and use.

Although the text follows a logical sequence, the chapters have been written to stand alone. Thus students will quickly understand any part of the text.

The placement of lengthy topics, such as database operations and macros, also has been divided into a logical format: important skill-building material appears first. This will make reading easy, and provide students with a textbook and an invaluable reference tool.

In each chapter, many examples highlight real-life situations. This will put Lotus, as a tool, into perspective and emphasize the specific commands or series of commands being discussed.

Each chapter ends with 15-40 review questions, which are divided into two groups. Group 1's questions reinforce the material covered in the chapter; group 2's exercises require hands-on participation from students. Answering group 2 questions will quickly make students acquainted with Lotus.

A comprehensive lab assignment ties in with the material discussed in the first 10 chapters. This assignment starts with basic Lotus operations, then uses advanced features throughout the chapters. The assignment will provide students with an excellent learning experience.

Appendix A covers basic DOS information, which will benefit novice and experienced users. The appendix provides information on hard disk management, directories, sub-directories, EDLIN, and the new operating system (OS/2).

Technical matters regarding Lotus operations are discussed in Appendix B. The material provides clear instructions for first-time Lotus installers.

Appendix C provides guidelines for file transfers to and from Lotus; its tips will help students avoid the frustration of trying to import or export data. Guidelines regarding file transfers between popular databases, spreadsheets, word processing packages, and BASIC programs will assist experienced users to extend their Lotus knowledge well beyond the basics.

Appendix D provides information on SIDEWAYS, a program that enables users to print wide worksheets. This appendix also includes valuable information on more than ten software packages that are compatible with Lotus 1-2-3. This information will assist users to utilize their Lotus worksheet in many advanced operations.

Appendix G contains answers to selected questions. Readers can use the questions to test themselves about specific topics.

This text teaches the functions of commands by using examples. With this method, commands are made clear to readers because the specific functions are placed in context rather than discussing them in the abstract. The limitations and strengths of the commands also are listed.

To be called "advanced," students must have a comprehensive knowledge of database operations, graphics, and Lotus macro commands. The text provides comprehensive coverage of these topics using many real-life examples. Five chapters have been devoted to macro design and use. This coverage highlights the power of Lotus as a super-programming language.

Every example and worksheet in the text is fully documented. By looking at the worksheet, readers will be able to understand the concept underlying a particular command or series of commands.

At the end of chapters, when appropriate, a series of misconceptions and solutions have been added. In some cases, the problems are caused by improper operating procedures or outright mistakes in operation. In any case, the misconceptions and solutions will guide readers and provide them with tips for avoiding and resolving common mistakes.

At the end of this text is a comprehensive command reference list. This will help readers review the entire Lotus command structure in a few minutes, and aid them to understand Lotus commands. It serves as a handy reference tool if users are unsure about the function of a command.

Versions of this material have been tested by groups of students, including college freshmen, sophomores, juniors and seniors, graduates, bankers, financial officers, and chief executive officers working for profit and nonprofit organizations. Classroom testing provided excellent feedback concerning the suitability of the material for different levels of students and other users.

Note to the Users:

This book has been written for a variety of audiences and assumes readers have different computer backgrounds. The following guidelines are suggested:

1. If you are not familiar with the disk operating system (DOS), study Appendix A. The first group of DOS commands in Table A-1 has been organized for novice DOS users; the second group of DOS commands has been selected for advanced DOS users.
2. If you just purchased a Lotus program, refer to Appendix B. This material will help you install Lotus on your system.
3. If you want to transfer files between Lotus and other programs such as dBase, VisiCalc, BASIC, etc., read Appendix C.
4. To refresh your memory regarding elementary Lotus materials, skim through chapters 1-4.
5. Advanced Lotus users, after a quick review of chapters 1-4, should proceed to the study of chapters 5-13. Chapters 12-13 provide numerous real-life examples of Lotus applications that utilize macros. Advanced Lotus users can develop the applications further.
6. Students interested only in Lotus macros should study chapters 9-13.
7. Students interested in Lotus database capabilities should study chapters 7-8.
8. For graphics users, chapter 5 provides comprehensive coverage of Lotus graphics. Although this text can be used to focus on and learn specific Lotus features, we hope you read the entire book. The text, studied as a whole, will show you the real power of Lotus when all the pieces are put together.

Acknowledgements

Several colleagues reviewed different versions of this manuscript and made constructive suggestions. Their help and comments are greatly appreciated.

Al Bird – University of Houston
Donnie Byers – Johnson County Community College
Dominic Ciaccio – Kankakee Community College
Robert Crews – Pan American University
Diane Drozd – College of DuPage
Pat Green – Temple Junior College
Mike Harris – Del Mar College
Robert McGlinn – Southern Illinois University
Beth Murphy – DePaul University
Beverly Oswalt – University of Central Arkansas
Roy Pipitone – Erie Community College

Jim Stacey – Ithaca College
Robert Taylor – Berkshire Community College
Mark Wayne – Chabot College
Louis Wolff – Moorpark College
Chuck Zebrowski – Texas Southmost College

Many different groups of people assisted me in completing this project. I am grateful to the students who attended my executive seminars and Lotus and MIS classes. They helped me fine-tune the manuscript during its various stages.

My students, John Nylon and Matthew Hightower, deserve special thanks for their assistance in running and debugging the majority of the macro exercises in chapter 13. Sylvia O'Brien deserves special recognition; her thoroughness and dedication made it easier to complete this project. Denise Simon, Theresa O'Dell, Lee Anne Dollison, and Janine Wilson, all of West Educational Publishing, were supportive and constructive in their suggestions concerning this project.

Last, but not least, I want to thank my family for their support and encouragement throughout my education.

1

An Overview of Lotus 1-2-3

1-1 Introduction

In this introductory chapter we will provide a quick review of Lotus, presenting a brief history, technical requirements, and different uses. We will also discuss types of data, priority of operations, and review a worksheet. This chapter should refresh your memory regarding some of the important aspects of Lotus 1-2-3.

1-2 What Is a Spreadsheet?

A *spreadsheet* is simply a table or matrix of rows and columns, very similar to an accounting journal. The intersection of each row and column is called a *cell*. A cell can hold any type of data, including numbers, formulas, texts, and so forth. The major difference between an electronic spreadsheet and an accounting journal is the enhanced flexibility, speed, and accuracy provided by an electronic spreadsheet.

Theoretically, the number of applications that can be handled by an electronic spreadsheet is unlimited. In general terms, any application that can fit into a row and column setting can be handled by a spreadsheet program. This includes such applications as balance sheets, income statements, budgeting analyses, mailing lists, databases, and sales analyses.

The size and sophistication of a spreadsheet depends upon the type of program. Some are dedicated spreadsheets such as VisiCalc, while some are integrated packages such as Lotus and Framework that perform many more applications than just spreadsheet analysis. We will discuss these applications in the next section.

1-3 Spreadsheets Prior to Lotus

The spreadsheet era began in 1978 when Robert Frankston, Dan Bricklin, and Dan Fylstra designed and marketed VisiCalc, the most popular microcomputer software prior to Lotus.

VisiCalc was very impressive for its time. The package, designed to perform spreadsheet analysis, included a matrix of 254 rows and 63 columns, many commands, and several built-in functions such as formulas for performing different tasks. However, it had some serious shortcomings. Earlier versions of VisiCalc did not have Boolean operations such as OR, AND, NOT, and IF. Furthermore, it performed very limited graphics and database operations.

Some of these limitations were improved in later versions of VisiCalc. A DIF (Data Interchange Format) utility program developed by Software Arts translated VisiCalc spreadsheets to other programs for graphics, databases, and word processing applications. VisiTrend/VisiPlot and VisiFile could communicate with VisiCalc through the DIF utility. Yet there was still a need for a more sophisticated spreadsheet program.

SuperCalc (by Sorcim Corporation), a CP/M-based program introduced in 1980, was an improvement on VisiCalc. This package also included 254 rows and 63 columns.

Later releases of VisiCalc, ProCalc, and SuperCalc tried to eliminate the shortcomings of the earlier VisiCalc. Integrated packages were introduced that could perform spreadsheet analysis, data management, graphics, word processing, and communication operations. These new packages included Multiplan (by Microsoft Corp.) Context MBA (by Context Management Systems), Framework (by Ashton-Tate), and Lotus 1-2-3 (by Lotus Development Corporation). Some experts believe Lotus is not a true integrated package because it does not have word processing and communication capabilities. This is by no means a serious problem because Lotus files can communicate with several popular word processing programs, as well as with some communication packages. Data transfer between Lotus and other software will be discussed in Appendix C.

1-4 Lotus: The Ultimate Spreadsheet

Lotus 1-2-3 Release 1 was introduced in 1982. Within six months it was upgraded to Release 1A and in mid-1985, Release 2 appeared on the market. Later Release 2.01, a simple upgrade over Release 2.0, was introduced. Release 3, which is considered to be a major release, is expected to be introduced in 1988. Lotus Development Corporation has been continuously improving this product. After VisiCalc, Lotus has been one of the best sellers of all time.

Lotus includes three functions in one. Besides spreadsheet analysis, it is able to perform graphics and data management operations.

Lotus Release 2 features a spreadsheet of 8,192 rows and 256 columns, which equals 2,097,152 cells. To utilize this capacity, a huge main memory is needed. At the present time there is no microcomputer that can use this spreadsheet without upgrading its memory.

By using a series of commands and built-in functions, Lotus can perform some very impressive operations. Its data management functions are quite effective. Since the database generated by Lotus resides in RAM, the speed of manipulation is impressive (see Chapters 7 and 8).

The Lotus graphics function is also relatively sophisticated. Using spreadsheet data, Lotus can generate bar, pie, stacked-bar, line, and XY graphs. Again, since the data for graphics is provided by the spreadsheet component of Lotus, the speed of calculation and redrawing is very high. As you will see in Chapter 5, doing what-if analysis with Lotus graphics is fast and simple.

Release 2 of Lotus increased the size of the worksheet from 2,048 rows to 8,192 rows and added many new functions. By itself, Lotus can serve as a forecasting package (see the discussion of data regression in Chapter 8).

1-5 New Upgrade: Release 2.01

There are specific technical improvements in Release 2.01 as compared to Release 2, but they are minor and will not change the way you have been using Release 2. These specific improvements are as follows:

1. File retrieval time is faster than before.
2. Labels (nonnumeric data) are now equal to zero in mixed formulas.
3. Financial functions can have positive as well as negative arguments.
4. COMMAND.COM (see Appendix B) is not required on the utility disk.
5. A fractional number can be defined specifically (in Release 2, financial functions ignored any fractional portion of the term argument).

There are also some minor changes in driver installation and installation for hard disk systems. If you are using Release 2.01, we advise you to spend a few minutes reading its brief manual. We will talk about the differences between Release 2.01 and Release 1A in Appendix E.

1-6 Most Recent Version: Release 3

Release 3 is the most recent version of Lotus 1-2-3. We have gathered the following information from Lotus Development Corporation.

1-2-3 Release 3 has been rewritten in C to provide support for multiple hardware platforms. The product will be compatible (file and macro) with all previous releases of 1-2-3, and will read and write Release 2.X files directly.

1-2-3 Release 3 is character-based and will support DOS 2.X, 3.X, and OS/2 operating environments in the same package. The DOS version will be compatible with the Lotus/Intel/Microsoft (LIM) Expanded Memory Specification, version 4. This will allow 1-2-3 to support up to 32 megabytes of expanded memory under LIM.

Enhancements have been made to all areas of the product, including spreadsheet, graphics, database, printing, and usability.

Spreadsheet:

- Three-dimensional worksheets.

- Multiple files in memory.

- Formulas linked with files on disk as well as in memory.

- Increased size of the working area in 1-2-3 Release 3 to 256 worksheets, each containing 256 columns by 8,192 rows.

- Spreadsheet auditing and range and formula annotation.

- Automatic cell formatting.

- Techniques to maximize calculation speed: minimum recalculation of spreadsheet cells that are dependent on what's been changed, and background recalculation to allow the user to continue working in the spreadsheet.

Graphics:

- "Hot graph" window (automatic updating of an on-screen graph when the related worksheet is changed).

- Support for new graph types including open-high-low-close, mixed line and bar, area charts, and horizontal graphs.

- Support for graphic metafiles.

- Control over colors, fonts, hatching patterns, and size of graphs.

- Support for customization options such as logarithmic scaling and two Y-axes.

Database:

- Direct access to external databases (1-2-3 database functions performed on databases without having to translate external files or leave 1-2-3).

- Sorting on multiple keys (up to 256).

- Simple resorting from database entries.

Printing:

- Graphics printed directly from the 1-2-3 menu.

- Text and graphics printed on the same page.

- Support for PostScript devices.

- Print queuing.

Usability:

- Not copy protected.

- Network capabilities, including file reservation.

- Undo command.

- Keystroke recorder for easy macro creation.

Lotus Extended Applications Facility

Release 3 will have built-in hooks to support a new application programming language, currently referred to as the Lotus Extended Applications Facility. This facility goes far beyond the capabilities of macros and will allow users to extend and customize various Lotus applications. Available separately as a tool kit, this facility will replace the current Developer Tools and provide a more powerful and easy method for creating add-ins.

Multiple Environments

Lotus also has under development several other compatible versions of 1-2-3 including 1-2-3/G, designed for OS/2 and Presentation Manager; 1-2-3 for Apple Computer's Macintosh family of machines; and 1-2-3/M designed to run on IBM mainframes with the same familiar user interface as 1-2-3 for the PC.

1-2-3 is the only spreadsheet that will be available in a range of environments — offering the user consistent commands, an efficient way to manage and consolidate information, and standardized training, support, and custom applications development.

1-7 Lotus Technical Requirements

Lotus is written in assembly language, the closest language to machine language. This has improved the speed of calculation in Lotus as compared to earlier spreadsheet programs. Lotus is available for PCs or PC-compatibles such as the IBM PC, NEC Advanced PC, Wang Professional, AT & T 6300, Zenith Data System, Texas Instruments Professional Computer, and so forth.

Two 360K double-sided disk drives are needed or a hard disk. Your computer must also have a minimum of 256K of RAM. Remember, Lotus Release 2 requires almost 192K of RAM to load (if it is loaded directly to the memory without going through the Lotus Access System). A color or monochrome display with Hercules graphics or another graphics adapter is also needed if you want to use the graphics capability. The operating system must be either PC or MS DOS, version 2 and above (see Appendix A).

1-8 Lotus Access System

When your entire package is installed (see Appendix B), you can access any part of Lotus 1-2-3 through the Lotus Access System. All Lotus operations are stored on the System disk except instructions for printing graphics, which is done by the PrintGraph disk. To start the Lotus Access System, put the DOS disk in drive A. At the A> prompt, pull DOS out and put the Lotus System disk in drive A. Type Lotus and hit **Return**. Your screen will display the material shown in Figure 1–1.

You can choose any of the options shown in the figure either by moving the cursor to one of the options and pressing the **Return** key or by typing the first letter of the option name. The last option, Exit, takes you out of the Lotus Access System and puts you back at the DOS A> prompt.

To get into the main section of Lotus, first put the System disk in drive A. Then you can either go through the Lotus Access System or type 123 at the A> prompt. If your computer has 256K of RAM memory, the latter option will give you approximately 15K more memory.

Figure 1–1 Lotus Access System

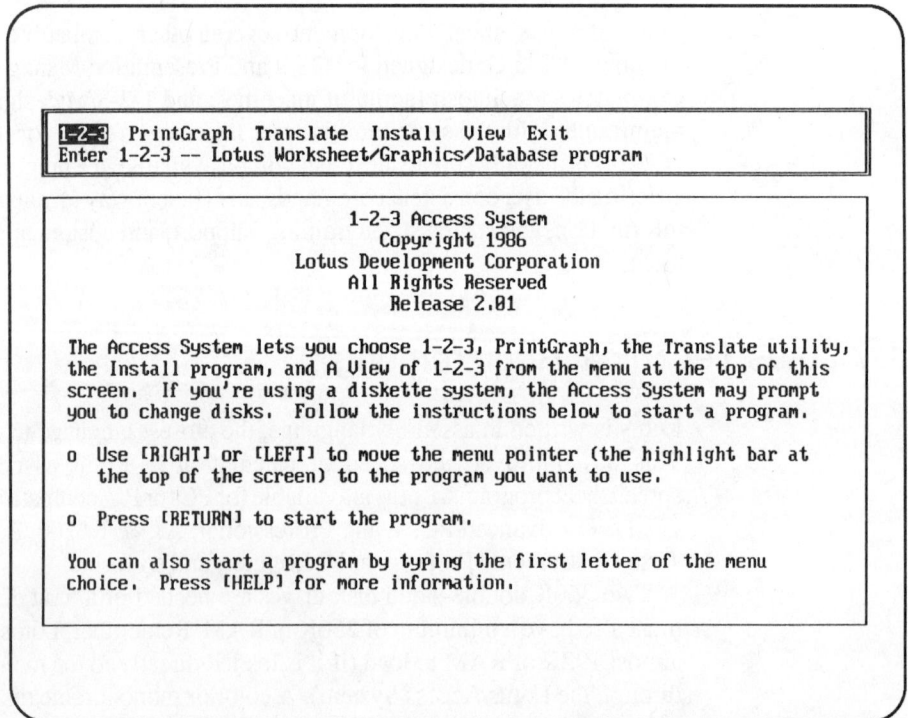

```
 ┌──────────────────────────────────────────────────────────────┐
 │ 1-2-3  PrintGraph  Translate  Install  View  Exit              │
 │ Enter 1-2-3 -- Lotus Worksheet/Graphics/Database program       │
 └──────────────────────────────────────────────────────────────┘

 ┌──────────────────────────────────────────────────────────────┐
 │                    1-2-3 Access System                         │
 │                      Copyright 1986                            │
 │                 Lotus Development Corporation                  │
 │                     All Rights Reserved                        │
 │                       Release 2.01                             │
 │                                                                │
 │  The Access System lets you choose 1-2-3, PrintGraph, the Translate utility, │
 │  the Install program, and A View of 1-2-3 from the menu at the top of this │
 │  screen.  If you're using a diskette system, the Access System may prompt │
 │  you to change disks.  Follow the instructions below to start a program. │
 │                                                                │
 │  o  Use [RIGHT] or [LEFT] to move the menu pointer (the highlight bar at │
 │     the top of the screen) to the program you want to use. │
 │                                                                │
 │  o  Press [RETURN] to start the program. │
 │                                                                │
 │  You can also start a program by typing the first letter of the menu │
 │  choice.  Press [HELP] for more information. │
 └──────────────────────────────────────────────────────────────┘
```

When you are in Lotus, you can always access the on-line Help menu by just pressing the F1 key. Remember, to access the Help menu, you must have a diskette in your default drive. Any diskette will do. The Help menu will appear. You have access to more than 200 screens of the Help menu. Figure 1–2 shows an example of the Help menu.

You can move around the Help menu by using the cursor. If you look at the bottom left corner of this menu, you will see the words Help Index. The Help Index will give you several options. Figure 1–3 shows the Help Index menu. Point the cursor to any of these options and press the **Return** key. The section on Error Messages, for example, tells you how and when an error might occur and how to resolve the error. To leave the Help menu, just press the **Escape (ESC)** key.

To return to the Lotus Access System, invoke the main menu by pressing the question mark key (the slash key on the IBM keyboard or its equivalent on other keyboards) and then choose the Quit option. This option gives you two choices, NO or YES. If you choose YES, you will return to the Lotus Access System.

If you do not want to access 1-2-3 and its companion programs from the Lotus Access System, you can access any of them directly from DOS. To do so, at the A> prompt do the following:

- To access 1-2-3, type 123, assuming the 1-2-3 System disk is in drive A.

- To access a view of 1-2-3, type VIEW, assuming the View of 1-2-3 disk in drive A.

Figure 1–2 A Sample Screen of the Help Menu

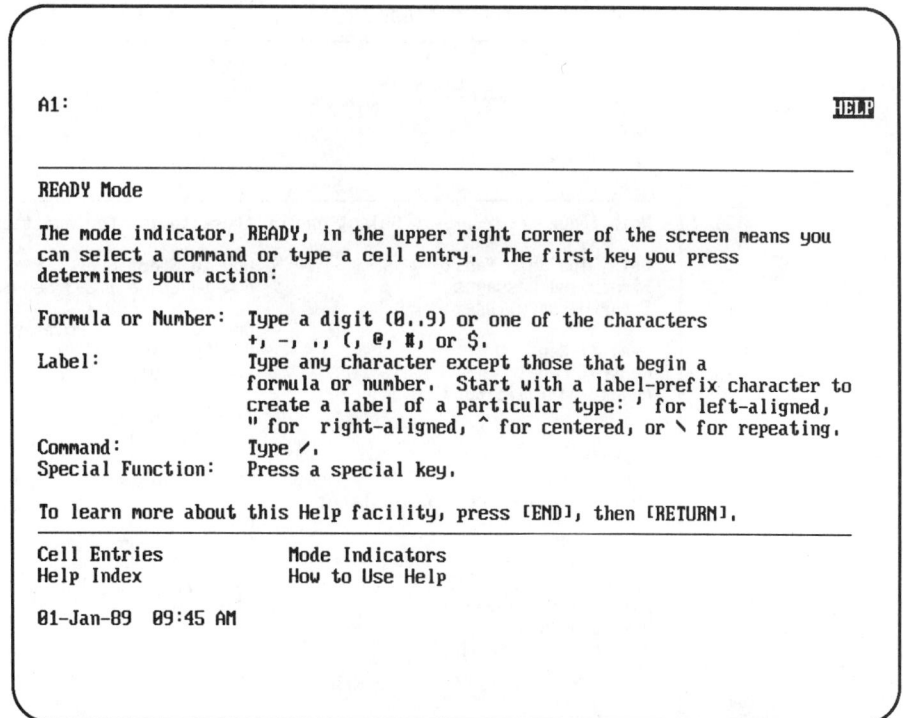

```
A1:                                                                    HELP


READY Mode

The mode indicator, READY, in the upper right corner of the screen means you
can select a command or type a cell entry.  The first key you press
determines your action:

Formula or Number:   Type a digit (0..9) or one of the characters
                     +, -, ., (, @, #, or $.
Label:               Type any character except those that begin a
                     formula or number.  Start with a label-prefix character to
                     create a label of a particular type: ' for left-aligned,
                     " for  right-aligned, ^ for centered, or \ for repeating.
Command:             Type /.
Special Function:    Press a special key.

To learn more about this Help facility, press [END], then [RETURN].

Cell Entries          Mode Indicators
Help Index            How to Use Help

01-Jan-89  09:45 AM
```

- To access PrintGraph, type PGRAPH, assuming the PrintGraph disk is in drive A.

- To access Translate, type TRANS, assuming the Utility disk is in drive A.

- To access Install, type INSTALL, assuming the Utility disk is in drive A.

- To access Access, type LOTUS, assuming the 1-2-3 System disk in in drive A.

1-9 What Lotus Can Do for You

The number of applications handled by Lotus is practically unlimited. Lotus can be used in any discipline, although its major applications have been in the areas of finance and accounting. In the next sections we will provide you with an overview of some of the more common Lotus applications. Chapters 12 and 13 present specific applications in the areas of finance, accounting, production, forecasting, and so on.

1-10 Lotus as a Decision Support System (DSS) Tool

In the past couple of years, Lotus has been utilized and evaluated as a *Decision Support System (DSS) tool*. A DSS tool or product is any package that can help a

Figure 1–3 Help Index Menu

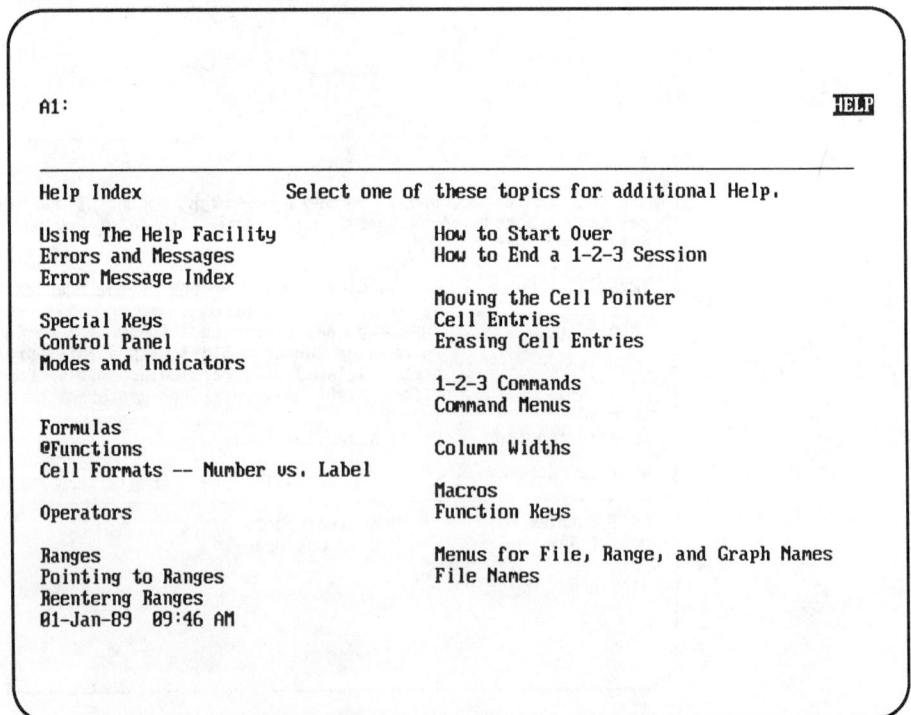

```
A1:                                                              HELP


     Help Index              Select one of these topics for additional Help.

     Using The Help Facility           How to Start Over
     Errors and Messages               How to End a 1-2-3 Session
     Error Message Index
                                       Moving the Cell Pointer
     Special Keys                      Cell Entries
     Control Panel                     Erasing Cell Entries
     Modes and Indicators
                                       1-2-3 Commands
                                       Command Menus
     Formulas
     @Functions                        Column Widths
     Cell Formats -- Number vs. Label
                                       Macros
     Operators                         Function Keys

     Ranges                            Menus for File, Range, and Graph Names
     Pointing to Ranges                File Names
     Reenterng Ranges
     01-Jan-89  09:46 AM
```

decision maker in making decision, or making a better decision. It must be able to perform what-if analysis, goal-seeking operations, sensitivity analysis, and modeling analysis. As you will see throughout this book, Lotus can perform any of these functions. Some of these capabilities are readily available in the Lotus command structure. Others can be done by developing a series of macros (see Chapters 9–11). Let us explain these major functions.

1-11 Using Lotus for What-If Analysis

What-if analysis calculates the effects of a change in one variable over other variables or the entire worksheet. A simple example is a break-even analysis. The break-even point (see Chapter 11) is the number of units generated in which total cost is equal to total revenue. For example, if the fixed cost of the operation is $500, the variable cost of a unit is $10, and the selling price is $15, the break-even point would be 100 units. At this point the company will neither lose nor gain. Above this point, the company will gain; below this point, the company will lose. Lotus can help you discover what will happen to the break-even point if the selling price is increased to $17; or what will happen to the break-even point if the variable costs are decreased by $3.

This feature can be used in a much more complex environment. Think about a budgeting problem. Let us say you have projected the budget of your company for the next five years. Suddenly you notice that the projected income for 1991 will be reduced by five percent. What is the impact of this income reduction on the entire budget? Thousands of accurate calculations must be done in order to answer this question. But if the budget is on a Lotus spreadsheet, this amazing program can perform all the recalculations almost instantly with no errors! Just change the old value to the new value and press the **Return** key.

What-if analysis can be done with graphics as well. Change any data item and press the F10 (Graph) key in READY mode and your graph will be redrawn instantly (see Chapter 5).

As you will see in Chapter 8, Lotus provides you with table-handling procedures; that in itself is a good application of what-if analysis. You can monitor the impact of one or two variables on the entire worksheet, or on a specific range.

1-12 Using Lotus for Goal-Seeking Analysis

Goal-seeking analysis is the reverse of what-if analysis. Here you may ask a question such as, "In order to generate $5,000,000 of total sales, how much should I advertise?" If you build an advertising model (Lotus provides you with the facilities to do this), performing such goal-seeking analyses will be easy.

Goal-seeking can be done by changing one variable or many variables; it depends on the complexity of your model. Remember, by using Lotus macros (see Chapters 9–11) you can build fairly complex mathematical models. When the model is built, leave the rest of the calculations to the speed and accuracy of Lotus.

1-13 Using Lotus for Sensitivity Analysis

Sensitivity analysis basically means monitoring the range, elasticity, or variation within a model. Let us say that you are paying $15 per hour to the workers on the assembly line. If the workers ask for more money, how much more can you pay and still make a profit? Sensitivity analysis studies the range of variation for a variable and calculates its effect over the entire system. Again, Lotus will provide you with such a facility.

1-14 Building an Integrated DSS Using Lotus

By combining a powerful spreadsheet, database management, and graphics, Lotus can be used as an integrated DSS package.

The database component can be used for storing data. Basic database operations (see Chapters 7–8) can be performed. Data can be organized in different orders, sorted, or searched. This data can be used for modeling analysis. Lotus Release 2 has provided you with many different models. Many of the built-in functions, especially the financial functions, can be used directly. The data matrix and data regression commands can be used for building sophisticated forecasting models (see Chapter 8). When the analysis and model building is done, the graphics portion of Lotus provides you with five different graphs. Since all operations (database, spreadsheet, and graphics) are performed within one package, the speed and effectiveness are amazingly high.

1-15 Types of Data

Throughout your Lotus program you will see three types of data:

- numbers

- formulas

- labels

Numbers (values) are any data items starting with the digits 0 through 9, -, +, $, or (. Numbers can be up to 240 characters long but cannot include spaces or commas. They can have up to 15 decimal places. Very small and very large numbers are presented in scientific notation.

For those of you who have forgotten scientific notation, following are some examples:

Regular Numbers		Scientific Notation Equivalent	
5000	=	5E+3	$5 * 10^3$
2500000	=	25E+5	$25 * 10^5$
.0000006	=	6E-07	$6 * 10^{-7}$
.00007	=	7E-05	$7 * 10^{-5}$

Formulas must begin with the digits 0 through 9, ., +, -, (, @, #, or $, and can be up to 240 characters long. For example, +A7+AB is a valid Lotus formula. Formulas cannot contain spaces. If the first part of the formula is a cell address, the formula must start with a plus sign (+).

Data items that are neither formulas nor numbers are considered *labels*. Labels can be up to 240 characters long. They either begin with a prefix (see the next section) or start with characters that are not included in the starting position of numbers or formulas. However, labels can be made up of numeric digits (for example, phone numbers, street address), as long as this data will not be used in any arithmetic operations. To enter numeric data as a label, precede it with a label prefix. Long labels occupy the next right cell(s). If the next right cell is already occupied, Lotus will truncate the label on the screen but not in memory.

1-16 Types of Label Prefixes

Labels may begin with four different prefixes indicating whether they are left-justified, right-justified, or centered. By default, Lotus will left-justify a label. Following are the types of prefixes:

' (apostrophe)   left-justified

" (double quotation) right-justified

^ (caret)   centered (this character is the uppercase of key 6, i.e., press the **Shift** key and then key 6)

\ (backslash)repeat the same character until the length of the cell is filled out

Remember, prefixes are used only for labels. Numbers are always right-justified and don't need a prefix.

1-17 Arithmetic Operations in Lotus

Lotus, like any other programming language, follows a series of rules to perform arithmetic operations. These priority rules are as follows:

1. Expressions inside parentheses have the highest priority.
2. Exponentiation (raising to power) has the next highest priority.
3. Multiplication and division have the third highest priority.
4. Addition and subtraction have the fourth highest priority.
5. When there are two or more operators with the same priority, Lotus proceeds from left to right.

The following examples should make this clear. First, Lotus uses * (asterisk) for multiplication, ^ (caret) for exponentiation, and / (slash) for division. If A=5, B=10, C=2, calculate the following:

1. A+B/C   = 10
2. (A+B)/C =   7.5
3. A*B/C   = 25
4. (A*B)/C = 25
5. A^C/2   = 12.50

1-18 Entering Formulas

You can enter formulas by typing. This process is straightforward. However, you must remember to start a formula with a plus sign, +.

Another way to enter formulas is called *pointing*. Let us say that in Figure 1–4 we would like to add cells A1, B1, C1, and D1 and store the result in cell G1 by pointing. Do the following:

1. Move the cursor to cell G1 and enter a + sign.
2. Move the cursor to cell A1 (you will see A1 in the control panel), then add another + sign.
3. Move the cursor to cell B1, then add another + sign.
4. Move the cursor to cell C1, then add another + sign.
5. Move the cursor to cell D1.

Now you are done adding; just press the **Return** key. You will see that the result, 10, is stored in cell G1.

Figure 1–4 Adding the Contents of Four Different Cells by Pointing

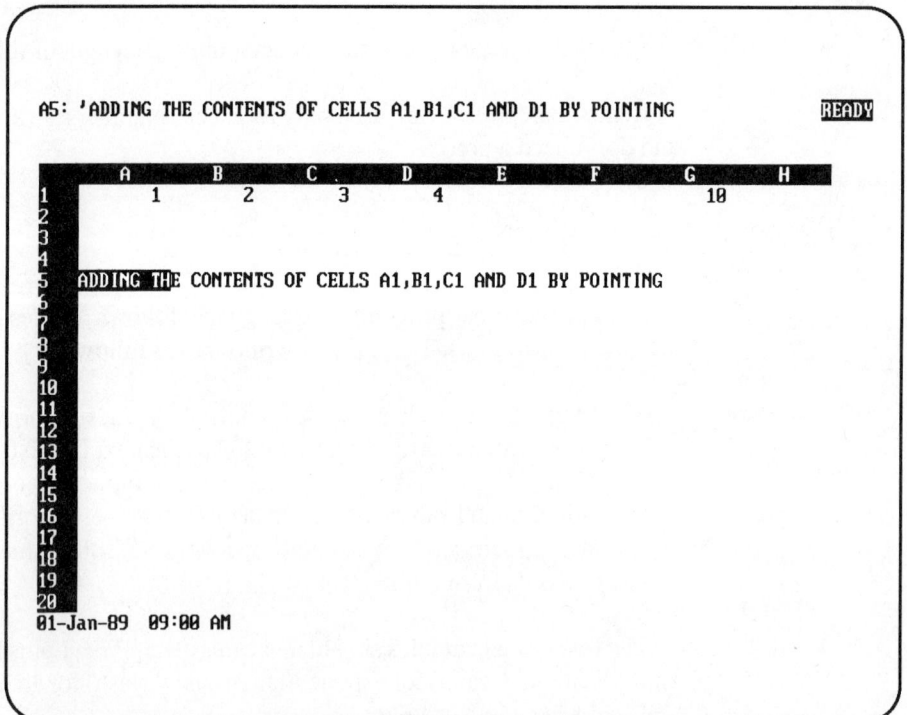

When you design a formula, remember to always use the cell address instead of the cell value (A1 vs 1 or B1 vs 2 in this example). The reason for this is that you can change the contents of the cells and the result would be automatically recalculated. If you use values instead of cell addresses, you have to change the formula whenever you change the values.

Pointing can be very helpful if you are dealing with long, complicated formulas. You can transfer the content of a cell to another cell by just starting with a plus sign in the destination cell, moving the cursor to the target cell, and pressing the **Return** key. Pointing is more accurate since we humans are prone to make transpositions and typographical errors.

1-19 Control Panel

The first three lines from the top of a worksheet are called the *control panel*. The first line usually gives you four types of information. Let us examine Figure 1–5.

The first item on the first line is the cell address. This is the present position of the cursor. In our case, cell D16 is the present cell. This position can be changed by using one of the arrows in READY mode.

The second item gives the format of the present cell. In our case it is C4, meaning currency with four decimal places (discussed in Chapter 2).

The third item is the column width of the present cell. In this case it is 20 characters (discussed in Chapter 2).

Figure 1–5 A Sample Worksheet

```
D16: (C4) [W20] 500000                                        READY

          A        B        C           D            E
1              THIS IS AN EXAMPLE OF AN UNFORMATTED INCOME STATEMENT
2
3                                      1984         1985
4
5    Sales                             500000       650000
6        Cost of Goods Sold           -225000      -310000
7    Gross Profit                      275000       340000
8        Expenses                     -200000      -230000
9    Net Income                         75000       110000
10
11
12              THIS IS AN EXAMPLE OF THE CURRENCY FORMAT
13
14                                      1984         1985
15
16   Sales                        $500,000.0000   $650,000
17       Cost of Goods Sold      ($225,000.0000) ($310,000)
18   Gross Profit                 $275,000.0000   $340,000
19       Expenses                ($200,000.0000) ($230,000)
20   Net Income                   $75,000.0000    $110,000
01-Jan-89  09:01 AM                                   CAPS
```

The fourth item is the content of the present cell. This can be labels, numbers, formulas, etc. In our case it is 500000.

The second line of the control panel provides you with the main menu.

The third line of the control panel lists either options available to the menu that can be chosen by the cursor, or the menu selected by the present position of the cursor.

1-20   Indicators

In the upper right corner of Figure 1–5, at the lower right, and at the lower left you will see information called *indicators*. There are three types of indicators.

Mode Indicators

This indicator appears at the upper right corner of the worksheet. There are 11 types of mode indicators, as follows:

WAIT   Lotus is executing or processing a command. Wait until this indicator goes off before performing any task. For example, you may have to wait while Lotus recalculates a balance sheet after changing one of the figures.

VALUE   The user is entering a number or a formula; for example, +A1+A2 or 655.

READY   Lotus is ready to accept the next command or the next action. For example, in this mode you can enter data onto the worksheet, call the menu, and so on.

POINT   The cell pointer is pointing to a cell or a range. For example, if you copy the contents of cell A1 to B1..B10 and you are at the FROM or TO choices of the Copy command, the indicator mode shows POINT (discussed in Chapter 2).

MENU   The Lotus menu is being displayed. For example, when you press the / key (the question mark key) in order to invoke the main menu, the indicator shows MENU.

LABEL   Indicates that the user is entering a label. This means any nonnumeric data. For example, if you type I AM BUSY, you will see LABEL as the indicator.

HELP   Indicates that the user has invoked the HELP facility. To see this, press F1.

FIND   This indicator is displayed when the /Data Query Find operation is in progress (see Chapter 7).

FILES   This indicator appears whenever a File menu is invoked; for example, /File Save or /File Retrieve (see Chapter 2).

ERROR   This indicator appears whenever an error occurs. For example, if you try to save a file in Drive B and it does not have any disk, you will receive the ERROR indicator. To clear the error indicator, press either **Return** or **Escape**.

EDIT   This indicator appears when you perform any kind of editing. To see this, press F2.

Status Indicators

Status indicators appear at the lower right corner of the worksheet. There are 10 of these indicators, as follows:

SST   This indicator, which means single step, appears when a macro is being executed one step at a time. As we discuss in Chapter 9, you can execute a Lotus macro one step at a time for debugging purposes.

STEP   When this indicator appears, it means the single step mode has been turned on. To turn the step on, press Alt and F2 at the same time. To leave STEP mode, press Alt and F2 again.

SCROLL   Shows that the **Scroll Lock** key is on. If you move the cursor down, the worksheet will scroll.

OVR   This indicator appears if the **Insert** key is on. This is used when you perform some editing task.

NUM   Indicates that the **Num Lock** key is on. When this key is on, the arrow keys serve as a numeric pad (a calculator) and cannot be used for moving the cursor around the worksheet.

END   Indicates that the **End** key is on. This is used in combination with any of the arrow keys.

CMD   Appears during the execution of a macro. As soon as the macro execution is over, this indicator will disappear.

CIRC   This indicator appears if a cell is referring to itself. For example, if you type +A11 in cell A11, you will see CIRC. This will happen only if the recalculation order is natural. (For different types of recalculation, see Chapter 2.)

CAPS   Indicates that the **Caps Lock** key is on. To turn it off, press the key again. You will see CAPS in Figure 1–5.

CALC   Indicates that the worksheet needs to be recalculated. If you press F9 this indicator will disappear.

Date and Time Indicators

This indicator appears at the lower left corner of the screen. You can change this format by using/Worksheet Global Default Other or delete the indicator with / Worksheet Global Default Other Clock None.

1-21   Function Keys

Lotus utilizes the IBM-type keyboard function keys very effectively. These keys make it much easier for you to perform different tasks. Some of these keys are used individually, such as F1 through F10; some of them are used in conjunction with other keys, such as F2 + Alt for STEP. Following are descriptions of these keys.

F1 (Help)   Accesses the Lotus on-line help facility.

F2 (Edit)   Shifts Lotus into EDIT mode. The contents of the current cell will be displayed in the control panel and the cursor will be positioned at the end of the cell's content. Now you can perform any editing. When you are done, hit the **Return** key.

F3 (Name)   Displays all the range names in POINT mode. If you press this key a second time, you will receive a full screen listing of all the range names. This is helpful if you would like to know all the range names before issuing another name (discussed in Chapter 2).

F4 (Abs)   In POINT mode, changes an address from absolute, to mixed, to relative. The cycle can continue (discussed in Chapter 2).

F5 (GoTo)   Gives you the opportunity to move to any location in the worksheet.

F6 (Window)   Moves the cursor between two split screens (discussed in Chapter 2).

F7 (Query)   Performs most recent /Data Query operation (discussed in Chapter 7).

F8 (Table)   Operates the last /Data Table command, e.g., recalculates the present table (discussed in Chapter 8).

F9 (Calc)   Recalculates the worksheet. All formulas will be calculated into their most recent values (discussed in Chapters 2 and 10).

F10 (Graph)   In READY mode, redraws the most recent graph. This is very handy for What-If analysis performed on a graph by changing different variables.

Alt + F1 (Compose)   In conjunction with other keys, used to generate international characters. For example, try Alt+F1+((left parenthesis).

Alt + F2 (Step)   Switches Lotus into single step mode for debugging a macro.

1-22 Special Keys

In addition to function keys, some other very useful keys are:

Backspace   Erases a character or a range.

Backtab (←)   In READY mode, moves the cursor one screen to the left. In EDIT mode, moves the cursor five positions to the left.

Tab (→)   In READY mode, moves the cursor one screen to the right. If the **Shift** and **Tab** keys are pressed together, they move the cursor one screen to the left. In EDIT mode, moves the cursor five positions to the right.

Break   Cancels the current operation. To activate this key, hold down the **Ctrl** key while pressing the **Break** key.

Delete (Del)   In EDIT mode, erases the current character.

Escape   Cancels the current operation, e.g., gets you out of Lotus menu, erases a line, and so on.

Alt (Macro)   In conjunction with a macro name, it will invoke that macro.

Period (.)   When you try to enter a range, it anchors the cursor if it is unanchored for pointing (discussed in Chapter 2).

Return   Finalizes the operation: entering data, issuing a command, and so on.

Summary

This chapter provided a quick review of Lotus 1-2-3. We presented several Lotus applications and discussed Lotus as an integrated DSS product. We also presented types of data, types of label prefixes, arithmetic operations, and different indicators and function keys. This chapter should refresh your memory regarding Lotus fundamentals.

Review Questions

1.* Name some spreadsheet packages prior to lotus.
2. What are the technical requirements of Lotus?
3. What is the Lotus Access System?
4. How do you access the Help Index menu?
5. How do you access the PrintGraph program?
6. What are some typical applications of Lotus?
7. What is a DSS?
8.* How and why can Lotus be used as an integrated DSS product?
9. What are some examples of what-if analysis? Of goal-seeking analysis?
10. How many types of data can be used by Lotus?
11. How many label prefixes does Lotus have?
12. What is the priority of operations?
13. Which operation has the highest priority?
14. Which operation has the lowest priority?
15. What are the indicators?
16.* How many types of indicators does Lotus have?
17. List the 10 function keys used by Lotus.
18. What are the special keys?
19. Give some uses of the special keys.
20. Using the Lotus Help Index, get a listing of all the function keys. What is the specific use of each function key?
21. Using the Lotus Help Index, get a listing of all the functions in Lotus. How many different functions are supported by Lotus?
22. Get Lotus started. Enter 2, 4, 6, 8, and 10 into cells A1 through A5, respectively. Using the pointing technique generate the sum of these cells and store the result in cell H1. What are the advantages of pointing compared with entering a formula directly?
23.* Give three examples of what-if analysis performed by Lotus. Generate a simple worksheet and perform a what-if analysis on the worksheet.
24. Generate a simple advertising model. In your model, relate the total sales to the amount of money spent on advertising. Now perform a goal-seeking analysis by changing the amount of the advertising budget to generate different levels of total sales.
25.* Using Lotus compute the following calculations:

    A1=10, A2=20, A3=30

    . A1 * A2/A3

    . (A1 + A2)/A3

    . A1/A2/A3

26. Get Lotus started. By pressing the / (slash) key, start the menu. What is the control panel? Generally speaking, how many lines of information are available in the control panel?
27. Figure 1–5 shows the time and date for this worksheet. Using the appropriate command, erase this information.
28. Generate as many mode indicators as you can. How do you generate EDIT as your mode indicator?
29. Generate a simple worksheet that includes the following information:

   . cells A1 through A15, 15 student names

   . cells B1 through B15, 15 Lotus test scores

   Now calculate the average of these 15 scores. First enter the formula directly, then use pointing.
30. Now split the screen vertically. On the second screen type a second test score for the same group of students and calculate their averages.

* These questions are answered in Appendix G.

Misconceptions and Solutions

M — Lotus provides a very large spreadsheet, 8,192 rows by 256 columns. At the present time there is no way to use this entire facility with a typical PC because of the memory requirements.

S — To utilize most of this facility, some computers can be upgraded to a bigger memory, up to four megabytes. This can be done with either Intel Above Board or AST Rampage Board.

M — Lotus has been written in 8088 assembler language. This means its processing power is higher than that of other spreadsheets. Even so, this speed will not be high enough to deal with very large spreadsheets.

S — Install an 8087 or 80287 coprocessor chip. It will immensely increase the speed of calculation. This will be very helpful when your worksheet includes a lot of mathematical calculations, sorts, table handling, and so forth.

M — When you perform editing you can move back and forth by using left or right arrows. This may be time-consuming with long labels.

S — Use the **Home** key to move to the beginning of the label and use the **End** key to move to the end of the label.

M — Nonnumeric data that starts with numbers, e.g., 29 Avenue, will be considered numeric data. You can always watch the mode indicator at the top right corner of the screen. This will tell you what type of data you are entering. The mode indicator for numbers is VALUE; for labels, LABEL.

S — Enter such data with one of the label prefixes.

M — Cell addresses, e.g., A5, A69, will be considered nonnumeric data by Lotus.

S — These values must be preceded by a plus sign (+A9) or any other numeric characters from 0 to 9, +, -, ., (, $, #, or @.

M — Entering long formulas may be time-consuming; also, accuracy may be jeopardized.

S — Use the pointing technique to enter long formulas.

M — Sometimes your arrow keys do not move.

S — Hit the **Esc** key to return to READY mode. If the arrow keys still do not work, check to see if the **Num Lock** key is on. If this is the case, press the **Num Lock** key again.

M —You are entering a formula and at the end you press the Return key. Lotus gives you a beep and you cannot get out of EDIT mode.

S — Check your parentheses to make sure that every left parenthesis is matched with a right one.

M — One commonly used method of entering a data item on the worksheet is pressing the **Return** key. This process may be slow.

S — Use several other keys in order to enter a data item. You may use the **Arrow** keys, **Home**, and the **Window** key (F6).

M — There are two options when choosing a selection from a menu. You can move the cursor to the option and then press the **Return** key, or you can type the first letter of the option. In this case, you may skip a menu if you press the **Return** key.

S — When you are choosing an option by typing the first letter of the option, don't press the Return key. Lotus automatically does this for you.

Comprehensive Lab Assignment

Design the following worksheet for the students in your Lotus class.

	A	B	C	D	E	F	G	H
1	Name	Major	Sex	Standing	Age	Test 1	Test 2	Test 3
2	Brown	MIS	M	JR	20	90	85	75
3	Jones	CS	M	JR	25	95	70	60
4	Smith	ACC	F	SO	19	85	90	90
5	Rudd	MKT	F	SO	20	99	85	100
6	Gerlads	MIS	F	SR	23	100	85	80
7	Moseley	CS	F	SR	28	80	90	100
8	Erb	CS	M	FR	18	80	90	100
9	Thomson	MIS	F	GD	35	95	80	80
10	Sapp	MGT	M	GD	45	200	90	65
11	Lopez	FIN	M	JR	22	95	92	95

1. Using the right label prefix, line up all the headings.
2. Save this worksheet under CHAPT1.

2

Lotus Commands Menu

2-1 Introduction

In this chapter we will review the Lotus commands menu. This includes worksheet and range commands. We will discuss relative, absolute, and mixed addressing and explain different types of format commands. We will also discuss file operations performed by Lotus. As you will see in later chapters, the operations performed by Lotus, from simple tasks to very complex ones, are accomplished by using these commands. Learn to understand the specific use of each command. At the end of the text, we have provided a summary of all the commands.

2-2 /Copy Command

The /Copy command enables you to copy a portion of a worksheet to another section of the same worksheet.

2-3 /Move Command

With the /Move command, you can move a portion of a worksheet to another section of the same worksheet.

2-4 Pointing

To define a range in a worksheet you have two options. First, you can type the address of a range, for example, a1..a5. Second, you can use pointing. To use the pointing technique, the mode indicator must be in POINT. At this time, press the **period** key . (>key). You have now anchored the first corner of the range. You can move the cursor in any direction until you have specified the range. When the desired range is established, press the **Return** key.

The **Esc** key removes the anchor from a range or breaks the pointing process. **Backspace, Home,** and **End** keys can also be used with pointing. For example, HOME anchors the present position of the cursor to cell A1.

2-5 Worksheet Global Commands

If you choose the Worksheet Global command from the main menu, you will see the following menu:

Format   Label-Prefix   Column-Width   Recalculation   Protection   Default   Zero

In the next sections we will explain these options.

2-6 /Worksheet Global Label-Prefix

If you choose /Worksheet Global Label-Prefix from the main menu, you will be presented with the following three choices:

Left   Right   Center

As we discussed in Chapter 1, either enter a label prefix manually or use these commands for inserting left, right, or center justification. Remember that by default, numbers are right-justified and labels are left-justified.

You should always issue the command and then type data into the worksheet. The command has no effect on data already entered in the worksheet.

2-7 /Worksheet Global Column-Width

This command enables you to set the column width for the entire worksheet. By default, the size of the column is nine characters. In many cases this default setting must be changed. For long names or labels you must extend the column width to more than nine characters. For short labels or numbers you may want to reduce this default setting. For example, for a Sex field you need a column width of one character, M or F. The column width can be changed to any number between 1 and 240, inclusive.

2-8 /Worksheet Global Recalculation

If you choose/Worksheet Global Recalculation from the main menu, you will be given the following menu:

Natural   Columnwise   Rowwise   Automatic   Manual   Iteration

In the *Natural* option, Lotus will recalculate all values that have impact over a particular formula first. For example, if a formula in cell A10 depends upon cell H35, Lotus first recalculates cell H35 and then goes to cell A10.

In the *Columnwise* option, all columns will be recalculated first, that is, from A to B to C, and from top to bottom.

In the *Rowwise* option, all rows will be recalculated first, row 1 to row 2, and so on from left to right.

In *Automatic*, Lotus recalculates the entire worksheet whenever you change any value. This is the default setting.

In the *Manual* option, Lotus recalculates the entire worksheet whenever you hit F9. This is a very useful option if you are dealing with a large worksheet and you do not want to spend a lot of time recalculating the worksheet for a minor change, or if you are making many changes but you don't want to see intermediate results.

In the *Iteration* option, Lotus uses an iteration number between 1 and 50 for Columnwise, Rowwise, and Natural options or whenever there is a circular reference (a cell is referring to itself). When the iteration number is reached, the calculation will stop.

2-9 /Worksheet Global Protection

This command works in conjunction with /Range Protect and /Range Unprotect to protect a worksheet or a portion of a worksheet from unwanted changes. When you issue this command, you will be given two choices: Enable or Disable. With the Enable facility on, only unprotected area can be accessed and modified. Remember, the /Worksheet Erase command can always erase your worksheet (protected or unprotected worksheet).

2-10 /Worksheet Global Default

When you choose /Worksheet Global Default from the main menu, you will be presented with the following menu:

Printer   Directory   Status   Update   Other   Quit

The Printer option will give all the settings for the printer, as follows:

• *Interface*   describes the connection between Lotus and your printer (parallel or serial)

• *Auto-LF*   tells you whether your printer automatically issues a line-feed after a carriage return

- *Left*   sets the left margin; default is 4
- *Right*   sets the right margin; default is 76
- *Top*   sets the top margin; default is 2
- *Bottom*   sets the bottom margin; default is 2
- *Pg-Length*   sets page length; default is 66
- *Wait*   allows you to pause
- *Setup*   specifies a string of control characters; default is a blank (see Chapter 3)
- *Name*   tells you which printer to use; default is the first printer

The Directory option tells you the current directory.

The Status option gives you the present default settings of your system, for example, left margin, right margin, and so forth. This is a helpful command to use periodically in order to find out the default settings of your system.

The Update option enables you to save current settings in the configuration file (123.CNF file). If you change the default drive from B: to A: or C:, you must use/ Worksheet Global Default Update in order to save these new settings. If you do not do this, the next time you access your worksheet, your current directory will be B:. If you do not want to save this new change, you must use /Worksheet Global Default Quit to leave the menu.

The Other option will give the following choices:

- *International*   Under this option you get Punctuation, Currency, Date, Time, and Quit. Punctuation describes the characters used by Lotus for thousands separators, argument separators, etc. Currency tells you the sign used for currency, e.g., $. Date specifies different date options. Time will give you four different time formats. Quit will put you back into the previous menu.
- *Help*   This option is used for accessing the Help facility. You have two choices: Instant and Removable. If you choose the Instant option, Lotus provides you with Help when you hit F1. If you choose the Removable option, Lotus closes the Help facility whenever you leave. To make this change permanent, you have to use the Update command.
- *Clock*   This option gives you the format for the date and time presented in the lower left portion of your screen. There are three options: Standard, International, and None. The Standard option is the default setting. If you choose the International option, you must use the international settings for date (D4) and time (D9), as discussed later in this chapter. If you choose None, the date and time will not be displayed on the screen. This is nice if you do not want to see these items all the time.

2-11 /Worksheet Global Zero

This command gives you the option of displaying or suppressing zeros in the worksheet. If you invoke /Worksheet Global Zero, you will be given No and Yes options. Choosing Yes will suppress the display of zero. Remember, the zero will still be in the memory.

2-12 /Worksheet Insert

This command allows you to insert either a row or a column into your worksheet. This can be very helpful during database operations discussed in Chapter 7. To activate this command, type /Worksheet Insert. Lotus gives you the options of Column or Row. Choose either Row or Column, then hit the **Return** key. Lotus will ask for the cell address of the row or the column. For column or row insertion all you need is the address of one cell. For example, D1..D1 will insert a blank in column D if the option chosen was Column. A1..A1 will insert a blank in row 1 if the option chosen was Row.

2-13 /Worksheet Delete

This command allows you to delete rows or columns. When you invoke /WD you will be given two options: Row and Column. When you delete a row or column with this command, the deleted area will be closed up.

2-14 /Worksheet Column

If you type Worksheet Column from the main menu, you will be given the following options:

Set-Width   Reset-Width   Hide   Display

Set-Width allows you to change the width of a column. The default setting is nine characters. You can extend the size of a column from 1 to 240 characters, inclusive. Reset-Width allows you to return the column width to its default setting.

The Hide option allows you to hide a portion of the worksheet without erasing anything. This command is useful in report generation. You may hide data that you do not want to print and redisplay it after printing.

The Display option redisplays the hidden columns, which will be marked by asterisks next to the column letters.

2-15 /Worksheet Erase

This command allows you to erase the entire worksheet. If you invoke /Worksheet Erase, you will be given two options: Yes and No. The Yes option erases the worksheet. Be careful. Be sure that this is what you want to do. If you haven't saved it, the erased worksheet is gone for good.

2-16 /Worksheet Titles

The Worksheet Titles command freezes rows or columns along the top or left side of the screen. This enables you to see either the top portion, the side portion, or both, of your worksheet as you move around it. If you use/Worksheet Titles, you will be given the following options:

>   Both   Horizontal   Vertical   Clear

• *Both* freezes the rows above and the columns to the left of the cursor. To see the effect of this command, all the data must be to the left and above the cursor position.

• *Horizontal* freezes the rows above the cursor. This means you can move around the cursor vertically in the worksheet, but the row or rows above the cursor are fixed.

• *Vertical* freezes the columns to the left of the cursor. This means you can move around the cursor horizontally in the worksheet but the column or columns to the left of the cursor are fixed.

• *Clear* unfreezes the worksheet.

2-17 /Worksheet Window

Using /Worksheet Window allows you to split the screen to view two versions of a worksheet, formatted and unformatted, at the same time. When you invoke / Worksheet Window you will be given the following choices:

>   Horizontal   Vertical   Sync   Unsync   Clear

The Horizontal option creates a split screen with two horizontal windows. To produce such a worksheet, move the cursor to a particular row (row 2 or any row below this), then type /WWH. If you invoke this command in row 1 you will hear a beep. This means you cannot split the screen in row 1.

The Vertical option creates a split screen with two vertical windows. To produce such a worksheet, move the cursor to a particular column (column B or any column to the right of column B), then type /WWV.

The Unsync option allows independent movement in either window.

The Clear option removes the second window from your worksheet.

To move the cursor between the two windows, press F6. The default for scrolling is Sync.

2-18 /Worksheet Status

This command provides you with information about available memory, recalculation method, current format, label prefix, column width, zero suppression, and global protection. This can be very helpful when you want to erase some unwanted data, speed up the processing time by changing the recalculation method, get a view of the current settings, and so on.

2-19 /Worksheet Page

This command inserts a page break into the worksheet, useful when writing reports. When you print a worksheet, a new page will start at the page break. To use this command, move the cursor to the row below where you want the page break, then issue the /Worksheet Page command. The location of the break will be given by ::, which must be positioned in column A.

2-20 /Range Protect

You can protect a portion of your worksheet from being deleted by using the /Range Protect command. This means that you will not be able to erase this portion accidentally. To use this command, first you must use /Worksheet Global Protection Enable in order to turn on the protection facility. Now you can remove the protection from any range in the worksheet with the /Range Unprotect command, enter data into the range, and then protect it using /Range Protect command. If a range is protected and you try to erase its contents, you will get an error message.

2-21 /Range Label

As we discussed in Chapter 1, Lotus enters numbers by default as right-justified and labels by default as left-justified. The arrangement for labels can be changed either by including a label prefix manually or by using /Range Label, Left, Right, or Center. These commands change the label prefix of a cell that contains labels (nonnumeric data). They do not have any effect on numbers.

2-22 /Range Erase

This command can be used for erasing a specified portion of a worksheet. (Remember, it cannot erase a protected area of a worksheet.) To erase a single cell, move the cursor to that particular cell, type /Range Erase, and then press the **Return** key.

2-23 /Range Name Create

To perform any Lotus operations in a certain range, two options are available. Let us say you are trying to add the contents of cells A1, A2, A3, and A4. You can refer to these four cells as A1..A4 or you can give this range a name; then from this point you may refer to the range by using its name. To name a range you have to use the /Range Name Create command. A range name can have up to 14 characters. Try to use meaningful names and avoid names such as A14 or G23. These names are misleading because you do not know if they are cell addresses or range names.

You can use /Range Name Label to name an adjacent cell. With this option you can use Right, Down, Left, and Up. For example, if cell G1 contains "Commission Rate" as the name for cell H1. Naturally, you can use Up, Left, and Down options, depending upon where the desired cell and cursor are at any specific time.

To delete a range name use /Range Name Delete. This will erase a specific range name. To erase all the range names in your worksheet, you must use /Range Name Reset. What happens if you duplicate a range name? Lotus assigns the most recent range to the specific range name. To get a listing of all the range names and their addresses, use /Range Name Table. This command will give you the name of all the ranges in your current worksheet in alphabetical order. Remember to position the cursor in a blank area of the worksheet so the table does not overwrite good data. To issue this command all you need is the upper left corner cell of the table, which will show all range names. From this point on you will get the listing of all the range names.

When you try to use a new range name, if you are not sure which names have been utilized, press F3 in the POINT mode. This will give all the range names that are already in your worksheet. Remember, whenever you save a worksheet the range names will also be saved.

Using range names can be much easier than using range addresses. For example, if you are designing a balance sheet, your total assets would be the sum of current assets and fixed assets. All you need to use is the @SUM function. Type in the following formula: @SUM (current asset, fixed asset). (All Lotus functions will be discussed in Chapter 4.)

2-24 /Range Justify

This command treats a continuous column of text as a line. You can use it to break a long title or heading into several shorter ones. The shorter titles will be lined up in one or several columns; it is up to you how many columns will be occupied. In Figure 2–1 we give several examples of this command. All you need to do is type your title and use the /Range Justify command. Remember, if there is data underneath the line that you are justifying, that data will be also justified and moved down. Therefore, your data won't be destroyed.

2-25 /Range Input

This command can be used to limit user input to a particular unprotected portion of the worksheet; thus, it can be very helpful during data-entry routines. If you use the command /Range Input and specify a range, you can move the cursor only to the unprotected cells in the range.

To show how the /Range Input command works, get Lotus started. Use / Worksheet Global Protection Enable in order to protect the entire worksheet. At this point, you cannot enter any data into this worksheet; all of it is protected.

```
A1: [W9] 'THIS WORKSHEET SHOWS EXAMPLES OF THE /RANGE JUSTIFY PROCEDURE    READY

           A        B        C        D        E        F        G        H
 1   THIS WORKSHEET SHOWS EXAMPLES OF THE /RANGE JUSTIFY PROCEDURE
 2
 3
 4   EXAMPLE
 5   I HAVE LEARNED SO MUCH ABOUT LOTUS 1-2-3 ALREADY
 6
 7   EXAMPLE OF RANGE JUSTIFY 1 COLUMN -- e.g., /RJ A8..A8(HIT RETURN)
 8   I HAVE
 9   LEARNED
10   SO MUCH
11   ABOUT
12   LOTUS
13   1-2-3
14   ALREADY
15
16   EXAMPLE OF RANGE JUSTIFY 2 COLUMNS -- e.g., /RJ A17..B17(HIT RETURN)
17   I HAVE LEARNED SO
18   MUCH ABOUT LOTUS
19   1-2-3 ALREADY
20
01-Jan-89  09:51 AM
```

Figure 2–1 Example of /Range Justify Command

Use the /Range Unprotect command to remove protection from range A1..A10. You can now enter data into this range with no problem. Now use the /Range Input command and define A1..A5 as your input range. At this point you can only move back and forth between A1 and A5, inclusive. There is no way to get out of this area. Using this technique, you can limit beginning users to a specified portion of your worksheet so that they cannot mistakenly erase or damage your worksheet.

Several keys can be used with the /Range Input command. These include **Backspace, Down, Edit, End, Escape, Help, Home, Left, Return, Right,** and **Up. End** will move the cursor to the end of the Input range, Home will move the cursor to the beginning of the Input range, and so on. To terminate the /Range Input command, press **Escape** or **Return** without typing any data.

2-26 /Range Transpose

This command exchanges the rows and columns of a given range; rows become columns and columns become rows. For example, a two-by-three table (two rows and three columns) becomes a three-by-two table (three rows and two columns). All you need to do is to use the /Range Transpose command. Lotus will ask you for the original range. Specify the range and hit the **Return** key. Now Lotus asks you the range for the transposed table. Specify only the upper left corner cell of the range and hit the **Return** key. Be careful. If you direct the transposed table to a part of a worksheet that is already occupied, you will lose that portion of data.

2-27 /Range Value

This command converts formulas in a given range to their numeric values. Let us assume cells A1 and A2 contain values 5 and 10. Cell A3 contains +A1+A2. If you want to copy the exact value of this formula and not the formula itself, you must use the /Range Value command first in order to translate the formula to its numerical value, then do the copying.

2-28 Relative Addressing

Lotus maintains the address of a particular cell and compares it to the origin of the worksheet. For example, in relation to a formula in cell E10, cell G4 is two columns to the right and six rows above cell E10. To make this clear, look at Figure 2–2. In cell B11 we have the formula +B9+B8+B7+B6. If we copy this formula to cell C11, Lotus is smart enough to recognize that in this cell we have to add +C9+C8+C7+C6. If we copy the same formula to cells D11 and E11, in cell D11 we will see +D9+D8+D7+D6 and in cell E11 we will see +E9+E8+E7+E6. This is called **relative addressing,** a powerful feature. It will make the task of copying a more efficient operation. Let us say you have sales data related to 100 different businesses in the first 100 columns of a worksheet. To calculate the sum of each column, all you need to do is to type a formula for one column and then copy the same formula to the other 99 columns.

Figure 2–2 An Example of Relative Addressing

```
A1: 'THIS WORKSHEET SHOWS ONE EXAMPLE OF THE RELATIVE ADDRESSING PROCEDURE  READY


         A         B         C         D         E         F         G         H
1   THIS WORKSHEET SHOWS ONE EXAMPLE OF THE RELATIVE ADDRESSING PROCEDURE
2
3   EXAMPLE
4                                   DIVISIONS
5   MONTHS     DIV 1     DIV 2     DIV 3     DIV 4
6   JAN          100       343       123       654
7   FEB          234       654       466       453
8   MAR          313       345       245       213
9   APR          321       368       907       790
10             ----------------------------------
11     TOTAL     968      1710      1741      2110
12             ==================================
13
14   IN CELL B11 WE USED THE FORMULA +B6+B7+B8+B9
15   THEN WE COPIED THIS FORMULA TO C11..E11
16
17
18
19
20
    01-Jan-89   09:51 AM
```

2-29 Absolute Addressing

There are many times when you must refer to an exact location or an exact value. Sometimes you may want to use some predefined numbers or ratios. In these cases you have to use **absolute addresses**. For example, in relation to a formula in cell E10, cell G4 is G4, when used as an absolute address.

To make this distinction clear, look at Figure 2–3. Five divisions of XYZ Company sold different amounts of a particular product. Your task is to calculate the percentage of total sales for each division. In cell C5, type formula +B5/B11. If you copy this formula to range C6..C9, you will get an error. The reason is that in every case the division unit must be divided by the total units currently in cell B11. Relative addressing will not work here. You have to make cell B11 absolute, meaning always fixed.

To make a cell absolute, put a dollar sign ($) in front of the row number and one in front of the column letter. You can either type ($) or use F4, the Abs function key. This key can change and show you four variations of relative, absolute, and mixed addressing. For example, if your cell address is A10 and in POINT mode you press F4 four times, you will see $A$10, A$10, $A10, and finally A10. Remember, to use this key you must be in POINT mode. The simplest way to enter POINT mode is to press the F5 function key (**GoTo** key).

Cell $B$11 is absolute. To make a range name absolute, precede it with a dollar sign, e.g., $ASSET.

In Figure 2–3, first we typed (+B5/$B$11) in cell C5, then copied this formula to range C6..C9.

Figure 2–3 An Example of Absolute Addressing

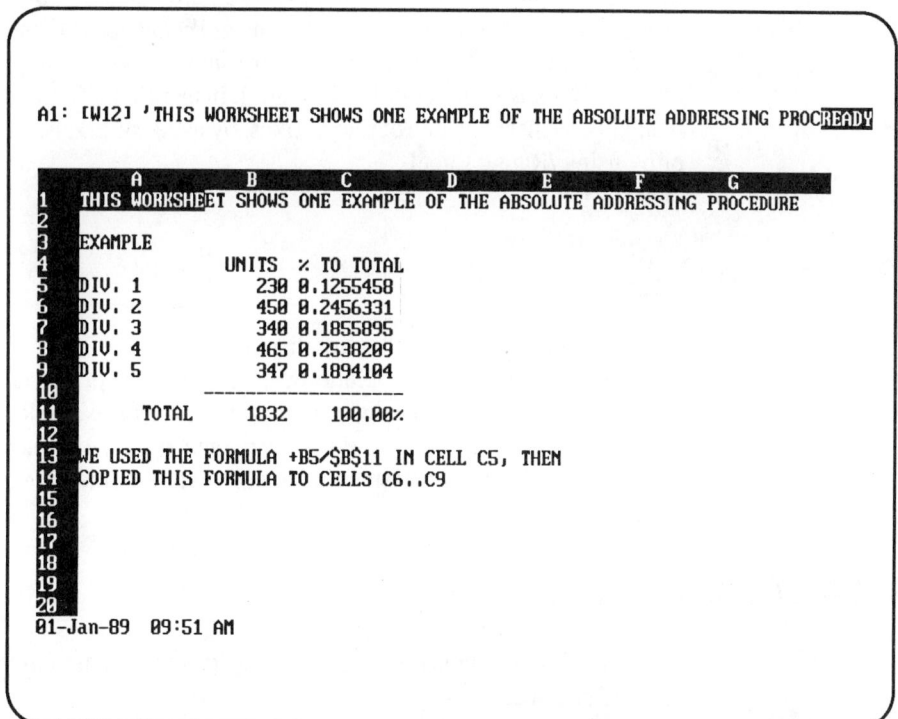

```
A1: [W12] 'THIS WORKSHEET SHOWS ONE EXAMPLE OF THE ABSOLUTE ADDRESSING PROC READY


         A          B        C         D        E        F        G
 1  THIS WORKSHEET SHOWS ONE EXAMPLE OF THE ABSOLUTE ADDRESSING PROCEDURE
 2
 3  EXAMPLE
 4                     UNITS  % TO TOTAL
 5  DIV. 1              230  0.1255458
 6  DIV. 2              450  0.2456331
 7  DIV. 3              340  0.1855895
 8  DIV. 4              465  0.2538209
 9  DIV. 5              347  0.1894104
10                   -----------------
11        TOTAL       1832   100.00%
12
13  WE USED THE FORMULA +B5/$B$11 IN CELL C5, THEN
14  COPIED THIS FORMULA TO CELLS C6..C9
15
16
17
18
19
20
01-Jan-89  09:51 AM
```

2-30 Mixed Addressing

There are cases when you want to have both relative and absolute addressing together. You can have either the row or the column fixed and the other absolute. For example, $A10 means that the column remains the same but the row changes; B$10 means that the row is fixed but the column changes. Figure 2–4 illustrates two examples of mixed addressing.

The first example in Figure 2–4 shows the discounted prices under different discount rates for two products whose original prices were $12 and $30.

The second example in this figure shows the same thing in a different format. Can you tell what is different?

2-31 Formats: Dressing Up Your Worksheet

To access the Format command in Lotus there are two options, either /Worksheet Global Format or /Range Format. /Global Format is used when the entire worksheet needs to be formatted. /Range Format is used if a specific portion of the worksheet is to be formatted. Figure 2–5 shows all the options available under the Format command. The options are Fixed, Scientific, Currency, ", ", General, +/-, Percent, Date, Text, and Hidden. The Reset option is used to change the existing setting to the global default setting.

2-32 General Option

The General option is the default Format command. You may check the worksheet status to verify this. In this format the insignificant zeros to the right of the decimal place are eliminated. Very large and very small numbers are presented in scientific notation. Labels (nonnumeric data) are left-justified. You can change this setting manually by inserting one of the prefixes, by using /Worksheet Global Label-Prefix, or by using /Range Label.

2-33 Fixed Option

The Fixed option format does not display commas or dollar signs in the formatted worksheet. Numbers can include up to 15 decimal places. If you specify fewer decimal places, the number will be rounded up. For example, if you specify three decimal positions, 6.7786 would be displayed as 6.779. This option is suitable for printing checks or financial statements, such as an income statement or balance sheet.

2-34 Scientific Option

The Scientific option is used for very large or very small numbers. You can specify up to 15 decimal places.

Figure 2–4 An Example of Mixed Addressing

```
A1: (G) [W9] 'THIS WORKSHEET SHOWS TWO EXAMPLES OF MIXED ADDRESSING          READY

        A.      B       C       D       E       F       G       H
1   THIS WORKSHEET SHOWS TWO EXAMPLES OF MIXED ADDRESSING
2
3   EXAMPLE #1
4                   DISCOUNTED PRICE AT X%
5   PRICE       0.05    0.15    0.25    0.35    0.45    0.55    0.65
6        12     11.4    10.2       9     7.8     6.6     5.4     4.2
7        30     28.5    25.5    22.5    19.5    16.5    13.5    10.5
8
9   WE USED THE FORMULA +$A$6*(1-B$5) IN CELL B6,THEN COPIED THIS FORMULA TO
10  CELLS C6..H6.WE USED FORMULA +$A$7*(1-B$5) IN CELL B7 THEN COPIED TO
11  CELLS C7..H7.
12  EXAMPLE #2              PRICES
13  DISCOUNT VALUE          60     100
14              0.05        57      95
15              0.15        51      85
16              0.25        45      75
17              0.35        39      65
18
19  WE USED THE FORMULA +$C$13*(1-$B14) IN CELL C14, +$D$13*(1-$B14) IN
20  CELL D14, THEN COPIED THE FORMULA TO CELLS C15..D17.
01-Jan-89  09:52 AM
```

Figure 2–5 Different Format Options Available in Lotus

```
A1:                                                                          MENU
Fixed  Scientific  Currency  ,  General  +/-  Percent  Date  Text  Hidden  Reset
Fixed number of decimal places (x.xx)
        A       B       C       D       E       F       G       H
1
2
3
4
5
6
7
8
9
10
11
12
13
14
15
16
17
18
19
20
01-Jan-89  09:52 AM
```

2-35 Currency Option

In the Currency option, the dollar sign will appear immediately to the left of the numbers. A comma (,) will separate every third digit. Negative numbers will appear in parentheses. The placement of the decimal is determined as in the other options. If the specified column width does not include enough space, a series of asterisks will be displayed (of course this is true for all the options).

2-36 Comma (,) Option

The comma option is very similar to Currency. The only difference is that the dollar sign is suppressed. This option is suitable for nonfinancial reports.

2-37 +/- Options

In the +/- format, a positive number will be presented with the plus sign (+), a negative number with the minus sign (-), and zero with a period. This option is considered a limited graphics option, making the job of comparing different numbers an easy task.

2-38 Percent Option

The Percent option presents numbers as a percentage of 100; for example, .05 = 5%. This option can be very useful when comparing a portion of data to the total; for example, the portion of total cost of production belonging to raw materials.

2-39 Date Options

Lotus allows five different formats for date. The beginning date in the Lotus calendar is December 31, 1899 and the last date in the calendar is December 31, 2099. December 31, 1899 is defined by Lotus as zero; January 1, 1900 equals 1; and December 31, 2099 equals 73050.

2-40 Time Options

Lotus has four different time options. In time formats fractional parts of serial numbers represent time (.000 = midnight, .5000 = noon, 20/24 = 8:00 PM and so on) as parts of a 24-hour period. You can use the @TIME and @NOW functions to generate these numbers.

2-41 Text Option

The content of each cell will be displayed as text using the Text option. For example, if cell A30 contains +H1*P1 (hours multiplied by pay rate), this formula will be displayed using the Text format. The Text option can be helpful in debugging lengthy formulas.

2-42 Hidden Option

The Hidden option is useful for hiding a portion of the worksheet or the entire worksheet. This format can generate reports that do not need to display a portion of the worksheet. (Remember that the hidden portion is still a part of your worksheet and is included in any calculations.) This format also provides security by hiding some portions of a worksheet from unauthorized users. To reveal the hidden portion, move the cursor to any other format option and press the **Return** key.

2-43 Override Option

As we mentioned earlier, the Format command can be accessed either by /Worksheet Global Format or /Range Format. /Range Format always has priority over /Worksheet Global Format. This means that the portion of the worksheet formatted by /Range Format is not affected by /Worksheet Global Format. Figure 2–6 illustrates this case. Column D in the upper worksheet was formatted by /Range Format Currency 0 (zero) Return D5..D9 Return. The lower worksheet was formatted by /Worksheet Global Format, (comma) 0 (zero) Return. As you see, column D is untouched. This is helpful for generating worksheets that use different formats for different tasks.

2-44 A Complete Example

To put the whole thing together we have created a final worksheet that uses the 17 Format options generated by Lotus to serve as a quick reference. Figure 2–7 demonstrates these options.

2-45 An Overview of File Operations

When you choose the File option from the main menu, you will be given the following choices:

Retrieve   Save   Combine   Xtract   Erase   List   Import   Directory

Figure 2–6 Example of Override Option

```
A1: ' COLUMN D HAS BEEN FORMATTED WITH THE /RANGE FORMAT CURRENCY  OPTION   READY

        A        B        C        D        E        F
1    COLUMN D HAS BEEN FORMATTED WITH THE /RANGE FORMAT CURRENCY  OPTION
2
3                                DIV. A    DIV. B    DIV. C
4
5    Sales                      $500,000   650000    800000
6      Cost of Goods Sold      ($225,000) -310000   -385000
7    Gross Profit               $275,000   340000    415000
8      Expenses                ($200,000) -230000   -261000
9    Net Income                 $75,000    110000    154000
10
11   THIS EXAMPLE SHOWS HOW THE /WORKSHEET GLOBAL FORMAT COMMA  OPTION DOES
12             NOT OVERRIDE THE /RANGE FORMAT CURRENCY  OPTION
13
14                               DIV. A    DIV. B    DIV. C
15
16   Sales                      $500,000   650,000   800,000
17     Cost of Goods Sold      ($225,000) (310,000) (385,000)
18   Gross Profit               $275,000   340,000   415,000
19     Expenses                ($200,000) (230,000) (261,000)
20   Net Income                 $75,000    110,000   154,000
01-Jan-89  09:59 AM
```

Figure 2–7 A Complete Example of All Format Options

```
E18: (T) [W12] +C7*C8                                        READY

        A        B        C        D        E        F        G
1    FORMAT OPTION       UNFORMATED         FORMATTED
2
3    GENERAL             25000              25000
4    FIXED               25000              25000.00
5    SCIENTIFIC          25000              2.50E+04
6    CURRENCY            25000              $25,000
7    ,                   25000              25,000
8    +/-                 6                  ++++++
9    D1                  31621              28-Jul-86
10   D2                  31621              28-Jul
11   D3                  31621              Jul-86
12   D4                  31621              07/28/86
13   D5                  31621              07/28
14   T1                  0.448263           10:45:30 AM
15   T2                  0.448263           10:45 AM
16   T3                  0.448263           10:45:30
17   T4                  0.448263           10:45
18   TEXT                150000             +C7*C8
19   HIDDEN              25000
20
01-Jan-89  10:00 AM
```

2-46 /File Save and Retrieve

The Save option enables you to save a Lotus file on a disk to make it permanent. A file can be saved under any valid file name (valid names are discussed in the next section). Remember that your disk must be formatted first (see Appendix A on formatting a disk.)

To save a new file, simply choose the /File Save option and enter a name. However, if you are working with an old file that has already been saved at least once and you try to save it again, Lotus will give you two options:

Cancel   Replace

If you choose the Cancel option, nothing will be saved and you return to the READY mode. Your old file will stay on the disk, untouched. If you choose the Replace option, the current worksheet will replace the old version on the disk, regardless of any difference in size.

To retrieve a file from a disk, choose the Retrieve option, then hit the **Return** key. Lotus will give you a listing of all your worksheet files. Either type the name of the file or move the cursor to a particular file and hit the **Return** key.

2-47 Lotus File Specifications

Lotus file specifications are very similar to those for DOS files (discussed in Appendix A). Lotus accepts any valid file name up to eight characters in length. Digits zero through nine and the underscore are accepted as part of a file name. Spaces are not allowed. The following are some examples of valid and invalid Lotus file names:

PAYROLL	Valid
PAY-ROLL	Valid
ROLL55	Valid
PARTNUMBER	Lotus cuts it to eight characters, then accepts it
PAY ROLL	Invalid (a space is not accepted)

Lotus generates and manipulates three types of files. These include Worksheet (WK1), Graph (PIC), and Print (PRN). Remember, Lotus Release 1A generates WKS as the extension and the Lotus student version generates WKE as the extension. Non-Lotus files are identified under Others (non-Lotus–type ASCII files, discussed in Appendix C). For example, when you save a worksheet, Lotus automatically attaches the extension WK1 to it. When you save a file, you can type your own extension. However, this file will not be retrieved automatically by Lotus nor will it show on your menu. To retrieve such a file, type the name with the extension. Any Lotus file created in version 1A can be retrieved when using version 2.0 but the opposite is not true. Version 2.0 files must be translated prior to retrieval when using version 1A. (For file translation, see Appendix C.)

Two wild card characters are accepted by Lotus: the question mark (?) and the asterisk (*). The question mark, used for one character only, means any character in a particular position. For example, B:\PAYROLL?.WK1 will give you all the files whose first seven characters are payroll and which are worksheet files. The asterisk, used for one or more characters, means any character at the end of the file name or extension. For example, B:*.WK1 will give you all the worksheet files (all files with extension WK1).

Lotus always starts its root directory with the drive name and a backslash (B:\). Within the root directory you can establish a subdirectory. (For more information on directories and subdirectories, see Appendix A.)

You can make your Lotus file self-booting. If you save your worksheet under AUTO123, Lotus will automatically load this file as soon as you start the spreadsheet.

To erase a permanent file, use the /File Erase command. But remember that if you erase a file, it is gone for good. You can use wild card characters to erase Lotus files in order to expedite the process, but this maximizes the danger of losing a file.

You can have one current file and many permanent files at any time. The current file is your current worksheet and permanent files are the files saved on your disk. If you retrieve another file, the current worksheet will be erased. If you do not want to lose this worksheet, you must save it before retrieving another file.

Lotus also allows you to save a file with a password. To do this, follow these steps:

1. Create or load a file.
2. Type File Save from the main menu.
3. Type your desired file name.
4. Hit the space bar.
5. Type P (for password).
6. Hit the Return key.
7. Type the desired password. Your password can be any of the LICS (Lotus International Character Set) characters, up to 15 characters. Do not use spaces. (See Appendix F for Lotus LICS.)
8. Hit the Return key.
9. Type the password again to verify it and hit the Return key.

If you change your mind, you can always change or delete the password. To delete a password but save the file itself, first retrieve the file with the present password. When you are ready to save it again (/File Save), you will be given the following message: B: Myfile.WK1 [PASSWORD PROTECTED] (Myfile.WK1 is any valid file name). Hit the backspace to erase the [PASSWORD PROTECTED], then hit the Return key. Now your file will be saved under the desired name, in this case Myfile. To change a password, first delete the password as we just did, hit the space bar, and type P followed by the Return key.

If you forget the password, you cannot retrieve the file. The password must be typed exactly as you created it every time you retrieve the file. Uppercase characters are considered to be different from lowercase characters.

2-48 /File Combine

The Combine option gives you three choices:

Copy   Add   Subtract

The Copy option enables you to copy an entire file or a portion of a file to the current worksheet. Be careful to remember the present position of the cursor; Copy can overwrite the current worksheet. This option gives you two choices:

Entire-File   Name/Specified-Range

Either the entire file or a specific range can be copied. Lotus will ask you for the name of the file, the range name, or range coordinates. Copy will not change the current worksheet if the cursor is in an empty location of the current worksheet.

The Add option enables you to add a file or a portion of a file to the current worksheet. Again, the position of the cursor is important. When you choose Add you will be given two choices:

Entire-File   Name/Specified-Range

You can choose either of these. The difference between Add and Copy is that Add adds the contents of the incoming file or range to the current worksheet. For example, if the cursor is at cell A1 and cell A1 contains 5, and if cell A1 from the incoming file contains 15, the final value of cell A1 in the current worksheet will be 20.

The Subtract option gives you the opportunity to subtract an entire file or a portion of a file from the current worksheet. Remember the present position of the cursor. In each of these three options the incoming data will be entered in the worksheet from the present position of the cursor to the right and down.

Remember, when you use the Add option, if an incoming file overlays a cell containing a label or a formula, Lotus discards the incoming value and retains the label or formula in the current worksheet. For example, if cell A1 in the current worksheet contains the label "COBOL", the incoming data will not have any effect on it.

2-49 /File Xtract

This option extracts and saves the entire worksheet or a portion of the current worksheet in a file on disk. Unlike Combine, Xtract does not change information in the current worksheet. Two options are given under Xtract: Formulas and Values. With the Formulas option, Lotus saves the worksheet with any formulas from the current worksheet to the extracted file. For example, if cells A1 and A2 contain 5 and 10 and cell A3 contains their sum, +A1+A2, then the Formulas option saves this worksheet and the formula.

With the Values option, Lotus saves the worksheet with only calculated values for formulas. In the above example, 15 will be extracted and saved with the worksheet, not +A1+A2. This means that you will not know how the value was obtained.

2-50 /File List, Erase, and Directory

With the /File List command you can get the listing of your entire directory. Your Lotus directory will include four types of files: WK1, PIC, PRN, and Others. You can choose any of these options and Lotus will give you a complete listing of files within any group.

The Erase option allows the deletion of files WK1, PIC, PRN, and Others. (Others includes all the files in your directory, both Lotus and non-Lotus files.)

The Directory option will tell you the current directory of your system. Usually your directory is in drive B, but it can be changed. To find the status of your directory, you can also use the /Worksheet Global Default Status command. This will display the current directory. If you have access to a hard disk, type /File Directory A: to access files on a floppy disk and then place the floppy disk in drive A. For example, if you have a hard disk and you are trying to use the disks provided with this book, you first have to issue /File Directory A:, then put one of the disks in drive A.

Summary

This chapter reviewed Lotus commands. Four categories of commands were discussed: Worksheet, Range, Format, and File commands. All Lotus operations are performed by these commands. We also discussed different types of addressing: relative, absolute, and mixed addressing. You should understand the specific use of each type of addressing.

Review Questions

1. What is the pointing technique? What are the advantages of this technique?
2. What does Global mean?
3.* What is the length of a column by default?
4. Can a protected worksheet be erased?
5. Which command is used to extend all the columns in the worksheet from 9 to 20?
6. Which command is used to freeze the horizontal and vertical headings?
7. How do you move between two split screens?
8. Is there any specific column for /Worksheet Page break or can it be any column?
9. Does the /Range Label command have any effect on the data already in the worksheet?
10.* What are the limitations of range names? Can they be of any length?
11. When you use the /Range Justify command, do you lose the data below the row that is being justified or will the data be moved down?

12. What are the applications of the /Range Input command? Of /Range Transpose?

13. What are the applications of the /Range Value command?

14. What is the difference between relative and absolute addressing?

15. What is mixed addressing?

16.* How many format options are available in Lotus?

17. What is the difference between currency and comma options?

18. What are the applications of the +/- options?

19.* How many date options are available?

20. How many time options are available?

21. How do you hide a column?

22. How do you know a column(s) is hidden?

23. What is the override option? Does /Range Format or /Worksheet Global Format have a higher priority?

24.* How many different files are supported by Lotus?

25. What are the extensions for different Lotus files?

26. What is a valid file name in Lotus?

27. How do you generate a password for a file?

28. What are the characteristics of a password?

29. What are the options under the /File Combine command?

30. What are the applications of the /File Xtract command?

31. What is the function of the Values option in the /File Xtract command?

32.* What is the function of the Text option in /File Xtract command?

33. Get Lotus started. Type COBOL in cell A1. By using pointing copy cell A1 into cells A1..H20.

34. Type BASIC in cell A1. By using pointing copy this cell in range A1..H1. Now by using the Move command, move this row of data into row A10..H10.

35. Erase the current worksheet by using /WEY. Now issue the /WGLC command. From now on all your data will be centered. Is this correct?

36.* By using /WGPE protect the entire worksheet. At this point, can you type any data into this worksheet? Can you erase this worksheet?

37. Type 5 in cells A1 and A2; in cell A3 type +A1-A2. The result must be zero. To suppress this zero, what command must be used?

38. Generate a worksheet as follows:

	A	B	C
1		Balance Sheet for Yellow Rose Company	
2			
3	Quarter 1		
4	Quarter 2		
5	Quarter 3		
6	Quarter 4		

Freeze both horizontal and vertical titles. How do you know these titles are frozen? How do you unfreeze these titles?

39. Generate a worksheet that includes 30 rows and 10 columns. Using /WP break this worksheet into two worksheets with 15 rows in each. To activate this command, is there any specific position for the cursor?

40. In cells A1 through A10 type 10 different names. These names are left-justified by default. By using the /RLC command center them. By using the appropriate command make these labels right-justified.

41. In an empty worksheet type:
"LOTUS CAN BE USED IN MANY DIFFERENT SETTINGS".
By using the /RJ command justify this message in column A. Justify it in columns A and B.

42. Generate a data entry area in range A1..H10. (The operator must be able to move the cursor only in this area.)

43. Generate a 5 by 10 worksheet (5 rows and 10 columns). Using the /RT command, transpose this worksheet. What are some of the real-life applications of the /RT command?

44. Type @NOW in cell A1. Generate five different date formats in this cell.

45. Type @TIME(11,40,30) in cell H1. Generate four different time formats in this cell.

46. Type 10 different numbers in cells A1 through A10. We would like to keep the format of cell A5 as currency, but the rest of the worksheet must be in comma format. How do you do this? Which command has the higher priority, Range or Worksheet?

47. Save the above worksheet with a password called Secret. Retrieve the file and change the password to Public.

48. Using the /File Combine command, copy a Lotus file into your current worksheet. Why is the position of the cursor so important when you use this command?

49. Using the /FX command, extract a portion of your current worksheet and save it into a file called New. What is the difference between /File Combine and /File Xtract? Which command may alter the current worksheet?

Misconceptions and Solutions

M — If you enter a new data item in a very large worksheet, Lotus immediately recalculates the entire worksheet. If you keep entering different values, this may slow down the entire process.

S — You can use /Worksheet Global Recalculation Manual. This turns the automatic recalculation off. Enter all your numbers, then press F9 (CALC).

M — When you use the /Move or /Copy commands to move or copy a data item or formula to a cell, the content of the cell will be replaced by the new data. Then any formula that refers to this cell will use this new value.

S — Direct the /Move or /Copy command to an empty cell or an area of the worksheet that does not have any relationship to your earlier formulas.

M — If you have a series of range names in a worksheet and delete a portion of that worksheet by using /Worksheet Delete or /Range Erase, your range becomes undefined, even though the names are still intact.

S — First check the addresses and listing of all your range names by using F3 in POINT mode. Then issue the command for erasing.

M — The /Move command does not transfer cell addresses in the same way that the /Copy command does. /Copy transfers relative addresses of cells. Absolute cell addresses will be transferred as absolute with /Copy but not with /Move. For example, in cells A1 and B1 type numbers 1 and 2 respectively, then use the formula $A$1+$B$1 in cell C1. Transfer this entire row to row 10 by using /Copy. You will see in cell C10 the same formula as in cell C1. If you move the original row to row 10, you will see $A$10+$B$10 in cell C10.

S — Don't try to transfer absolute addresses with the /Move command.

M — If you try to erase a portion of a row or a column of a worksheet, don't use /Worksheet Delete Row or /Worksheet Delete Column. These commands erase the entire row or the entire column.

S — Use Range Erase to erase a portion of a worksheet.

M — /Range Name Table will give you a listing of all the range names. This command may overwrite a part of your worksheet.

S — Before invoking this command, find an empty location in your worksheet. Then invoke the command.

M — You cannot use /Range Justify if any cells in a particular range are protected.

S — First use /Worksheet Global Protection Disable to turn off the protection facility, then use /Range Justify.

M — Using /Range Transpose, if a particular range contains formulas with relative addresses, Lotus won't adjust relative addresses to refer to the same cells.

S — Use the /Move command instead.

M — In the middle of your spreadsheet work you see the error message ILLEGAL CELL OR RANGE ADDRESS.

S — Check your range specification to see if this is what you wanted to do. You may have typed an undefined range.

M — You invoke a particular format command and stroke the **Return** key. The particular cell may give you a solid line of asterisks.

S — The cell is not wide enough. Use the appropriate command in order to widen the cell width.

M — When you save a file with a password, if you forget the password, you will never be able to retrieve that file.

S — Use a password that has a special meaning for you.

M — One of the options in the Lotus main menu is Quit. When you choose this option, you will leave Lotus and your work will not be saved.

S — Save your worksheet first; Lotus will not save your worksheet automatically.

M — FILE NOT FOUND is a common unfriendly error message.

S — Either the particular file is not on the disk or you spelled the name wrong. Type the right file name and possibly the drive identifier. If it still doesn't work, there should not be such a file.

M — You try to save or retrieve a file, but the mode indicator says DISK DRIVE NOT READY.

S — Check to see that there is a disk in your default drive, and that the door is closed.

M — You have done all the necessary planning, but are still running out of memory.

S — Replace formulas in the worksheet with values.

M — Working with large worksheets that involve many different ranges can be complicated.

S — One way to simplify and clarify some aspects of a complex worksheet is to use range names instead of range addresses; for example, current asset instead of A1..A10 in a typical worksheet.

M — Whenever you use the /Worksheet Titles command to perform any editing, you cannot use the arrow keys in order to enter the locked area for editing.

S — You can use the GoTo key (F5) in order to move to the locked area. Also, Titles do not pose any barrier to POINT technique.

M — /Range Justify can cause serious problems in a worksheet if there is data below the range being justified.

S — Use /Range Justify only for those labels that do not have anything underneath, that are only nonnumeric data. Otherwise some serious problems may occur.

M — To avoid all the intermediate results in a worksheet after several data entries, you should choose the manual recalculation method. However, if you are interested in seeing the result of some updates in only one cell, it may be a time-consuming process to press the F9 (Calc) key.

S — After changing any values, you can move the cursor to that particular cell, then press F2 (Edit key), then press the **Return** key. This cell will be updated immediately to its most recent value.

Comprehensive Lab Assignment

Retrieve CHAPT1 and perform the following:

1. Move all graduate students to the top of the worksheet.
2. Adjust the length of each column in order to display the data more clearly. For example, the length of the sex column should be only 1; major should be 5, etc.
3. Using /Worksheet Titles freeze both horizontal and vertical titles.
4. Generate an input data entry over the three test scores (this means the cursor must be able to move around only in this area).
5. Return input data entry to normal.
6. Move the entire worksheet down four rows.
7. Enter a title for the entire worksheet as follows:
   This worksheet illustrates the performance of a group of students in the Lotus class.
8. Using /Range Justify, justify this title into two lines.
9. Using the appropriate Format command, add one decimal to each test score.
10. Using /File Xtract, extract the name and major of all the students into a file called NAME.
11. Save the final worksheet under CHAPT2.
12. Save this file once again with a password. This time use SECRET as the password and IMPORTANT as the file name.
13. Retrieve IMPORTANT and change the password to SECRET1.

3

Report Generation

3-1 Introduction

In this chapter we discuss the /Print command, one that enables you to generate reports. Using this command and its subcommands, you can print directly to a printer or to a file for future printing. You have flexibility in determining the look of your report by specifying such aspects as margins and lengths. This command also assists you in generating reports that can be utilized later by other software such as databases, word processors, other spreadsheets, and so on (for more information see Appendix C). For printing wide worksheets Sideways, a software discussed in Appendix D can be used.

3-2 Printing to a File or a Printer

As mentioned earlier, a report can be printed directly to a printer or to a file. Since the commands are the same for both printer and file, we will only refer to the printer as the print device.

When you try to print to a file, a file name must be defined, following the rules discussed in Chapter 2. The file generated by the /Print command will use PRN as an extension, as opposed to WK1 (for worksheet) or PIC (for graphic files).

Files generated by /Print File can later be printed in DOS. At the A> prompt type TYPE filename.PRN. This file can be brought to the worksheet by the /File Import command; however, the file will lose its column and row structures. The reason for this transformation is that filename.PRN is an ASCII file (see Appendix C).

Whether printing to a printer or to a file, you have complete control over a file's size and format. This means that you can choose a specific range or ranges.

3-3 Overview of the /Print Command

When you invoke the /Print command, you will be given two options: Printer and File. Both have the following further options:

Range   Line   Page   Options   Clear   Align   Go   Quit

Range allows you to print either a specific portion of the worksheet or the entire worksheet. As usual, you can specify the range address or use pointing.

Line inserts a line or skips a line. If the printer is at the bottom of the report, this command will advance the printer to the next page.

Page skips a page or advances a page. If there is a footer, it will be printed at the bottom of the page.

Options includes several interesting choices:

Header   Footer   Margins   Borders   Setup   Pg-Length   Other   Quit

Header prints a line of text up to 240 characters below the top margin.

Footer prints a line of text up to 240 characters above the bottom margin.

Margins allows you to define Left, Right, Top, and Bottom margins.

Borders prints designated column or row headings on every page.

This can be either above or to the left of the specified range you are printing. With this option you can choose rows or columns. The areas you have identified as borders are not supposed to be included in your print range. If they are, you will get duplicate information.

Setup specifies the style and font size for a printer. The setup string, up to 39 characters, comes from a printer control code (you should consult your printer manual for specifics). It must begin with a backslash (\) and a three- or four-digit code. For example, \015 on an Epson FX80 prints compressed output.

Pg-Length defines the number of lines of text to be printed. This can be any number between 1 and 100.

Other options include several powerful commands:

As-Displayed   Cell-Formulas   Formatted   Unformatted

As-Displayed prints the report as it appears on the monitor.

Cell-Formulas prints the contents of each occupied cell in the specified print range, one cell per line.

Formatted restores the previous format settings for headers, footers, and page breaks.

Unformatted prints a specified range without headers, footers, and page breaks. This option can be very helpful when printing to a file.

The *Clear* command in the main menu provides you with the following options:

All   Range   Borders   Format

All cancels print range, borders, footers, and headers. Everything is returned to the default settings.

Range cancels the present print range.

Borders clears the present borders.

Format restores page length, margins, and setup settings to their default settings.

Align tells the printer that the user has positioned the paper at the top of a new page. This command should be used before printing a worksheet. If you do not use this command, there may be gaps in the middle of the report.

Go in the main menu executes the Print command.

Quit, as usual, gets you out of the Print menu.

3-4 Default Settings

In most cases, the printer's default settings should satisfy your needs (to see the entire default settings, use /Worksheet Global Default Printer). The default settings include the following:

Page Length	66 lines
Left Margin	4 characters from the left side of the paper
Right Margin	76 characters from the left side of the paper
Top Margin	2 lines from the top of the page
Bottom Margin	2 lines from the bottom of the page

As you have seen in the main menu of the /Print command, any of these settings can be changed, either temporarily or permanently. For temporary changes issue the command /Print Printer Options. Under Options you have:

Header   Footer   Margins   Borders Setup   Pg-Length   Other   Quit

For permanent changes first issue the command /Worksheet Global Default Printer. Change whatever you want, then choose /Worksheet Global Default Update.

3-5 Controlling Your Printer More Effectively

Several commands that we have already discussed can be used individually or collectively to enhance the effectiveness of your printer by reducing manual intervention and generating more readable output. You will see the enhanced features more clearly when you design a macro (discussed in Chapters 9–13) for printing and /or when you print to a file rather than to the printer.

/Print Printer Line skips a line. If you would like to skip a page, choose /Print Printer Page. After printing a report, select /Print Printer Align. This command will skip the printer to the beginning of a new page.

As we discussed in Chapter 2, /Worksheet Page gives a page break. This command will start a new page no matter how much of the present page is empty. When you use /Worksheet Page, you must check to see how many lines you have specified in /Print Printer Options Pg-Length. /Worksheet Page may not override this command *if* the number of lines specified by /Print Printer Options Pg-Length is less than the number of lines covered by /Worksheet Page.

3-6 Special Characters

Three special characters can be utilized for entering page numbers and the current date and for specifying the position of the header or footer, as follows:

(number sign)   Enter a page number starting at 1.

@ (at sign)   Enter current date in international format (month/day/year).

¦ (split vertical bar) Separate portions of the header or footer, either left, center, or right-justified. We show examples of this at the end of the chapter. Text by itself will be left-justified. Preceded by one split vertical bar it will be centered; preceded by two split vertical bars (¦¦), it will be right-justified.

3-7 Planning Your Printed Report More Accurately

A standard page is 66 lines; standard means 11 inches, or six lines per inch. By default, Lotus leaves two lines blank between the text and the header or footer. If your printed line is longer than the right margin, Lotus will wrap around to the next line. To avoid this, use compressed type in your setup string. Of the 66 lines, only 56 lines are available for the text.

Lines 1–2	Top margin
Line 3	Header, if any
Lines 4–5	Blank by default
Lines 6–61 (56 lines)	Your text
Line 64	Footer, if any
Lines 65–66	Bottom margin

Different printers have different setup options. With the Epson FX80 printer we used \015 to generate compressed output. To stop a printing session use the **Ctrl** and **Break** keys together. This may not stop the printer immediately, but it will stop as soon as its buffer is empty.

3-8 Printing Reports with Different Options

To show you how the /Print command works, we developed several examples. Figure 3–1 is a balance sheet for four quarters of Ocean City Tourist Attraction.

In Figure 3–2, we printed three worksheets in one report using the default option. This report was generated by using /Print, Printer, Range, A1..E52, Return, Align, Go. As you see, even the default setting will give you a readable report.

Figure 3–1 Ocean City Tourist Attraction Balance Sheet in Worksheet Form

```
A1: [W32] '                    OCEAN CITY TOURIST ATTRACTION                    READY

              A               B         C         D         E
   1                OCEAN CITY TOURIST ATTRACTION
   2            (1986-87  Figures in thousands of dollars)
   3       ------------------------------------------------------
   4                        Spring    Summer    Fall    Winter
   5       ------------------------------------------------------
   6   Current Assets
   7       Cash            $36,249   $42,495   $58,761   $72,300
   8       Accounts Receivable  26,700   23,821   22,545   22,768
   9       Inventory         8,000    7,625    9,025    8,475
  10                        -------   -------   -------   -------
  11   Total Current Assets  70,949   73,941   90,331  103,543
  12
  13   Fixed Assets
  14       Property, Plant and Equipment
  15           Land          49,121   48,700   45,600   40,410
  16           Building      82,212   82,212   79,100   78,275
  17           Leasehold Improvements  22,400   18,506   17,900   20,145
  18           Equipment      8,364    8,544    9,106    9,364
  19       Gross P, P and E  162,097  157,962  151,706  148,194
  20       Accumulated Depreciation  (48,814)  (37,600)  (36,945)  (29,725)
01-Jan-89  10:01 AM
```

Figure 3–1 (Continued)

```
A21: [W32]                                                              READY

              A               B         C         D         E
  21                        -------   -------   -------   -------
  22       Net P, P and E   113,283  120,362  114,761  118,469
  23
  24       Other Assets       545      489      513      606
  25
  26   Total Fixed Assets   113,828  120,851  115,274  119,075
  27
  28   Total Assets        $184,777 $194,792 $205,605 $222,618
  29                        =======   =======   =======   =======
  30
  31   ::
  32   Current Liabilities
  33       Accounts Payable  34,522   37,819   33,245   31,009
  34       Notes Payable     10,000   11,321    7,369    8,655
  35       Income Tax Payable  4,500    4,789    5,802    6,134
  36                        -------   -------   -------   -------
  37   Total Current Liabilities  49,022   53,929   46,416   45,798
  38
  39   Noncurrent Liabilities
  40       Long Term Debt    52,242   48,700   46,345   40,300
01-Jan-89  10:01 AM
```

```
A41: [W32]                                                          READY


                 A                    B        C        D        E
41
42  Total Liabilities              101,264  102,629   92,761   86,098
43
44  Stockholders' Equity
45     Common Stock                  2,555    2,644    2,750    2,936
46     Retained Earnings            80,958   89,519  110,094  133,584
47                                   ------   ------   ------   ------
48  Total Stockholders' Equity      83,513   92,163  112,844  136,520
49
50  Total Liabilities and Equity  $104,777 $194,792 $205,605 $222,618
51                                  =======  =======  =======  =======
52
53
54
55
56
57
58
59
60
    01-Jan-89  10:01 AM
```

Figure 3–1 (Continued)

In Figure3–3, we generated a page of a report with Header and Footer options. This report was generated by /Print, Printer, Range, A1..E52, Return, Options, Header¦¦, @, Return, Footer¦, Page #, Return, Pg-Length 66, Return, Margins Right 78, Return, Margins Top 4, Return, Margins Bottom 4, Return, Quit, Align, Go.

In Figure 3–4, we generated two pages of a report using a page break. We used the Borders Rows command under Options to show headings on both pages. This report was generated by /Print, Printer, Range A6..E52, Return, Options, Borders, Rows, A1..E5, Return, Quit, Align, Go.

In Figure 3–5, we used the Borders Columns command showing winter figures with column headings. In this case, Borders Columns was A6..A52 and Print Range was E3..E52. The report was generated by /Print, Printer, Range E3..E52, Return, Options, Borders, Columns A3..A52, Return, Quit, Align, Go.

In Figure3–6, we used the Compressed option to print the spring quarter. The setup character on the Epson FX80 is \015. The report was generated by /Print, Printer, Range A3..B52, Return, Options, Setup \015, Return, Quit, Align, Go.

In Figure 3–7 we displayed the spring quarter without enhancements. We used / Print, Printer, Range B3..B52, Return, Options, Other, As-Displayed, Quit, Align, Go.

In Figure 3–8 we displayed the spring quarter using cell formulas. We used /Print, Printer, Range B3..B52, Return, Options, Other, Cell-Formulas, Quit, Align, Go.

```
                     OCEAN CITY TOURIST ATTRACTION
                 (1986-87  Figures in thousands of dollars)
-------------------------------------------------------------------

                               Spring    Summer    Fall    Winter
-------------------------------------------------------------------

Current Assets
   Cash                       $36,249   $42,495  $58,761  $72,300
   Accounts Receivable         26,700    23,821   22,545   22,768
   Inventory                    8,000     7,625    9,025    8,475
                              -------   -------  -------  -------
Total Current Assets           70,949    73,941   90,331  103,543

Fixed Assets
   Property, Plant and Equipment
      Land                     49,121    48,700   45,600   40,410
      Building                 82,212    82,212   79,100   78,275
      Leasehold Improvements   22,400    18,506   17,900   20,145
      Equipment                 8,364     8,544    9,106    9,364
   Gross P, P and E           162,097   157,962  151,706  148,194
   Accumulated Depreciation  (48,814)  (37,600) (36,945) (29,725)
                              -------   -------  -------  -------
   Net P, P and E             113,283   120,362  114,761  118,469

   Other Assets                   545       489      513      606

Total Fixed Assets            113,828   120,851  115,274  119,075

Total Assets                 $184,777  $194,792 $205,605 $222,618
                              =======   =======  =======  =======


Current Liabilities
   Accounts Payable            34,522    37,819   33,245   31,009
   Notes Payable               10,000    11,321    7,369    8,655
   Income Tax Payable           4,500     4,789    5,802    6,134
                              -------   -------  -------  -------
Total Current Liabilities      49,022    53,929   46,416   45,798

Noncurrent Liabilities
   Long Term Debt              52,242    48,700   46,345   40,300
                              -------   -------  -------  -------
Total Liabilities            101,264   102,629   92,761   86,098

Stockholders' Equity
   Common Stock                 2,555     2,644    2,750    2,936
   Retained Earnings           80,958    89,519  110,094  133,584
                              -------   -------  -------  -------
Total Stockholders' Equity     83,513    92,163  112,844  136,520

Total Liabilities and Equity $184,777  $194,792 $205,605 $222,618
                              =======   =======  =======  =======
```

Figure 3–2 Ocean City Tourist Attraction Balance Sheet

```
                      OCEAN CITY TOURIST ATTRACTION
                  (1986-87  Figures in thousands of dollars)
          -------------------------------------------------------------

                                  Spring    Summer    Fall     Winter
          -------------------------------------------------------------
          Current Assets
            Cash                 $36,249   $42,495  $58,761   $72,300
            Accounts Receivable   26,700    23,821   22,545    22,768
            Inventory              8,000     7,625    9,025     8,475
                                 -------   -------  -------   -------
          Total Current Assets    70,949    73,941   90,331   103,543

          Fixed Assets
            Property, Plant and Equipment
              Land                49,121    48,700   45,600    40,410
              Building            82,212    82,212   79,100    78,275
              Leasehold Improvements 22,400 18,506   17,900    20,145
              Equipment            8,364     8,544    9,106     9,364
            Gross P, P and E     162,097   157,962  151,706   148,194
            Accumulated Depreciation (48,814) (37,600) (36,945) (29,725)
                                 -------   -------  -------   -------
            Net P, P and E       113,283   120,362  114,761   118,469

            Other Assets            545       489      513       606

          Total Fixed Assets     113,828   120,851  115,274   119,075

          Total Assets          $184,777  $194,792 $205,605  $222,618
                                 =======   =======  =======   =======


          Current Liabilities
            Accounts Payable      34,522    37,819   33,245    31,009
            Notes Payable         10,000    11,321    7,369     8,655
            Income Tax Payable     4,500     4,789    5,802     6,134
                                 -------   -------  -------   -------
          Total Current Liabilities 49,022  53,929   46,416    45,798

          Noncurrent Liabilities
            Long Term Debt        52,242    48,700   46,345    40,300
                                 -------   -------  -------   -------
          Total Liabilities      101,264   102,629   92,761    86,098

          Stockholders' Equity
            Common Stock           2,555     2,644    2,750     2,936
            Retained Earnings     80,958    89,519  110,094   133,584
                                 -------   -------  -------   -------
          Total Stockholders' Equity 83,513 92,163  112,844   136,520

          Total Liabilities and Equity $184,777 $194,792 $205,605 $222,618
                                 =======   =======  =======   =======
```

Figure 3–3 Ocean City Tourist Attraction: A Fancier Report!

Figure 3–4 Ocean City Tourist Attraction: With Borders Rows and Page Break

```
                  OCEAN CITY TOURIST ATTRACTION
             (1986-87  Figures in thousands of dollars)
-----------------------------------------------------------------

                         Spring   Summer    Fall    Winter
-----------------------------------------------------------------
Current Assets
   Cash                 $36,249  $42,495  $58,761  $72,300
   Accounts Receivable   26,700   23,821   22,545   22,768
   Inventory              8,000    7,625    9,025    8,475
                         -------  -------  -------  -------
Total Current Assets     70,949   73,941   90,331  103,543

Fixed Assets
   Property, Plant and Equipment
      Land               49,121   48,700   45,600   40,410
      Building           82,212   82,212   79,100   78,275
      Leasehold Improvements  22,400   18,506   17,900   20,145
      Equipment           8,364    8,544    9,106    9,364
   Gross P, P and E     162,097  157,962  151,706  148,194
   Accumulated Depreciation (48,814) (37,600) (36,945) (29,725)
                         -------  -------  -------  -------
   Net P, P and E       113,283  120,362  114,761  118,469

   Other Assets            545      489      513      606

Total Fixed Assets      113,828  120,851  115,274  119,075

Total Assets           $184,777 $194,792 $205,605 $222,618
                        ======= ======= ======= =======
```

Figure 3–4 (Continued)

```
                  OCEAN CITY TOURIST ATTRACTION
             (1986-87  Figures in thousands of dollars)
-----------------------------------------------------------------

                         Spring   Summer    Fall    Winter
-----------------------------------------------------------------
Current Liabilities
   Accounts Payable       34,522   37,819   33,245   31,009
   Notes Payable          10,000   11,321    7,369    8,655
   Income Tax Payable      4,500    4,789    5,802    6,134
                         -------  -------  -------  -------
Total Current Liabilities 49,022   53,929   46,416   45,798

Noncurrent Liabilities
   Long Term Debt         52,242   48,700   46,345   40,300
                         -------  -------  -------  -------
Total Liabilities        101,264  102,629   92,761   86,098

Stockholders' Equity
   Common Stock            2,555    2,644    2,750    2,936
   Retained Earnings      80,958   89,519  110,094  133,584
                         -------  -------  -------  -------
Total Stockholders' Equity 83,513   92,163  112,844  136,520

Total Liabilities and Equity $184,777 $194,792 $205,605 $222,618
                        ======= ======= ======= =======
```

```
------------------------------------------
                                    Winter
------------------------------------------
Current Assets
    Cash                            $72,300
    Accounts Receivable              22,768
    Inventory                         8,475
                                    -------
Total Current Assets                103,543

Fixed Assets
    Property, Plant and Equipment
        Land                         40,410
        Building                     78,275
        Leasehold Improvements       20,145
        Equipment                     9,364
    Gross P, P and E                148,194
    Accumulated Depreciation       (29,725)
                                    -------
    Net P, P and E                  118,469

    Other Assets                        606

Total Fixed Assets                  119,075

Total Assets                       $222,618
                                    =======


Current Liabilities
    Accounts Payable                 31,009
    Notes Payable                     8,655
    Income Tax Payable                6,134
                                    -------
Total Current Liabilities            45,798

Noncurrent Liabilities
    Long Term Debt                   40,300
                                    -------
Total Liabilities                    86,098

Stockholders' Equity
    Common Stock                      2,936
    Retained Earnings               133,584
                                    -------
Total Stockholders' Equity          136,520

Total Liabilities and Equity       $222,618
                                    =======
```

Figure 3–5 Ocean City Tourist Attraction: With Borders Columns

```
------------------------------------------
                              Spring
------------------------------------------
Current Assets
    Cash                      $36,249
    Accounts Receivable        26,700
    Inventory                   8,000
                              -------
Total Current Assets           70,949

Fixed Assets
    Property, Plant and Equipment
        Land                   49,121
        Building               82,212
        Leasehold Improvements 22,400
        Equipment               8,364
    Gross P, P and E          162,097
    Accumulated Depreciation  (48,814)
                              -------
    Net P, P and E            113,283

    Other Assets                  545

Total Fixed Assets            113,828

Total Assets                 $184,777
                              =======


Current Liabilities
    Accounts Payable           34,522
    Notes Payable              10,000
    Income Tax Payable          4,500
                              -------
Total Current Liabilities      49,022

Noncurrent Liabilities
    Long Term Debt             52,242
                              -------
Total Liabilities             101,264

Stockholders' Equity
    Common Stock                2,555
    Retained Earnings          80,958
                              -------
Total Stockholders' Equity     83,513

Total Liabilities and Equity $184,777
                              =======
```

Figure 3–6 Spring Quarter of Ocean City Tourist Attraction, Compressed

```
          ---------
           Spring
          ---------

          $36,249
           26,700
            8,000
          -------
           70,949


           49,121
           82,212
           22,400
            8,364
          162,097
          (48,814)
          -------
          113,283

              545

          113,828

         $184,777
         =======


           34,522
           10,000
            4,500
          -------
           49,022


           52,242
          -------
          101,264


            2,555
           80,958
          -------
           83,513

         $184,777
         =======
```

Figure 3–7 Spring Quarter of Ocean City Tourist Attraction As Is

```
B3:  \-
B4:  ^Spring
B5:  \-
B7:  (C0) 36249
B8:  (,0) 26700
B9:  (,0) 8000
B10: "-------
B11: (,0) @SUM(B7..B10)
B15: (,0) 49121
B16: (,0) 82212
B17: (,0) 22400
B18: (,0) 8364
B19: (,0) @SUM(B15..B18)
B20: (,0) -48814
B21: "-------
B22: (,0) +B19+B20
B24: 545
B26: (,0) +B22+B24
B28: (C0) +B11+B26
B29: "=======
B33: (,0) 34522
B34: (,0) 10000
B35: (,0) 4500
B36: "-------
B37: (,0) @SUM(B33..B35)
B40: (,0) 52242
B41: "-------
B42: (,0) +B37+B40
B45: (,0) 2555
B46: (,0) 80958
B47: "-------
B48: (,0) +B45+B46
B50: (C0) +B42+B48
B51: "=======
```

Figure 3–8 Spring Quarter of Ocean City Tourist Attraction: Cell-Formulas

Summary

Using the /Print command and its subcommands, you can generate reports. You can print to a printer or to a file for future printing. Margins, headers, and footers can be specified. Depending upon the type of printer you use, you can specify strings. This means you can print with different type sets, in compressed types, and so forth. The /Print command also gives you the Cell-Formulas option, which lets you print the "guts" of your worksheet in order to debug it or make further modifications.

Review Questions

1. What is the difference between printing to a file and printing to a printer?
2.* If you print to a file, how do you print the content of this file in DOS?
3. What are some of the advantages of printing to a file over printing to a printer?
4. What are the printer default settings?
5. What is the maximum and the minimum page length?
6.* Which character is used to display the current date?
7. What is the role of the Borders command?
8. How many ways can you split 58 lines of text into two pages?
9.* Does /Worksheet Page always override Pg-Length?
10.* What are some uses of the Cell-Formulas option?

11.   When do you use the Align option?

12.   How do you advance the printer to the top of a new page?

13.   What is the file extension of a file generated by /Print File?

14.* How many of the 66 lines of a page (by default) are available to you for writing text (excluding top and bottom margins)?

15.   How do you change default settings temporarily?

16.* How do you change default settings permanently?

17.   When and why do you use the Clear option?

18.   Generate a ten-row by five-column worksheet. Print this worksheet as follows:

- Using the **Shift** and **PrtSc** keys.

- Using /Print Printer with default settings.

- Using /Print Printer with top and bottom margins of eight.

- Using the Cell-Formulas option.

- Using the Compressed option.

Misconception and Solution

M — You try to use the /Print Printer command and receive an error message, PRINTER-ERROR.

S — Check your printer. It may be loosely connected, not connected at all, out of paper, or turned off!

Comprehensive Lab Assignment

Retrieve CHAPT2 and perform the following:

1.   Print the file using the **Shift** and **PrtSc** keys.

2.   Print the existing file into an ASCII file called CHAPT 3 (remember that the extension of this file will be PRN).

3.   Using the /PP command, print this file with default settings.

4.   Print the existing file with the given left and right margins.

5.   Using the appropriate commands, generate a page number and today's date on the printed file.

6.   Using the appropriate commands, generate a compressed output.

7.   Print the file using Cell-Formulas.

8.   Save the existing file under CHAPT3.

9.   Using /File Import, retrieve CHAPT3.PRN.

10.   Try to parse this file into its original fields (hint: see Appendix C).

4

Functions:
Lotus as a Modeling Language

4-1 Introduction

In this chapter we will review eight different categories of functions offered by Lotus. These include mathematical, financial, statistical, logical, string, date/time, and special functions. These functions make Lotus a powerful modeling tool. As you will see in Chapters 11–13, macro commands utilize these functions for effective macro-based application programs.

4-2 What Is a Lotus Function?

A Lotus *function* is a built-in formula for the calculation of a specific task. Lotus has eight function groups. Each has been designed to perform a unique task. For example, you have learned how to add the contents of cells A1, A2, A3 and A4 by adding +A1+A2+A3+A4. Instead of doing this, you could simply type @SUM(A1..A4). Now you can see how easy it is to perform the task using a function.

Every function follows this format:

@FUNCTION(argument1,argument2,...)

A function must begin with the at sign (@). Next comes the name of the function and one or a series of arguments in parentheses. The *argument* is the information Lotus needs in order to perform a task. Consider the function @SUM(X1,X2,X3). The function name is SUM and the arguments are X1, X2, and X3. Some functions, however, do not need any arguments.

4-3 Argument Types

Lotus accepts three types of arguments:

1. Numeric values. In the function @ABS(y), y is a value; @ABS(-5) = 5.
2. Range values. In the function @SUM(A1..A9), A1..A9 is the range address. In the function @SUM(Asset), Asset is a range name.
3. String values. In the function @UPPER("rose") = ROSE, rose is the string value. Remember, strings must be enclosed in double quotation marks.

Numeric values can have one of the following forms:

actual value	@ABS(-5)
cell address	@ABS(A11)
cell range name	@SUM(asset)
formula	@ABS((-20/4)/5)
function	@INT(@ABS(A11)+@SQRT(64))
combination	@INT(@SUM(A1..A10)+asset+2500)

Range values can have one of the following forms:

range name	@SUM(DIVISION1)
range address	@SUM(A1..A10)
combination	@SUM(DIVISION1,A1..A9,DIVISION9)

And finally, string values can have one of the following forms:

cell address	@LOWER(A1)
cell name	@LOWER(STREET) (remember street is a cell name)
actual value	@LOWER("I AM A STUDENT")
formula	@LENGTH("TITLE"&"SUB-TITLE")

When you are working with functions you must keep in mind the exact type of argument accepted by each function. For example, @SUM("TITLE") will cause an error because the @SUM function requires a numeric value or a range value, not a string value.

Seven functions do not require any arguments. These include @ERR, @FALSE, @NA, @NOW, @PI, @RAND, and @TRUE. We will talk about these later in this chapter.

The functions @CELL, @N, and @S require single-cell values as arguments; however, you must enter these values as a range, for example @N(A1..A1), or a cell address preceded by an exclamation mark, as in @N(!A1). We will discuss these later in this chapter.

4-4 Mathematical Functions

Lotus offers 17 mathematical functions. All except @PI require arguments. The arguments can be values, cell addresses, range names, formulas, or other functions. Arguments for sine, cosine, and tangent must be expressed in radians. (To convert degrees to radians, multiply the number of degrees by @PI/180.)

The trigonometric functions arc sine, arc cosine, and arc tangent return all angles in radians. (To convert radians to degrees, multiply the number of radians by 180/@PI.)

4-4-1 @ABS(A)

This function's argument must be numeric. The function always returns the positive value of the argument. Examples:

```
@ABS(5)     = 5
@ABS(0)     = 0
@ABS(-5)    = 5
@ABS("Happy Birthday") = ERR – invalid argument
```

4-4-2 @ACOS(A)

The function calculates the arc cosine of an angle and returns the angle, in radians, whose cosine is A. Argument A must be between -1 and +1. Examples:

```
@ACOS(.25)          = 1.318116 (radians)
@ACOS(-0.5)         = 2.094395 (radians)
@ACOS(1)*180/@PI    = 0 (degrees)
@ACOS(.75)*180/@PI  = 41.40962 (degrees)
@ACOS(9.5)          = ERR – invalid argument
```

4-4-3 @ASIN(A)

Argument A must be between -1 and +1. The function calculates the arc sine of an angle and returns the angle, in radians, whose sine is A. Examples:

```
@ASIN(0.25)         = 0.252680 (radians)
@ASIN(-0.5)         = -0.52359 (radians)
@ASIN(.5)*180/@PI   = 30 (degrees)
@ASIN(1)*180/@PI    = 90 (degrees)
@ASIN(9.5)          = ERR – invalid argument
```

4-4-4 @ATAN(A)

This function's argument can take any value. It calculates the two-quadrant arc tangent of an angle and returns the angle, in radians, whose tangent is A. Examples:

```
@ATAN(90)           = 1.559685 (radians)
@ATAN(-45)          = -1.54857 (radians)
@ATAN(1)*180/@PI    = 45 (degrees)
```

4-4-5 @ATAN2(A,B)

The arguments can take any numeric value. The function calculates the four-quadrant arc tangent of an angle and returns the angle, in radians, whose tangent is B/A. If both A and B are zero, the result is ERR. Examples:

@ATAN2(4,590)	= 1.564016
@ATAN2(-30, -60)	= -2.03444
@ATAN2(0, 0)	= ERR

4-4-6 @COS(A)

This function calculates the cosine of angle A, which must be measured in radians. The result is always between -1 and 1. Examples:

@COS(90*PI/180)	= 3.4E-19
@COS(60*@PI/180)	= 0.5

4-4-7 @EXP(A)

This function calculates the result of *e* (2.7182) to the *A*th power. The upper limit for A is 709; beyond this the result is too large to be stored by Lotus. Examples:

@EXP(0)	= 1
@EXP(1)	= 2.718281
@EXP(-2)	= 0.135335
@EXP(2)	= 7.389056
@EXP(1000)	= ERR – too large

4-4-8 @INT(A)

This function returns the integer portion of the argument, but it does not round the number. If you would like to round a number, either use the @ROUND function or simply add .50 to the argument of the @INT(A) function. Examples:

@INT(5.5645)	= 5
@INT(-6.45698)	= -6
@INT(9.9)	= 9
@INT(9.9+.50)	= 10

4-4-9 @LN(A)

Argument A must be greater than zero. The function calculates the natural logarithm of A. Examples:

@LN(58)	= 4.060443
@LN(1)	= 0
@LN(-5)	= ERR – invalid argument

4-4-10 @LOG(A)

Argument A must be greater than zero. The function calculates the logarithm (base 10) of A. Examples:

@LOG(25)	= 1.397940
@LOG(1)	= 0
@LOG(-5)	= ERR – invalid argument

4-4-11 @MOD(A,B)

Argument A can be any number; argument B can be any number except zero. The function calculates the remainder of A/B. The sign returned by this function will always be the same as the sign of A. Examples:

@MOD(13,7)	= 6
@MOD(11,3)	= 2
@MOD(-14,2)	= 0
@MOD(-15,4)	= -3
@MOD(15,-4)	= 3
@MOD(7,0)	= ERR – invalid argument

4-4-12 @PI

This function returns 3.141592 or PI, the ratio of the circumference of a circle to its diameter (2*PI*R/(2*R) = PI, where R is the radius of a circle).

4-4-13 @RAND

This function generates a random number between zero and one. You can use it to generate a random number between any range of numbers as follows:

@INT(@RAND*(U-L+1)+L)

where U is the upper bound, L is the lower bound. For example, if you are interested in a random number between 1000 and 100, your formula would be @INT(@RAND*(901)+100). This formula will return an integer between 100 and 1000.

4-4-14 @ROUND(A,n)

Argument n must be a value between -15 and +15. The function rounds argument A to n places. This function can round on either side of the decimal point. Examples:

@ROUND(2.435678,3)	= 2.436
@ROUND(5.567564,3)	= 5.568
@ROUND(145.267,-1)	= 150
@ROUND(145.267,-2)	= 100
@ROUND(145.267,-3)	= 0

4-4-15 @SIN(A)

This function returns the sine of angle A. The angle must be measured in radians. Examples:

@SIN(45*@PI/180)   = 0.707106
@SIN(60*@PI/180)   = 0.866025

4-4-16 @SQRT(A)

Argument A must be a positive number. The function returns the positive square root of A. Examples:

@SQRT(16)   = 4
@SQRT(25)   = 5
@SQRT(56)   = 7.483314
@SQRT(-4)   = ERR – invalid argument

4-4-17 @TAN(A)

Argument A must be measured in radians. The function returns the tangent of angle A. Examples:

@TAN(45*@PI/180)   = 1
@TAN(90*@PI/180)   = 2.9E+18
@TAN(180*@PI/180)   = -3.4E-19

Table 4-1 summarizes mathematical functions.

Table 4–1

MATHEMATICAL FUNCTIONS

@ABS(A)	Absolute value of A
@ACOS(A)	Arc cosine of A
@ASIN(A)	Arc sine of A
@ATAN(A)	2-quadrant arc tangent of A
@ATAN2(A,B)	4-quadrant arc tangent of B/A
@COS(A)	Cosine of A
@EXP(A)	E (2.718282) raised to A power
@INT(A)	Integer part of A
@LN(A)	Log of A base E
@LOG(A)	Log of A base 10
@MOD(A,B)	Remainder of A/B
@PI	PI (3.14159...)
@RAND	Random number between 0 and 1
@ROUND (A,n)	A rounded to n places
@SIN(A)	Sine of A
@SQRT(A)	Square root of A
@TAN(A)	Tangent of A

4-5 Financial Functions

Lotus has 11 financial functions. They can be utilized for cash flow analysis, investment analysis, loan installment, three methods of depreciation analysis, and many more. Before you use these functions, you should remember that term and interest rate must be expressed for the same time frame (for monthly payment, the yearly interest rate must be divided by 12 and the term must be multiplied by 12). Interest rate can be entered either as a percentage (10%) or as a decimal (.10). Lotus assumes ordinary annuity. This means that a payment is made at the end of each period and the annuity due is made at the beginning of each period.

4-5-1 @FV(payment,interest rate,term)

This function calculates the future value of a series of equal payments with a given interest rate over a period of time. The @FV function uses the following formula:

$$FV = Payment * \frac{(1 + interest)^{n-1}}{interest} \quad \text{where n = number of periods}$$

Figure 4–1 shows the future value of an IRA plan over 20 years with a $2,000 payment and an interest rate of 9 percent. This function can be very helpful for calculating the future value of an investment.

4-5-2 @PV(payment,interest rate,term)

This function calculates the present value of an investment. The payments must be equal. The function uses the following formula:

$$PV = Payment * \frac{(1 - (1 + interest)^{-n})}{interest} \quad \text{where n = term}$$

This function can be used for discounting a series of future income payments to today's value. Let us say somebody will pay you $5,000 for the next five years. How much can you sell this portfolio for today? Figure 4–2 shows an example of this function.

4-5-3 @IRR(estimate,range)

This function calculates the internal rate of return (IRR) of a series of cash inflows and outflows. Estimate can be any figure between zero and one. Range is the entire cash inflow and outflow of a particular investment. This function can be very helpful for investment analysis. Let us assume you have an investment portfolio that includes a series of cash outflows (initial cost, labor, raw materials, etc.) and a series of cash inflows (the income that may be generated by the investment). Let us assume that you have no money to invest in this project. You go to a bank for a loan. At what interest rate can you afford to implement the project? It depends on the internal rate of return. If the IRR is 12 percent and the bank is willing to lend you money at a rate less than 12 percent, you can proceed. At an interest rate of 12 percent you will neither lose nor gain and at a rate more than 12 percent you will lose. Figure 4–3 illustrates an example of this function.

Figure 4–1 Future Value of an IRA Investment

```
B6: 'INTEREST RATE OF 9% WILL BE USED TO DISCOUNT THE ANNUITY.                    READY

        A         B         C         D         E         F         G
1  ===================================================================
2                       @FV(PAYMENT,INTEREST RATE,TERM)
3  ===================================================================
4  IN THIS EXAMPLE,THE FUTURE VALUE OF AN ORDINARY ANNUITY  IS
5  CALCULATED.   THE ORDINARY ANNUITY PAYS $2,000  FOR A TERM OF 20
6  YEARS.   AN INTEREST RATE OF 9% WILL BE USED TO DISCOUNT THE ANNUITY.
7  CELL G15 CONTAINS @FV(A15,C15,E15).
8
9
10
11                        ANNUAL
12     YEARLY            INTEREST           TERM               FUTURE
13     PAYMENT             RATE          (IN YEARS)            VALUE
14   ===========        =========       ==========        ===============
15   $2,000.00            9.00%             20              $102,320.24
16
17
18
19
20
01-Jan-89   10:02 AM
```

Figure 4–2 Present Value of an Ordinary Annuity

```
G6: [W11]                                                                         READY

        A         B         C         D         E         F         G
1  ===================================================================
2                       @PV(PAYMENT,INTEREST RATE,TERM)
3  ===================================================================
4  IN THIS EXAMPLE,THE PRESENT VALUE OF AN ORDINARY ANNUITY IS
5  CALCULATED.   THE ORDINARY ANNUITY PAYS $10,000 FOR A TERM OF 10
6  YEARS.   AN INTEREST RATE OF 10% WILL BE USED TO DISCOUNT THE ANNUITY.
7  CELL G15 CONTAINS @PV(A15,C15,E15).
8
9
10
11                        ANNUAL
12     YEARLY            INTEREST           TERM               PRESENT
13     PAYMENT             RATE          (IN YEARS)            VALUE
14   ===========        =========       ==========        ===========
15   $10,000.00          10.00%             10              $61,445.67
16
17
18
19
20
01-Jan-89   10:02 AM
```

4-5-4 @NPV(interest rate,range)

This function calculates the present value of a series of future cash flows discounted at a fixed interest rate, assuming that each cash flow occurs at the end of each period. This function uses the following formula:

$$\Sigma \ \frac{Vi}{(1 + interest)^i}$$

where $Vi \ldots Vm$ = series of cash flows

m = number of cash flows

i = number of iterations (1 to m)

The cash inflows or outflows do not need to be equal. This function is very helpful for calculating today's worth of an investment that may generate different future cash inflows and outflows. Figure 4–4 illustrates an example of this function.

4-5-5 @PMT(principal,interest rate,term)

This function calculates the amount of the periodic payment on a loan, using the following formula:

$$PMT = principal \ \frac{interest \ rate}{1 - (interest \ rate + 1)^{-n}}$$

where n = term

This function is very helpful for determining the payments for a new car, house, boat, and so forth. Figure 4–5 illustrates an example of this function.

4-5-6 @CTERM(interest rate,future value,present value)

This function calculates the number of compounding periods an investment reaches from a given present value to a given future value with a given fixed interest rate. Lotus utilizes the following formula in this function:

$$\frac{LN \ (future \ value/present \ value)}{Ln \ (1 + interest \ rate)}$$

where Ln = natural logarithm

This function can be very helpful for future planning, let us say for your children's college expenses. It tells you how many years it will take to accumulate a certain amount of money. Figure 4–6 shows an example of this function.

4-5-7 @TERM(payment,interest rate,future value)

This function calculates the number of payment periods necessary to accumulate a given future value. All payments must be equal. The function uses the following formula:

$$\frac{LN \ (1 + (Future \ value * interest/payment))}{Ln \ (1 + interest \ )}$$

where Ln = natural logarithm

To calculate the term of an annuity that is due, the following formula should be used:

@TERM(payment, interest rate, future value/(1+ interest))

Figure 4–7 illustrates an example of this function.

Figure 4-3 Internal Rate of Return Analysis

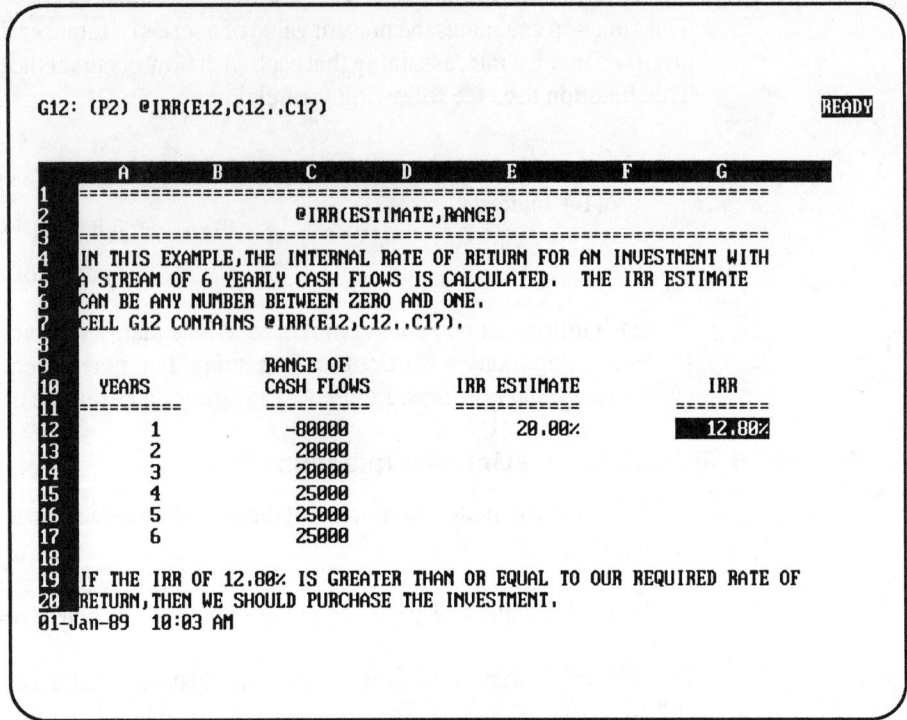

```
G12: (P2) @IRR(E12,C12..C17)                                              READY

        A         B         C         D         E         F         G
1  ================================================================
2                        @IRR(ESTIMATE,RANGE)
3  ================================================================
4  IN THIS EXAMPLE,THE INTERNAL RATE OF RETURN FOR AN INVESTMENT WITH
5  A STREAM OF 6 YEARLY CASH FLOWS IS CALCULATED.  THE IRR ESTIMATE
6  CAN BE ANY NUMBER BETWEEN ZERO AND ONE.
7  CELL G12 CONTAINS @IRR(E12,C12..C17).
8
9                      RANGE OF
10   YEARS            CASH FLOWS        IRR ESTIMATE           IRR
11  ==========        ==========        ============        =========
12      1               -80000             20.00%             12.80%
13      2                20000
14      3                20000
15      4                25000
16      5                25000
17      6                25000
18
19  IF THE IRR OF 12.80% IS GREATER THAN OR EQUAL TO OUR REQUIRED RATE OF
20  RETURN,THEN WE SHOULD PURCHASE THE INVESTMENT.
01-Jan-89  10:03 AM
```

Figure 4-4 Net Present Value Analysis

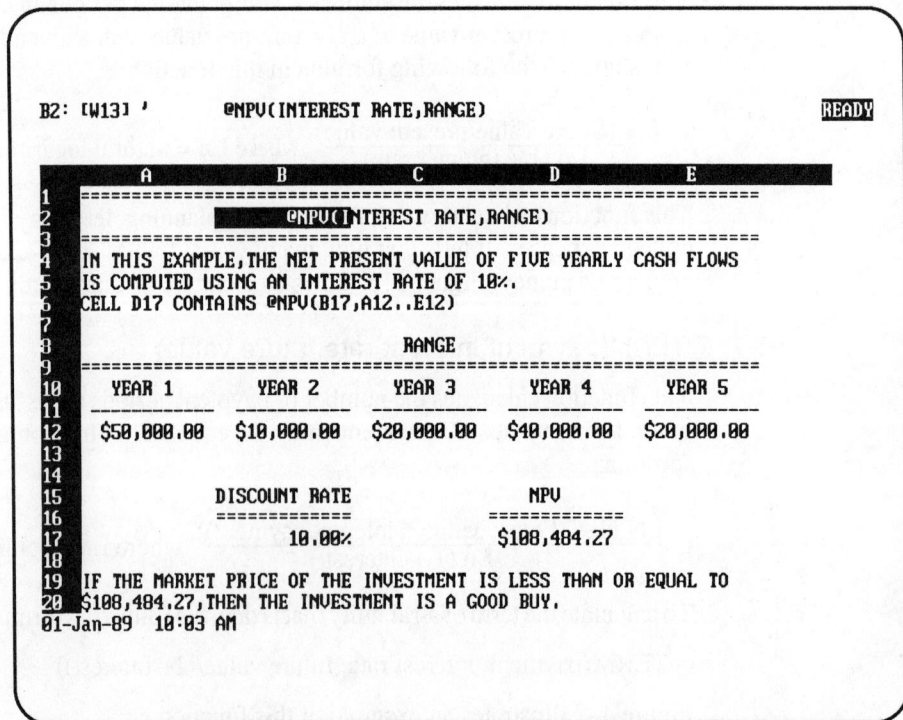

```
B2: [W13] '        @NPV(INTEREST RATE,RANGE)                              READY

        A           B           C           D           E
1  ================================================================
2                   @NPV(INTEREST RATE,RANGE)
3  ================================================================
4  IN THIS EXAMPLE,THE NET PRESENT VALUE OF FIVE YEARLY CASH FLOWS
5  IS COMPUTED USING AN INTEREST RATE OF 10%.
6  CELL D17 CONTAINS @NPV(B17,A12..E12)
7
8                              RANGE
9  ================================================================
10   YEAR 1      YEAR 2      YEAR 3      YEAR 4      YEAR 5
11  ----------  ----------  ----------  ----------  ----------
12  $50,000.00  $10,000.00  $20,000.00  $40,000.00  $20,000.00
13
14
15              DISCOUNT RATE              NPV
16              =============          =============
17                 10.00%               $100,484.27
18
19  IF THE MARKET PRICE OF THE INVESTMENT IS LESS THAN OR EQUAL TO
20  $100,484.27,THEN THE INVESTMENT IS A GOOD BUY.
01-Jan-89  10:03 AM
```

Figure 4–5 Payment Analysis of a Particular Loan

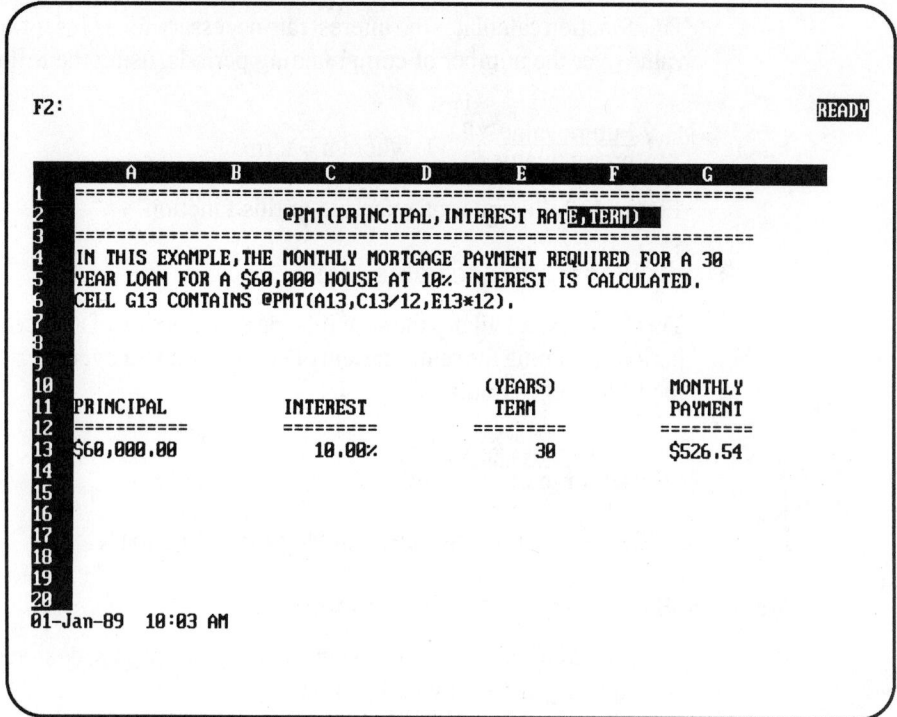

```
F2:                                                                    READY

         A        B        C        D        E        F        G
1  ====================================================================
2                    @PMT(PRINCIPAL,INTEREST RATE,TERM)
3  ====================================================================
4  IN THIS EXAMPLE,THE MONTHLY MORTGAGE PAYMENT REQUIRED FOR A 30
5  YEAR LOAN FOR A $60,000 HOUSE AT 10% INTEREST IS CALCULATED.
6  CELL G13 CONTAINS @PMT(A13,C13/12,E13*12).
7
8
9
10                                          (YEARS)          MONTHLY
11 PRINCIPAL             INTEREST             TERM            PAYMENT
12 =========             ========            =========       =========
13 $60,000.00            10.00%                 30           $526.54
14
15
16
17
18
19
20
01-Jan-89   10:03 AM
```

Figure 4–6 Number of Compounding Periods Analysis

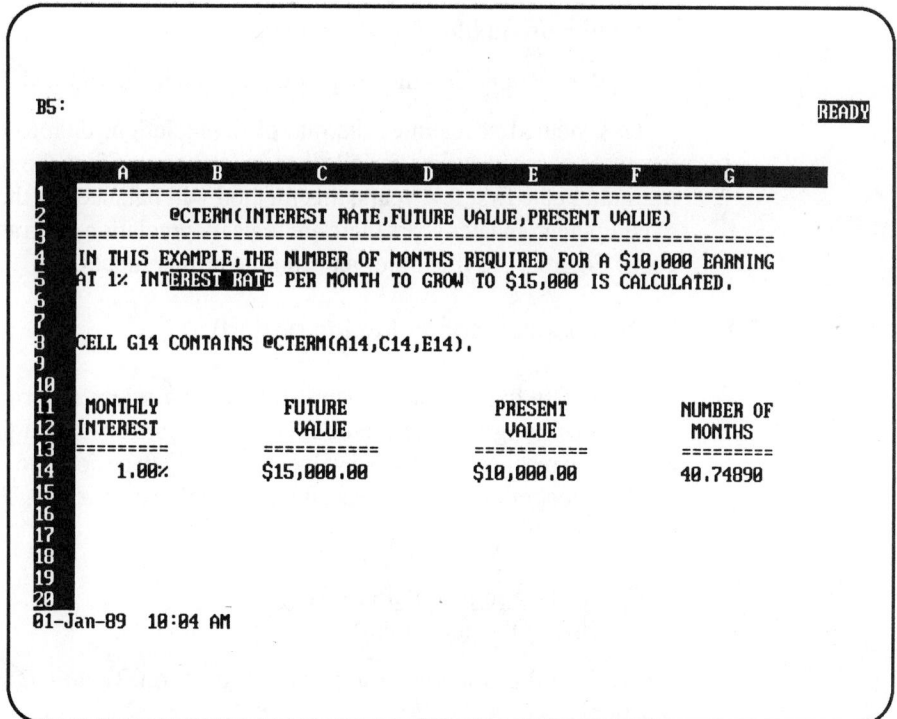

```
B5:                                                                    READY

         A        B        C        D        E        F        G
1  ====================================================================
2              @CTERM(INTEREST RATE,FUTURE VALUE,PRESENT VALUE)
3  ====================================================================
4  IN THIS EXAMPLE,THE NUMBER OF MONTHS REQUIRED FOR A $10,000 EARNING
5  AT 1% INTEREST RATE PER MONTH TO GROW TO $15,000 IS CALCULATED.
6
7
8  CELL G14 CONTAINS @CTERM(A14,C14,E14).
9
10
11 MONTHLY               FUTURE              PRESENT         NUMBER OF
12 INTEREST              VALUE               VALUE            MONTHS
13 =========            ==========           ==========      =========
14   1.00%              $15,000.00           $10,000.00      40.74890
15
16
17
18
19
20
01-Jan-89   10:04 AM
```

4-5-8 @RATE(future value,present value,term)

This function calculates the interest rate necessary for a present value to reach a future value over the number of compounding periods, using the following formula:

$$\left(\frac{\text{Future value}}{\text{present value}}\right)^{\frac{1}{n}} -1 \quad \text{where } n = \text{term}$$

Figure 4–8 illustrates an example of this function.

4-5-9 @SLN(cost,salvage value,life)

This function calculates the straight-line depreciation of a piece of equipment for one period, assuming the same amount of depreciation for every period. The function uses the following formula:

$$\frac{(\text{Cost - Salvage Value})}{\text{useful life of the asset}}$$

Figure 4–9 illustrates an example of this function.

4-5-10 @SYD(cost,salvage value,life,period)

This function calculates the sum-of-the-years'-digits depreciation for a selected period using the following formula:

$$\frac{(\text{Cost - Salvage Value}) * (\text{Useful life} - P + 1)}{(n * (n + 1)/2)}$$

where n = useful life of the equipment

P = period for which depreciation is being computed

This method accelerates the rate of depreciation; therefore, more depreciation expenses occur in earlier periods than in later ones. Since the maintenance costs are minimal in the first few years, this method will balance out the total cost of a piece of equipment. In later years there are fewer depreciation costs and more maintenance costs. Figure 4–10 illustrates an example of this function.

4-5-11 @DDB(cost,salvage value,life,period)

This function calculates the depreciation for a selected period of time, using the double-declining-balance method. Depreciation stops when the book value of the equipment reaches the salvage value. At any given period, the book value is equal to the total cost minus total depreciation over all prior periods. This function uses the following formula:

$$\frac{(\text{Book value in that period} * 2)}{(\text{life of the equipment})}$$

Figure 4–11 illustrates an example of this function. Table 4–2 summarizes financial functions.

Figure 4–7 Number of Payment Periods Analysis

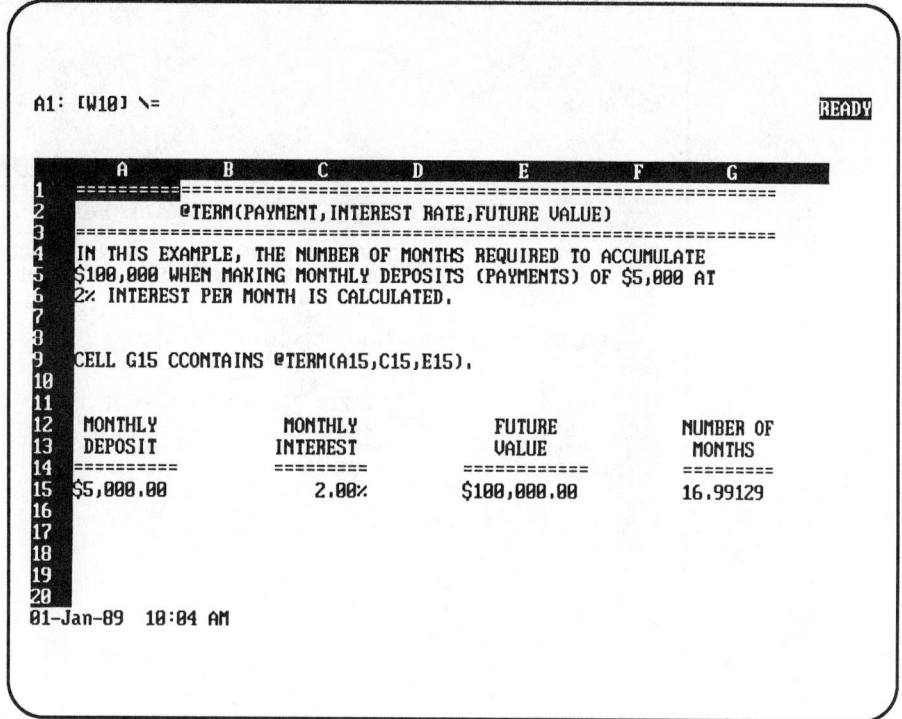

```
A1: [W10] \=                                                          READY

        A         B         C         D         E         F        G
1  ==================================================================
2            @TERM(PAYMENT,INTEREST RATE,FUTURE VALUE)
3  ==================================================================
4  IN THIS EXAMPLE, THE NUMBER OF MONTHS REQUIRED TO ACCUMULATE
5  $100,000 WHEN MAKING MONTHLY DEPOSITS (PAYMENTS) OF $5,000 AT
6  2% INTEREST PER MONTH IS CALCULATED.
7
8
9  CELL G15 CCONTAINS @TERM(A15,C15,E15).
10
11
12 MONTHLY             MONTHLY             FUTURE            NUMBER OF
13 DEPOSIT             INTEREST            VALUE             MONTHS
14 ==========          ==========          ============      =========
15 $5,000.00             2.00%             $100,000.00        16.99129
16
17
18
19
20
01-Jan-89  10:04 AM
```

Table 4–2

FINANCIAL FUNCTIONS

@FV(payment, interest rate, term)	Future value of annuity invested at a certain interest rate for a number of periods
@PV(payment, interest rate, term)	Present value of annuity invested at a certain interest rate for a number of periods
@IRR(estimate, range)	Internal rate of return for range of cash flows — supply estimate interest rate between 0 and 1
@NPV(interest rate, range)	Net present value of future cash flows at constant interest rate
@PMT(principal, interst rate, term)	Loan payment based on principal, at certain interest rate over a number of periods
@CTERM(interest rate, future value, present value)	Compounded term of an investment reaches from a given present value to a given future value with a given fixed interest rate
@TERM(payment, interest rate, future value)	Number of payment periods necessary to accumulate a given future value
@RATE(future value, present value, term)	Interest rate necessary for a present value to reach a future value
@SLN(cost, salvage value, life)	Straight-line depreciation
@SYD(cost, salvage value, life, period)	Sum-of-years'-digits depreciation
@DDB(cost, salvage value, life, period)	Double-declining-balance depreciation

---

Figure 4–8 Interest Rate Analysis

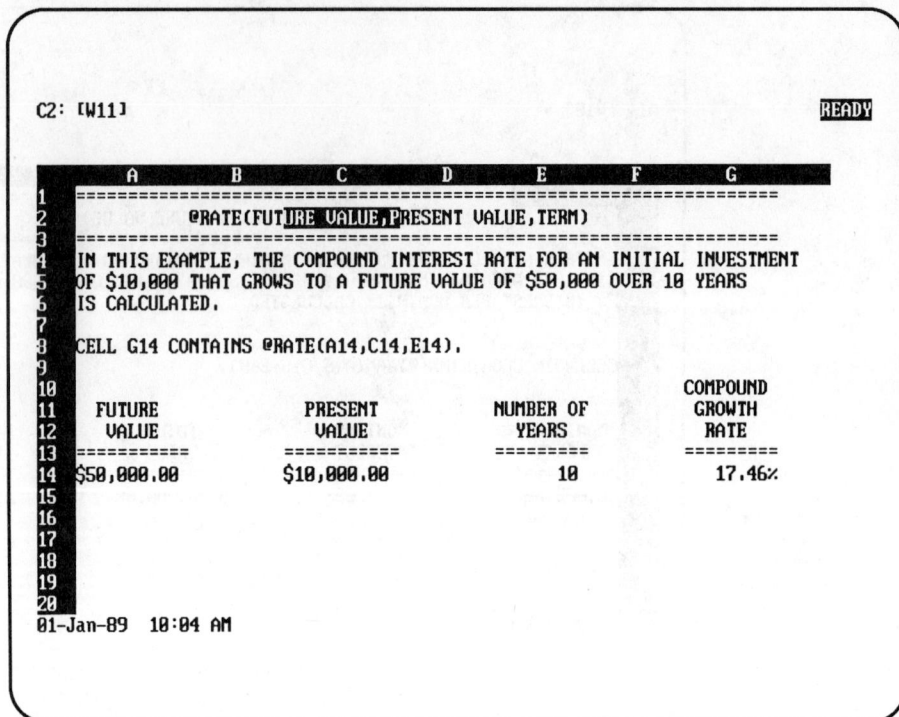

```
C2: [W11]                                                                READY

        A         B         C         D         E         F         G
1  ====================================================================
2              @RATE(FUTURE VALUE,PRESENT VALUE,TERM)
3  ====================================================================
4  IN THIS EXAMPLE, THE COMPOUND INTEREST RATE FOR AN INITIAL INVESTMENT
5  OF $10,000 THAT GROWS TO A FUTURE VALUE OF $50,000 OVER 10 YEARS
6  IS CALCULATED.
7
8  CELL G14 CONTAINS @RATE(A14,C14,E14).
9
10                                                            COMPOUND
11    FUTURE             PRESENT           NUMBER OF           GROWTH
12    VALUE               VALUE              YEARS              RATE
13  ==========          ==========         =========          =========
14  $50,000.00          $10,000.00             10              17.46%
15
16
17
18
19
20
01-Jan-89  10:04 AM
```

Figure 4–9 Straight-Line Depreciation

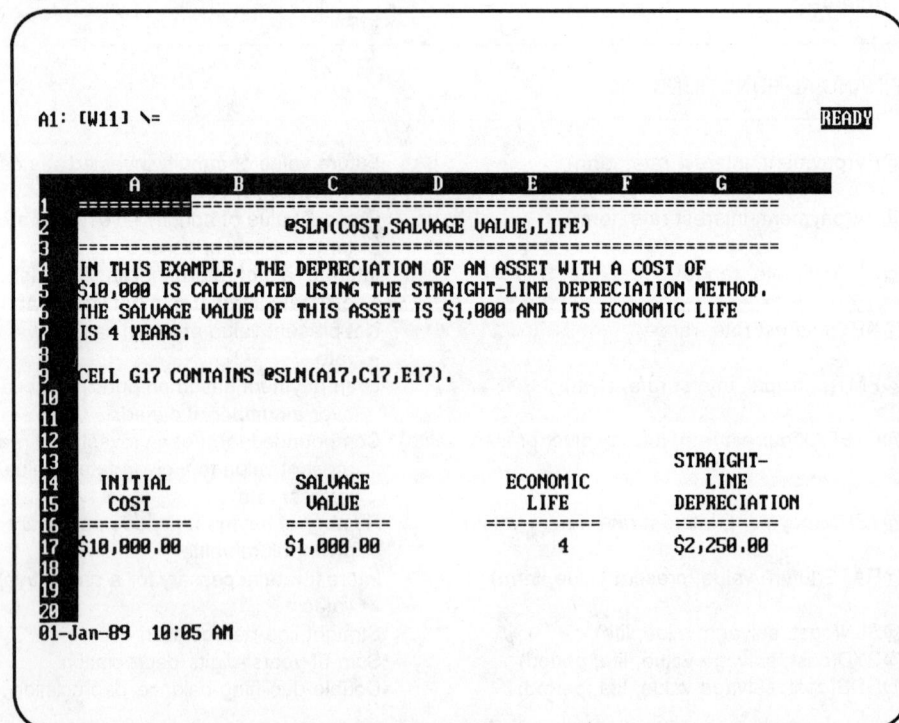

```
A1: [W11] \=                                                             READY

        A         B         C         D         E         F         G
1  ====================================================================
2              @SLN(COST,SALVAGE VALUE,LIFE)
3  ====================================================================
4  IN THIS EXAMPLE, THE DEPRECIATION OF AN ASSET WITH A COST OF
5  $10,000 IS CALCULATED USING THE STRAIGHT-LINE DEPRECIATION METHOD.
6  THE SALVAGE VALUE OF THIS ASSET IS $1,000 AND ITS ECONOMIC LIFE
7  IS 4 YEARS.
8
9  CELL G17 CONTAINS @SLN(A17,C17,E17).
10
11
12
13                                                          STRAIGHT-
14    INITIAL            SALVAGE           ECONOMIC            LINE
15     COST               VALUE              LIFE          DEPRECIATION
16  ==========          ==========         ==========         ==========
17  $10,000.00          $1,000.00              4            $2,250.00
18
19
20
01-Jan-89  10:05 AM
```

Figure 4–10 Sum-of-the-Years'-Digits Depreciation

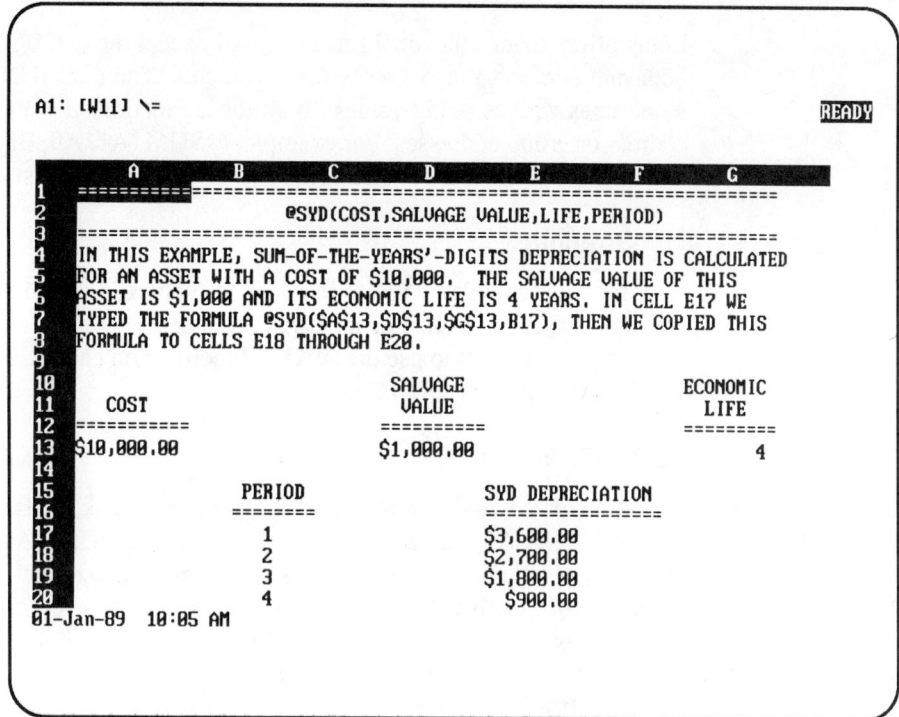

```
A1: [W11] \=                                                    READY

        A        B        C        D        E        F        G
1  =====================================================================
2                      @SYD(COST,SALVAGE VALUE,LIFE,PERIOD)
3  =====================================================================
4  IN THIS EXAMPLE, SUM-OF-THE-YEARS'-DIGITS DEPRECIATION IS CALCULATED
5  FOR AN ASSET WITH A COST OF $10,000.  THE SALVAGE VALUE OF THIS
6  ASSET IS $1,000 AND ITS ECONOMIC LIFE IS 4 YEARS. IN CELL E17 WE
7  TYPED THE FORMULA @SYD($A$13,$D$13,$G$13,B17), THEN WE COPIED THIS
8  FORMULA TO CELLS E18 THROUGH E20.
9
10                                SALVAGE                    ECONOMIC
11    COST                        VALUE                        LIFE
12  ==========                  ==========                  ==========
13 $10,000.00                   $1,000.00                            4
14
15               PERIOD                    SYD DEPRECIATION
16               ========                  =================
17                  1                          $3,600.00
18                  2                          $2,700.00
19                  3                          $1,800.00
20                  4                            $900.00
01-Jan-89  10:05 AM
```

Figure 4–11 Double-Declining-Balance Depreciation

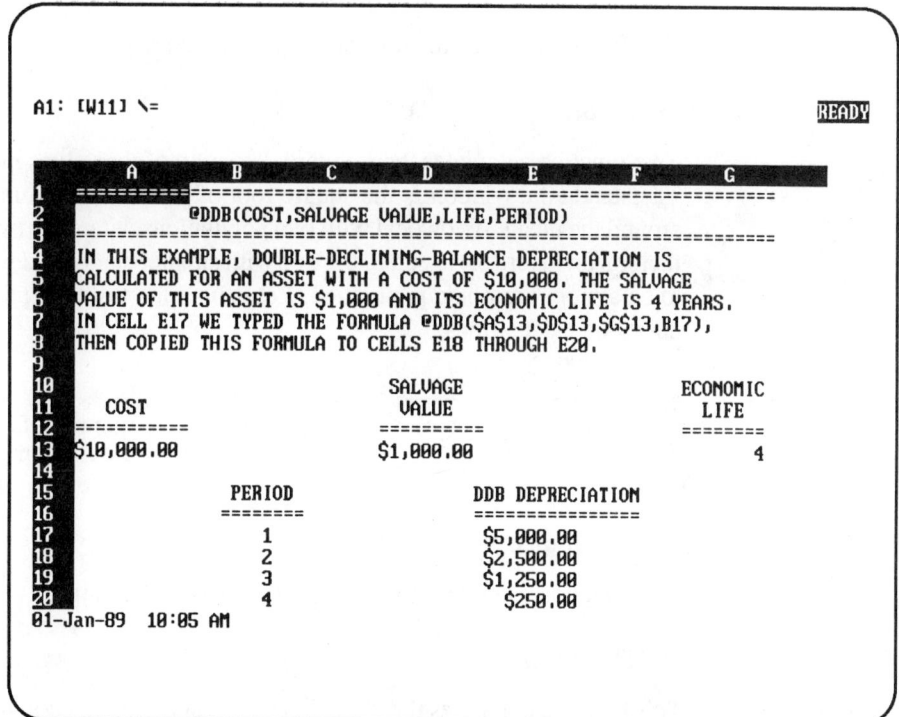

```
A1: [W11] \=                                                    READY

        A        B        C        D        E        F        G
1  =====================================================================
2                      @DDB(COST,SALVAGE VALUE,LIFE,PERIOD)
3  =====================================================================
4  IN THIS EXAMPLE, DOUBLE-DECLINING-BALANCE DEPRECIATION IS
5  CALCULATED FOR AN ASSET WITH A COST OF $10,000. THE SALVAGE
6  VALUE OF THIS ASSET IS $1,000 AND ITS ECONOMIC LIFE IS 4 YEARS.
7  IN CELL E17 WE TYPED THE FORMULA @DDB($A$13,$D$13,$G$13,B17),
8  THEN COPIED THIS FORMULA TO CELLS E18 THROUGH E20.
9
10                                SALVAGE                    ECONOMIC
11    COST                        VALUE                        LIFE
12  ==========                  ==========                  ========
13 $10,000.00                   $1,000.00                            4
14
15               PERIOD                    DDB DEPRECIATION
16               ========                  =================
17                  1                          $5,000.00
18                  2                          $2,500.00
19                  3                          $1,250.00
20                  4                            $250.00
01-Jan-89  10:05 AM
```

4-6 Statistical Functions

Lotus offers seven statistical functions. All except the @COUNT function accept both numeric and range values for arguments. The @COUNT function accepts numeric as well as string values. In all these functions arguments can be a single address or group addresses. For example, @SUM (A1..A9, B5, ASSET) is valid.

Lotus considers a blank cell used as an argument in the list as the value zero.

4-6-1 @AVG(range)

This function calculates the average of all values included in the list or range. Examples: @AVG (A1..A15) or @AVG(Asset).

If you do not want to use the @AVG function you can use its equivalent, which is @SUM(range)/@COUNT(range).

4-6-2 @COUNT(range)

This function counts the number of occupied (nonblank) cells in the range. For example, if cells A1, A2, and A5 are occupied, @COUNT(A1..A5) = 3. If range includes only blank cells, the result is zero; for example, if cells A1 through A5 are all empty, @COUNT(A1..A5) = 0. However, if you use @COUNT(A10), even if A10 is empty, you still receive 1.

4-6-3 @MAX(range)

This function returns the maximum value in the range.

4-6-4 @MIN(range)

This function returns the minimum value in the range.

4-6-5 @STD(range)

This function calculates the standard deviation of the values included in the range. The standard deviation is the square root of the variance, a measure of deviation around the mean. If you deal with two populations, let us say two sales regions, and their mean (average) is equal, the one with smaller standard deviation is considered to be a more harmonic population. Lotus uses the following formula for standard deviation calculations:

$$\sqrt{\frac{(\text{Value i} - \text{average})^2}{n}} \quad \text{where} \quad \begin{array}{ll} n & = \text{number of items in the range} \\ \text{value i} & = \text{the } i\text{th item in the range} \end{array}$$

4-6-6 @SUM(range)

This function calculates the sum of all values in the range.

4-6-7 @VAR(range)

This function computes the variance of the values included in the range. Lotus uses the following formula in this function:

```
C7: '@SUM(A7..A19)  =                                              READY


        A        B          C           D          E          F          G
1  ================================================================
2  IN THIS EXAMPLE, THE STATISTICAL FUNCTIONS BELOW WILL BE
3  CALCULATED.
4  ================================================================
5
6
7      -500              @SUM(A7..A19)  =          1300
8      -400
9      -300              @AVG(A7..A19)  =           100
10     -200
11     -100              @MIN(A7..A19)  =          -500
12        0
13      100              @MAX(A7..A19)  =           700
14      200
15      300              @VAR(A7..A19)  =        140000
16      400
17      500              @STD(A7..A19)  =      374.16573
18      600
19      700              @COUNT(A7..A19)=            13
20
01-Jan-89   10:06 AM
```

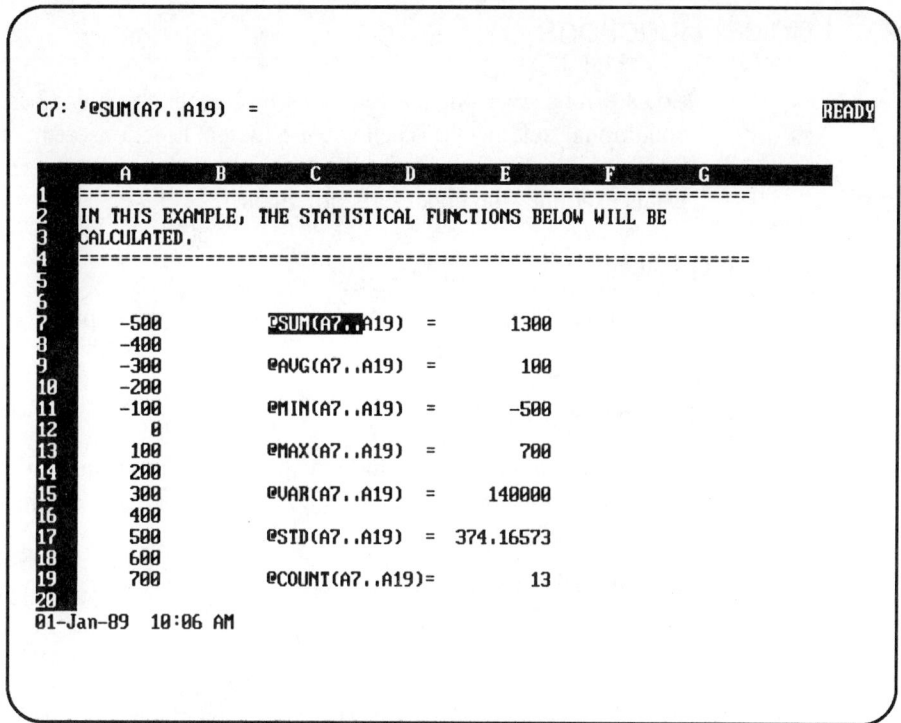

Figure 4–12 Statistical Functions

$$\sum \frac{(\text{Value i - average})^2}{n} \quad \text{where Value i} = \text{the } i\text{th item in the range}$$
$$n = \text{number of items in the range}$$

The formulas for variance and standard deviation are for a population (the entire group). To calculate the variance and standard deviation of the sample (random sample), use the following formulas:

Variance   = @COUNT(range)/(@COUNT(range)-1) * @VAR (range)

Standard Deviation = @SQRT(@COUNT(range)/(@COUNT(range)-1))* @STD(range)

Figure 4–12 illustrates an example of these seven statistical functions. Table 4–3 summarizes statistical functions.

Table 4–3

STATISTICAL FUNCTIONS

@AVG(range)	Average of values in the range
@COUNT(range)	Number of nonblank entries in the range
@MAX(range)	Maximum value in the range
@MIN(range)	Minimum value in the range
@STD(range)	Population standard deviation of items in the range
@SUM(range)	Sum of the values in the range
@VAR(range)	Population variance of values in the range

4-7 Logical Functions

Lotus offers seven logical functions that generate values based on the results of conditional statements. When you use logical functions, remember that a blank cell has the value of zero. If you use a range name that represents a multiple cell range, Lotus examines the upper left corner cell.

4-7-1 @FALSE

This function returns the logical value zero. For example, if you type @FALSE in cell A1, you will get zero.

4-7-2 @IF(condition,A,B)

The condition must be a numeric value or one that results in a numeric value. The function returns the value A if the condition is true or the value B if the condition is false. Examples:

    @IF(3<0,"A","B")   B
    @IF((10+5)/2<10,"T","F")   T

@IF(A9>200, C10, D10) – means if the value in cell A9 is greater than 200, then use the value in cell C10, otherwise use the value in cell D10.

@IF(A10<>30 #AND#A20="NO", E10, E20) – contents of A10 and A20 will be evaluated then either E10 or E20 will be used.

4-7-3 @ISERR(A)

This function examines cell A to see if it contains the value ERR. The function will return one if cell A contains the value ERR; otherwise it returns zero. Examples:

    @ISERR(5/0) =   1
    @ISERR(2/2) =   0

In the first example the value 1 is returned because 5/0 is invalid.

4-7-4 @ISNA(A)

This function tests A to see if it contains the value NA (not available). The function returns one if A contains the value NA; otherwise, it returns zero. Let us say in cell A15 we have stored function @NA, @ISNA(A15) = 1, and @ISNA(A16) = 0. Cell A16 can contain anything except @NA. This function is used to show a particular number is not available to calculate a formula, therefore it shows NA in the current cell and in all other cells that depend on a particular formula. This is useful for building worksheets when they need values that are not yet defined.

4-7-5 @ISNUMBER(A)

This function tests cell A to see if it contains a numeric value. The function returns one if cell A contains a number or a calculation (formula) resulting in a numeric value; otherwise it returns zero. Examples:

@ISNUMBER(5)	=	1
@ISNUMBER("7")	=	0
@ISNUMBER(68/8+@SQRT(16))	=	1
@ISNUMBER("PORTLAND")	=	0

4-7-6 @ISSTRING(A)

This function is similar to @ISNUMBER(A), but it tests for a string. It returns one if A is a string, otherwise it returns zero. Examples:

| @ISSTRING(7) | = | 0 |
| @ISSTRING("LOTUS") | = | 1 |

4-7-7 @TRUE

This function returns the logical value one. Let us assume cell A10 contains the string "BASIC". Then @IF(A10="BASIC",@TRUE,@FALSE) = 1, so TRUE or 1 are the same. Table 4–4 summarizes logical functions.

Table 4–4

LOGICAL FUNCTIONS

@FALSE	Returns logical value 0
@IF(condition, A,B)	Returns A if condition is TRUE, and B if condition is FALSE
@ISERR(A)	Returns TRUE (1) if A contains the value ERR; otherwise FALSE (0)
@ISNA(A)	Returns TRUE (1) if A contains the value NA; otherwise FALSE(0)
@ISNUMBER(A)	Returns TRUE (1) if A contains a numeric value; otherwise FALSE (0)
@ISSTRING(A)	Returns TRUE (1) if A contains a string value; otherwise FALSE (0)
@TRUE	Returns the logical value 1

4-8 String Functions

Lotus offers 19 string functions that are extremely helpful for nonnumeric manipulations. If a string is used as an argument, it must be enclosed in a pair of quotation marks. The characters of strings enclosed in quotation marks are numbered starting from zero. For example, string "DISK" is numbered from zero to 3.

4-8-1 @CHAR(A)

Argument A can be any numeric value between 0 and 255. The function returns the ASCII/LICS character corresponding to the number A (see Appendix F). For values outside this range, you get ERR. If your argument is a decimal, Lotus will convert it to an integer. Examples:

| @CHAR(77) | = | M |
| @CHAR(100) | = | d |

@CHAR(81.5)   =   Q
@CHAR(280)   =   ERR

(ASCII, American Standard Code for Information Interchange, is a data presentation code accepted by a majority of computer manufacturers. LICS, Lotus International Character Set, includes numbers 0 to 255 for all the codes and characters accepted by Lotus.)

4-8-2 @CODE(string)

This function returns the ASCII/LICS code number for the first character in the string (argument). If the argument is not a string, you will get ERR. Examples:

@CODE("TEST")   =   84
@CODE("T")   =   84
@CODE("PASCAL")   =   80
@CODE("JONES")   =   74
@CODE(65)   =   ERR

4-8-3 @CLEAN(string)

Strings imported with the /File Import command, especially if they are imported by modem from a different site, may contain nonprintable characters or noise (ASCII codes below 32). This function eliminates the nonprintable characters from the strings. The argument of this function must be a string value or a cell address that contains a string value. The cell address cannot be a range.

4-8-4 @EXACT(String1,String2)

This function compares two strings to see if they are identical. If they are, the function returns one, otherwise it returns zero. Remember, uppercase and lowercase characters are different. Both arguments must be strings, otherwise you get ERR. Examples:

@EXACT("TRYOUT","TRYOUT")   = 1
@EXACT("TRYOUT","TRYUT")   = 0
@EXACT("555","555")   = 1
@EXACT("555",555)   = ERR

4-8-5 @FIND(Search String,String,Start Number)

This function searches for a string starting from a specified position. It returns the exact position of the first occurrence of the desired string. If the search fails, you get ERR. The starting number must be either zero or positive. If the starting number is not an integer, Lotus considers only the integer part. Examples:

@FIND("LOTUS","LOTUS IS POWERFUL",0) = 0
@FIND("LOTUS","ONE OF THE BEST SPREADSHEETS IS LOTUS",10)
= 32
@FIND("HAPPY","WE HAVE LEARNED SO MUCH ALREADY",0) =
ERR
@FIND("M", "I HAD A GOOD MONTH IN MEXICO",15.6) = 22

4-8-6 @LEFT(String,m)

This function returns the first m characters in the string. Examples:

@LEFT("COBOL",3)	= COB
@LEFT("HAPPINESS IS HERE",5)	= HAPPI

4-8-7 @LENGTH(String)

This function returns the number of characters included in the string. Examples:

@LENGTH("LESSON")	= 6
@LENGTH("YESTERDAY WAS SUNNY")	= 19
@LENGTH("")	= 0
@LENGTH(555)	= ERR

4-8-8 @LOWER(String)

This function converts all the letters in the string to lowercase. Examples:

@LOWER("Portland")	= portland
@LOWER("PORTLAND")	= portland

4-8-9 @MID(String,Start Number,m)

This function extracts m characters from a string after skipping the start number characters. Examples:

@MID("JACKSON",2,5)	= CKSON
@MID("I AM GOING HOME NOW",6,60)	= OING HOME NOW
@MID("LOTUS DOES GRAPHICS",0,5)	= LOTUS

4-8-10 @N(RANGE)

This function returns the value of the upper left corner of a particular range as a number. For example, if values 100, 200, 300, and 400 are stored in cells A1, A2, A3, and A4, then @N(A2..A4) will return 200.

4-8-11 @PROPER(String)

This function puts a string into proper order by converting the first letter of each word to a capital letter and the rest to lowercase letters. Examples:

@PROPER("SUSAN BROWN")	= Susan Brown
@PROPER("Susan BROWN")	= Susan Brown

4-8-12 @REPEAT(String,m)

This function repeats a particular string m times. Examples:

@REPEAT("HB",2)	= HBHB
@REPEAT("BH",1)	= BH
@REPEAT("I AM HAPPY",2)	= I AM HAPPY I AM HAPPY

4-8-13 @REPLACE(Original String, Start Number,m, New String)

This function removes m characters in an original string beginning at the start number and then inserts a new string in the same position in the original string. Examples:

@REPLACE("ATTENTION",1,3,"XXXXX")   =   AXXXXXNTION
@REPLACE("ATTENTION",1,-1,11XXXXX)   =   ERR

In the first example, position zero is at A, position one is at T, so TTE will be removed and five Xs will be inserted. The second example is invalid. Why?

4-8-14 @RIGHT(String,m)

The function returns the last m characters in a particular string. M must be >= 1. Examples:

@RIGHT("FORTRAN",3)   =   RAN
@RIGHT("DATABASE",1)   =   E

4-8-15 @S(Range)

This function returns the value in the upper left corner cell of the range as a string value (if the cell contains a value). For example, if cells A1, A2, A3, and A4 contain strings SUE, JACKSON, BOB, and JACK, the following can be seen:

@S(!A1)   =   SUE
@S(A2..A3)   =   JACKSON
@S(A1..A4)   =   SUE

4-8-16 @STRING(Y,m)

In this function, m specifies the number of decimal places from 0 to 15. M must be >= 0. The function converts a number Y to a string with m places to the right of the decimal point. In order to convert a string to its numeric equivalent, use @VALUE. Examples:

@STRING(125.8735,3)   =   125.874
@STRING(125.87,0)   =   126
@STRING(125.87,-1)   =   ERR

4-8-17 @TRIM(String)

This function eliminates excess space characters from a particular string. Examples:

@TRIM("IT   HAS   BEEN   A   LONG   DAY")   = IT HAS BEEN A LONG DAY
@TRIM("THIS   IS   A   TEST")   = THIS IS A TEST

4-8-18 @UPPER(String)

This function converts all the letters in a string to uppercase. Examples:

@UPPER("First Computer")   =   FIRST COMPUTER
@UPPER("happy")   =   HAPPY

4-8-19 @VALUE(String)

This function converts a string to a numeric value. Examples:

@VALUE("12 4/3")	=	13.3333333333
@VALUE("1.567E+5")	=	156700
@VALUE("15.55")	=	15.55
@VALUE("-10/-2*2")	=	ERR

Table 4–5 summarizes string functions.

Table 4–5

___

STRING FUNCTIONS

___

@CHAR(A)	Returns ASCII/LICS character represented by A (see Appendix F)
@CODE(string)	Returns ASCII/LICS code for first character in the string
@CLEAN(string)	Eliminates nonprintable characters from the string
@EXACT(string1, string2)	Compares two strings
@FIND(search string, string, start number)	Position at which the first occurrence of search string begins in the string
@LEFT(string,m)	Returns m leftmost characters in the string
@LENGTH(string)	Returns length of the string
@LOWER(STRING)	Changes the string to lowercase
@MID(string, start number, m)	Returns m characters of the string beginning with character start number
@N(range)	Numeric value in upper left corner cell in range
@PROPER(string)	Changes string to initial caps
@REPEAT(string,m)	Duplicates string m times
@REPLACE(original string, start number, m, new string)	m characters removed from original string, replaced with new string at start number
@RIGHT(string,m)	Returns m rightmost characters in the string
@S(range)	Returns string value of a cell in the range)
@STRING(y,m)	Returns numeric value y as a string, with m decimal places
@TRIM(string)	Removes leading/trailing spaces from the string
@UPPER(string)	Changes the string to uppercase
@VALUE(string)	Converts a string to a numeric value

___

4-9 Date and Time Functions

___

Lotus offers 11 date and time functions. These functions generate or use numbers to represent dates and times, so that you can use them in calculations. Before you use these functions, remember the following:

1. Any date between January 1, 1900 and December 31, 2099 inclusive is valid and has an equivalent integer serial number.
2. The first serial number is 1, the last is 73050.
3. January 1, 1900 is equivalent to 1 and December 31, 2099 is equivalent to 73050.

4. Each hour of the day has a serial number as well, e.g., midnight = 0, noon = .50, etc.
5. The following functions generate serial numbers: @DATE, @DATEVALUE, @NOW, @TIME, and @TIMEVALUE
6. The following functions use serial numbers: @DAY, @MONTH, @YEAR, @HOUR, @MINUTE, and @SECOND

4-9-1 @DATE(Year,Month,Day)

This function returns the serial number corresponding to a certain year, month, or day. Remember, since there was no February 29, 1900 (we did not have leap year then), Lotus assigns a date number to this particular day. This does not invalidate any of your calculations, unless you use any dates between January 1 and March, 1, 1900. (Remember, D1 through D5 are five date options provided by Lotus, discussed in Chapter 2.) Examples:

@DATE(87,7,1)	=	31959	Equivalent in D1	=	01-Jul-87
@DATE(86,12,1)	=	31747	" " D2	=	01-DEC
@DATE(87,6,1)	=	31929	" " D3	=	Jun-87
@DATE(87,10,1)	=	32051	" " D4	=	10/01/87
@DATE(87,10,1)	=	32051	" " D5	=	10/01

4-9-2 @DATEVALUE(Date String)

This function, similar to @DATE, returns the serial number of a date written as a string. The difference is that @DATEVALUE uses a single string value as its argument. The date string must be in one of the five date formats discussed in section 2–39. Examples:

@DATEVALUE("01-JUL-87") =	31959
@DATEVALUE("01-DEC") =	29556
@DATEVALUE("JUN-87") =	31929
@DATEVALUE("10/01/87") =	32051
@DATEVALUE("02-JUN-86") =	32565

4-9-3 @DAY(Date Number)

This function returns the day of the month (1 through 31) of the argument. Examples:

@DAY(@DATE(87,9,1)) =	1
@DAY(31700) =	15

4-9-4 @MONTH(Date Number)

This function returns a month (1 through 12) of the year in the string. Examples:

@MONTH(@DATE(87,9,1)) =	9
@MONTH(31625) =	8

4-9-5 @YEAR(Date Number)

This function returns any year between 0 to 199 of the argument. Examples:

@YEAR(@DATEVALUE("1-SEP-87")) =   87
@YEAR(31629)   =   86

4-9-6 @NOW

This function returns the current date and time. Example:

We typed @NOW on our Lotus worksheet. The function returned 29221.02, indicating January 1, 1980 at 12:36 A.M. The integer part is the date and the decimal portion is the time.

Other examples:

@INT(@NOW)   = 29221
@YEAR(29221)   = 80
@MONTH(29221)   = 1
@DAY(29221)   = 1

One good application of the @NOW function is to generate the serial number for DATE function. Assume that during the log-on time you have entered the correct date and time to the computer. Now, you can convert this serial number to any of the five Date formats.

To generate the time portion, you should do the following:

@NOW-@INT(@NOW), then use any of the four TIME formats.

4-9-7 @TIME(Hour,Minute,Second)

In this function hour must be between 0 and 23, minute must be between 0 and 59 and second must be between 0 and 59. The function returns a serial number between 0 and 1 for hour, minute, and second. The serial number is a fraction of a day. Examples: (Remember T1 through T4 are hour time options provided by Lotus, discussed in Chapter 2)

@TIME(10,52,40) = 0.453240 is equal to 10:52:40 A.M.. T1
@TIME(2,10,59)   = 0.90960   "   "   "   02:10 A.M.   T2
@TIME(22,50,50) = 0.951967 "   "   "   22:50:50   T3
@TIME(23,45,10) = 0.989699 "   "   "   23:45   T4
@TIME(30,30,30) = ERR

4-9-8 @TIMEVALUE(Time String)

This function returns a serial time number for the string. It is similar to @TIME except that the argument here is only one string. The time string must be in one of the four accepted Lotus time formats and must be enclosed in double quotes. Examples:

@TIMEVALUE("12:30:45") = 0.5213541667
@TIMEVALUE("12:30")   = 0.5208333333

4-9-9 @HOUR(Time Number)

This function extracts and returns the hour from a time number. The returned value is between 0 and 23; 0 refers to midnight and 23 to 11:00 P.M. Examples:

@HOUR(0.1876736111) = 4
@HOUR(31774.5)   = 12

4-9-10 @MINUTE(Time Number)

This function extracts and returns the minutes from a time number. The returned value is between 0 and 59. Examples:

@MINUTE(0.1567)   = 45
@MINUTE(12)   = 0

4-9-11 @SECOND(Time Number)

This function extracts and returns the seconds from a time number. The returned value is between 0 and 59. Examples:

@SECOND(0.639)   =   10
@SECOND(@TIME(10,10,10))   =   10

Table 4–6 summarizes date and time functions.

Table 4–6

DATE AND TIME FUNCTIONS

Functions that generate serial numbers:

@DATE(year,month,day)	Serial number of year, month, day
@DATEVALUE(date string)	Serial number of date
@NOW	Serial number at current date and time
@TIME(hour,minute,second)	Serial number of time between 0 and 1
@TIMEVALUE(time string)	Serial number of time

Functions that accept serial numbers as input:

@DAY(date number)	Returns day number (1-31) of date-number
@HOUR(time number)	Returns hour number (0-23) of time-number
@MINUTE(itme number)	Returns minute number (0-59) of time-number
@MONTH(date number)	Returns month number (1-12) of date-number
@SECOND(time number)	Returns second number (0-59) of time-number
@YEAR(date number)	Returns year number (0-199) of date-number

4-10 Special Functions

Lotus offers 11 special functions, most of which are used for searching for a value in a table.

4-10-1 @@(Cell Address)

The argument of this function can be a cell address written as a label, a range name, or a string formula whose value is a cell address or cell name. This function returns the content of the cell referenced by the cell address. Let us say cell A10 contains label H20 and cell H20 contains 200. Then @@(A10) returns 200.

4-10-2 @CELL(Attribute,Range)

This function returns the attribute of a cell or range from the attribute table (see Table 4–7). The attribute must be enclosed in double quotation marks; uppercase or lowercase does not matter. If you use a single cell as range, you must express it as a range (A1..A1 or !A1). If the range includes more than one cell, Lotus uses the upper left corner of the given range. To update cell attributes, you must press F9, the **CALC** function key. Figure 4–13 illustrates the following examples of this function:

@CELL("row",A10..A10)	=	10
@CELL("ADDRESS",A3..A3)	=	$A$3
@CELL("CONTENTS",!A7)	=	HELLO
@CELL("FORMAT",!A10)	=	G
@CELL("PREFIX",!A5)	=	"
@CELL("WIDTH",!A10)	=	9
@CELL("TYPE",'!A3)	=	V

4-10-3 @CELLPOINTER(Attribute)

This function returns attribute information about the current cell. It is very useful for testing the content of a cell; for example, finding out if a cell holds a value or is blank. Examples:

@CELLPOINTER("width") = 9 (by default each column width is 9 characters in length)

If the current row is row 30, then

@CELLPOINTER("ROW") = 30

4-10-4 @CHOOSE(Y,V0,V1,V2...Vn)

This function uses the numeric value of Y to return an item from the list V0 to Vn. The first value in the list is 0; therefore if Y = 2, @CHOOSE will select the third item. You can have up to 240 numeric or string values in the list. Examples:

@CHOOSE(3,10,17,25,29,35,38,41)	=	29
@CHOOSE(0,10,17,25,29,35,38,41)	=	10
@CHOOSE(3,"TONY","SAM","JOE","STEVE")	=	STEVE

4-10-5 @COLS(Range)

This function returns the number of columns in a specific range. Examples:

@COLS(A1..C1)	=	3
@COLS(A1..H20)	=	8

Table 4–7 Attribute Table for the @CELL Function

ATTRIBUTE	THE CALCULATED RESULT
"ADDRESS"	Returns the current cell address, e.g., A10
"COL"	Returns the current column number (1 to 256)
"CONTENTS"	Returns the content of the current cell:
	b for blank cell
	v for numeric value or formula
	L for label or string
"FORMAT"	Returns the current numeric formula of a given address:
	F0 to F15 for fixed, 0 to 15 decimal places
	S0 to S15 for scientific, 0 to 15 decimal places
	C0 to C15 for currency, 0 to 15 decimal places
	G for general
	P0 to P15 for percent
	D1 to D5 for date 1 to date 5 and D6 to D9 for Time 1 to Time 4 format (see Chapter 2)
	T for Text
	A blank if the content of the cell is an empty string
"PREFIX"	Returns the current label prefix:
	' (apostrophe) for left-justified
	" for right-justified
	∧ for centered
"PROTECT"	Returns the protection status:
	1 if it is protected
	0 if it is not protected
"ROW"	Returns the current row number (1 to 8192)
"TYPE"	Returns the data type in a cell:
	b for blank
	v for numeric value or formula
	L for label or string
"WIDTH"	Returns the current column width (1 to 240)

```
A1: 'CONTENT                                                        READY

        A        B        C        D        E        F        G        H
 1   CONTENT              Description of a column
 2                        This cell is blank
 3       555             This cell has a numeric value
 4   HARRY               This cell has a label
 5       LOTUS           This cell is right-justified
 6       HI              This cell is centered
 7   HELLO               This cell is protected
 8       55.00           This cell is fixed-formatted to 2 decimal places
 9   5.00E+03            This cell is scientific-formatted to 2 decimal places
10       19078           This cell shows the date format (D1)
11   2+2                 This cell shows the text format
12                        This cell shows the hidden format
13
14
15
16
17
18
19
20
01-Jan-89  10:06 AM
```

Figure 4–13 Sample Worksheet for the @CELL Function

4-10-6 @ERR

This function returns the numerical value ERR. This cannot be substituted with the label ERR, e.g., "ERR".

4-10-7 @HLOOKUP(Y,Range,Row Number)

This function performs a horizontal table search beginning with row zero and comparing the value of Y to each cell in the top row of a specified range. As soon as it finds a number larger than Y, it stops and backs up one cell. It moves down the specified row number and returns the content of the appropriate cell. If there is an exact match to Y, the search stops at that cell without backtracking. Then it moves down the specified row number and returns the content of the appropriate cell. If Y (the search value) is smaller than the first value, the function returns ERR. If Y is larger than all the values, the search stops at the last cell in the top row of the range without backtracking. Then it moves down the specified row number and returns the content of the appropriate cell. Remember, the top row of the table used by @HLOOKUP must be sorted in ascending order; this is row 0. Figure 4–14 illustrates this function. Examples:

@HLOOKUP(475,B4..H9,2) = 12
@HLOOKUP(850,B4..H9,3) = 15

@HLOOKUP(450,B4..H9,5)   =   20
@HLOOKUP(375,B4..H9,1)   =   18
@HLOOKUP(150,B4..H9,3)   =   ERR

4-10-8 @INDEX(Range, Column Number, Row Number)

This function returns the content of the cell located at the intersection of the column and row number in a specified range. The first row and column numbers are 0. If the argument is out of range (the row or column number is larger than the table), you get an ERR. We have used the data in Figure 4–14 for this function for the following examples:

@INDEX(A4..H9,0,0)   =   0
@INDEX(A4..H9,1,2)   =   13
@INDEX(A4..H9,5,5)   =   16
@INDEX(A4..H9,5,15) =   ERR

4-10-9 @NA

This function returns the numeric value NA whenever a particular number is not available in order to complete a formula. The function can be helpful for alerting the user. For example, if cell A10 contains 100, then @IF(A10/2>25,@NA,"I AM BUSY")   =   NA

Figure 4–14 Horizontal Table Search with the @HLOOKUP Function

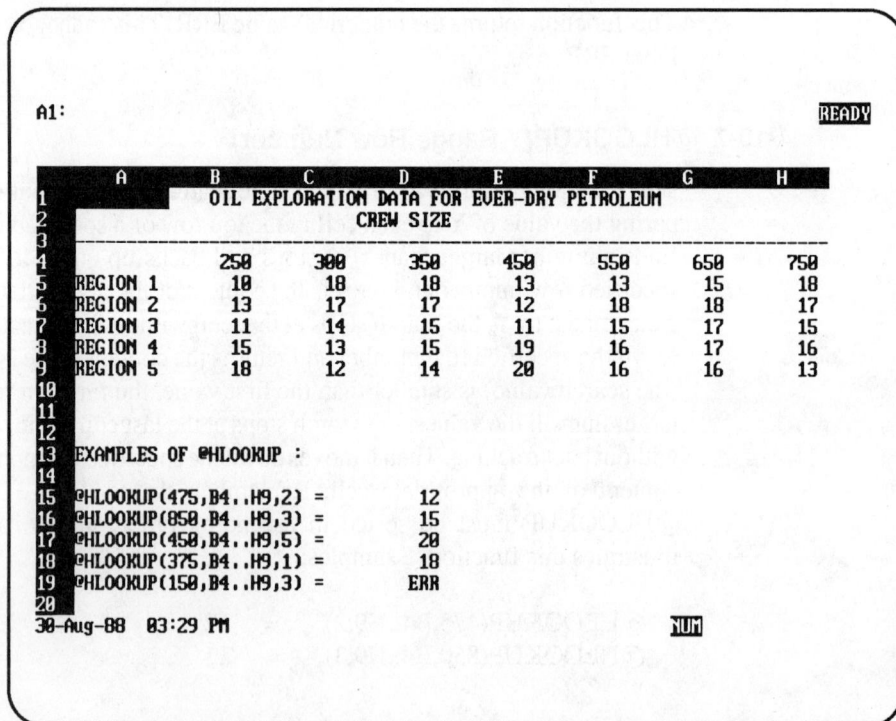

4-10-10 @ROWS(Range)

This function returns the number of rows in a given range. If we use data from Figure 4–14, we will see the following:

@ROWS(A3..D9)   =   7
@ROWS(A6..E4)   =   3
@ROWS(A6..H20)   =   15

4-10-11 @VLOOKUP(Y, Range, Column Number)

This function, similar to @HLOOKUP, performs a vertical search.

The function compares the value of Y to each cell in the first column of a specified range. As soon as it finds a number larger than Y in a cell, it backs up one cell. @VLOOKUP moves across the specified column number and returns the content of the appropriate cell. If there is an exact match to Y, the search stops at the cell (no backup will take place), then moves across the specified column number and returns the content of the appropriate cell. If the search value is smaller than the first value in the search column, the function returns ERR. If Y is larger than all the values, the search stops at the last cell in the first column of the range, then moves across the specified column number and returns the content of the appropriate cell. Remember, the first column in the table is column 0 and the values in the first column (e.g., the index column) must be in ascending order. The following examples are illustrated in Figure 4–15.

Figure 4–15 Vertical Table Search with the @VLOOKUP Function

B3:   READY

	A	B	C	D	E	F	G	H
1			COMMISSION TABLE					
2								
3	TOTAL SALES		GROUP #1	GROUP #2	GROUP #3	GROUP #4	GROUP #5	GROUP #6
4	20000		2000	2100	2200	2300	2400	2500
5	25000		3000	3100	3200	3300	3400	3500
6	30000		4000	4100	4200	4300	4400	4500
7	34000		5000	5100	5200	5300	5400	5500
8	40000		6000	6100	6200	6300	6400	6500
9	45000		7000	7100	7200	7300	7400	7500
10	50000		8000	8100	8200	8300	8400	8500
11								
12	EXAMPLES OF @VLOOKUP:							
13								
14	@VLOOKUP(26500,A4..G10,2) =		3000					
15	@VLOOKUP(45000,A4..G10,3) =		7100					
16	@VLOOKUP(37300,A4..G10,4) =		5200					
17	@VLOOKUP(41000,A4..G10,5) =		6300					
18	@VLOOKUP(47000,A4..G10,6) =		7400					
19	@VLOOKUP(19000,A4..G10,1) =		ERR					
20	@VLOOKUP(50000,A4..G10,7) =		ERR					

01-Jan-89   10:07 AM

$$
\begin{array}{ll}
\text{@VLOOKUP(26500,A4..G10,2)} & = 3000 \\
\text{@VLOOKUP(45000,A4..G10,3)} & = 7100 \\
\text{@VLOOKUP(37300,A4..G10,4)} & = 5200 \\
\text{@VLOOKUP(41000,A4..G10,5)} & = 6300 \\
\text{@VLOOKUP(47000,A4..G10,6)} & = 7400 \\
\text{@VLOOKUP(19000,A4..G10,1)} & = \text{ERR} \\
\text{@VLOOKUP(50000,A4..G10,7)} & = \text{ERR}
\end{array}
$$

Table 4–8 summarizes special functions.

Table 4–8

SPECIAL FUNCTIONS

@@(cell address)	Returns contents in the cell referenced by cell address
@CELL(attribute*,range)	Returns information about the attribute in the upper left corner cell of range** (see Table 4–7)
@CELLPOINTER(attribute*)	Returns information about the attribute of the highlighted cell
@CHOOSE(y,v0,v1,...vn)	Returns Yth argument in list v0, v1,...vn
@COLS(range)	Returns number of columns in range
@ERR	Returns value of ERR (error)
@HLOOKUP(y,range,row number)	Performs horizontal table lookup
@INDEX(range, column number, row number)	Returns value of the cell in the range at the intersection of column and row
@NA	Returns value NA (NOT AVAILABLE)
@ROWS(range)	Returns number of rows in the range
@VLOOKUP(y,range,column)	Performs vertical table lookup

*   String argument to @CELLPOINTER can be "ROW", "COL", "WIDTH","PREVIX", "ADDRESS", "TYPE", "FORMAT", "CONTENTS" (uppercase or lowercase). See TAble 4–7.

**   Specify single cell as a range, e.g., A2..A2 or !A2.

Summary

In this chapter we have discussed Lotus functions. These eight groups of functions enable you to perform a variety of operations. Some of these functions, such as the financial functions, have more versatile uses; others, such as special and string functions, are used in more advanced applications. As you will see in Chapters 11 through 13, a variety of these functions are used effectively with Lotus macros for performing numerous tasks.

Review Questions

1.   What is a Lotus function?
2.   What is a function argument?
3.   How many types of arguments are there?
4.* Do all the functions need an argument?
5.   How many mathematical functions are available in Lotus?
6.* Can the argument of @SQRT function be negative?

7. Which function is used to round 6.2782 to 6.28?
8. How many financial functions are supported by Lotus?
9. If you want to buy a car, which financial function may be helpful to you?
10. What are some of the applications of the @IRR function?
11.* What is the difference between the @NPV and @PV functions?
12. How many statistical functions are supported by Lotus?
13. Which function in this group may accept numeric as well as string values?
14. Which function is used to calculate the average of a range?
15. What are some of the applications of logical functions?
16.* How many logical functions are supported by Lotus?
17. What are some to the applications of string functions?
18. Can you do arithmetic with date and time functions?
19. Which date and time functions generate serial numbers?
20. What are special functions?
21. What are some of the practical uses of the @HLOOKUP and @VLOOKUP functions?
22.* Which function uses the attribute table?
23. In @HLOOKUP or @VLOOKUP what will happen if the search value does not exist in the table?
24. What is @ABS(-5)?
25. What is @EXP(10)?
26. What is @MOD(18,5)?
27.* What is @ROUND(167.292,2)?
28. What is @SQRT(-4)?
29. Calculate the future value of an IRA plan of $2,000 for 30 years with a fixed interest rate of 10%.
30. What is the @IRR of the following investment portfolio: -200,000; -150,000; -50,000; 65,000; 180,000; 200,000; and 300,000
31. What are the acceptable values for the estimate in the @IRR function?
32. Calculate the NPV of the portfolio given in problem 30 with a fixed interest rate of 12%.
33.* What is the monthly payment of a $200,000 house (with no down payment), with an interest rate of 8.75% and a 30-year mortgage plan?
34. Calculate the depreciation of an equipment for the next five years using straight-line, sum-of-the-years' digits, and double-declining-balance methods and the following data:

    cost   = 20,000

    salvage value   = 2,000

    useful life   = 5 years

35.* Calculate the seven statistical functions on the following data:

    2, 69, 37, 220, 165, 1, 62, and 95

36. What is the result of @EXACT("BASIC", "basic")?
37. What is the result of @LEFT("JACKSON",2)?
38. What is the result of @LENGTH(666)?

39.   What is the result of @MID("JACKSON", 2, 3)?
40.   What is the result of @REPEAT("Lotus", 4)?
41.   Generate today's date by using the @NOW function. Now modify this function to generate the current time (Hint: you have to use the @INT function.)
42.   Using the @HLOOKUP and @VLOOKUP functions, generate a simple tax table. Your tax table should include 10 different groups of income and should allow eight different deductions. Now calculate tax for different income levels and different deductions.

Misconceptions and Solutions

M — Usually the interest rate in a mortgage problem is stated as yearly and the payment is monthly. Using a yearly interest rate and monthly payment will cause mistakes in payment calculation.

S — Divide the yearly interest rate by 12 and multiply the number of years by 12. This adjustment will calculate the correct payment.

M — You are entering a function. When you try to enter the function by pressing the **Return** key, Lotus gives you a beep.

S — Check the syntax of any @ functions that you have used to be sure you have typed the name and the syntax of the function correctly. Also check to see if the number of left and right parentheses are matched.

Comprehensive Lab Assignment

Retrieve CHAPT3 and perform the following:

1.   Add an additional column to the worksheet (column I); give the title Total to the column.
2.   Using the @SUM function, calculate the total score of each student and store the result in this column.
3.   Generate another column (column J); give the title Statistics to this column.
4.   Generate the seven statistical functions for the total scores of all the students.
5.   Using the @NOW and @INT functions, generate the exact time and date in cell E19.
6.   Save this worksheet under CHAPT4.

5

Graphics: Converting Figures into Pictures

5-1 Introduction

In this chapter, we will study the types of graphs generated by Lotus, which include pie charts, and bar, line, stacked-bar, and XY graphs. Specific applications of each graph will illustrate its use. In Chapter 6 we will discuss how to print your graph on a graphic printer and/or plotter.

5-2 Why Graphics?

In today's competitive world, business executives and decision makers need to obtain information in the most effective and efficient way. Graphs achieve these goals by condensing massive amounts of data into simple, understandable form.

Lotus generates five different types of graphs:

1. Line graphs show changes in data over time. These graphs are suitable for time series analysis, in which one variable is time and the others could be such items as total sales, total cost, total advertising budget. Using line graphs, you can easily depict budget trends, total sales trends, administrative cost trends, and so forth.

2. Bar graphs emphasize differences between data items. For example, a bar graph can compare the total sales of five products of a particular company, the oil production from five oil wells, or the student population of six state universities.

3. XY graphs show relationships between two sets of data. This might be amount of sales and advertising budget, or years of education and yearly income.

4. Pie charts compare parts to the whole. For example, you can compare advertising expenses to total sales expenses.

5. Stacked-bar graphs compare different sets of data by arranging them on top of each other. This helps to visualize the meaning of the data.

There are many graphics packages on the market. Some may offer more variety and more sophistication compared to Lotus graphics. However, since Lotus graphs are based on the data available in the spreadsheet, they can be drawn fast and what-if analysis can be performed quickly. You can change data items, press F10 in READY mode, and the entire graph will be redrawn immediately.

5-3 Overview of Lotus Graphics

To set up a graph, first invoke Graph from the main menu. The following options will be presented:

Type X A B C D E F   Reset View Save Options Name Quit

Type indicates the graphs generated by Lotus: line, bar, XY, stacked-bar, and pie chart.

The X range is used for labeling the X-axis and is also used in the pie chart and the XY graph.

A, B, C, D, E, F indicates six different data ranges, allowing you to plot up to six ranges at the same time in all graphs except the pie chart.

Reset is used if you want to change the graph parameters. This means that all the previous data ranges, settings, and so forth will be erased.

View is used to display the graph on the screen if your computer has graphics capabilities.

Save is used to save a graph to be printed with the PrintGraph program.

Options gives you choices for dressing up your graph.

Name is used to name graph settings. Remember that a single worksheet can generate many different graphs with different names.

Finally, Quit is used to get back to the worksheet.

To create and display a graph, follow this procedure:

1. Select /Graph.
2. Select Type.
3. Select a graph type: line, bar, XY, stacked-bar, or pie chart.
4. Select one or more data ranges (X and/or A through F).
5. Specify the data for each range either by pointing or by typing the address.
6. Select View to display the graph type.
7. Press any key to return to the worksheet and the graph main menu.

5-4 Creating a Simple Pie Chart

Sunset Travel Agency has the following three expenses as part of its operating costs for 1986–1987. Enter the expenses into a worksheet.

Utilities   1850
Rent   1250
Supplies   700

Now plot these expenses using a pie chart.

Figure 5–1 shows this graph. It was generated with the commands /Graph, Type, Pie, X (A4..A6), Return, A (C4..C6), Return, View.

5-5 Saving the Graph Parameters

Once the graph is created, you may give it a name for later reference. In order to save a graph parameter, type /Graph Name Create. You can save a graph parameter under any name having up to 14 characters. After the graph is saved, you can change the parameters and save it under another name if you want. Don't forget to save (/File Save) the worksheet as well, because if you forget to save your worksheet, your graph will be lost. In addition, if you forget to name your graph (/Graph Name Create) and save only your worksheet, your graph will be lost.

To make a graph active (bring it back to memory), use /Graph Name Use. You can have only one graph active at one time. However, a worksheet can generate as many graphs as you want.

Figure 5–1 Worksheet for a Simple Pie Chart

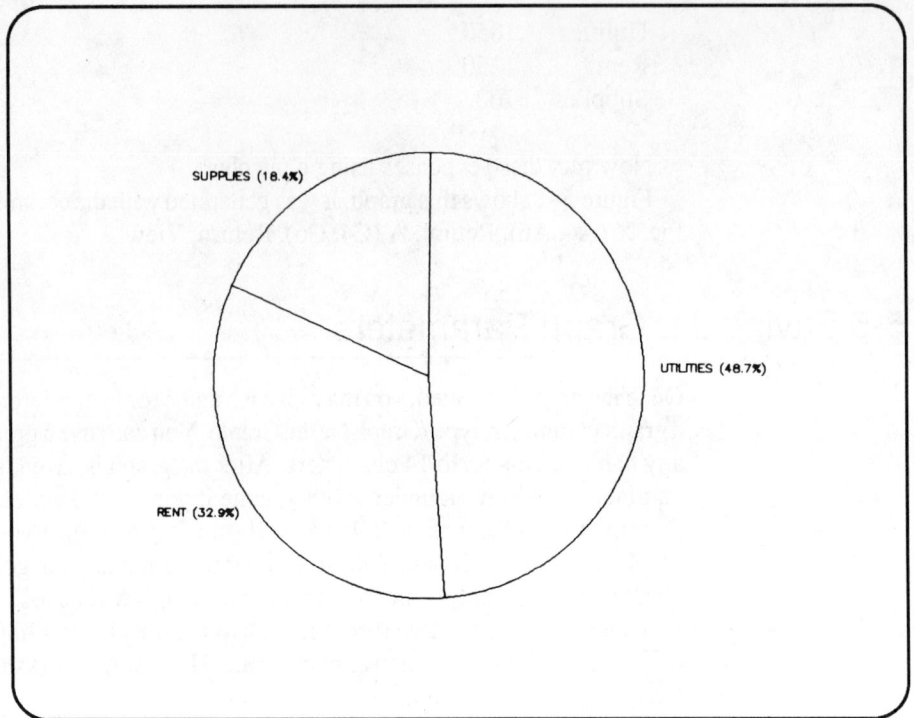

Figure 5–1 (Continued)

5-6 Deleting a Graph

To delete a graph, use /Graph Name Delete. Lotus will display all graph names for the current worksheet. You can either type the name to be deleted or move the cursor to the name and press **Return**. The graph is deleted. If you want to delete all the graphs under the current worksheet, use /Graph Name Reset. Be careful. When you issue this command all the graphs under the current worksheet will be gone and there is no way to retrieve them.

5-7 Saving a Graph for Printing

The Lotus spreadsheet program is not capable of printing your graph. To print your graph, first you must save it using /Graph Save. Lotus creates a graphic file on your disk with PIC as the extension. Now you can use the PrintGraph disk for printing your graph. When the graph is saved in a graphic file you can access it only from the PrintGraph program.

5-8 Pie Chart – a Second Look

As we mentioned earlier, pie charts are very useful for comparing some data to the whole. To activate the pie chart from the main menu, first select /Graph. Then from the Type menu choose Pie. To draw a pie chart, you need one data range. After you specify your data range, choose View and the graph will appear.

Figure 5–2 shows a pie chart of a simple regional analysis. Sales for each region are compared with total sales. This graph was generated by using /Graph, Type, Pie, X (A11..A13), Return, A (E11..E13), Return, View.

Figure 5–3 uses the same data for a sales performance analysis. This time the performance of each salesperson is compared with total sales. This graph was generated with /Graph, Type, Pie, X (B10..D10), Return, A (B15..D15), Return, View.

Generating a Pie Chart Using Crosshatches

Lotus can generate eight different crosshatches, which make data comparison an easy task. Each crosshatch has its own shape, and with color graphics, each crosshatch has a unique color. (We will discuss color later in this chapter.) Figure 5–4 illustrates these crosshatches. This figure was generated by using the commands /Graph, Type, Pie, X (B2..I2), Return, A (B3..I3), Return, B (B6..I6), Return, View.

To generate a crosshatch, you have to define a separate data range outside your original data range. The location of this new data range is not important. However, you must call this data range the B range. This means you must choose the B range, then specify the address of the data in your worksheet. In this data range you can enter any number between 0 to 8 inclusive. Codes 0 or 8 indicate an unshaded wedge.

Regional Analysis Using Crosshatches

In Figure 5–5 we show you another example of the pie chart with crosshatches. This figure performs regional analysis on the data shown in this worksheet. This figure was generated with /Graph, Type, Pie, X (A12..A14), Return, A (E12..E14), Return, B (B18..D18), Return, View.

Exploding a Pie Chart

Sometimes you may be interested in highlighting or "exploding" a portion or portions of a pie chart. Lotus provides you with a facility to perform this task. You can explode one or all portions of your pie chart. To do so, add 100 to the codes of your crosshatches. In Figure 5–6 we added 100 to cell B18. Now this cell contains 101.

This will explode that particular section of the pie with its original crosshatch. This figure was generated with /Graph, Type, Pie, X (A12..A14), Return, A (E12..E14), Return, B (B18..D18), Return, View.

Figure 5–7 illustrates a pie chart with all its components exploded. This figure was generated by using /Graph, Type, Pie, X (A12..A14), Return, A (E12..E14), Return, B (B18..D18), Return, View.

Figure 5–2 Regional Analysis Using a Pie Chart

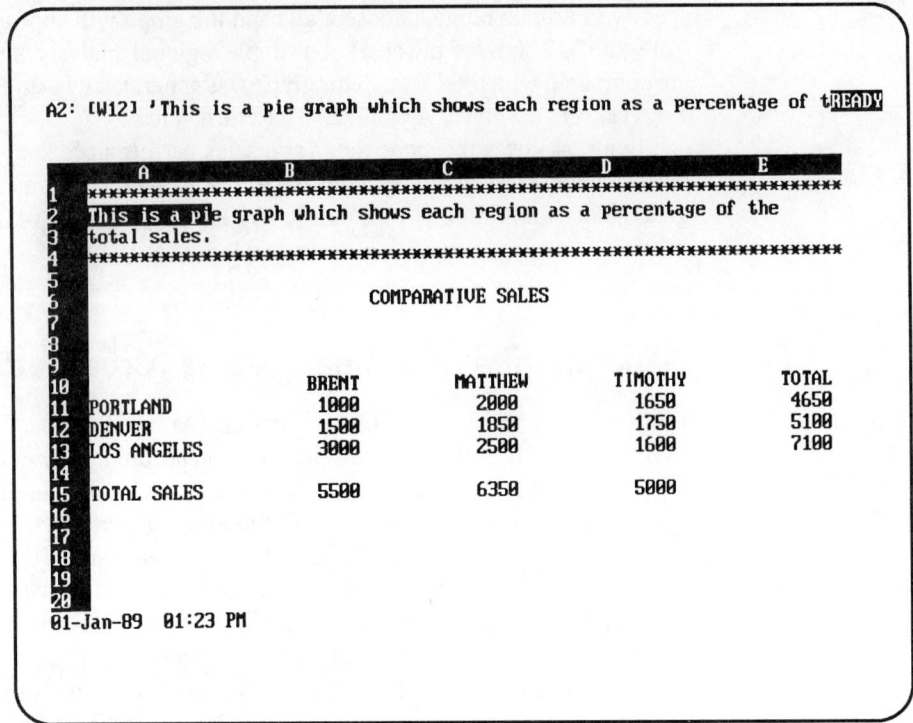

A2: [W12] 'This is a pie graph which shows each region as a percentage of t READY

```
          A           B            C            D            E
     ****************************************************************
1    This is a pie graph which shows each region as a percentage of the
2    total sales.
3    ****************************************************************
4
5                      COMPARATIVE SALES
6
7
8
9
10                     BRENT        MATTHEW      TIMOTHY      TOTAL
11   PORTLAND          1000         2000         1650         4650
12   DENVER            1500         1850         1750         5100
13   LOS ANGELES       3000         2500         1600         7100
14
15   TOTAL SALES       5500         6350         5000
16
17
18
19
20
     01-Jan-89   01:23 PM
```

Figure 5–2 (Continued)

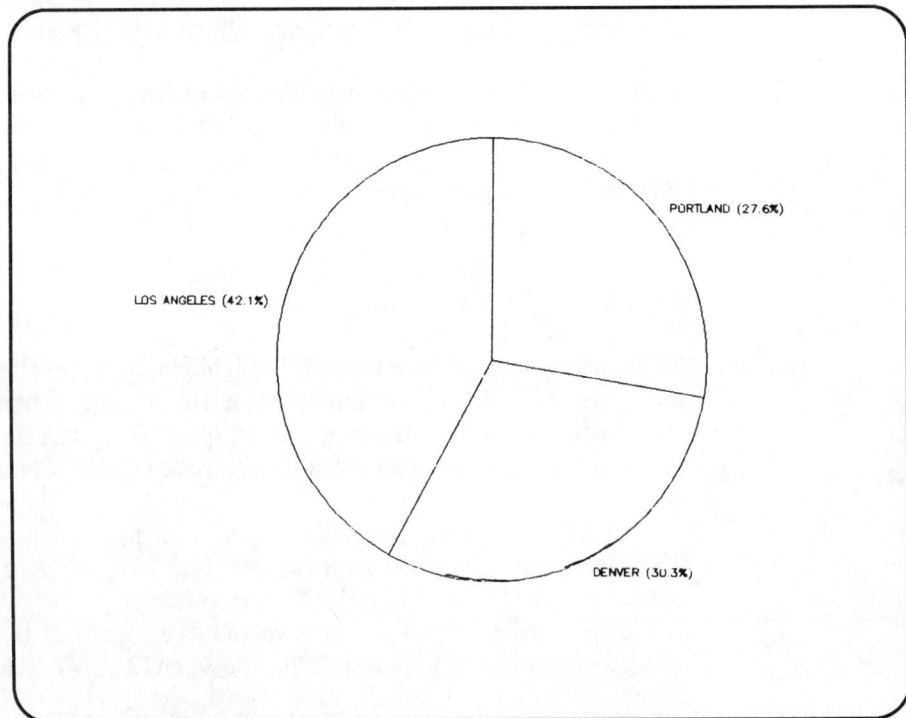

PORTLAND (27.6%)

LOS ANGELES (42.1%)

DENVER (30.3%)

Figure 5–3 Sales Performance Analysis Using a Pie Chart

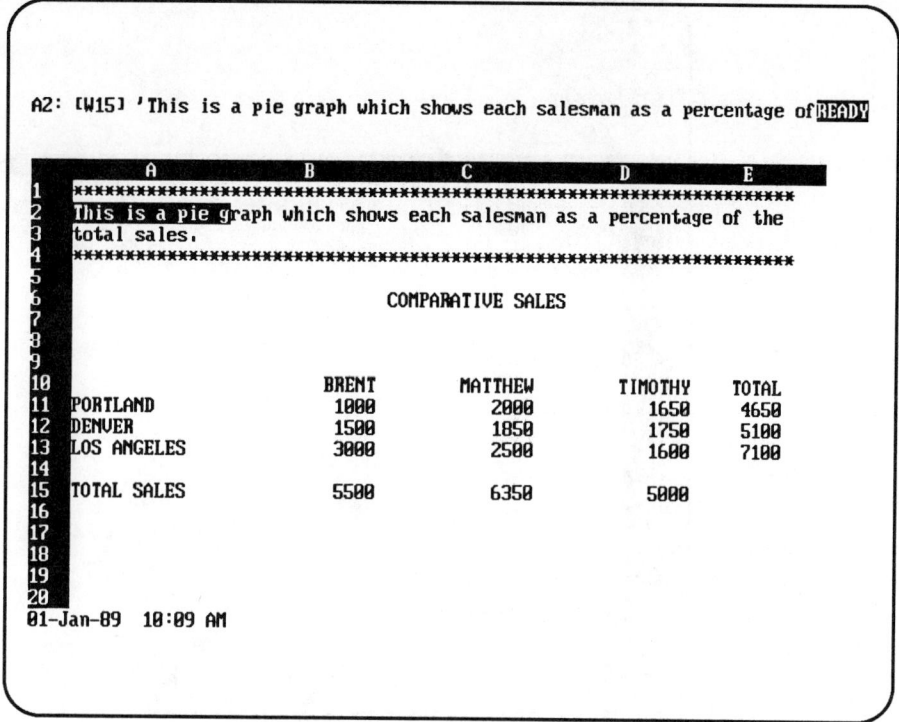

```
A2: [W15] 'This is a pie graph which shows each salesman as a percentage of READY

            A            B            C            D            E
1  ***************************************************************************
2  This is a pie graph which shows each salesman as a percentage of the
3  total sales.
4  ***************************************************************************
5
6                          COMPARATIVE SALES
7
8
9
10                      BRENT        MATTHEW      TIMOTHY      TOTAL
11 PORTLAND             1000         2000         1650         4650
12 DENVER               1500         1850         1750         5100
13 LOS ANGELES          3000         2500         1600         7100
14
15 TOTAL SALES          5500         6350         5000
16
17
18
19
20
01-Jan-89  10:09 AM
```

Figure 5–3 (Continued)

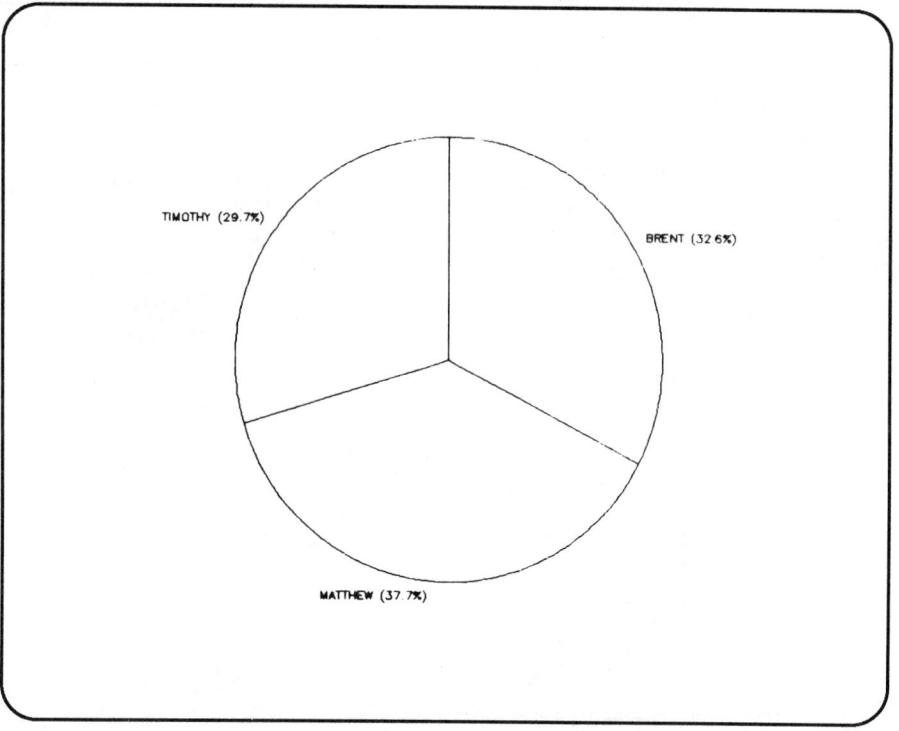

Figure 5–4 Crosshatch Options

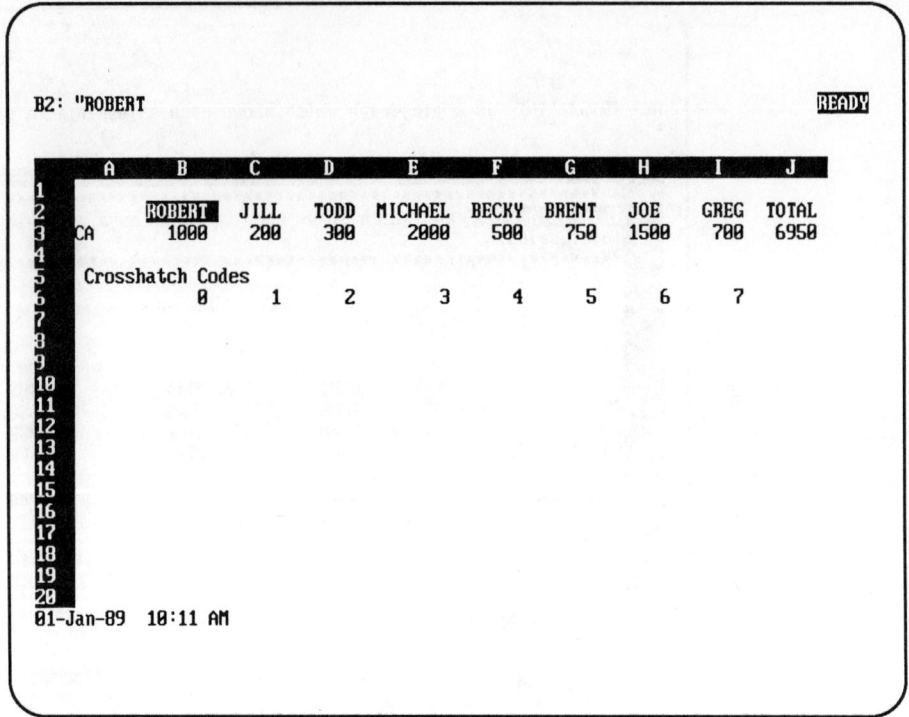

```
B2: "ROBERT                                                       READY

         A     B      C      D      E       F       G      H      I      J
1
2             ROBERT  JILL   TODD  MICHAEL  BECKY  BRENT   JOE   GREG  TOTAL
3      CA      1000   200    300    2000    500    750    1500   700   6950
4
5      Crosshatch Codes
6              0      1      2       3       4       5      6      7
7
8
9
10
11
12
13
14
15
16
17
18
19
20
       01-Jan-89  10:11 AM
```

Figure 5–4 (Continued)

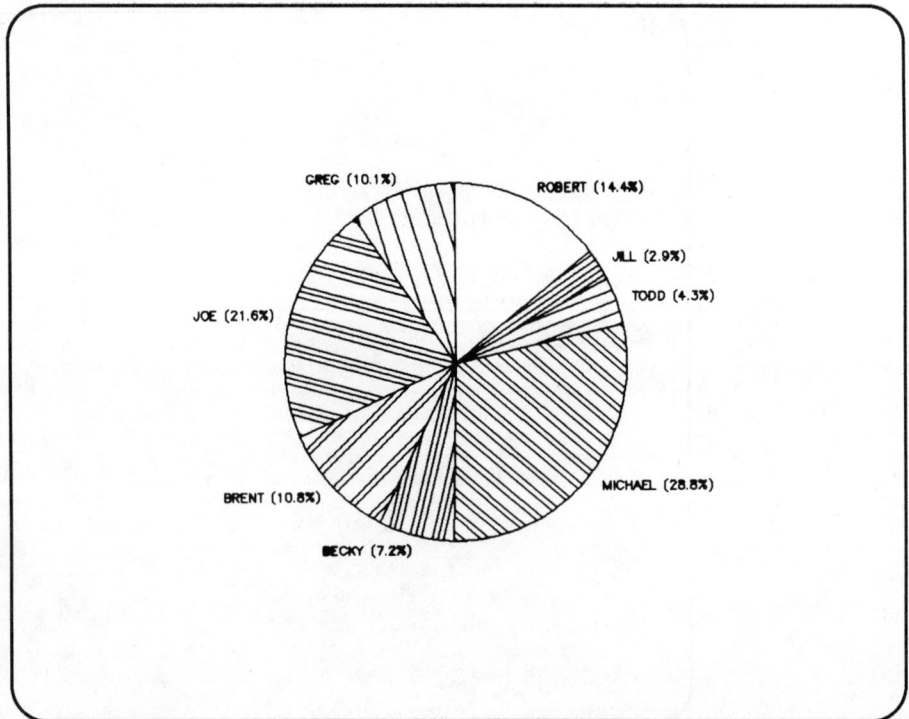

Figure 5–5 Regional Analysis Using Crosshatches

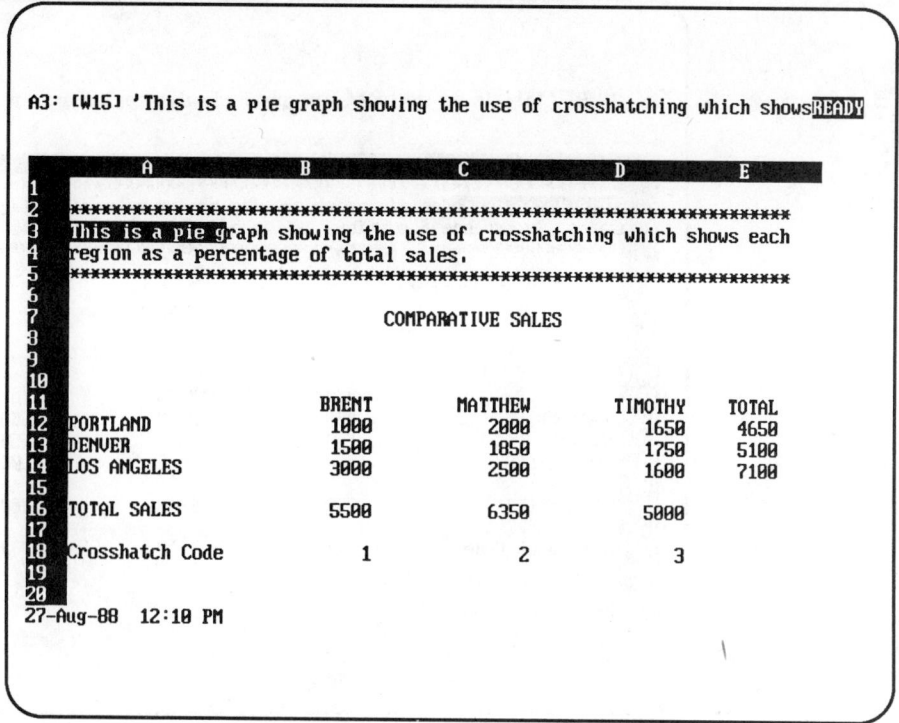

```
A3: [W15] 'This is a pie graph showing the use of crosshatching which shows READY

         A              B            C              D          E
1
2  ************************************************************************
3  This is a pie graph showing the use of crosshatching which shows each
4  region as a percentage of total sales.
5  ************************************************************************
6
7                        COMPARATIVE SALES
8
9
10
11                     BRENT        MATTHEW       TIMOTHY     TOTAL
12 PORTLAND            1000          2000          1650       4650
13 DENVER              1500          1850          1750       5100
14 LOS ANGELES         3000          2500          1600       7100
15
16 TOTAL SALES         5500          6350          5000
17
18 Crosshatch Code        1             2             3
19
20
27-Aug-88   12:10 PM
```

Figure 5–5 (Continued)

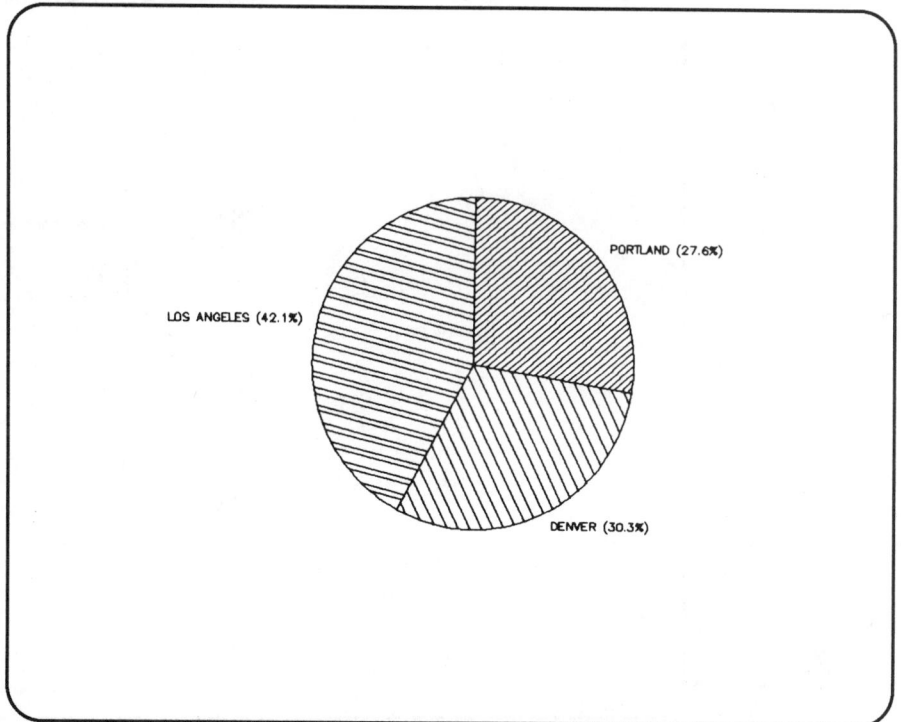

Figure 5–6 Exploding One Section of a Pie Chart

```
A2: [W15] 'This is an exploded pie graph showing region as a percentage of   READY

         A          B          C          D          E
1   *****************************************************************
2   This is an exploded pie graph showing region as a percentage of total
3   sales. To explode a portion, 100 is added to the crosshatch code.
4   *****************************************************************
5
6
7                        COMPARATIVE SALES
8
9
10
11                   BRENT      MATTHEW    TIMOTHY    TOTAL
12  PORTLAND         1000       2000       1650       4650
13  DENVER           1500       1850       1750       5100
14  LOS ANGELES      3000       2500       1600       7100
15
16  TOTAL SALES      5500       6350       5000
17
18  Crosshatch Code   101          2          3
19
20
    01-Jan-89   10:11 AM
```

Figure 5–6 (Continued)

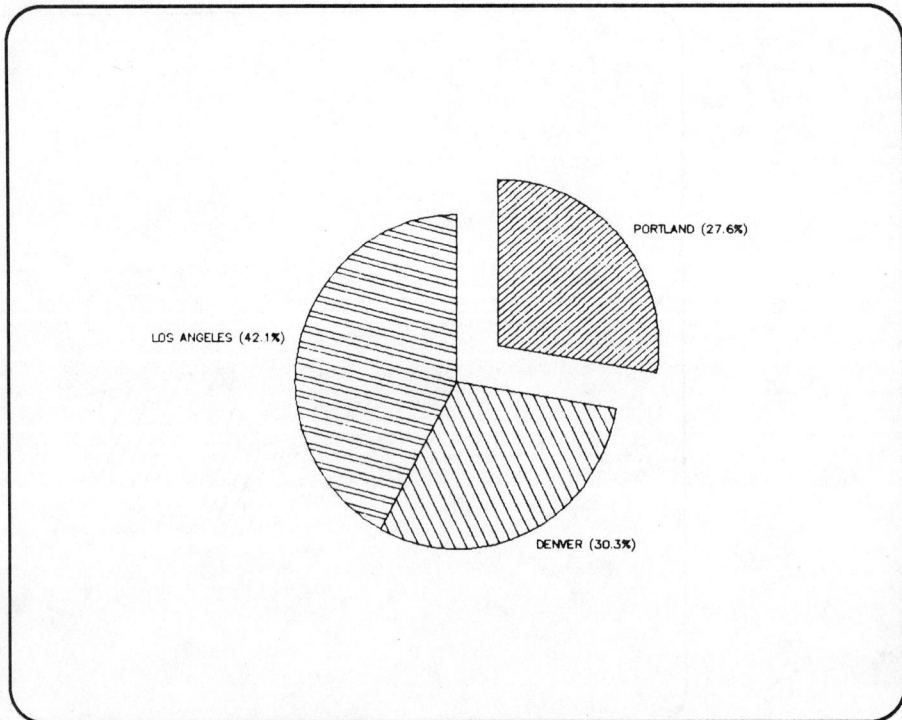

Figure 5–7 Explosion of the Entire Pie Chart

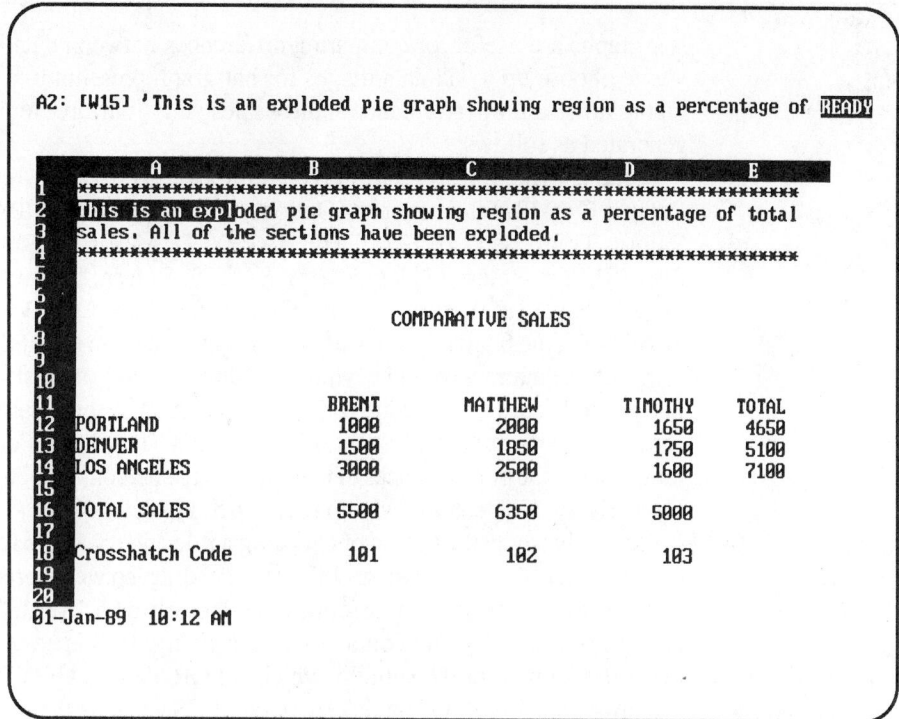

```
A2: [W15] 'This is an exploded pie graph showing region as a percentage of  READY

           A            B            C            D            E
1  ***************************************************************************
2  This is an exploded pie graph showing region as a percentage of total
3  sales. All of the sections have been exploded.
4  ***************************************************************************
5
6
7                          COMPARATIVE SALES
8
9
10
11                     BRENT        MATTHEW      TIMOTHY      TOTAL
12  PORTLAND           1000         2000         1650         4650
13  DENVER             1500         1850         1750         5100
14  LOS ANGELES        3000         2500         1600         7100
15
16  TOTAL SALES        5500         6350         5000
17
18  Crosshatch Code     101          102          103
19
20
01-Jan-89  10:12 AM
```

Figure 5–7 (Continued)

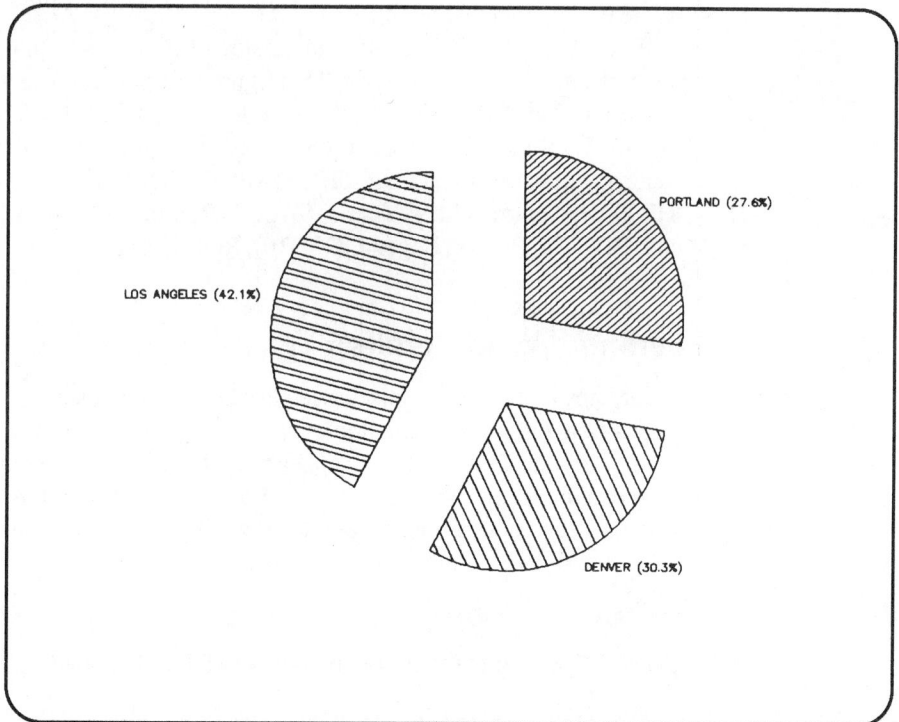

5-9 Bar Graphs

Bar graphs are useful for comparing differences between data items. Lotus allows you to choose up to six data ranges for bar graph presentation. Figure 5–8 is a bar graph showing the performance of three salespersons in three regions. This graph was generated as follows:

/Graph, Type, Bar, X (B10..D10), Return, A (B11..D11), Return, B (B12..D12), Return, C (B13..D13), Return, Options, Titles, First, COMPARATIVE SALES, Return, Titles, Second, FOR THE HAPPY TRAVELER, Return, Titles, X-axis, SALESMEN, Return, Titles, Y-axis, SALES, Return, Legend, A (\A11), Return, Legend, B (\A12), Return, Legend, C (\A13), Return, Quit, View.

As usual, the Graph option was chosen from the main menu. The type chosen was Bar. The X data range can be whatever labels you are interested in showing on the X-axis. In Figure 5–8, we have chosen the names of three salesmen. The A range shows the performance of Brent, Matthew, and Timothy in Portland. The B and C ranges show the performances of these three salespersons in Denver and Los Angeles respectively. You can include up to six such labels.

Lotus gives you the option of choosing a title and a subtitle for the graph. Choose Options, then Titles, then First. This is the heading, so we entered COMPARATIVE SALES. To enter this heading, either type it or use a backslash (\) followed by a cell address or a range name containing the heading. In this case, \C6 will do it. The Second option is for the subtitle, which is FOR THE HAPPY TRAVELER.

Now you choose the X-axis. We put SALESMEN on the X-axis and SALES for the Y-axis. To make the presentation clearer, you can choose up to six legends. We chose Legend A for PORTLAND, B for DENVER, and C for LOS ANGELES. These items can be either typed or entered with a backslash followed by the cell reference or range name.

Figure 5–9 is a slightly different version of Figure 5–8. In this figure we display the performance of each region. This figure was generated as follows:

/Graph, Type, Bar, X (A11..A13), Return, A (B11..B13), Return, B (C11..C13), Return, C (D11..D13), Return, Options, Titles, First, COMPARATIVE SALES, Return, Titles, Second, FOR THE HAPPY TRAVELER, Return, Titles, X-axis, REGION, Return, Titles, Y-axis, SALES, Return, Legend, A(\B10), Return, Legend, B(\C10), Return, Legend, C(\D10), Return, Quit, View.

Setting Scale Limits

So far, the graphs we have discussed have been plotted using automatic scaling. This means that Lotus always automatically fits your data in the X and Y axes; for example, your first data item appears first and the last data item appears last. However, there may be cases where you are interested in highlighting a portion of the graph or in changing the automatic scaling. If you issue the command /Graph Options Scale, the following menu will be illustrated:

Y scale   X scale   Skip

Choose Y scale and the following menu will be illustrated:

Automatic   Manual   Lower   Upper   Format   Indicator   Quit

Figure 5–8 Bar Graph for Sales Performance Analysis

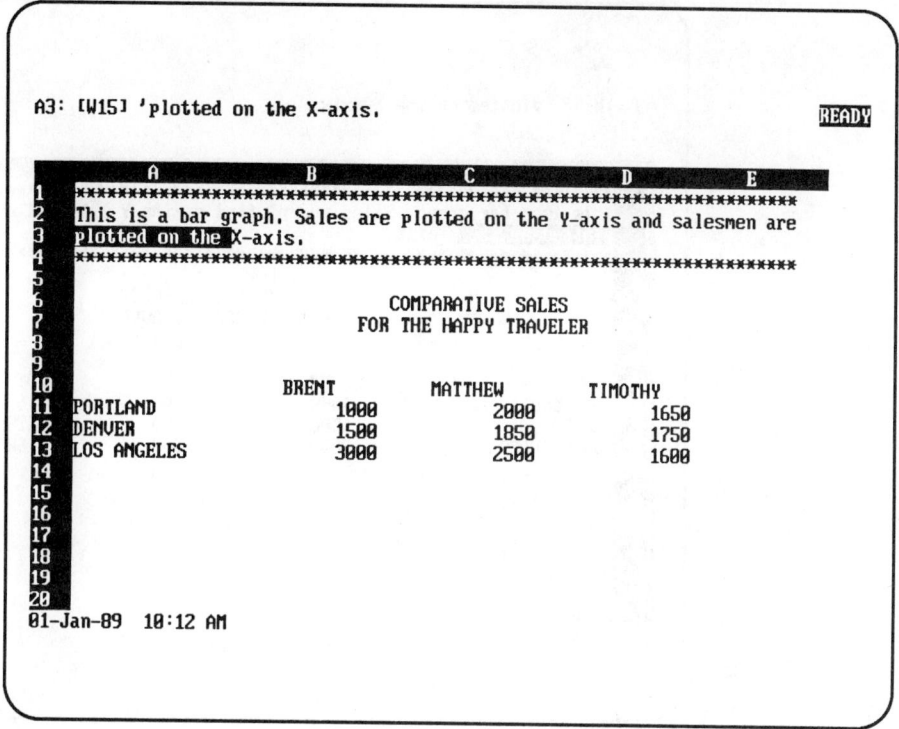

A3: [W15] 'plotted on the X-axis. ▮READY▮

	A	B	C	D	E
1	***				
2	This is a bar graph. Sales are plotted on the Y-axis and salesmen are				
3	plotted on the X-axis.				
4	***				

```
                         COMPARATIVE SALES
                        FOR THE HAPPY TRAVELER

                     BRENT        MATTHEW        TIMOTHY
PORTLAND             1000          2000           1650
DENVER               1500          1850           1750
LOS ANGELES          3000          2500           1600
```

01-Jan-89 10:12 AM

Figure 5–8 (Continued)

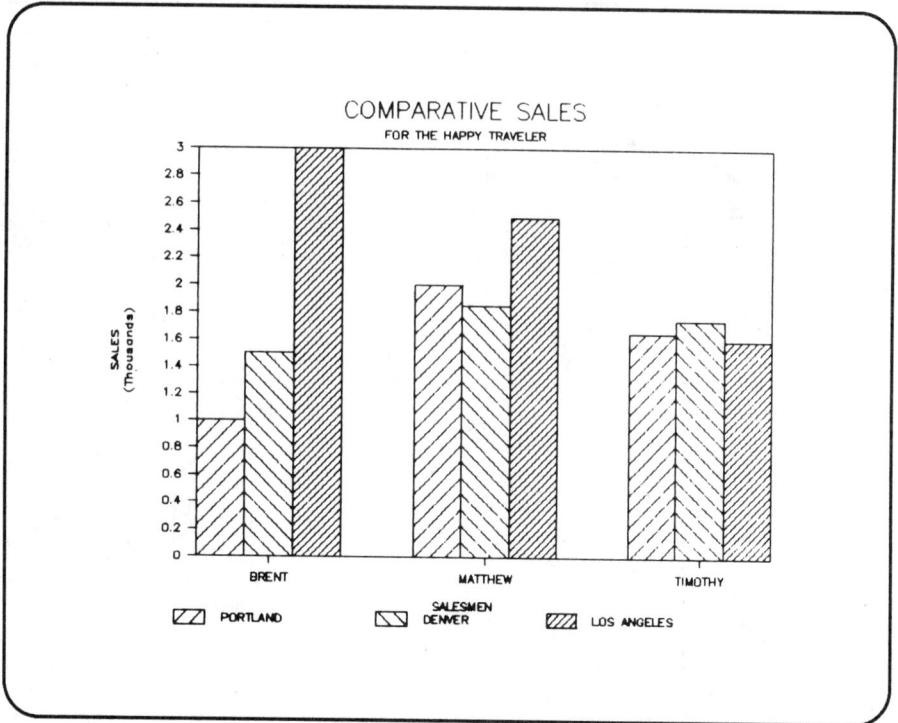

Figure 5–9 Bar Graph for Regional Analysis

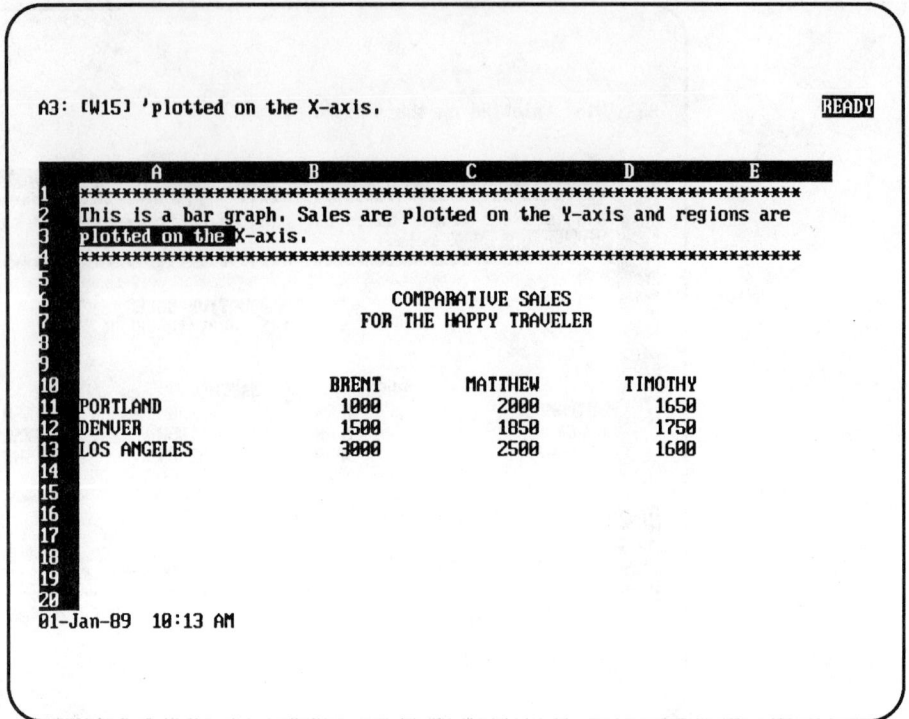

```
A3: [W15] 'plotted on the X-axis.                              READY

        A           B           C           D           E
1  *************************************************************
2  This is a bar graph. Sales are plotted on the Y-axis and regions are
3  plotted on the X-axis.
4  *************************************************************
5
6                       COMPARATIVE SALES
7                      FOR THE HAPPY TRAVELER
8
9
10                     BRENT      MATTHEW     TIMOTHY
11 PORTLAND            1000        2000        1650
12 DENVER              1500        1850        1750
13 LOS ANGELES         3000        2500        1600
14
15
16
17
18
19
20
01-Jan-89  10:13 AM
```

Figure 5–9 (Continued)

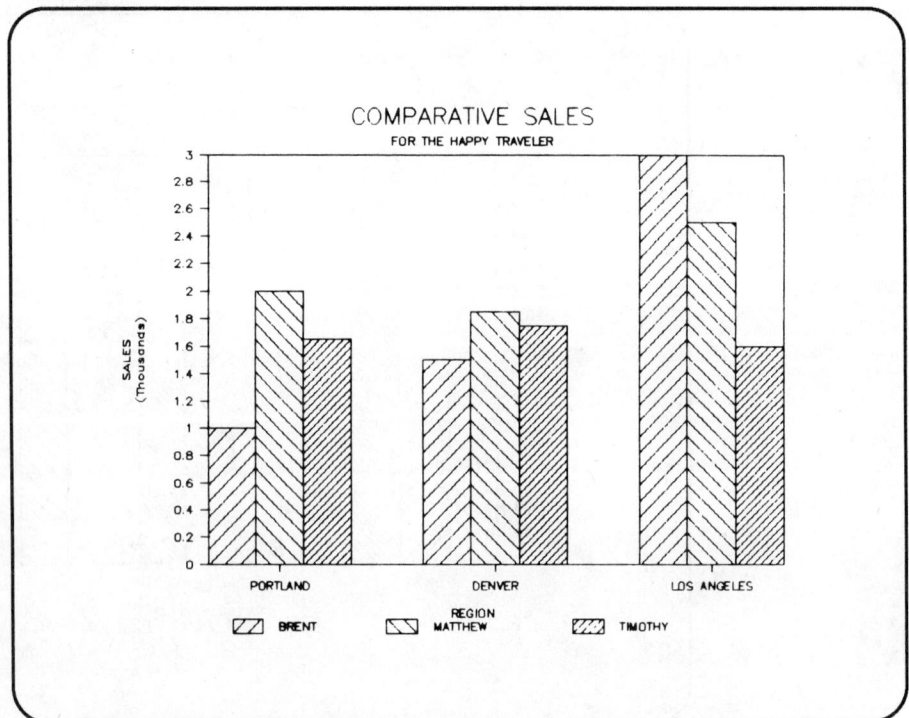

If you choose Manual, you will be given all the other choices. The Format option is the same as /Range Format or /Worksheet Global Format. This means you can format your number(s) in the X or Y axis.

Figure 5–10 shows an example of a manual scale. This figure was generated as follows:

/Graph, Type, Bar, X (B11..D11), Return, A (B12..D12), Return, B (B13..D13), Return, C (B14..D14), Return, Options, Legend, A (\A12), Return, Legend, B (\A13), Return, Legend, C (\A14), Return, Titles, First, COMPARATIVE SALES, Return, Titles, Second, FOR THE HAPPY TRAVELER, Return, Titles, X-axis, SALESMEN, Return, Titles, Y-axis, SALES, Return, Scale, Y-scale, Manual, Lower (-1,000), Return, Upper (4,000), Return, Quit, Quit, View.

The Indicator option allows you to suppress the scale indicator, or, more simply put, Lotus rescales the axis in order to fit the data. If your scale is too low and there are large differences between your data ranges you may see only a portion of your data. Figure 5–11 illustrates this case. This graph was generated as follows:

/Graph, Type, Bar, X (B11..D11), Return, A (B12..D12), Return, B (B13..D13), Return, C (B14..D14), Return, Options, Legend, A (\A12), Return, Legend, B (\A13), Return, Legend, C (\A14), Return, Titles, First, COMPARATIVE SALES, Return, Titles, Second, FOR THE HAPPY TRAVELER, Return, Titles, X-axis, SALESMEN, Return, Titles, Y-axis, SALES, Return, Scale, Y scale, Manual, Lower (-1000), Return, Upper (2000),Return, Quit, Quit, View.

5-10 Line Graphs

Line graphs are very useful when you want to observe the performance of one variable over a period of time; for instance, a company's total advertising budget for the years 1976 to 1987. The Format option is used to draw lines or symbols in line or XY graphs. When the Format option is chosen, the following menu will be presented:

Graph   A B C D E F   Quit

The Graph option sets the format for all ranges, while options A-F are used to set the format for a particular range. Lines, Symbols, Both, and Neither are choices under the Graph option. Lines will draw lines between data points; Symbols will draw symbols at data points; Both will draw both lines and symbols; and Neither will display data labels only.

Horizontal and vertical grid lines can be used to make graphs easier to read. These lines can be drawn by using the Grid option. A choice of horizontal grid lines, vertical grid lines, or both are available for the flexible presentation of line graphs.

The Data Labels option is used to specify a label corresponding to the data range. Up to six data ranges can be labeled. These labels can be aligned in five convenient ways relative to data points: center, left, above, right, or below.

Figure 5–12 is an example of a line graph. This figure shows the total sales for Alpha-Talk Company from 1975 to 1986. The graph was generated as follows:

/Graph, Type, Line, X (C11..C15), Return, A (F11..F15), Return, Options, Titles, First, ALPHA-TALK COMPANY, Return, Titles, X-axis, YEAR, Return, Titles, Y-axis, TOTAL SALES, Return, Format, Graph, Lines, Quit, Quit, View.

Figure 5–10 Manual Scaling of Sales Performance Analysis

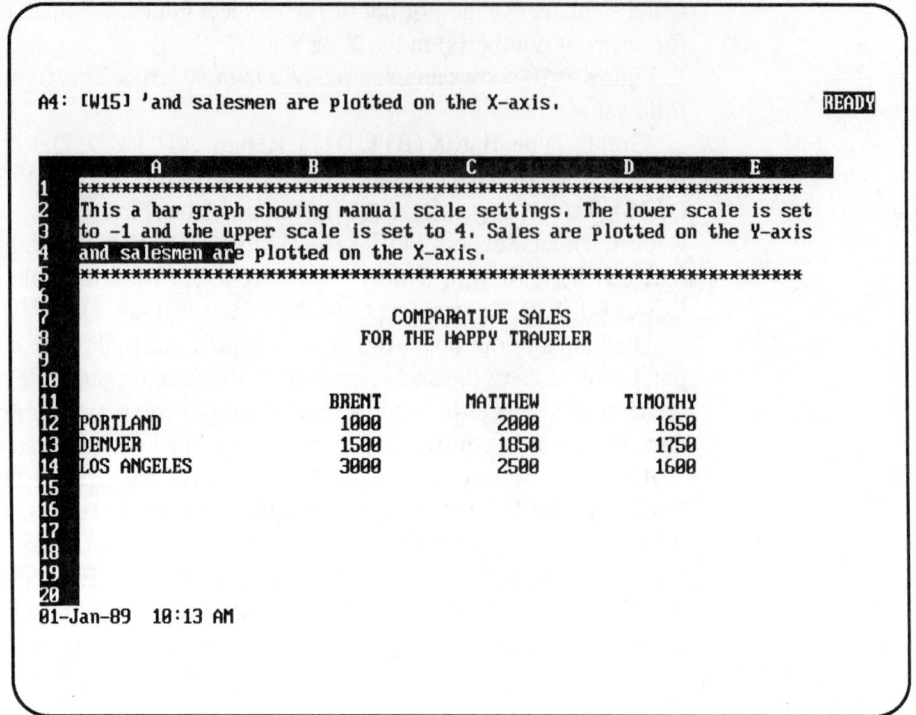

```
A4: [W15] 'and salesmen are plotted on the X-axis.                    READY

           A          B          C          D          E
1  *********************************************************************
2  This a bar graph showing manual scale settings. The lower scale is set
3  to -1 and the upper scale is set to 4. Sales are plotted on the Y-axis
4  and salesmen are plotted on the X-axis.
5  *********************************************************************
6
7                              COMPARATIVE SALES
8                            FOR THE HAPPY TRAVELER
9
10
11                    BRENT        MATTHEW        TIMOTHY
12 PORTLAND           1000          2000           1650
13 DENVER             1500          1850           1750
14 LOS ANGELES        3000          2500           1600
15
16
17
18
19
20
01-Jan-89  10:13 AM
```

Figure 5–10 (Continued)

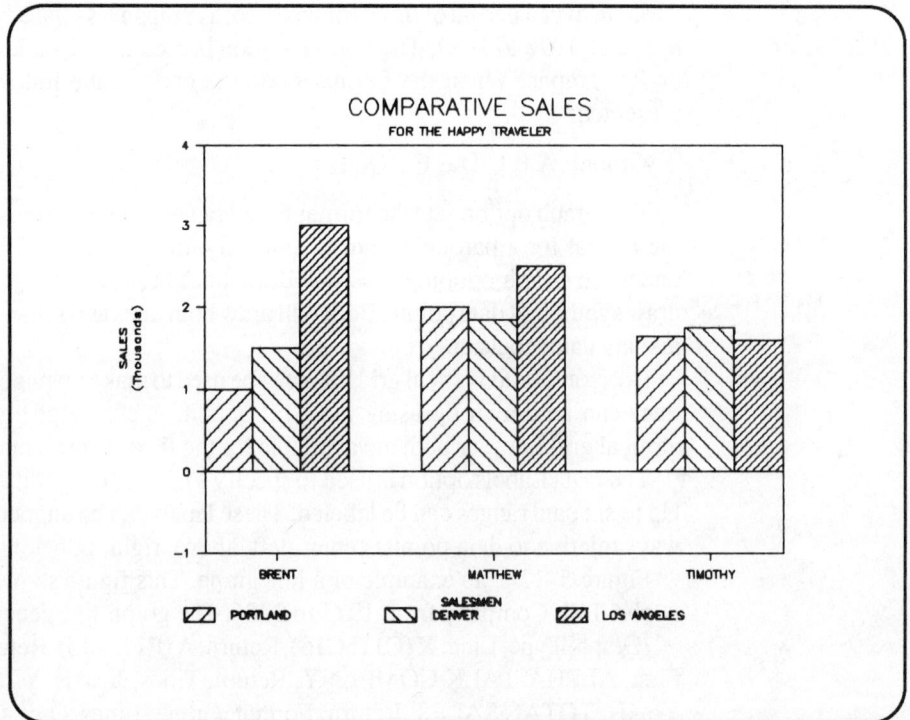

COMPARATIVE SALES
FOR THE HAPPY TRAVELER

Figure 5–11 Manual Scaling of Sales Performance

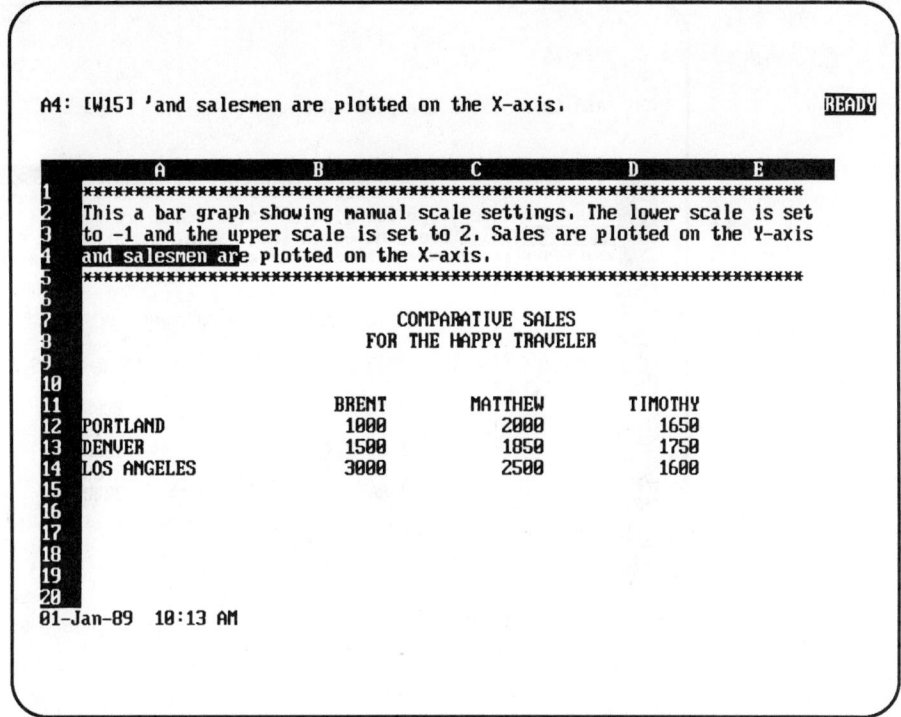

```
A4: [W15] 'and salesmen are plotted on the X-axis.                    READY

            A            B            C            D            E
1  ****************************************************************************
2  This a bar graph showing manual scale settings. The lower scale is set
3  to -1 and the upper scale is set to 2. Sales are plotted on the Y-axis
4  and salesmen are plotted on the X-axis.
5  ****************************************************************************
6
7                          COMPARATIVE SALES
8                        FOR THE HAPPY TRAVELER
9
10
11                      BRENT        MATTHEW       TIMOTHY
12 PORTLAND             1000          2000          1650
13 DENVER               1500          1850          1750
14 LOS ANGELES          3000          2500          1600
15
16
17
18
19
20
01-Jan-89   10:13 AM
```

Figure 5–11 (Continued)

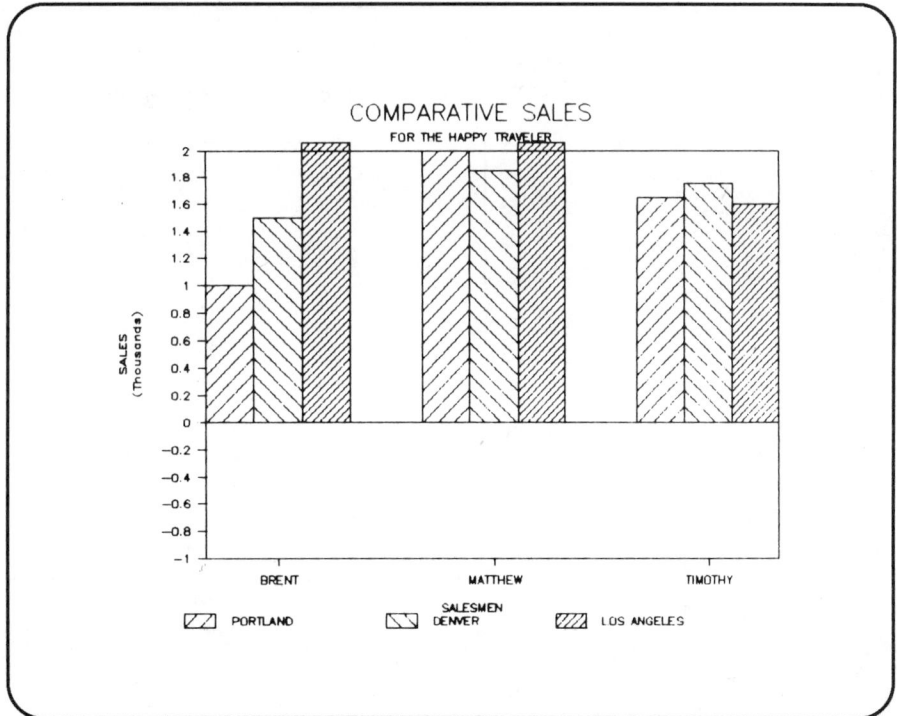

COMPARATIVE SALES
FOR THE HAPPY TRAVELER

Figure 5–12 Line Graph with Lines Only

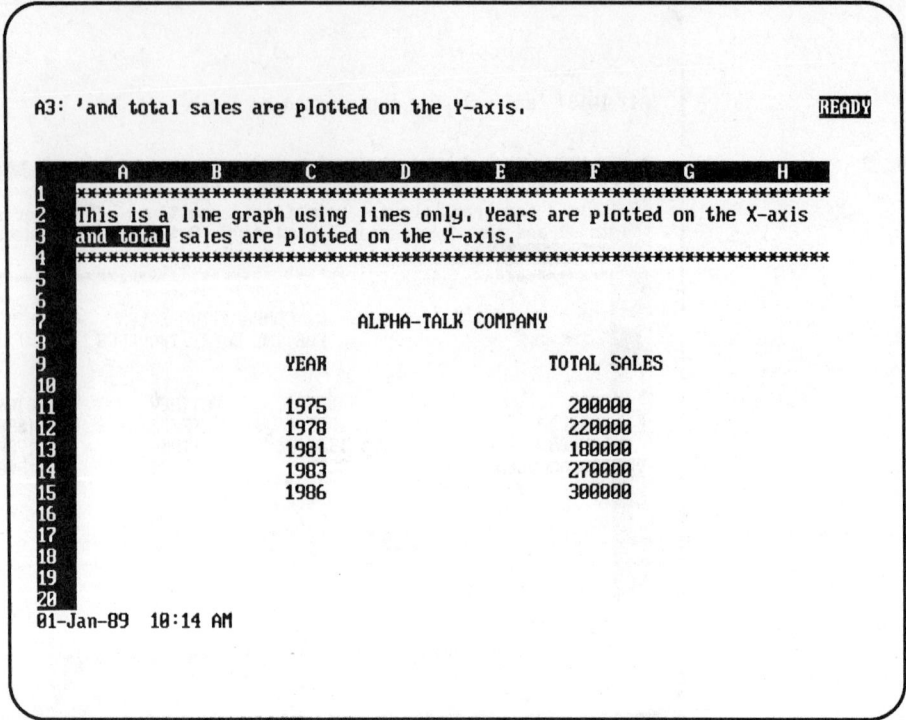

```
A3: 'and total sales are plotted on the Y-axis.                    READY

         A      B      C      D      E      F      G      H
1   ****************************************************************
2   This is a line graph using lines only. Years are plotted on the X-axis
3   and total sales are plotted on the Y-axis.
4   ****************************************************************
5
6
7                          ALPHA-TALK COMPANY
8
9                  YEAR                      TOTAL SALES
10
11                 1975                        200000
12                 1978                        220000
13                 1981                        180000
14                 1983                        270000
15                 1986                        300000
16
17
18
19
20
01-Jan-89   10:14 AM
```

Figure 5–12 (Continued)

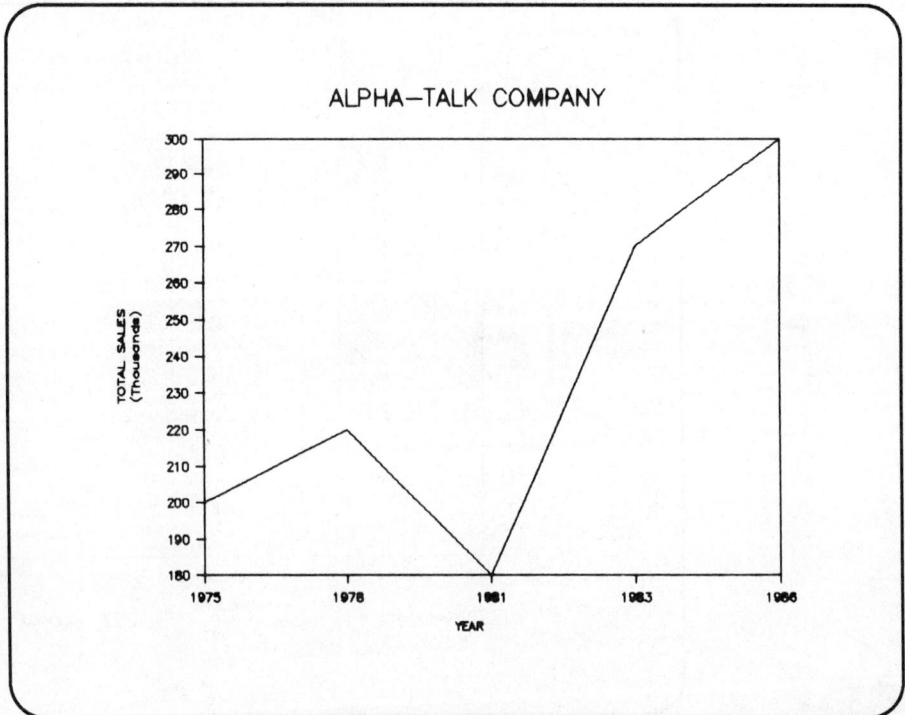

ALPHA-TALK COMPANY

Line Graph with Lines and Symbols

Figure 5–13 displays the same data as Figure 5–12 except that we have chosen both lines and symbols. This graph was generated as follows:

/Graph, Type, Line, X (C11..C15), Return, A (F11..F15), Return, Options, Titles, First, ALPHA-TALK COMPANY, Return, Titles, X-axis, YEAR, Return, Titles, Y-axis, TOTAL SALES, Return, Format, Graph, Both, Quit, Quit, View.

Line Graph with Lines, Symbols, and Grids

Figure 5–14 plots the same data as Figures 5–12 and 5–13 but uses a vertical grid. This figure was generated as follows:

/Graph, Type, Line, X (C12..C16), Return, A (F12..F16), Return, Options, Titles, First, ALPHA-TALK COMPANY, Return, Titles, X-axis, YEAR, Return, Titles, Y-axis, TOTAL SALES, Return, Grid, Vertical, Format, Graph, Both, Quit, Quit, View.

Figure 5–15 shows the same data, this time on a horizontal grid. This figure was generated as follows:

/Graph, Type, Line, X (C12..C16), Return, A (F12..F16), Return, Options, Titles, First, ALPHA-TALK COMPANY, Return, Titles, X-axis, YEAR, Return, Titles, Y-axis, TOTAL SALES, Return, Grid, Horizontal, Format, Graph, Both, Quit, Quit, View.

Figure 5–16 displays the same data once again. This time, we are using both vertical and horizontal grids. This figure was generated as follows:

/Graph, Type, Line, X (C12..C16), Return, A (F12..F16), Return, Options, Titles, First, ALPHA-TALK COMPANY, Return, Titles, X-axis, YEAR, Return, Titles, Y-axis, TOTAL SALES, Return, Grid, Both, Format, Graph, Both, Quit, Quit, View.

Figure 5–17 displays the same graph, this time using only symbols. This graph was generated as follows:

/Graph, Type, Line, X (C12..C16), Return, A (F12..F16), Return, Options, Titles, First, ALPHA-TALK COMPANY, Return, Titles, X-axis, YEAR, Return, Titles, Y-axis, TOTAL SALES, Return, Grid, Both, Format, Graph, Symbols, Quit, Quit, View.

Figure 5–18 displays the same data. This time, however, neither lines nor grids are used, just symbols. This figure was generated as follows:

/Graph, Type, Line, X (C11..C15), Return, A (F11..F15), Return, Options, Titles, First, ALPHA-TALK COMPANY, Return, Titles, X-axis, YEAR, Return, Titles, Y-axis, TOTAL SALES, Return, Format, Graph, Symbols, Quit, Quit, View.

Figure 5–19 displays a line graph that plots an advertising budget for twelve periods, using symbols. This figure was generated as follows:

/Graph, Type, Line, X (A7..A18), Return, A (B7..B18), Return, Options, Format, Graph, Both, Quit, Titles, First, SUNSHINE TRAVEL, Return, Titles, X-axis, YEAR, Return, Titles, Y-axis, PERCENTAGE OF ADVERTISING BUDGET, Return, Quit, View.

Figure 5–20 displays the same data as Figure 5–19, however, this time we have used the Skip option. This option lets you skip every *n*th label on the X axis. The graph was generated as follows:

Figure 5–13 Line Graph with Lines and Symbols

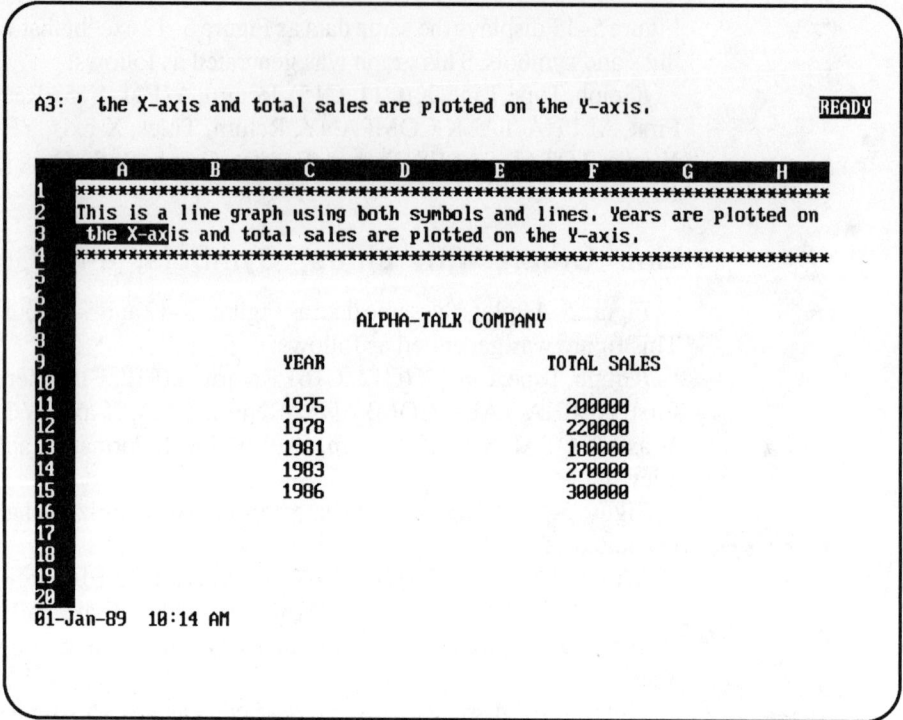

```
A3:  ' the X-axis and total sales are plotted on the Y-axis.              READY

            A         B         C         D         E         F        G         H
1  **********************************************************************************
2  This is a line graph using both symbols and lines. Years are plotted on
3  the X-axis and total sales are plotted on the Y-axis.
4  **********************************************************************************
5
6
7                           ALPHA-TALK COMPANY
8
9                   YEAR                      TOTAL SALES
10
11                  1975                         200000
12                  1978                         220000
13                  1981                         180000
14                  1983                         270000
15                  1986                         300000
16
17
18
19
20
01-Jan-89   10:14 AM
```

Figure 5–13 (Continued)

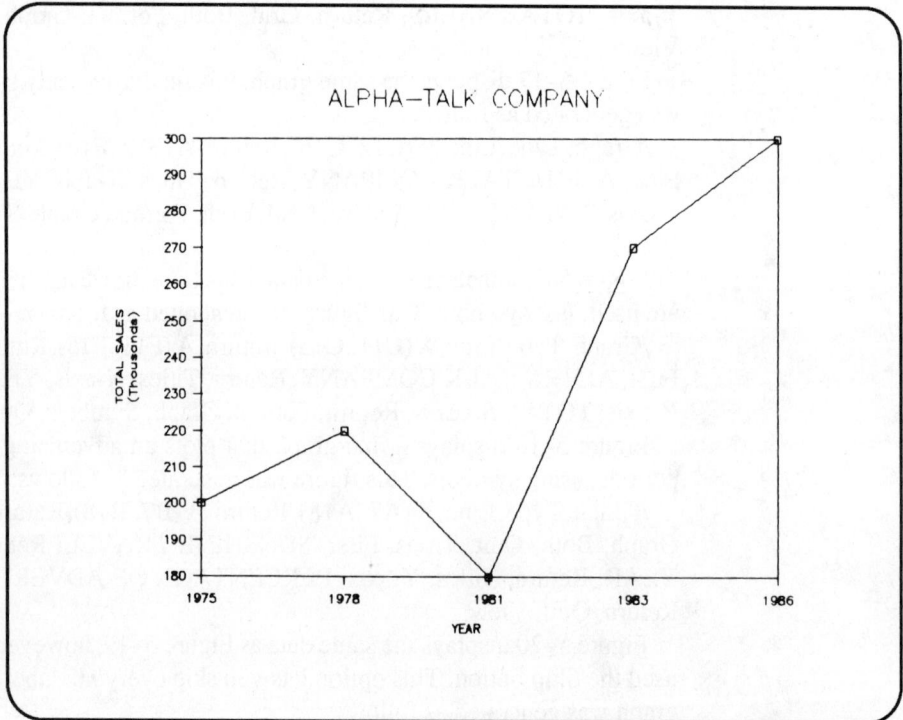

Figure 5-14 Line Graph with Both Lines and Symbols and a Vertical Grid

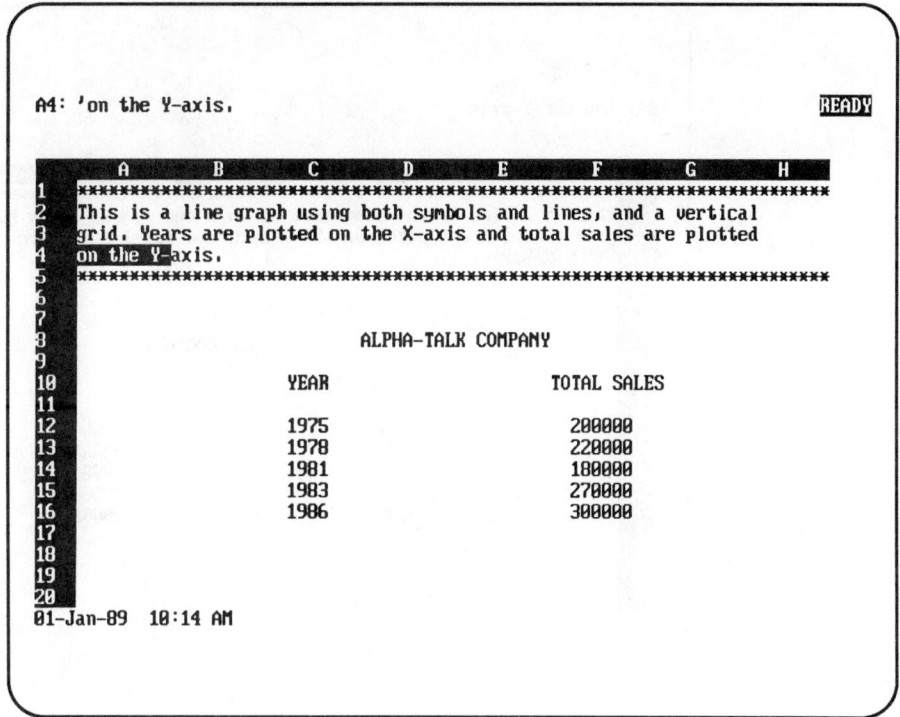

```
A4: 'on the Y-axis.                                              READY

         A       B      C      D      E      F      G      H
1   ************************************************************************
2   This is a line graph using both symbols and lines, and a vertical
3   grid. Years are plotted on the X-axis and total sales are plotted
4   on the Y-axis.
5   ************************************************************************
6
7
8                        ALPHA-TALK COMPANY
9
10       YEAR                          TOTAL SALES
11
12       1975                          200000
13       1978                          220000
14       1981                          180000
15       1983                          270000
16       1986                          300000
17
18
19
20
01-Jan-89  10:14 AM
```

Figure 5-14 (Continued)

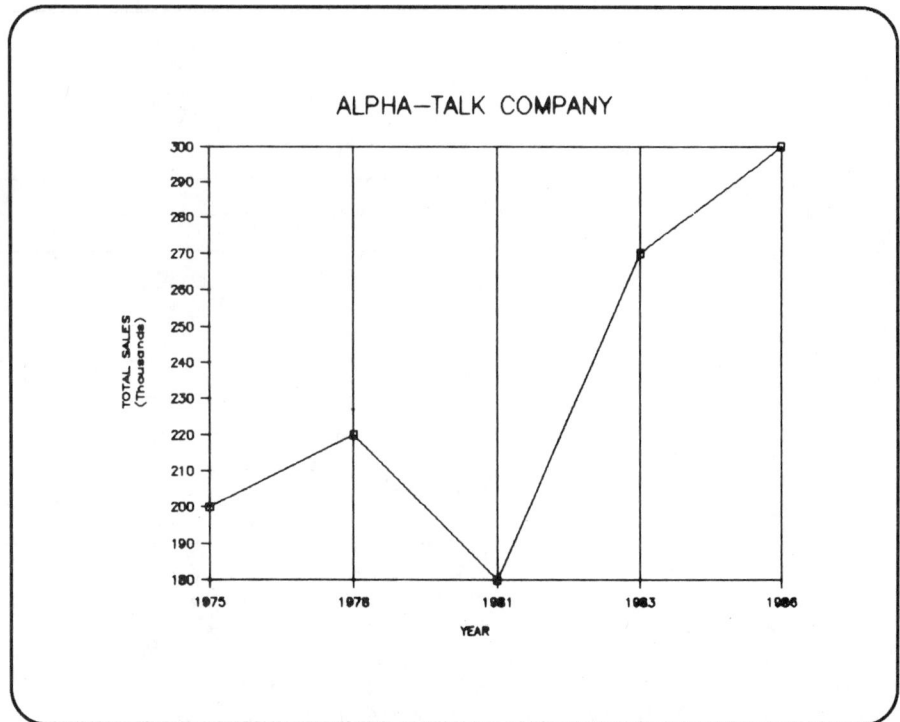

ALPHA-TALK COMPANY

Figure 5–15 Line Graph with Both Lines and Symbols and a Horizontal Grid

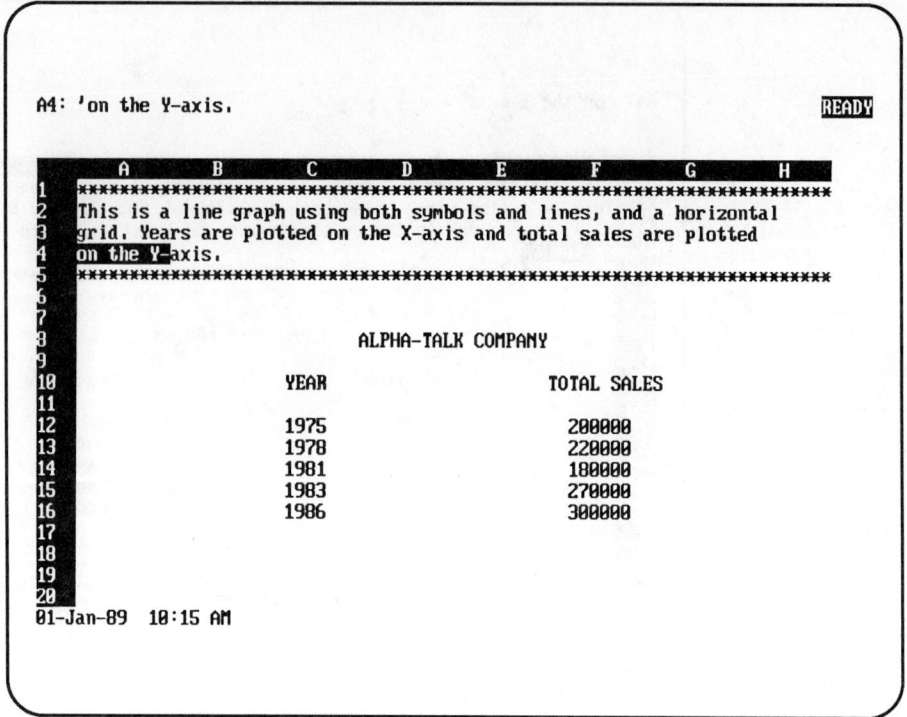

A4: 'on the Y-axis.   READY

```
         A        B        C        D        E        F        G        H
1  ***************************************************************************
2  This is a line graph using both symbols and lines, and a horizontal
3  grid. Years are plotted on the X-axis and total sales are plotted
4  on the Y-axis.
5  ***************************************************************************
6
7
8                             ALPHA-TALK COMPANY
9
10                 YEAR                        TOTAL SALES
11
12                 1975                          200000
13                 1978                          220000
14                 1981                          180000
15                 1983                          270000
16                 1986                          300000
17
18
19
20
01-Jan-89   10:15 AM
```

Figure 5–15 (Continued)

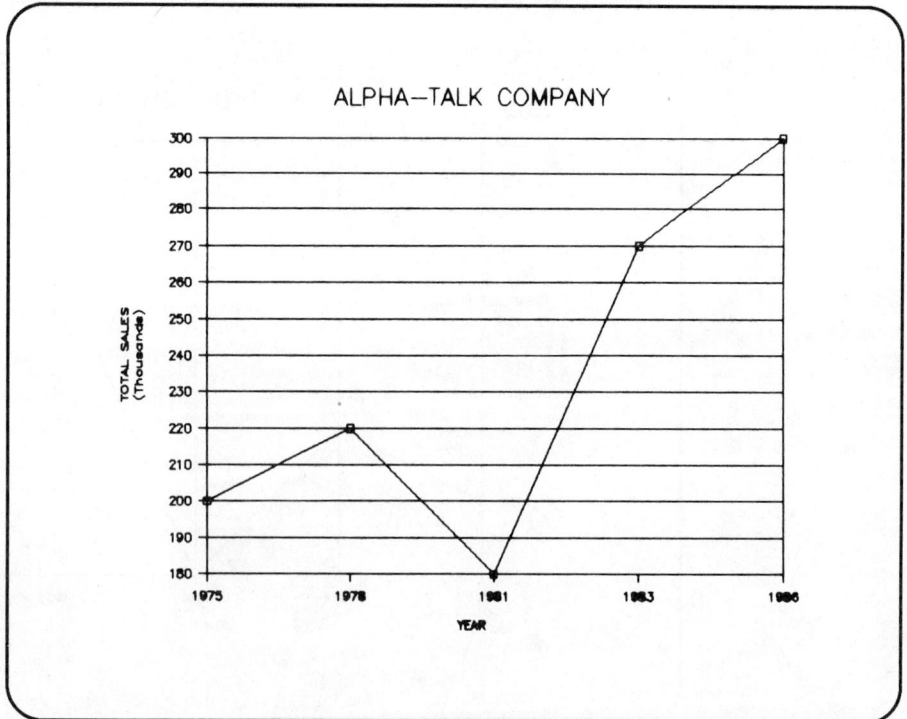

ALPHA—TALK COMPANY

Figure 5–16 Line Graph with Lines, Symbols, Vertical, and Horizontal Grids

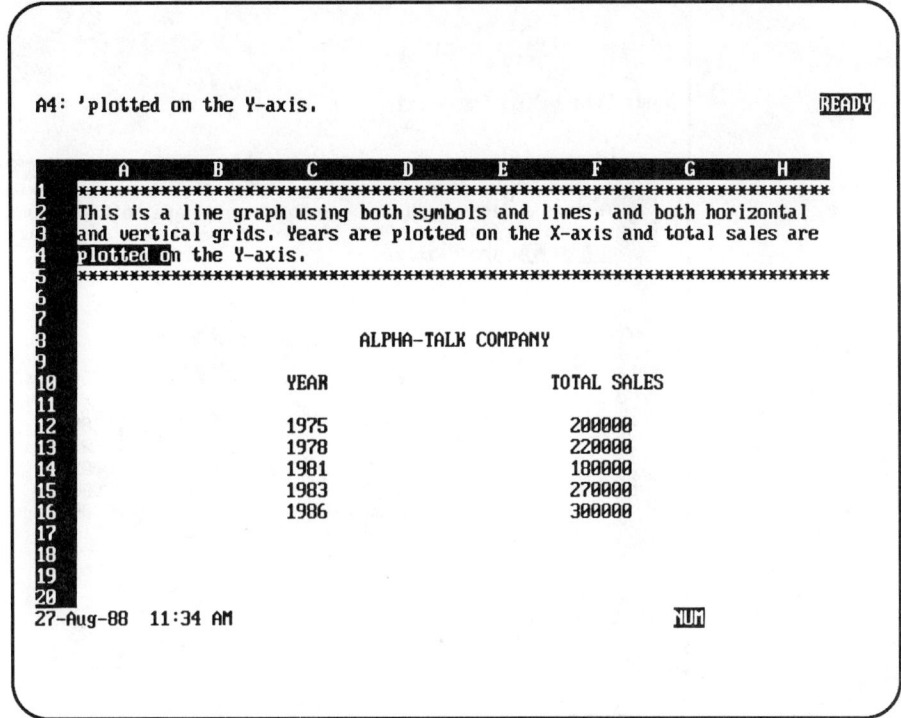

```
A4: 'plotted on the Y-axis.                                        READY

        A       B       C       D       E       F       G       H
1 ****************************************************************************
2 This is a line graph using both symbols and lines, and both horizontal
3 and vertical grids. Years are plotted on the X-axis and total sales are
4 plotted on the Y-axis.
5 ****************************************************************************
6
7
8                        ALPHA-TALK COMPANY
9
10       YEAR                          TOTAL SALES
11
12       1975                            200000
13       1978                            220000
14       1981                            180000
15       1983                            270000
16       1986                            300000
17
18
19
20
27-Aug-88  11:34 AM                                              NUM
```

Figure 5–16 (Continued)

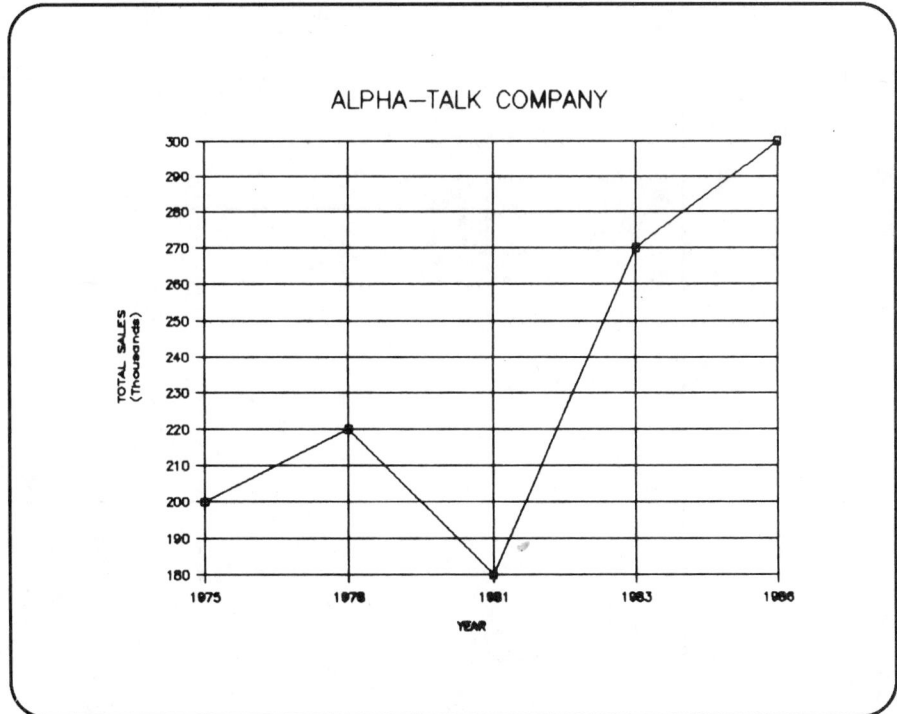

Figure 5–17 Line Graph with Symbols and Vertical and Horizontal Grids

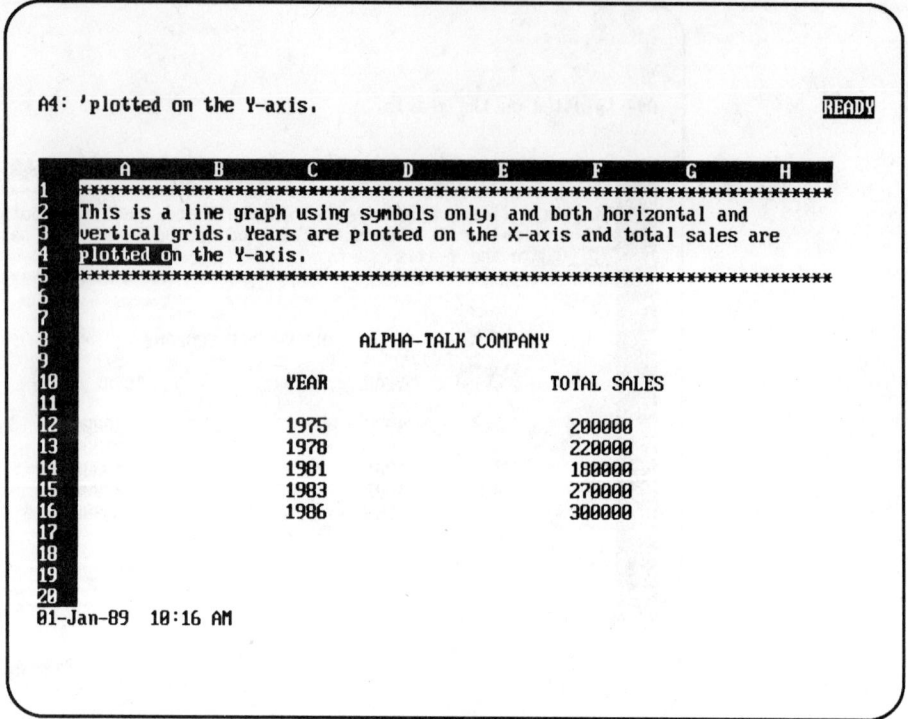

```
A4: 'plotted on the Y-axis.                                        READY

        A       B       C       D       E       F       G       H
1  ***********************************************************************
2  This is a line graph using symbols only, and both horizontal and
3  vertical grids. Years are plotted on the X-axis and total sales are
4  plotted on the Y-axis.
5  ***********************************************************************
6
7
8                            ALPHA-TALK COMPANY
9
10                 YEAR                    TOTAL SALES
11
12                 1975                      200000
13                 1978                      220000
14                 1981                      180000
15                 1983                      270000
16                 1986                      300000
17
18
19
20
01-Jan-89  10:16 AM
```

Figure 5–17 (Continued)

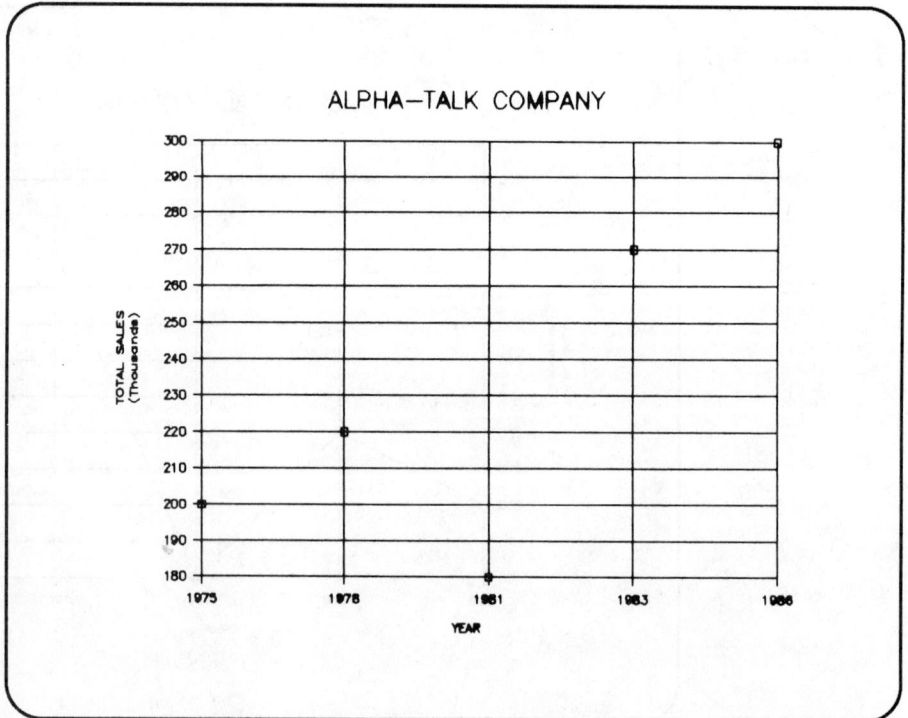

ALPHA-TALK COMPANY

Figure 5–18 Line Graph with Symbols Only

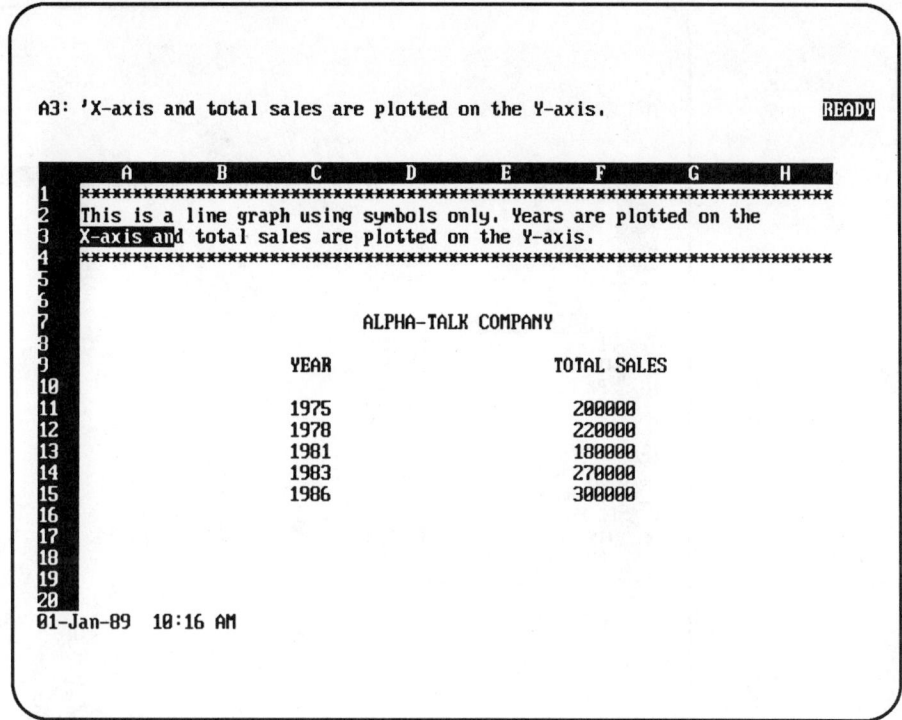

```
A3: 'X-axis and total sales are plotted on the Y-axis.                    READY

        A        B        C        D        E        F        G        H
1   *****************************************************************************
2   This is a line graph using symbols only. Years are plotted on the
3   X-axis and total sales are plotted on the Y-axis.
4   *****************************************************************************
5
6
7                           ALPHA-TALK COMPANY
8
9                   YEAR                      TOTAL SALES
10
11                  1975                      200000
12                  1978                      220000
13                  1981                      180000
14                  1983                      270000
15                  1986                      300000
16
17
18
19
20
01-Jan-89   10:16 AM
```

Figure 5–18 (Continued)

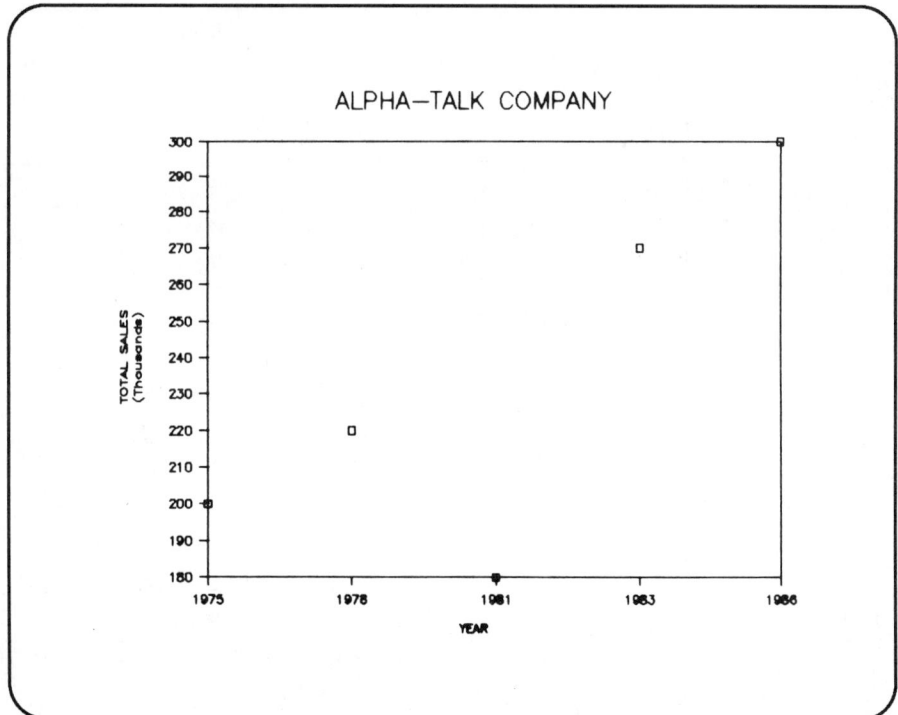

Figure 5–19 Line Graph of Advertising Budget without Skip Options

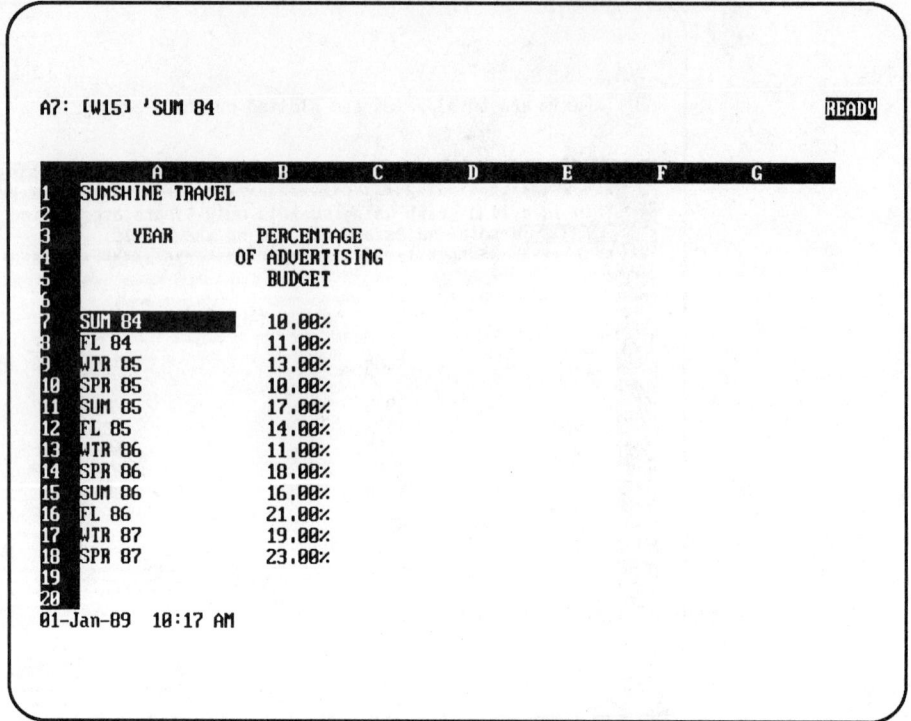

```
A7: [W15] 'SUM 84                                              READY

       A              B       C       D       E       F       G
1  SUNSHINE TRAVEL
2
3       YEAR         PERCENTAGE
4                    OF ADVERTISING
5                    BUDGET
6
7  SUM 84            10.00%
8  FL 84             11.00%
9  WTR 85            13.00%
10 SPR 85            10.00%
11 SUM 85            17.00%
12 FL 85             14.00%
13 WTR 86            11.00%
14 SPR 86            18.00%
15 SUM 86            16.00%
16 FL 86             21.00%
17 WTR 87            19.00%
18 SPR 87            23.00%
19
20
01-Jan-89  10:17 AM
```

Figure 5–19 (Continued)

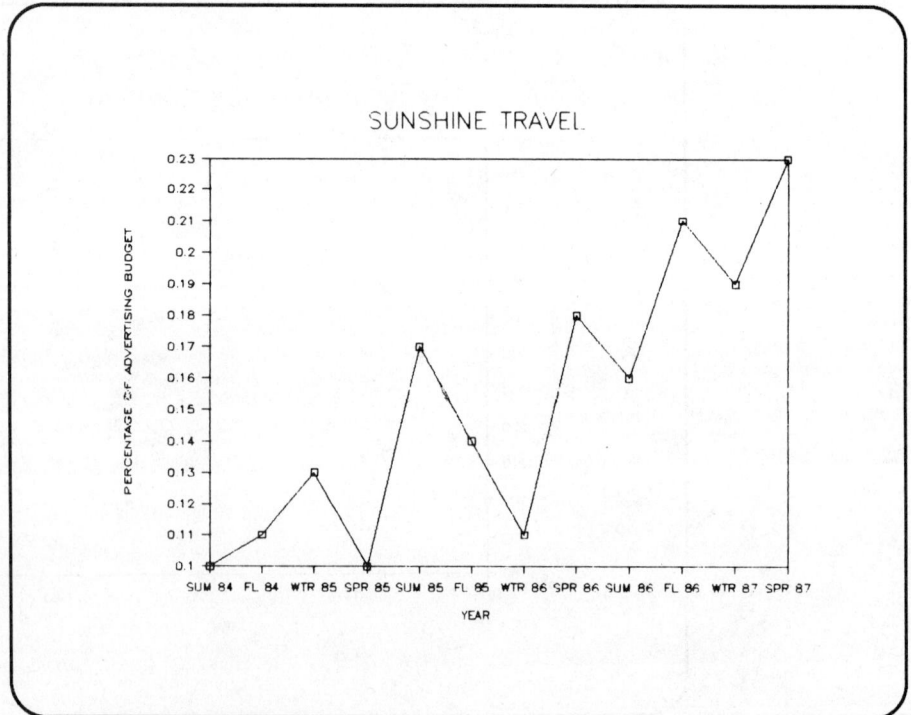

SUNSHINE TRAVEL

Figure 5–20 Line Graph of Advertising Budget with Skip Options

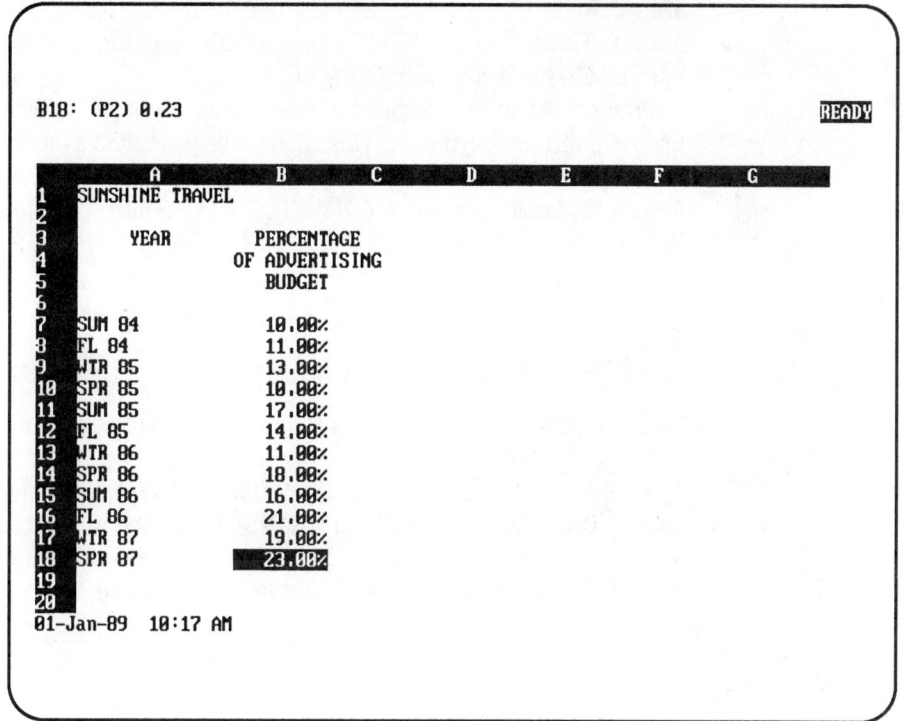

Figure 5–20 (Continued)

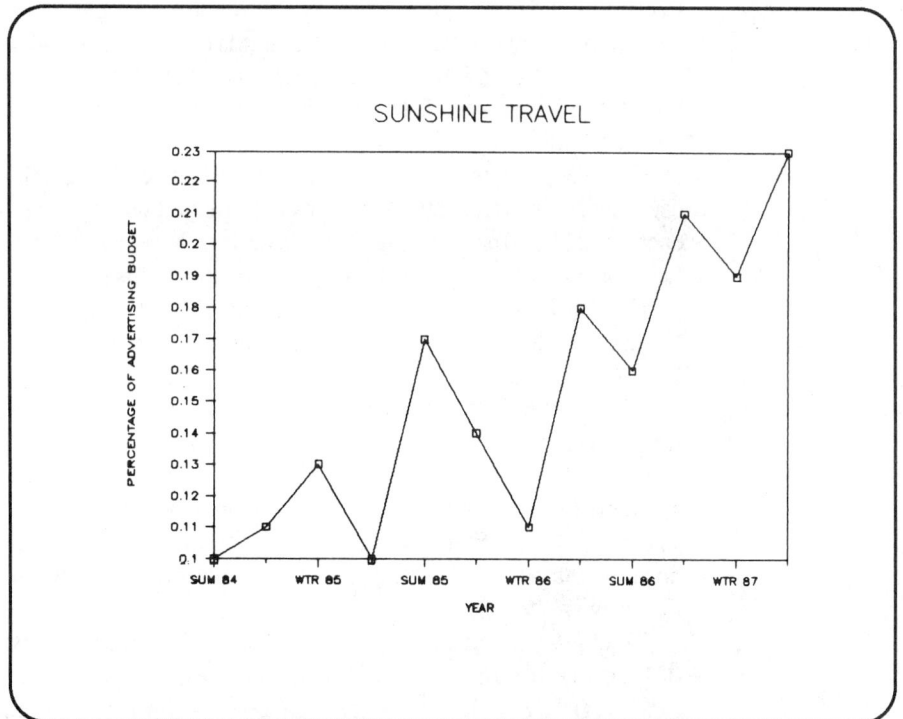

/Graph, Type, Line, X (A7..A18), Return, A (B7..B18), Return, Options, Scale, Skip, 2, Return, Titles, First, SUNSHINE TRAVEL, Return, Titles, X-axis, YEAR, Return, Titles, Y-axis, PERCENTAGE OF ADVERTISING BUDGET, Return, Format, Graph, Both, Quit, Quit, View.

Figure 5–21 compares the total sales of two divisions using a line graph with two lines and different symbols. This figure was generated as follows:

/Graph, Type, Line, X (A4..A13), Return, A (C4..C13), Return, B (E4..E13), Return, Options, Legend, A (DIVISION #1), Return, Legend, B (DIVISION #2), Return, Format, Graph, Both, Quit, Titles, X-axis, YEAR, Return, Titles, Y-axis, TOTAL SALES, Return, Quit, View.

Line Graph with Lines, Symbols, and Data Labels

Figure 5–22 plots the same data as Figure 5–19, but this time data labels are used. This graph was generated as follows:

/Graph, Type, Line, X (A7..A18), Return, A (B7..B18), Return, Options, Format, Graph, Both, Quit, Titles, First, SUNSHINE TRAVEL, Return, Titles, X-axis, YEAR, Return, Titles, Y-axis, PERCENTAGE OF ADVERTISING BUDGET, Return, Data-Labels, A (B7..B18), Return, Above, Quit, Scale, Skip, 2, Return, Quit, View.

5-11 Stacked-Bar Graph

In a stacked-bar graph, Lotus displays the corresponding value from each data range stacked on the top of the preceding data item in each bar. You can build a stacked-bar graph with six corresponding data items on top of each other. Shadings or colors represent each data item. When you define your data ranges, A corresponds to the lowest and F corresponds to the highest. As usual, the X range is used for data labels on the X-axis.

Figure 5–23 illustrates an example of the stacked-bar graph. The performance of each salesperson in the three regions is displayed with the regions stacked on top of each other. The first bar shows Brent's performance in Portland (the bottom portion), Denver (the middle), and Los Angeles (the top). This graph is generated as follows:

/Graph, Type, Stacked-Bar, X (B11..D11), Return, A (B12..D12), Return, B (B13..D13), Return, C (B14..D14), Return, Options, Legend, A (\A12), Return, Legend, B (\A13), Return, Legend, C (\A14), Return, Titles, First, COMPARATIVE SALES, Return, Titles, X-axis, SALESMEN, Return, Titles, Y-axis, SALES, Return, Quit, View.

Figure 5–24 is a different version of Figure 5–23. The performance of each salesperson in the same region is compared with the performances of the other salespeople. The first bar from the left shows Brent's performance (the bottom portion) compared with Matthew and Timothy in Portland. This graph is generated as follows:

/Graph, Type, Stacked-Bar, X (A12..A14), Return, A (B12..B14), Return, B (C12..C14), Return, C (D12..D14), Return, Options, Legend, A (\B11), Return, Legend, B (\C11), Return, Legend, C (\D11), Return, Titles, First, COMPARATIVE

Figure 5–21 Comparative Sales Analysis of Two Divisions

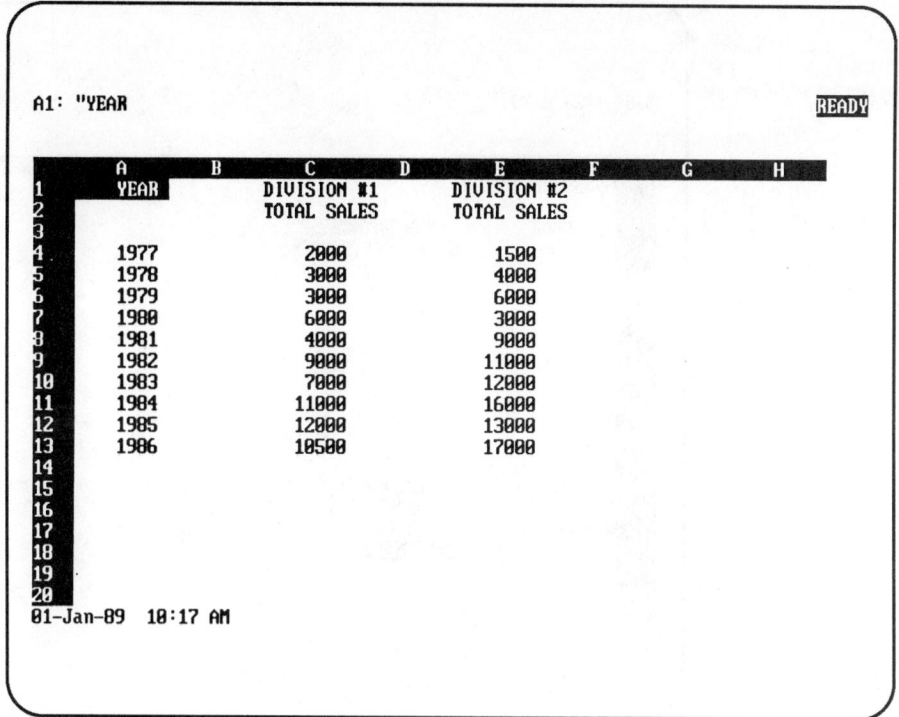

```
A1: "YEAR                                                        READY

        A       B       C       D       E       F       G       H
1     YEAR              DIVISION #1     DIVISION #2
2                       TOTAL SALES     TOTAL SALES
3
4     1977              2000            1500
5     1978              3000            4000
6     1979              3000            6000
7     1980              6000            3000
8     1981              4000            9000
9     1982              9000            11000
10    1983              7000            12000
11    1984              11000           16000
12    1985              12000           13000
13    1986              10500           17000
14
15
16
17
18
19
20
01-Jan-89   10:17 AM
```

Figure 5–21 (Continued)

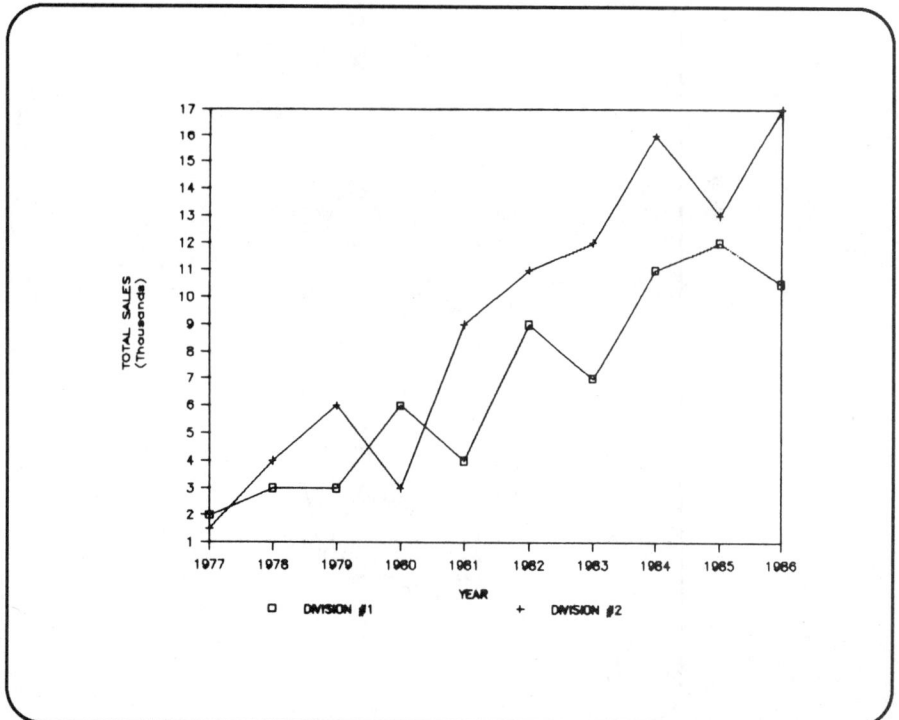

Figure 5–22 Total Budget for Advertising Using Data Labels

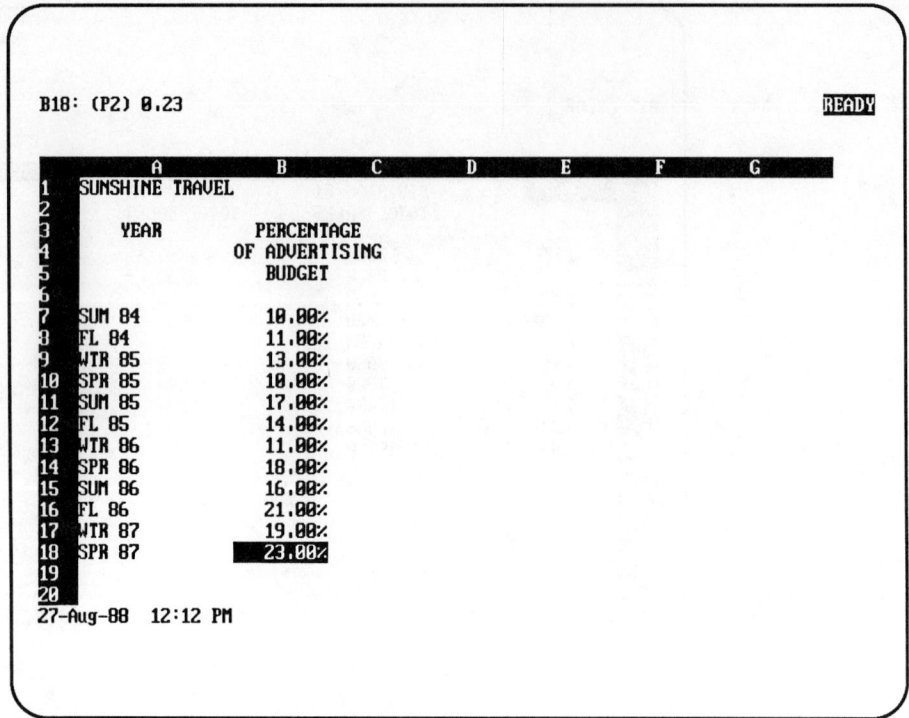

```
B18: (P2) 0.23                                              READY

          A           B        C       D       E      F       G
1  SUNSHINE TRAVEL
2
3      YEAR          PERCENTAGE
4                    OF ADVERTISING
5                    BUDGET
6
7  SUM 84            10.00%
8  FL 84             11.00%
9  WTR 85            13.00%
10 SPR 85            10.00%
11 SUM 85            17.00%
12 FL 85             14.00%
13 WTR 86            11.00%
14 SPR 86            18.00%
15 SUM 86            16.00%
16 FL 86             21.00%
17 WTR 87            19.00%
18 SPR 87            23.00%
19
20
27-Aug-88   12:12 PM
```

Figure 5–22 (Continued)

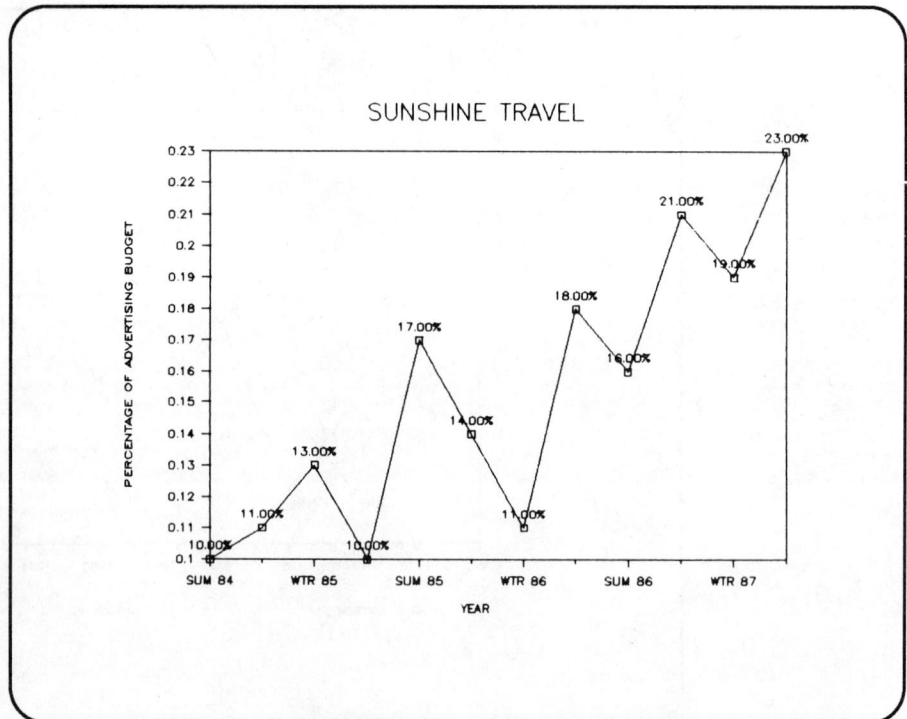

Figure 5–23 Comparative Sales in Three Regions using Stacked-Bar

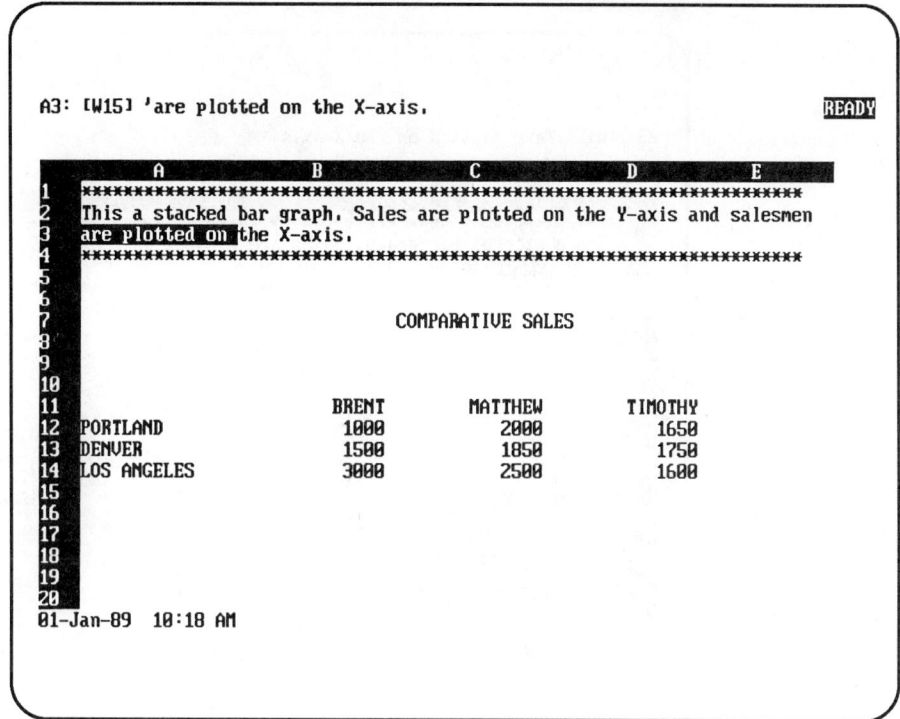

```
A3: [W15] 'are plotted on the X-axis.                                READY

          A              B              C              D              E
1  *********************************************************************
2  This a stacked bar graph. Sales are plotted on the Y-axis and salesmen
3  are plotted on the X-axis.
4  *********************************************************************
5
6
7                              COMPARATIVE SALES
8
9
10
11                      BRENT          MATTHEW        TIMOTHY
12 PORTLAND             1000           2000           1650
13 DENVER               1500           1850           1750
14 LOS ANGELES          3000           2500           1600
15
16
17
18
19
20
01-Jan-89  10:18 AM
```

Figure 5–23 (Continued)

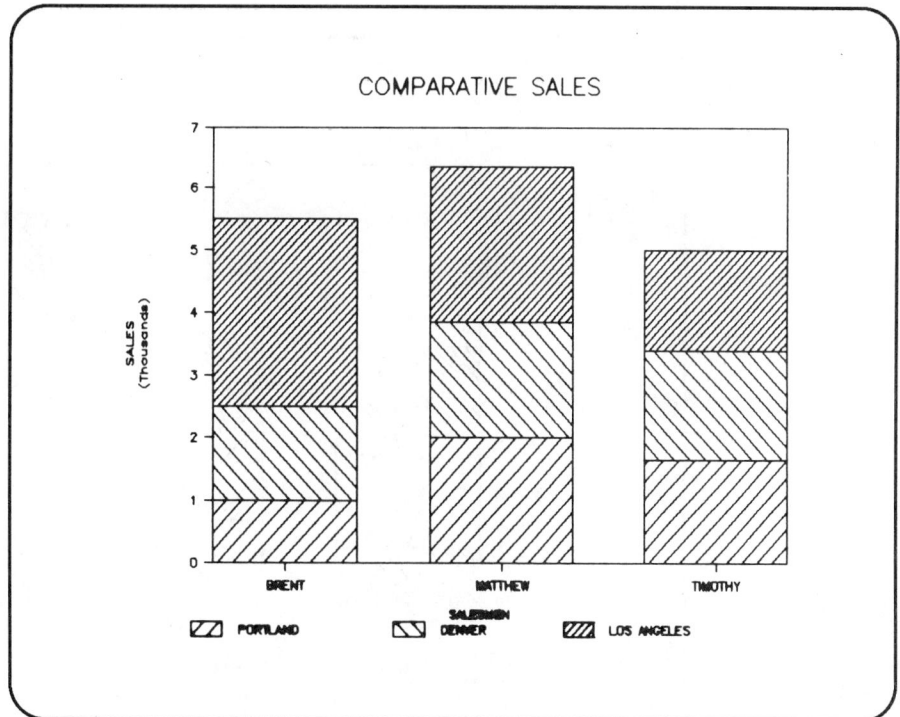

Figure 5–24 Comparative Sales for Three Salesmen in Three Regions using Stacked-Bar

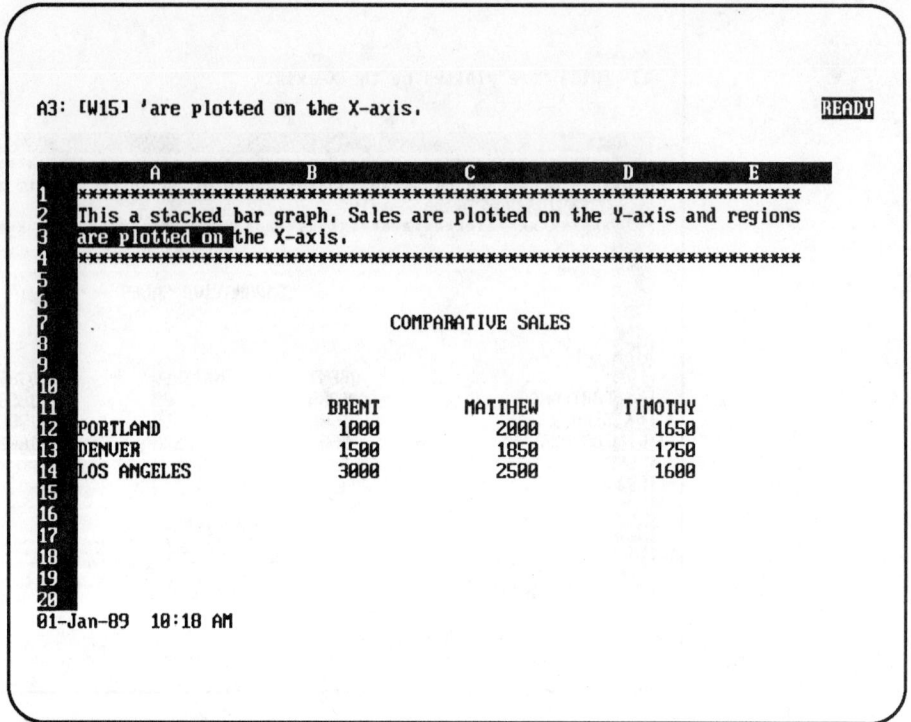

```
A3: [W15] 'are plotted on the X-axis.                                    READY

              A              B              C              D         E
1   ****************************************************************************
2   This a stacked bar graph. Sales are plotted on the Y-axis and regions
3   are plotted on the X-axis.
4   ****************************************************************************
5
6
7                               COMPARATIVE SALES
8
9
10
11                          BRENT         MATTHEW        TIMOTHY
12  PORTLAND                 1000          2000           1650
13  DENVER                   1500          1850           1750
14  LOS ANGELES              3000          2500           1600
15
16
17
18
19
20
01-Jan-89   10:18 AM
```

Figure 5–24 (Continued)

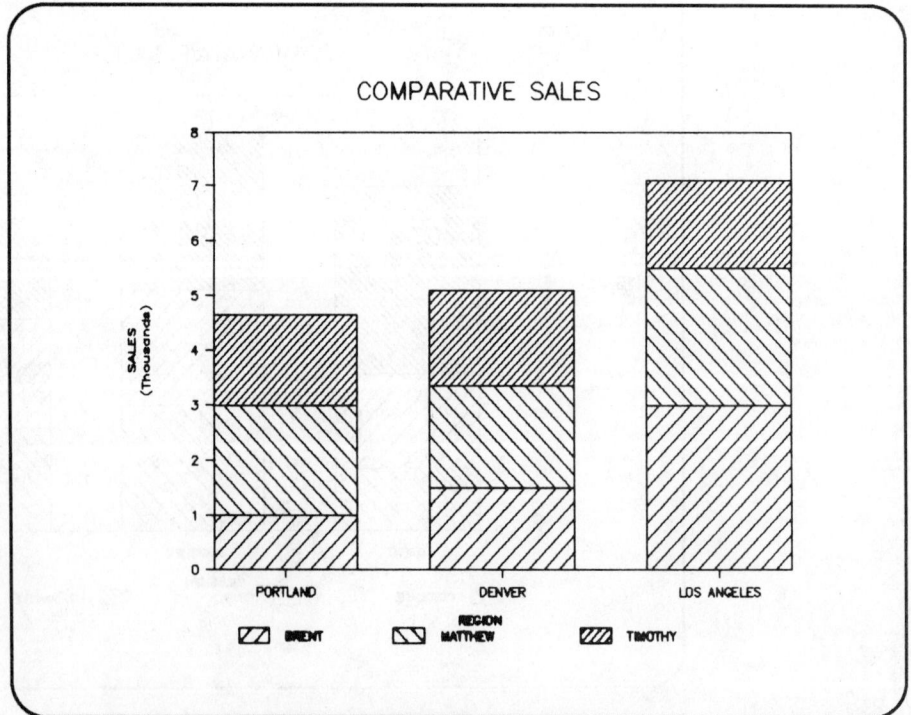

COMPARATIVE SALES

SALES, Return, Titles, X-axis, REGION, Return, Titles, Y-axis, SALES, Return, Quit, View.

Figure 5–25 is another example of a stacked-bar graph. Here we have used manual scaling. Since the scale was not big enough, a portion of the bar lies outside the scale. This figure was generated as follows:

/Graph, Type, Stacked-Bar, X (B11..D11), Return, A (B12..D12), Return, B (B13..D13), Return, C (B14..D14), Return, Options, Legend, A (\A12), Return, Legend, B (\A13), Return, Legend, C (\A14), Return, Titles, First, COMPARA-TIVE SALES, Return, Titles, X-axis, SALESMEN, Return, Titles, Y-axis, SALES, Return, Scale, Y Scale, Manual, Lower (-1000), Return, Upper (4000), Return, Quit, Quit, View.

5-12 XY Graphs

In an XY graph, Lotus pairs each value from the X data range with the corresponding data from each of the A–F ranges to plot the graph. You can generate up to six data ranges in a XY graph. Lotus uses different symbols to show each distinct range. Figure 5–26 is one example of an XY graph. Total sales are shown on the Y-axis and advertising on the X-axis. Remember, in an XY graph, one of your data ranges must be the X range. In a line graph there is no restriction in choosing a data range. This is the major difference between a line graph and an XY graph. We have used both lines and symbols. This was generated as follows:

/Graph, Type, XY, X (C11..C16), Return, A (A11..A16), Return, Options, Titles, First, SALES AND ADVERTISING, Return, Titles, X-axis, ADVERTISING, Return, Titles, Y-axis, TOTAL SALES, Return, Format, Graph, Both, Quit, Quit, View.

5-13 Miscellaneous

We have not talked about the color option yet because many Lotus users do not have access to color graphics. However, the /Graph Options Color command provides this facility. This command displays data range bars, graph lines, and symbols in different colors only if your monitor is capable of displaying color graphics.

/Graph Options B&W displays data ranges in contrasting monochrome cross-hatches. You should use /Graph Options B&W *only* if you have previously selected /Graph Options Color and want to return to a monochrome display.

5-14 A Comprehensive Model

To wrap up this chapter we have presented a comprehensive model for Happy Traveler Merchant. A portion of an income statement is presented in Figure 5–27. The following eight graphs (presented in Figures 5–28-1 through 5–28-8) will be illustrated:

1. A pie chart with crosshatches for total expense (in five groups).
2. A stacked-bar graph for six months of five expenses. The X-axis shows months and the Y-axis shows total expense.

Figure 5–25 Sales Analysis Using Stacked-Bar with Manual Scaling

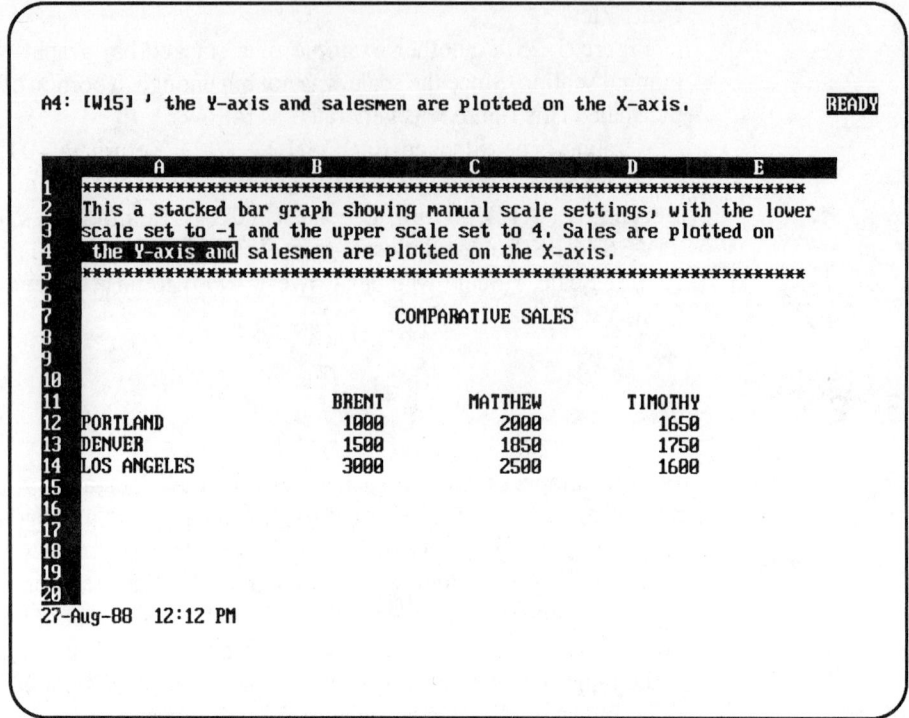

```
A4: [W15] ' the Y-axis and salesmen are plotted on the X-axis.              READY

          A              B            C            D            E
*********************************************************************
This a stacked bar graph showing manual scale settings, with the lower
scale set to -1 and the upper scale set to 4. Sales are plotted on
 the Y-axis and salesmen are plotted on the X-axis.
*********************************************************************

                         COMPARATIVE SALES

                    BRENT        MATTHEW      TIMOTHY
PORTLAND            1000         2000         1650
DENVER             1500         1850         1750
LOS ANGELES        3000         2500         1600

27-Aug-88   12:12 PM
```

Figure 5–25 (Continued)

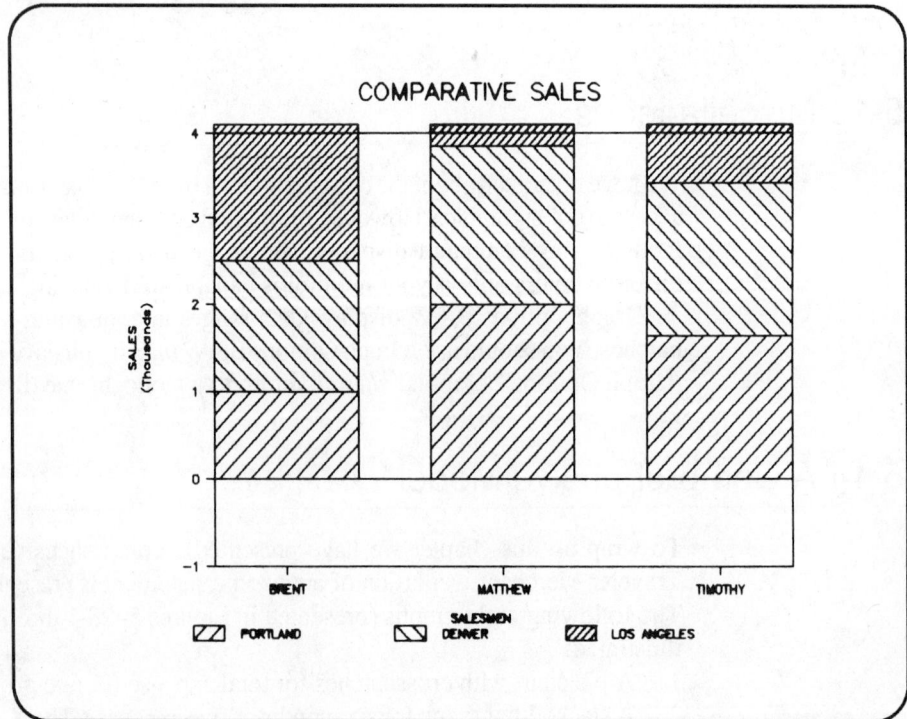

COMPARATIVE SALES

Figure 5–26 XY Graph for Total Sales and Advertising

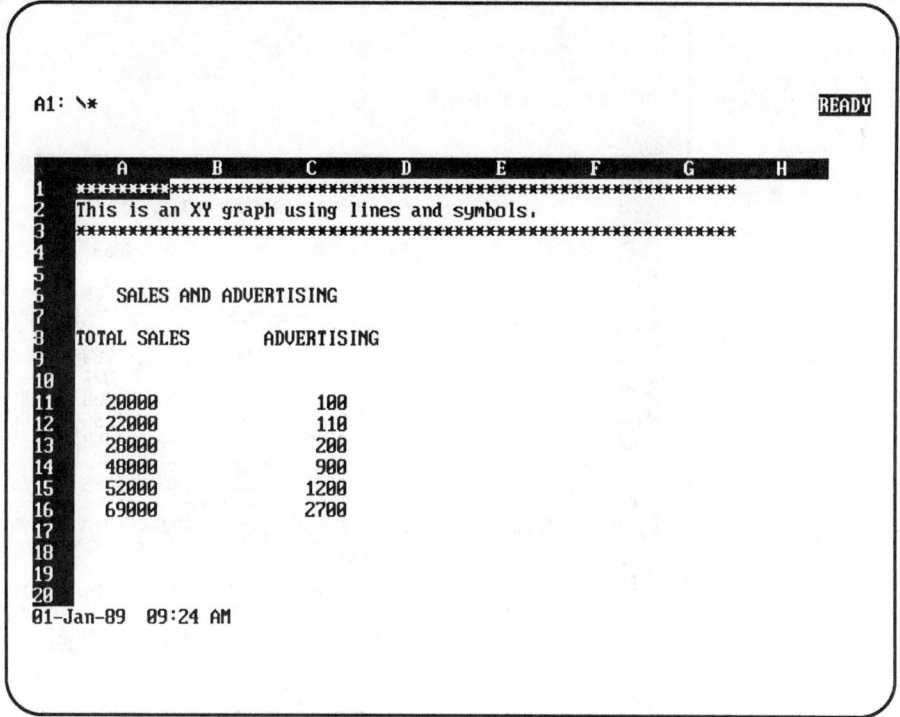

```
A1: \*                                                          READY

        A      B      C      D      E      F      G      H
1  *********************************************************************
2  This is an XY graph using lines and symbols.
3  *********************************************************************
4
5
6      SALES AND ADVERTISING
7
8  TOTAL SALES        ADVERTISING
9
10
11     20000              100
12     22000              110
13     28000              200
14     48000              900
15     52000             1200
16     69000             2700
17
18
19
20
01-Jan-89   09:24 AM
```

Figure 5–26 (Continued)

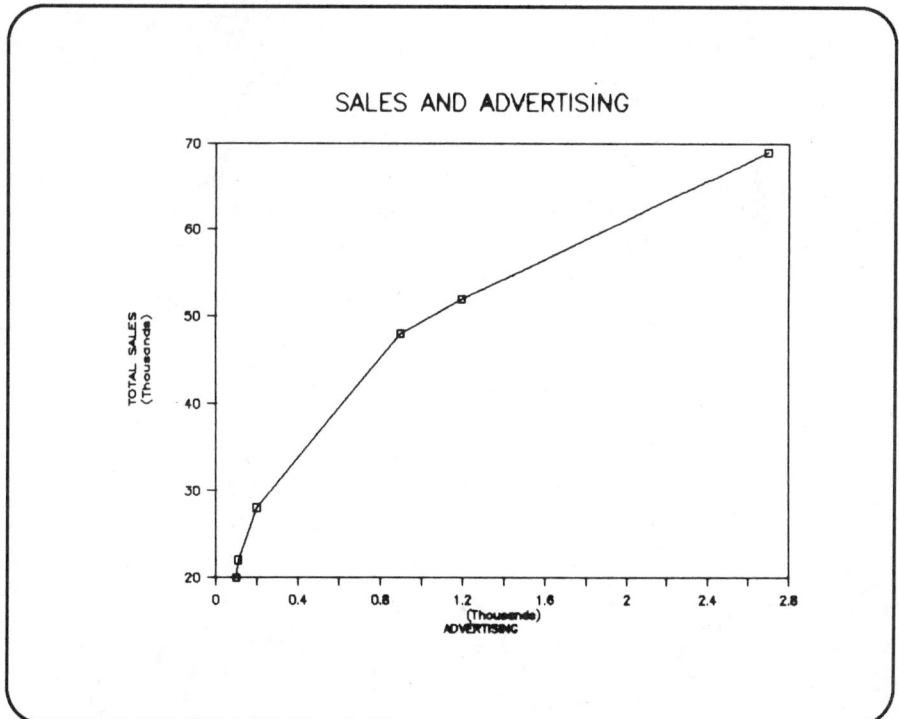

SALES AND ADVERTISING

Figure 5–27 A Partial Income Statement for Happy Traveler Merchant

```
I8: [W7] 'crosshatches                                                   READY

        A       B       C       D       E       F       G       H       I
1
2                       HAPPY TRAVELER MERCHANT
3
4               JAN     FEB     MAR     APR     MAY     JUNE    TOTAL
5
6   SALES     $2,000  $2,100  $1,900  $1,750  $2,200  $2,500  $12,450
7   ==========================================================Code for
8   EXPENSES                                                     crosshatches
9    Raw Mat.   600     650     590     550     600     700    3690      1
10   Labor      300     275     310     200     310     375    1850      2
11   Rent       150     175     140     120     150     200     935      3
12   Electric    75     100      95     100     145     165     680      4
13   Advert.     50      65      70      75     100     150     510      5
14  ------------------------------------------------------------
15  Total Exp.  1175    1265    1205    1125    1305    1590    7665
16  ==========================================================
17  Total Pro.  $825    $835    $695    $625    $895    $910  $4,785
18  ------------------------------------------------------------
19  Code for
20  exploded Pie chart      101     102     103     104     105     106
27-Aug-88  12:13 PM
```

Figure 5–28–1 Happy Traveler Merchant in Action

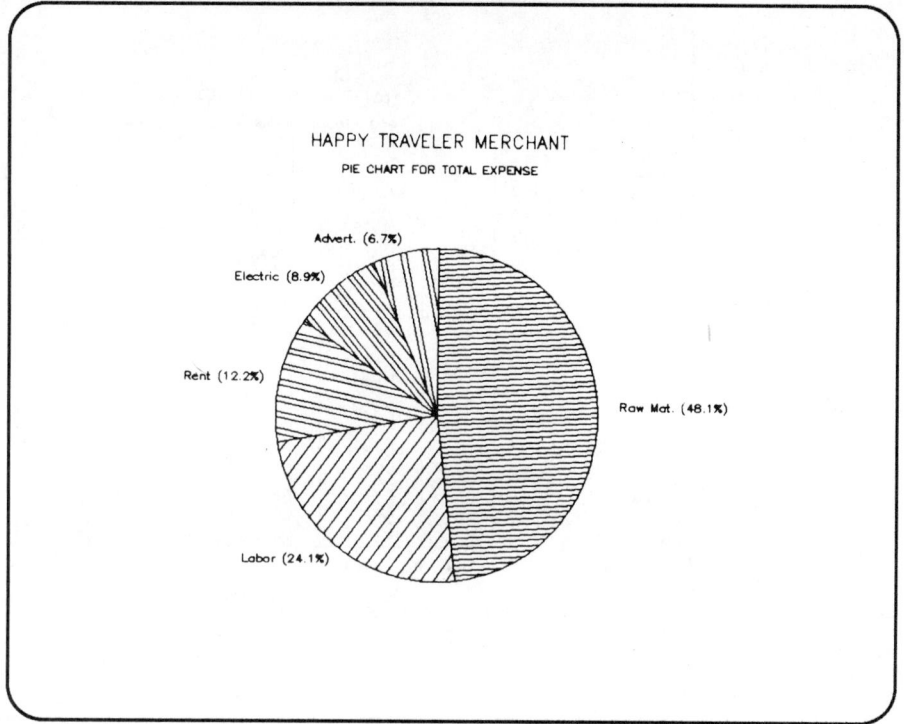

HAPPY TRAVELER MERCHANT

PIE CHART FOR TOTAL EXPENSE

Advert. (6.7%)
Electric (8.9%)
Rent (12.2%)
Raw Mat. (48.1%)
Labor (24.1%)

Figure 5–28–1 (Continued)

```
/Graph Type Pie
        X    A9..A13 Return
        A    H9..H13 Return
        B    I9..I13 Return
        Options Titles First "HAPPY TRAVELER MERCHANT" Return
                Titles Second "PIE CHART FOR TOTAL EXPENSE" Return
                Quit

        View
```

Figure 5–28–2

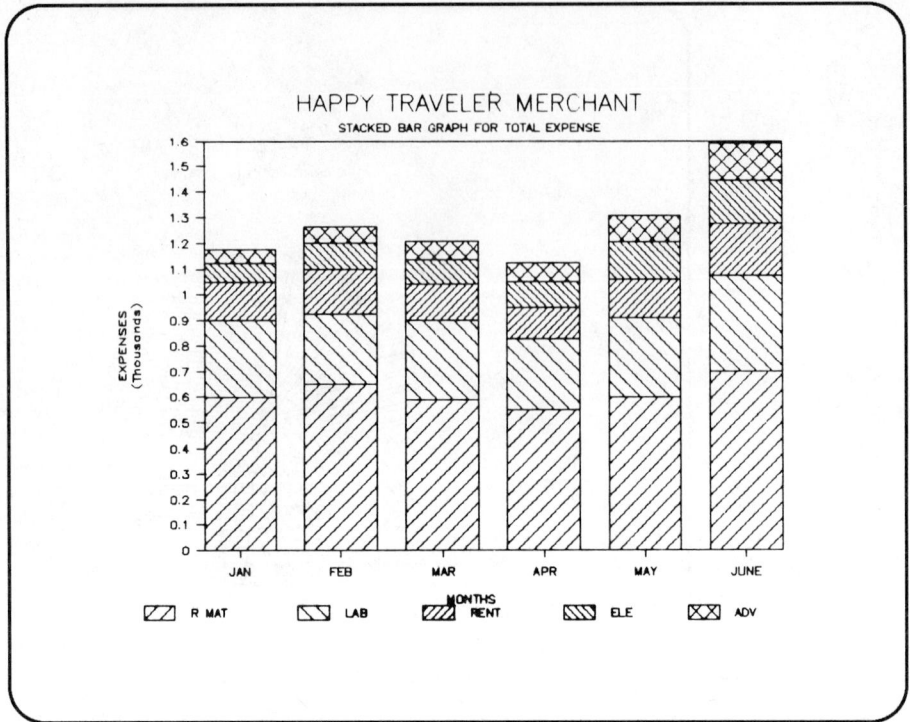

Figure 5–28–2 (Continued)

```
/Graph Type Stacked-Bar
      X   B4..G4 Return
      A   B9..G9 Return
      B   B10..G10 Return
      C   B11..G11 Return
      D   B12..G12 Return
      E   B13..G13 Return

      Options Legend A      "R MAT" Return
              Legend B      "LAB" Return
              Legend C      "RENT" Return
              Legend D      "ELE" Return
              Legend E      "ADV" Return
              Titles First  "HAPPY TRAVELER MERCHANT" Return
              Titles Second "STACKED BAR GRAPH FOR TOTAL EXPENSE"
                            Return
              Titles X-axis "MONTHS" Return
              Titles Y-axis "EXPENSES" Return
              Quit

      View
```

Figure 5-28-3

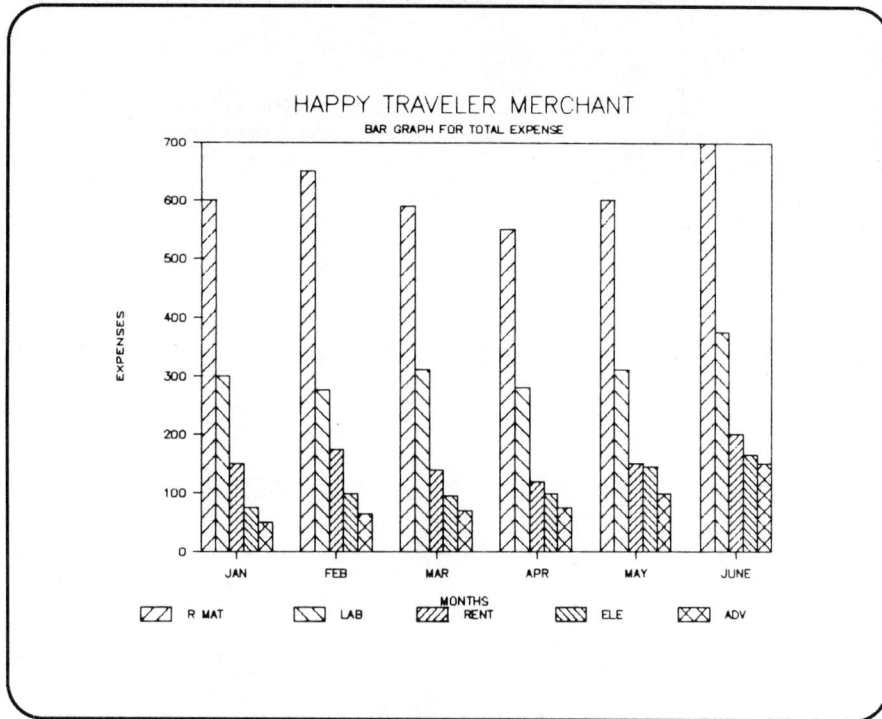

Figure 5-28-3 (Continued)

```
/Graph Type Bar
        X    B4..G4 Return
        A    B9..G9 Return
        B    B10..G10 Return
        C    B11..G11 Return
        D    B12..G12 Return
        E    B13..G13 Return

        Options Legend A        "R MAT" Return
                Legend B        "LAB" Return
                Legend C        "RENT" Return
                Legend D        "ELE" Return
                Legend E        "ADV" Return
                Titles First    "HAPPY TRAVELER MERCHANT" Return
                Titles Second   "BAR GRAPH FOR TOTAL EXPENSE" Return
                Titles X-axis   "MONTHS" Return
                Titles Y-axis   "EXPENSES" Return
                Quit

        View
```

Figure 5–28–4

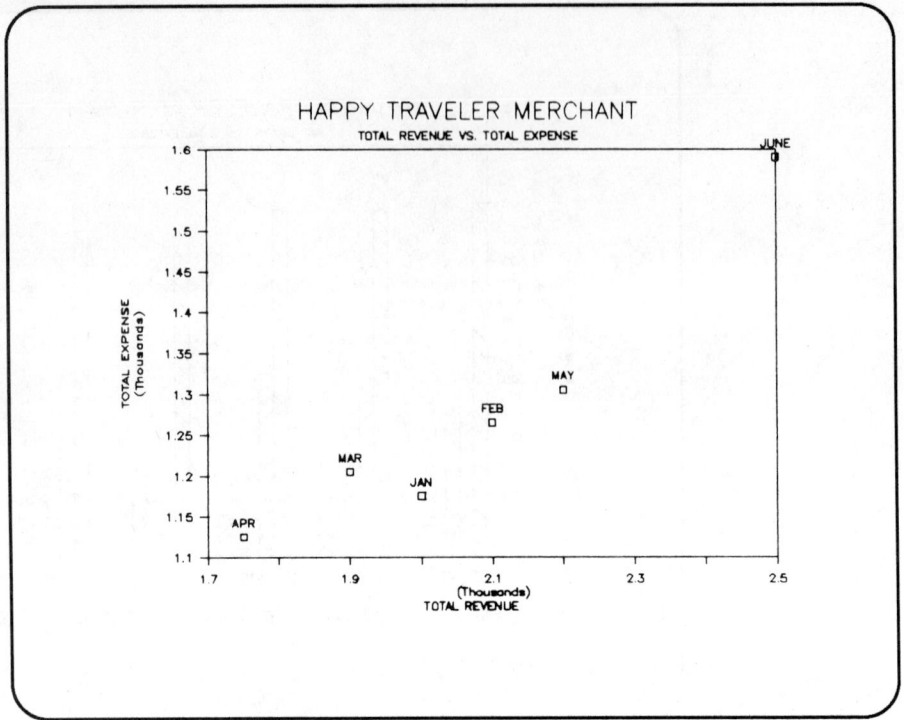

HAPPY TRAVELER MERCHANT
TOTAL REVENUE VS. TOTAL EXPENSE

Figure 5–28–4 (Continued)

```
/Graph Type XY

        X    B6..G6 Return
        A    B15..G15 Return

        Options Format  A Symbols
                        Quit
                Titles  First  "HAPPY TRAVELER MERCHANT" Return
                Titles   Second "TOTAL REVENUE VS. TOTAL EXPENSE"
                                Return
                Titles  X-axis "TOTAL REVENUE" Return
                Titles  Y-axis "TOTAL EXPENSE" Return
                Data labels A B4..G4  Return Above
                        Quit
                Quit

        View
```

Figure 5–28–5

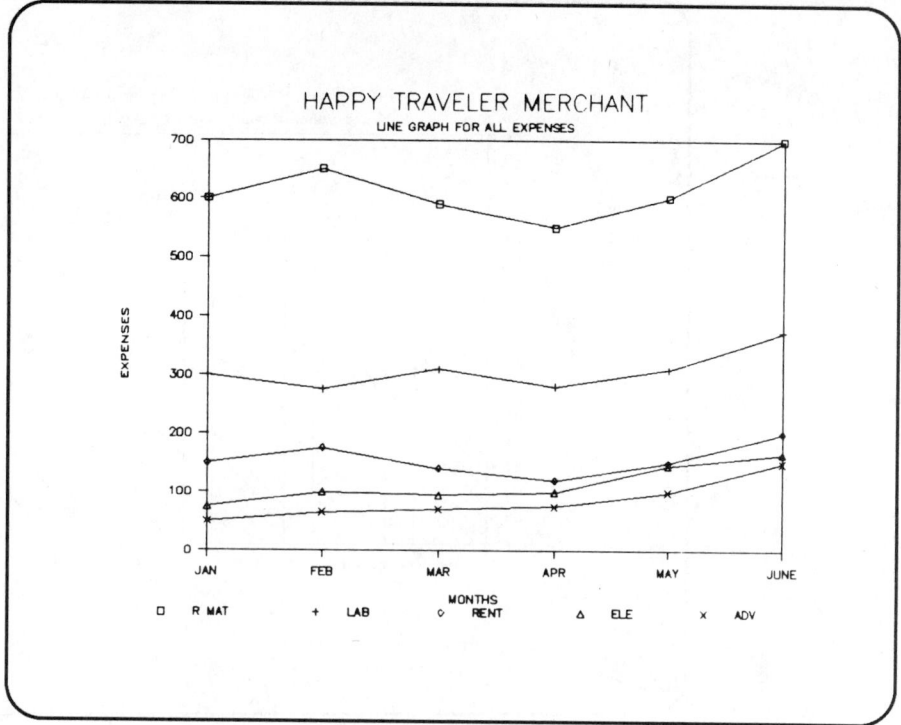

Figure 5–28–5 (Continued)

```
/Graph Type Line
        X    B4..G4 Return
        A    B9..G9 Return
        B    B10..G10 Return
        C    B11..G11 Return
        D    B12..G12 Return
        E    B13..G13 Return

        Options Legend   A      "R MAT" Return
                Legend   B      "LAB" Return
                Legend   C      "RENT" Return
                Legend   D      "ELE" Return
                Legend   E      "ADV" Return
                Titles First    "HAPPY TRAVELER MERCHANT" Return
                Titles Second   "LINE GRAPH FOR ALL EXPENSES" Return
                Titles X-axis   "MONTHS" Return
                Titles Y-axis   "EXPENSES" Return
                Quit

        View
```

Figure 5–28–6

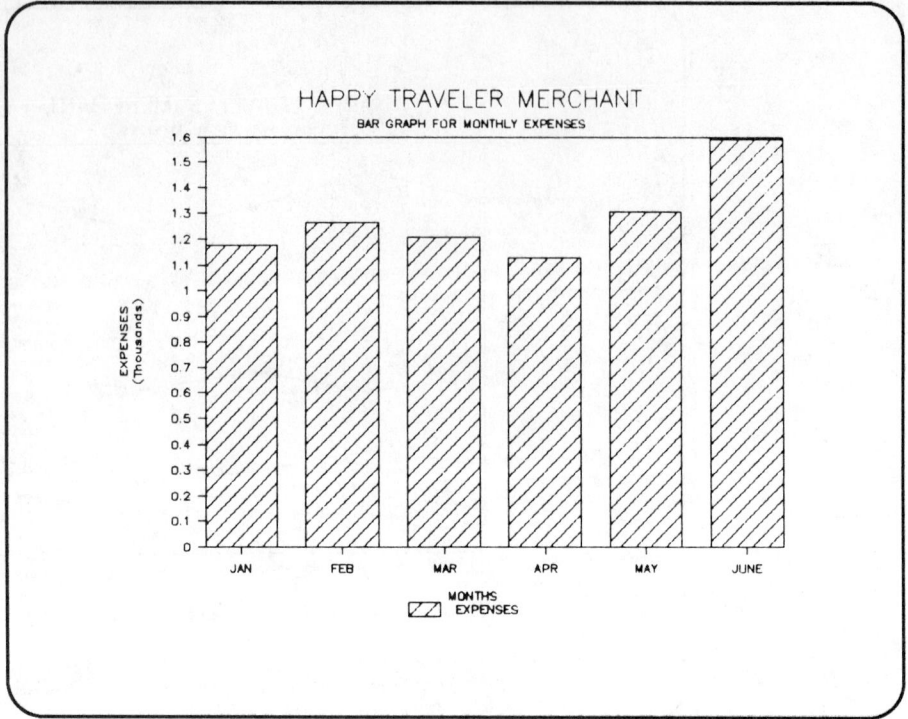

Figure 5–28–6 (Continued)

```
/Graph Type Bar
        X    B4..G4 Return
        A    B15..G15 Return

        Options Legend   A      "EXPENSES" Return
                Titles First    "HAPPY TRAVELER MERCHANT" Return
                Titles Second   "BAR  GRAPH  FOR  MONTHLY  EXPENSES"
                                 Return
                Titles X-axis   "MONTHS" Return
                Titles Y-axis   "EXPENSES" Return
                Quit

        View
```

Figure 5–28–7

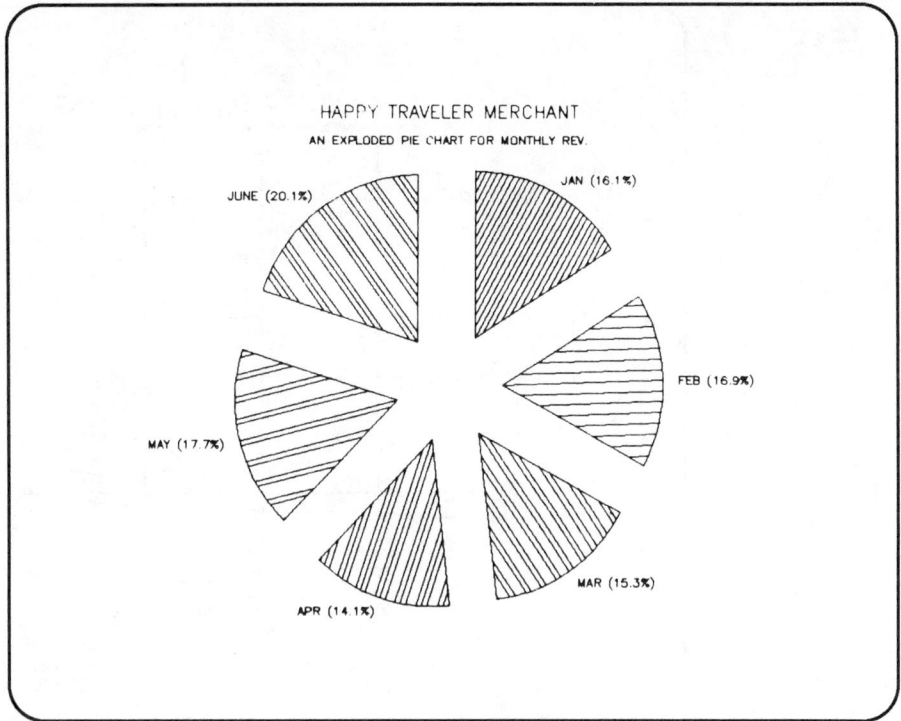

HAPPY TRAVELER MERCHANT

AN EXPLODED PIE CHART FOR MONTHLY REV.

Figure 5–28–7 (Continued)

```
/Graph Type Pie
    X    B4..G4        Return
    A    B6..G6        Return
    B    D20..I20      Return
    Options Titles  First  "HAPPY TRAVELER MERCHANT" Return
            Titles  Second "AN EXPLODED PIE CHART FOR MONTHLY
                           REV." Return
         Quit

    View
```

Figure 5–28–8

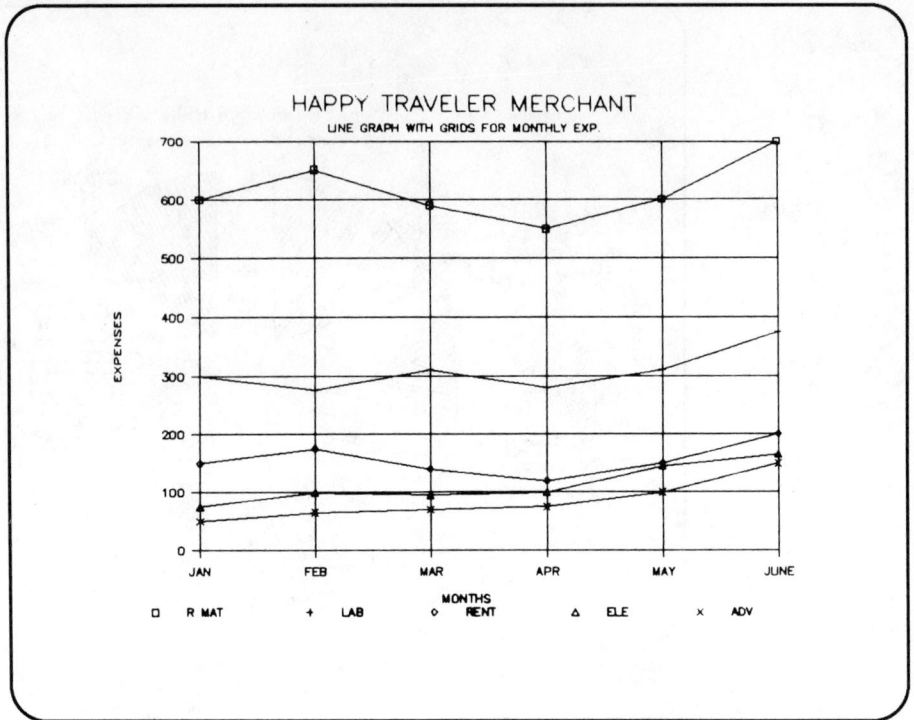

HAPPY TRAVELER MERCHANT
LINE GRAPH WITH GRIDS FOR MONTHLY EXP.

Figure 5–28–8 (Continued)

```
/Graph Type Line
     X    B4..G4    Return
     A    B9..G9    Return
     B    B10..G10  Return
     C    B11..G11  Return
     D    B12..G12  Return
     E    B13..G13  Return

     Options  Legend  A      "R MAT" Return
              Legend  B      "LAB" Return
              Legend  C      "RENT" Return
              Legend  D      "ELE" Return
              Legend  E      "ADV" Return
              Titles  First  "HAPPY TRAVELER MERCHANT" Return
              Titles  Second "LINE GRAPH WITH GRIDS FOR MONTHLY
                             EXP." Return
              Titles  X-axis "MONTHS" Return
              Titles  Y-axis "EXPENSES" Return
              Grid    Both
              Quit

     View
```

3. A bar graph with multiple ranges; on the X-axis different months, on the Y-axis the total of different expenses.
4. An XY graph with symbols and data labels. This graph displays total revenue vs. total expense.
5. A line graph of five different expenses over time using different symbols.
6. A simple bar chart for total monthly expenses.
7. An exploded pie chart for total revenue of six different months.
8. A line graph like Figure 5–28–5, but with horizontal and vertical grids.

Summary

Lotus can generate five different graphs: pie charts, bar graphs, stacked-bar graphs, XY graphs, and line graphs. As you can see from the examples, Lotus has a very impressive graphics operation. The last section of this chapter presented a comprehensive model of the variety of information that can be illustrated in Lotus graphics.

Review Questions

1. How many types of graphs can be generated by Lotus?
2. What is the unique application of each type?
3.* What are some of the limitations of Lotus graphics?
4.* What is the difference between XY graphs and line graphs?
5. How many data ranges can be used in Lotus graphics?
6.* What are the specific uses of the X range?
7. How do you save a graph for printing?
8.* Can your graph and your worksheet be saved under the same name?
9.* Can you retrieve a graphic file (e.g., PIC) from a system disk?
10. How do you delete a graph?
11.* How many different graphs can be generated by a worksheet?
12. What are the choices available under Options in the graph menu?
13.* How many types of grids can you have?
14. How many symbols are available for line graphs?
15. What are data labels? What are their applications?
16.* What is the Scale option?
17. Why do you use the Scale option?
18.* What are the uses of legends?
19. How many different legends can you have?
20. What is the function of the reset command in the graph menu?
21. Generate any sets of data comparable to Figure 5–27. Create the eight different graph types as we did in the comprehensive model for Happy Traveler Merchant.

Misconceptions and Solutions

M — When you invoke /Graph Name Delete, Lotus immediately erases the present graph settings and automatically returns you to the graph options menu. There is no confirmation step.

S — Before you use /GND, make sure this is what you want to do.

M — /GNR erases all the named graphs for a particular worksheet. If you issue this command there is no confirmation step.

S — Before issuing this command make sure this is what you want to do.

M — Sometimes no matter what you do, your graph does not show on the screen.

S — Check Graph, Options, Format, Graph, Neither. You may have accidentally formatted your graph to display neither lines nor symbols!

Comprehensive Lab Assignment

Retrieve CHAPT4 and perform the following:

1. Generate a line graph of the total scores of all the students. Name the graph G1, save it under G1, and save the worksheet under CHAPT5.
2. Generate a bar graph for three tests. This graph should compare the total scores of three tests. Name this graph G2 and save it under G2. Save the worksheet under CHAPT5.
3. Generate a stacked-bar for three test scores for six selected students. Name this graph G3, save it under G3, and save the worksheet under CHAPT5.
4. Generate a pie chart comparing the total scores of each test. Name the graph G4, save it under G4, and save the worksheet under CHAPT5.
5. Generate a cross-hatch pie chart.
6. Explode the pie chart.
7. Generate a final line graph from the total scores of each student with heading and subheading (any title); label both X and Y axes.
8. Name this graph G5, save it under G5, and save the final worksheet under CHAPT5.

6

The Print Graph Program

6-1 Introduction

In this chapter, we will explain how graphs generated on the screen can be transferred to graphic printers or plotters and how to generate hard copies of the graphs we studied in Chapter 5. We give an overview of the PrintGraph menu, discussing how to start it and how to exit from it. We explain ways you can control the look of your graph by specifying size, angle, typeface style, and so on. If you have access to a color printer or plotter, you will learn how to generate beautiful color graphics using 1-2-3 and the PrintGraph programs.

6-2 What Is the PrintGraph Program?

As you have seen so far, Lotus operations are stored on the 1-2-3 System disk. The only function not stored on the System disk is the PrintGraph program, which is stored on a separate disk. The reason for storing this program on a separate disk is to keep 1-2-3 at a manageable size. This program enables you to generate hard copies from graphs on your monitor. Using PrintGraph is possible only if you have access to a plotter or if your printer is capable of printing graphics as well as text.

To use the PrintGraph program, first save your graph with the /Graph Save command. Then exit from 1-2-3, and enter PrintGraph.

6-3 Starting PrintGraph

You can get PrintGraph started either from DOS or from the Lotus Access System. To load PrintGraph from DOS, at the A> prompt, put the PrintGraph disk in drive A, type PGRAPH, and press the **Return** key. If you are using a driver other than the default 1-2-3 set, you must type PGRAPH and the driver set, e.g., PGRAPH Name.

To load PrintGraph from the Lotus Access System, move the cursor to PrintGraph, hit the **Return** key, and follow the prompt. To exit from the PrintGraph program, choose the Exit option from the PrintGraph main menu. This will return you either to the Lotus Access System or to the DOS A> prompt.

6-4 Overview of the PrintGraph Main Menu

When you get the PrintGraph program started, you will see the main menu, as shown in Figure 6–1. This menu gives you six options as follows:

Image-Select   Settings   Go   Align   Page   Exit

You can use Left and Right arrows to move around the menu and press the **Return** key to select an option.

The Image-Select option allows you to choose one or more graphs to be printed. When you get the listing of your graph directory, move the cursor to the desired graph and hit the space bar. Your graph will be marked by a # sign. This means the graph is a candidate for printing. To remove the # sign, press the space bar again and the # sign will disappear. Later, if you want to print another graph, first remove the # sign from the present graph and choose your next candidate. If you don't remove the #, you will always print the first graph. Figure 6–2 shows the graph menu and the candidate for printing. This menu also tells you the date when a graph was generated, the time, and the size of the graph in bytes.

At this time, you can display your graph on the monitor (if you have graphics capability) by pressing F10.

The Settings option monitors the settings for the PrintGraph program. This includes size, fonts, color, and so forth.

Go starts the printing.

Align tells PrintGraph if the paper is positioned at the top of the page.

Page advances the paper to the top of the next page.

Exit gets you out of the PrintGraph program. You will return to DOS or to the Lotus Access System.

When you choose a graph from your graph directory for printing, remember that you cannot change any of the graph parameters in the PrintGraph program. If you want to make any changes, you must exit from PrintGraph, get into 1-2-3, retrieve your worksheet file, make the changes on the file, and save it by using /Graph Save. Also remember that a PIC (graphic) file cannot be retrieved in a 1-2-3 worksheet. You have to retrieve the worksheet file that generated the corresponding PIC file in the 1-2-3 worksheet (this file has the WK1 extension).

Figure 6–1 The PrintGraph Main Menu

Copyright 1986 Lotus Development Corp. All Rights Reserved. Release 2.01 MENU

Select graphs for printing
Image-Select Settings Go Align Page Exit

GRAPH	IMAGE OPTIONS			HARDWARE SETUP
IMAGES	Size		Range Colors	Graphs Directory:
SELECTED	Top	.395	X	A:\
	Left	.750	A	Fonts Directory:
	Width	6.500	B	A:\
	Height	4.691	C	Interface:
	Rotate	.000	D	Parallel 1
			E	Printer Type:
	Font		F	
	1 BLOCK1			Paper Size
	2 BLOCK1			Width 8.500
				Length 11.000
				ACTION OPTIONS
				Pause: No Eject: No

Figure 6–2 A Sample of Graphs Directory and a Candidate for Printing

Copyright 1986 Lotus Development Corp. All Rights Reserved. Release 2.01 POINT

Select graphs for output

PICTURE	DATE	TIME	SIZE
CH5-1	01-01-80	2:26	1191
CH5-10	01-01-80	2:34	2359
CH5-11	01-01-80		3167
CH5-12	01-01-80	2:36	578
CH5-13	01-01-80	2:36	728
CH5-14	01-01-80	2:36	778
CH5-15	01-01-80	2:37	858
CH5-16	01-01-80	2:37	908
CH5-17	01-01-80	2:38	868
CH5-18	01-01-80	2:38	688
CH5-19	01-01-80	2:38	1215
CH5-2	01-01-80	2:29	1200
CH5-20	01-01-80	2:39	1134
CH5-21	01-01-80	2:39	1516
CH5-22	01-01-80	2:46	1302
CH5-23	01-01-80	2:40	2779
CH5-24	01-01-80	2:40	2636
CH5-25	01-01-80	2:41	2632

[SPACE] turns mark on and off
[RETURN] selects marked pictures
[ESCAPE] exits, ignoring changes
[HOME] goes to beginning of list
[END] goes to end of list
[UP] and [DOWN] move cursor
    List will scroll if cursor
    moved beyond top or bottom
[GRAPH] displays selected picture

6-5 More on the Settings Command

When you choose Settings from the main menu, you will be given the following options:

Image   Hardware   Action   Save   Reset   Quit

Let us briefly explain these options.

6-6 Hardware Considerations

When you choose Settings Hardware, the following menu will be presented to you (see Figure 6–3):

Graphs-Directory   Fonts-Directory   Interface   Printer   Size-Paper Quit

PrintGraph automatically searches drive A for the Graphs and Fonts directories. You can change these directories to drive B by typing B:. With hard disk systems you have to change the default to C drive, or the drive where you have stored your graphs. This procedure is done during the installation of your system (see Appendix B). If you look back at Figure 6–1, you will see the default settings as follows:

Graphs Directory: A:
Fonts Directory: A:
Interface: Parallel 1; etc.

Your interface can be either parallel or serial. If you specify a serial interface for hardware settings (e.g., Settings, Hardware, Interface), you must also specify the baud rate setting of your printer. The baud rate is the speed at which data is transferred. Choose the fastest baud rate available for your printer. The following are baud rates in order of increasing speed:

Setting	Baud Rate
1	110
2	150
3	300
4	600
5	1,200
6	2,400
7	4,800
8	9,600
9	19,200

You must configure the serial printer to the following settings:

Setting	Value
Data bits	8
Stop bits	For baud 110, 2; otherwise,1
Parity	None

Remember, these settings must be changed on your printer, not in the PrintGraph program.

```
Copyright 1986 Lotus Development Corp.  All Rights Reserved. Release 2.01  MENU

Select graphs for printing
Image-Select  Settings  Go  Align  Page  Exit

    GRAPH       IMAGE OPTIONS                      HARDWARE SETUP
    IMAGES      Size              Range Colors      Graphs Directory:
    SELECTED     Top        .395  X                  A:\
                 Left       .750  A                 Fonts Directory:
                 Width     6.500  B                  A:\
                 Height    4.691  C                 Interface:
                 Rotate     .000  D                  Parallel 1
                                  E                 Printer Type:
             Font                 F
             1  BLOCK1                              Paper Size
             2  BLOCK1                               Width       8.500
                                                     Length     11.000

                                                  ACTION OPTIONS
                                                   Pause: No   Eject: No
```

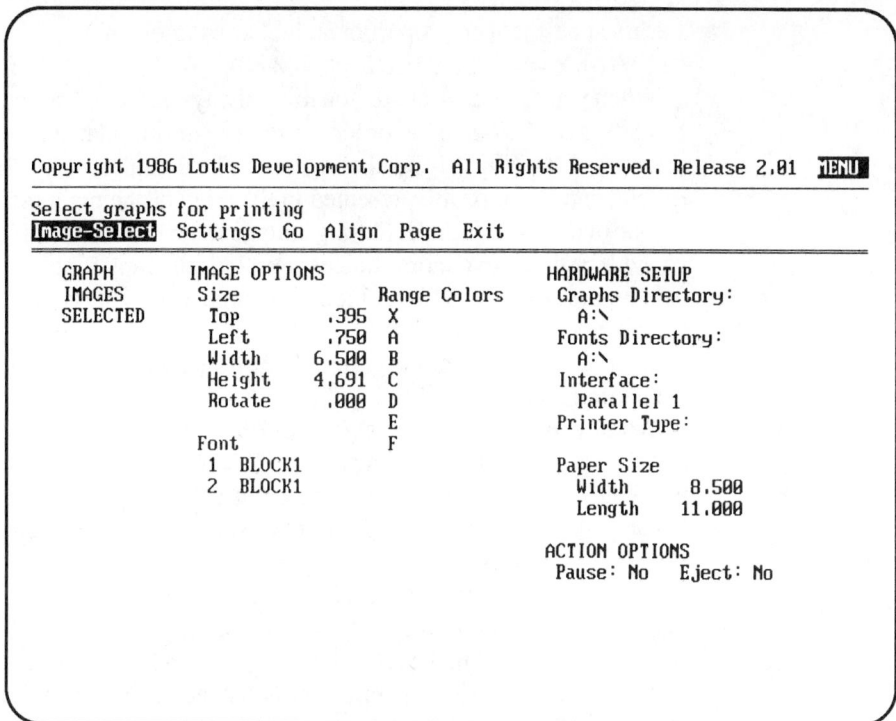

Figure 6–3 The Menu for Settings Hardware

The Size-Paper option in this menu will give you the following three options:

Length   Width   Quit

These options can change the default settings of PrintGraph.

6-7 The Image Option

The Image option will give the following menu:

Size   Font   Range-Colors   Quit

Choosing the Size option, you can select Full, Half, Manual, or Quit.

With the Full and Half options, PrintGraph will automatically fit your graph onto the entire page or onto half of the page and will set the height and width of the graph accordingly.

The Manual option enables you to change top and left margins manually. It also defines the width, height, and rotation of the graph, from zero to 90 degrees.

The Rotation option sets the number of degrees that the graph is turned counter-clockwise. If PrintGraph sets a graph size automatically, it preserves the aspect ratio or the ratio of graph width to graph height, approximately 1.385 to 1 for X– and Y–axes, respectively. Therefore, remember that if you change either X or Y, the other axis must be changed proportionately. For example, if X = 4, then Y = 2.88 (X/Y = 1.385/1, 4/Y = 1.385, Y = 4/1.385 = 2.88).

When you draw a pie chart, you must always maintain the standard aspect ratio of 1.385(X-axis)/1(Y-axis) in order to preserve the circular shape, otherwise you may end up with an ellipse instead of a circle. The default settings for Top, Left, Width, Height, and Rotation are presented in the body of the main menu (see Figure 6–1).

One of the options under Settings Image is the Font option. If this option is chosen you will be given two more choices, 1 or 2. Both graph fonts 1 and 2 have 11 options (see Figure 6–4). In the Font menu, the higher the option, the darker the print; for example, SCRIPT2 is darker than SCRIPT1. You can choose Font 1 for the heading and Font 2 for the rest of the graph. If you don't choose Font 2, PrintGraph will print the entire graph in Font 1.

When you choose Settings, Image, Range-Colors, PrintGraph displays a menu that shows the graph ranges, X and A to F. This setting depends on the type of printer that you are using; you will see different colors only with color printers. Range-Colors can be selected only if you have specified a particular printer or plotter by choosing Hardware, Printer.

Printing a colored pie chart is done in a slightly different way from the other types of graphs. The colors of the wedges are defined by the values in the B range when you save your graph using the /Graph Save command. If you recall from chapter 5, the B range was used for generating crosshatches in B range. Value 1 in the 1-2-3 worksheet corresponds to the X range in PrintGraph, value 2 to A, value 3 to B and so forth up to value 7 of the B range in the 1-2-3 worksheet to F in PrintGraph. Besides the color black, there are nine other colors: red, green, blue, orange, lime, gold, turquoise, violet, and brown.

6-8 The Action Option

One of the options under Settings is Action. If you choose Action from this menu, you will be given the following three choices:

Pause　　Eject　　Quit

The Action option monitors the operations of PrintGraph telling you what PrintGraph does between printing. You can choose Pause or Eject. If you choose the Pause option, you will be given two choices: Yes or No.

The Yes option makes PrintGraph pause. This is useful if you would like to change some of your settings after printing a graph. If you choose the No option, PrintGraph will not pause between printing graphs. This is useful if you are not going to change any of your settings from graph to graph.

The Eject option controls whether PrintGraph automatically advances the paper or not. If you choose this option, you will be given two more choices: Yes or No. Yes will give you one graph per page. No is used if you want more than one graph per page.

```
Copyright 1986 Lotus Development Corp. All Rights Reserved. Release 2.01  POINT

Select font 1


        FONT NAME      SIZE
        ---------------------          [SPACE] turns mark on and off
     #  BLOCK1         5732            [RETURN] selects marked font
        BLOCK2         9273            [ESCAPE] exits, ignoring changes
        BOLD           8624            [HOME] goes to beginning of list
        FORUM          9727            [END] goes to end of list
        ITALIC1        8949            [UP] and [DOWN] move cursor
        ITALIC2       11857               List will scroll if cursor
        LOTUS          8679               moved beyond top or bottom
        ROMAN1         6855
        ROMAN2        11598
        SCRIPT1        8132
        SCRIPT2       10367
```

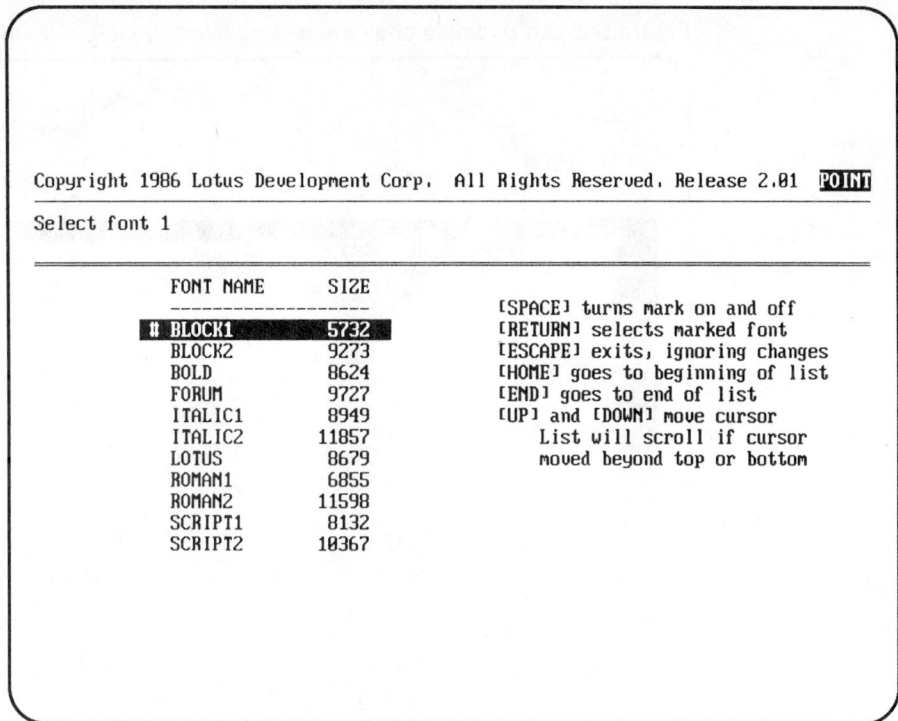

Figure 6–4 The Font Menu

If PrintGraph cannot fit the second graph on the same page, it advances to the next page automatically.

6-9 Save and Reset Options

Under the Settings menu, there are three other options: Save, Reset, and Quit.

The Save option can be used if you wish to save some of the present settings and use them in another session. If you do not choose this option, PrintGraph will not remember the most recent settings, which you may have changed during the last session. Therefore, it reads from the PGRAPH.CNF file (the default settings).

The Reset option is the opposite of Save. It replaces the current settings with those in the PGRAPH.CNF file(the default settings).

The Quit option will let you exit from this menu.

6-10 An Example of the Final Product

To wrap up this chapter, we developed an example using several of the options we have talked about. Look at Figure 6–5. First, by using Settings, Hardware, Printer, we chose the printer, in this case an IBM Graphics printer. Then we chose Image-Select (settings were the default values). Finally, we chose Go.

Figure 6–5 An Example of a Graph Generated by Default Settings

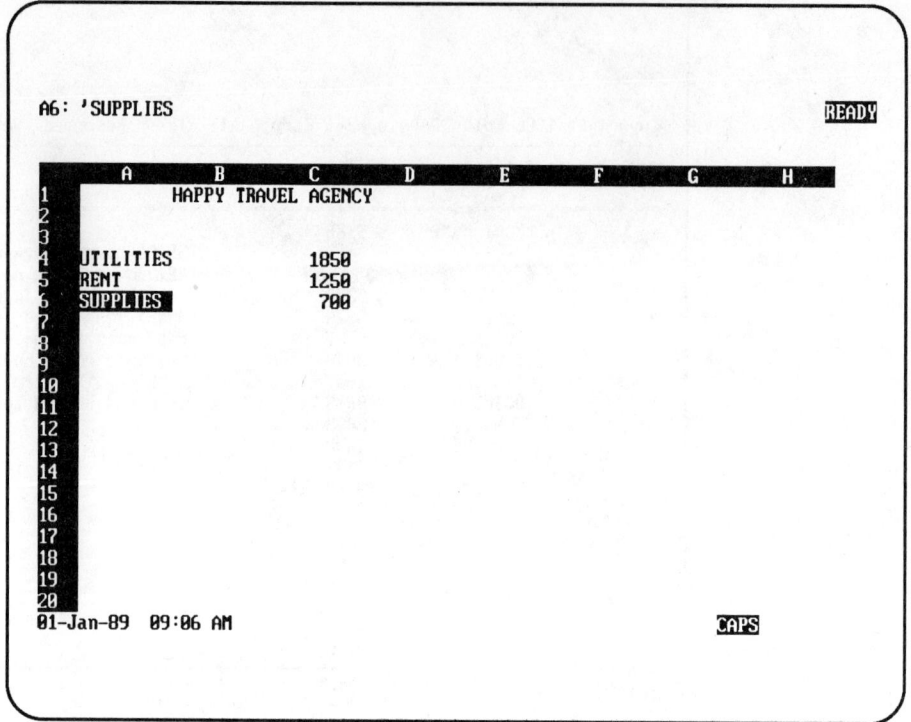

```
A6: 'SUPPLIES                                                    READY

        A      B      C      D      E      F      G      H
1              HAPPY TRAVEL AGENCY
2
3
4   UTILITIES          1850
5   RENT               1250
6   SUPPLIES            700
7
8
9
10
11
12
13
14
15
16
17
18
19
20
01-Jan-89  09:06 AM                                        CAPS
```

Figure 6–5 (Continued)

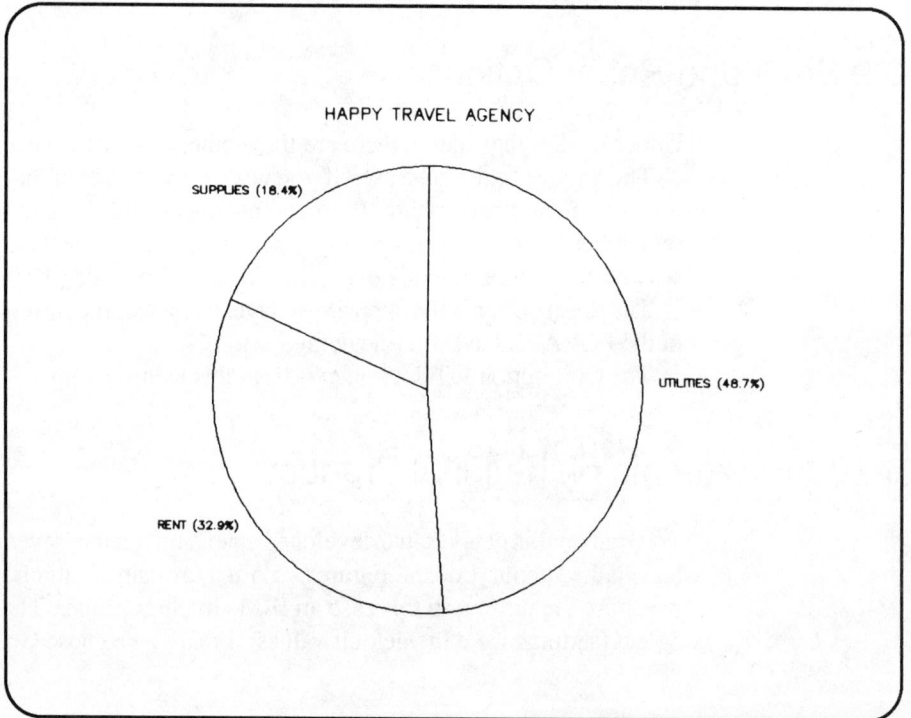

HAPPY TRAVEL AGENCY

SUPPLIES (18.4%)

UTILITIES (48.7%)

RENT (32.9%)

Summary

This chapter reviewed the PrintGraph program. This is the only program not included on the main 1-2-3 Systems disk. PrintGraph allows you to generate hard copies of the graphs you have created on your monitor with different settings. You can specify the size of the paper, the angle, the typeface, the size of the graph. The Font option provides you with 11 typefaces for the graph. If you have access to a color printer or plotter, you can generate color graphics.

Remember that at installation time, you must specify the type of printer and /or plotter you are using. As you will see in Appendix B, you can use a wide variety of printers and plotters with Lotus. If yours is not on the list, you may want to contact the Lotus Development Corporation.

Review Questions

1. How do you start PrintGraph?
2. How do you exit from PrintGraph?
3.* When you exit from PrintGraph, do you return to DOS or to the Lotus Access System?
4. What is the purpose of Image-Select in the main menu?
5.* Can you see your graph on the monitor using the PrintGraph program?
6. Can a PIC file (a graphic file) be retrieved in a 1-2-3 worksheet?
7.* How do you modify a graph's parameters in the PrintGraph program?
8. What is the purpose of the Align command in the main menu?
9. How many choices are available under the Font options?
10. How many colors are supported by the PrintGraph program?
11. What is the aspect ratio? What is this ratio in the default setting?
12.* Does the aspect ratio have to be fixed for pie charts? If yes, why?
13. How do you change the Graph directory from A drive to B drive?
14. How many interfaces are available?
15. The baud rate is required for which type of interface?
16.* What are the maximum and minimum baud rates?
17. What choices are available under Action?
18.* What does Pause do?
19. What does Eject do?
20. What is the purpose of Save and Reset in the Settings menu?
21. The following are oil production figures for Exatec Oil Company:

   1981 200,000 barrels
   1982 250,000 barrels
   1983 350,000 barrels
   1984 400,000 barrels
   1985 450,000 barrels
   1986 400,000 barrels
   1987 475,000 barrels

   Design and print a line graph, a bar graph, and a pie chart for this data.

Misconception and Solution

M — In a PrintGraph session, if you change some of the default settings and want to use these settings later, PrintGraph will not save these settings automatically.

S — Use the Settings Save command in order to save the current settings to the PGRAPH.CNF file before you exit from the PrintGraph session.

Comprehensive Lab Assignment

Get the PrintGraph program started and perform the following:

1. Generate a hard copy of G1, G2, G3, G4, and G5, generated in Chapter 5.
2. Change the Font options and generate the same graphs again.
3. Generate an oval-shaped pie chart.

7

Database Operations/Part One: Lotus as an Electronic File Cabinet

7-1 Introduction

In this chapter we will discuss the principles of database management using Lotus, including file creation, updating, sorting, and searching. We will use examples to illustrate the major database operations. Chapter 8 discusses advanced database operations.

7-2 What Is a Database?

In simple terms, a *database* is an organized collection of data stored in a central location. We all have used many databases, but we may not have called them that. A telephone directory is a good example of a database, one that has been organized alphabetically.

A better example of a database is the Yellow Pages. This database is also organized alphabetically; however, it is organized internally as well. If you are looking for a restaurant, you go to the *R* section, find *Restaurants*, and then search alphabetically for a particular restaurant.

In computer terminology, we call a database a collection of files, or more specifically, a collection of a series of integrated files. A *file* is a collection of records. A *record* is a collection of related fields, and a *field* is a collection of characters.

Your name, age, or occupation is an example of a field. If you put several name, age, and occupation fields together, you have constructed a record. Putting several student records together would establish a student file. At the same time, you can have a staff file, a faculty file, and so on. The collection of all these files is a database.

Most small and medium-size businesses use file cabinets to store their data. File cabinets are organized using a series of manila folders. Data in each folder is organized alphabetically, numerically, or by some other organizational scheme. Such a file cabinet and the information it contains can be called a manual database.

There are several differences between a manual and an automated database. An automated database is faster, more accurate, and occupies less space than a manual database.

7-3 Lotus as a Database

Lotus 1-2-3 offers some basic database capabilities. Using Lotus as a database management system, you can store up to 8,192 records. Each record can include up to 256 fields; each field can include up to 240 characters. However, compared to database packages such as dBASE III Plus or R-BASE 5000, Lotus offers limited database capabilities.

The size of a database depends on the size of the memory in your computer (RAM). Each character is equal to one byte of memory. So 1,000 records, each with 200 characters, is equal to 200,000 bytes, or approximately 195K. Lotus Release 2 requires 215K of memory if you load it from the Lotus Access System. If 1-2-3 is loaded directly, the memory requirement is approximately 192K.

Since a database generated by Lotus resides in RAM, processing speed is extremely fast. Using Lotus as a database is also helpful when you import files from other programs to perform database operations (for information on file transfer, see Appendix C).

7-4 Basic Database Operations Using Lotus

The Lotus database is simply an expansion of the spreadsheet. This spreadsheet includes 8,192 rows (records) and 256 columns (fields). Major database operations are:

- Database creation

- Database update

- Database sort

- Database search

Database creation simply means putting labels, formulas, or figures in different cells, something we have been doing all along. If the length of a particular field is larger than nine characters (the default value), it can be modified by using /Worksheet Global Column-Width or /Worksheet Column Set-Width.

Database update includes changing the content of a particular field (simple editing), insertion of a new record or field (/Worksheet Insert Row or /Worksheet Insert Column, respectively), deletion of a record or field (/Worksheet Delete Row or /Worksheet Delete Column, respectively), deletion of an entire database (/ Worksheet Erase Yes), or deletion of a portion of a database (/Range Erase).

You can sort your database in either ascending or descending order by using a primary key and a secondary key. A *primary key* is the first field chosen for a sort operation; for example, last name. The *secondary key* is the second field chosen for a sort operation; for example, sex. Finally, you can do any type of search using different criteria.

Other complex database operations, such as the join operation (putting two databases side by side), can be performed with the /File Combine command. A merge operation (adding one database to the bottom of another one) can also be performed by using the /File Combine command. For other database operations, such as label generation or managing multiple databases, macros (discussed in Chapters 9–11) can be developed.

7-5 Your First Database

Figure 7–1 shows an example of a database. This database has 15 records, each with six fields. Each field starts with a field name. The field name must be a label; however, it can be a numeric label such as "5" or "9", etc. The field name can be more than one line in length but only the last row will be considered the field name. Field names must be unique.

Figure 7–1 has been created in the same fashion as other worksheets. Numbers and figures are right-justified and labels are left-justified.

7-6 Sorting Your Database

The database can be sorted by any field, in ascending or descending order. To access the Sort command, choose Data from the main menu and then select the Sort command. The Sort command has the following options:

Data-Range   Primary-Key   Secondary-Key   Reset   Go   Quit

The data-range usually includes all data items in your database, though in reality you can include only a portion of your database. The field names must not be included in the data-range, otherwise it will be considered as a part of the database itself and will be mixed up with data items.

The primary-key is the first key for the Sort operation. Any field in your database may be selected as the primary-key. The secondary-key is another field that may be used for a Sort operation.

Reset is used when you decide to change the parameter of your database. When you choose the Reset command all current settings will go back to the default setting. For example, if your previous data range was A1..A50, after choosing the Reset

```
A1: [W12]                                                       READY

         A            B           C    D      E           F         G
1                   MY FIRST DATABASE
2
3    FIRST NAME   LAST NAME     AGE  SEX  OCCUPATION     INCOME
4    Randy        Alexander      36   M   Professor      $40,000
5    Fay          Alexander      30   F   Mayor          $30,000
6    Adam         Alexander      31   M   Engineer       $30,000
7    Andrea       Byan           36   F   Teacher        $31,000
8    Moe          Byan           40   M   Officer        $40,000
9    Bob          Adam           32   M   Engineer       $72,000
10   Anna         Adam            4   F   Unemployed     $11,000
11   Vicki        Adam            9   F   Unemployed     $12,000
12   Paula        Bobby          55   F   Housewife      $20,000
13   Jack         Jones          69   M   Artist         $19,000
14   Mary         Fishler        30   F   Interpreter    $19,000
15   Sue          Hayword        22   F   Student        $10,000
16   Tammy        Smith          29   F   Student        $10,000
17   Jacky        Brown          72   F   Engineer       $52,000
18   Lora         Jones          30   F   Nurse          $31,000
19
20
01-Jan-89   09:00 AM
```

Figure 7–1 An Example of a Database

command your data range will be erased. Now you have to define a new database range.

Go executes the Sort operation. And finally, Quit will let you leave the menu.

Figure 7–2 shows Figure 7–1 after having been sorted by last name. This figure was generated as follows:

/Data, Sort, Data-Range A4..F18, Return, Primary-Key, B4..B18, Return, A, Return, Go

By default, Lotus sorts in descending order. If you do not want this default setting, type A (ascending) and press the **Return** key. Otherwise, hit Return without typing anything; this means you are choosing the default setting. The order in which Lotus performs a sort is determined by a collating sequence. You may choose one of three collating sequences during the install operations (see Appendix B):

- Numbers first

- Numbers last

- ASCII

Uppercase and lowercase letters have the same value. As a general rule, nonlabel, nonnumeric, and composed characters (F1 + Alternate) fall at the end of the listing. (For ASCII codes see Appendix F.) As a general rule do not leave any empty row or column in your database.

```
A1: [W12] 'This database has been sorted by last name.                    READY


           A            B           C    D    E              F           G
    1  This database has been sorted by last name.
    2
    3  FIRST NAME   LAST NAME   AGE  SEX  OCCUPATION     INCOME
    4  Anna         Adam          4   F   Unemployed     $11,000
    5  Bob          Adam         32   M   Engineer       $72,000
    6  Vicki        Adam          9   F   Unemployed     $12,000
    7  Adam         Alexander    31   M   Engineer       $30,000
    8  Fay          Alexander    30   F   Mayor          $30,000
    9  Randy        Alexander    36   M   Professor      $40,000
   10  Paula        Bobby        55   F   Housewife      $20,000
   11  Jacky        Brown        72   F   Engineer       $52,000
   12  Andrea       Byan         36   F   Teacher        $31,000
   13  Moe          Byan         40   M   Officer        $40,000
   14  Mary         Fishler      30   F   Interpreter    $19,000
   15  Sue          Hayword      22   F   Student        $10,000
   16  Jack         Jones        69   M   Artist         $19,000
   17  Lora         Jones        30   F   Nurse          $31,000
   18  Tammy        Smith        29   F   Student        $10,000
   19
   20
   01-Jan-89  07:02 PM
```

Figure 7–2 Figure 7–1 Sorted by Last Name

7-7 Sorting with Two Keys

There are instances when you want to sort a database using two fields. The Yellow Pages, for example, has been sorted by business type and within each type, businesses are sorted alphabetically. In Figure 7–3, we sorted the original database (Figure 7–1) using two keys. The primary-key is sex and the secondary-key is age. Within each group, individuals are sorted by age. Figure 7–3 was generated as follows:

/Data, Sort, Data-Range A4..F18, Return, Primary-Key, D4..D18, Return, A, Return, Secondary-Key, C4..C18, Return, A, Return, Go

7-8 Search Operations

In search operations we are interested in a specific record or series of records that meet certain criteria. For example, in a student grade file we might want to search for all students who have a GPA greater than 3.60, or in an employee file, employees who hold a master's degree. To conduct a search operation, access Data from the main menu and then choose Query. Under Query we have:

Input   Criterion   Output   Find   Extract   Unique   Delete   Reset   Quit

Input includes the entire database, including the field names. For example, in Figure 7–1 the Input range is A3..F18.

```
A1: [W12] 'This database has been sorted by sex and age.              READY

        A            B          C   D      E              F        G
1   This database has been sorted by sex and age.
2
3   FIRST NAME   LAST NAME    AGE  SEX OCCUPATION      INCOME
4   Anna         Adam           4   F  Unemployed      $11,000
5   Vicki        Adam           9   F  Unemployed      $12,000
6   Sue          Hayword       22   F  Student         $10,000
7   Tammy        Smith         29   F  Student         $10,000
8   Mary         Fishler       30   F  Interpreter     $19,000
9   Lora         Jones         30   F  Nurse           $31,000
10  Fay          Alexander     30   F  Mayor           $30,000
11  Andrea       Byan          36   F  Teacher         $31,000
12  Paula        Bobby         55   F  Housewife       $20,000
13  Jacky        Brown         72   F  Engineer        $52,000
14  Adam         Alexander     31   M  Engineer        $30,000
15  Bob          Adam          32   M  Engineer        $72,000
16  Randy        Alexander     36   M  Professor       $40,000
17  Moe          Byan          40   M  Officer         $40,000
18  Jack         Jones         69   M  Artist          $19,000
19
20
01-Jan-89  07:07 PM
```

Figure 7–3 Figure 7–1 Sorted by Sex and Age

The criterion range is a part of the worksheet entered separately outside the database range, which includes the name of the field and the criterion we are searching for. The criterion range must have field names identical to those used in the database; therefore, the Copy command is optimal for creation of the criterion range field names. For example, in our database (Figure 7–1), the criterion range for all the engineers would be:

OCCUPATION
Engineer

Occupation is the field name in which we have a field containing Engineer. Up to 32 fields can be considered for the search in the criterion range.

The output range is a selected portion of a worksheet outside the database range used to store records based on the criterion range. It must contain the names of the fields in the database which you want to extract (uppercase or lowercase doesn't matter).

The Find option is used to choose a record or a series of records based on the criterion range (output range is not needed with the Find option). To use the Find option all you need to define is the Input range and the Criterion range, and then choose the Find option. When the option is executed, the selected records will be highlighted.

With the Extract option, a portion of a database can be copied to the output range, based on the criterion range (assuming you have already defined the output range).

The Unique option is used in order to extract only a unique portion of a database. In this case, duplicate records will not be chosen. For example, if you would like to choose one representative of each occupation, only one engineer will be selected, one professor, and so forth.

The Delete option is used to erase a portion of a database, based on the criterion range. The following section illustrates these options.

7-9 Search with Single Criterion

In Figure 7–4 we have searched the database on the left side of the figure for all engineers. This example was generated as follows:

/Data, Query, Input A5..D13, Return, Criterion F6..F7, Return, Find

As you see, when you choose the Find option, the cursor will point to the first record that meets a particular criterion. If you move the cursor down to the records below the first selected one, you will see it point to the next candidate (if there is any). This will continue until all the candidates are highlighted. Now, if you try to move the cursor farther down, you will hear a beep. This means there are no more candidates to be highlighted.

To demonstrate the actual output we have used the Extract option. Figure 7–5 was generated as follows:

Figure 7–4 Example of Search with Single Criterion (All Engineers)

```
A1: [W12] 'This database is being searched for engineers, and we are using READY


        A        B    C      D              E        F      G
1  This database is being searched for engineers, and we are using the
2  Find option.
3
4
5  FIRST NAME    AGE  SEX OCCUPATION                CRITERION RANGE
6  Randy         36   M   Professor                 OCCUPATION
7  Adam          31   M   Engineer                  Engineer
8  Joe           40   M   Officer
9  Bob           32   M   Engineer
10 Paula         55   F   Housewife
11 Mary          30   F   Interpreter
12 Jacky         72   F   Engineer
13 Lora          30   F   Nurse
14
15
16
17
18
19
20
01-Jan-89  07:12 PM
```

/Data, Query, Input A5..D13, Return, Criterion F6..F7, Return, Output A16..D20, Return, Extract

Remember, the output range does not need to include the entire range for the extracted output (assuming you have enough empty space for the extracted data). If you copy only the names of the fields from the database and specify the first line of the output range, that would be adequate. The first line of the output range is always the row containing the name of the fields for the extracted output.

7-10 Search for Either Criterion

There are numerous occasions when you are interested only in a couple of criteria; either one would be acceptable. For example, you might look for an employee with a bachelor's degree *or* 17 years of experience, or a student who is majoring in MIS *or* computer science. In computer terminology this is called an OR condition (either condition is acceptable). (The opposite is the AND condition, meaning that all the conditions must be met.) The OR criteria must be in a vertical line; that is, in a column. The AND criteria must be in a horizontal line; that is, in a row. In Figure 7–6, we searched the database for individuals who are either engineers or teachers. This figure was generated as follows:

/Data, Query, Input A3..E11, Return, Criterion G4..G6, Return, Output A15..E20, Return, Extract

Figure 7–5 Example of Search with Single Criterion (All Engineers) with Output Range

```
A1: [W12] 'This database is being searched for all engineers, and we are usREADY

        A           B    C    D            E         F         G
1   This database is being searched for all engineers, and we are using the
2   Extract option.
3
4
5   FIRST NAME    AGE  SEX OCCUPATION            CRITERION RANGE
6   Randy          36   M  Professor             OCCUPATION
7   Adam           31   M  Engineer              Engineer
8   Moe            40   M  Officer
9   Bob            32   M  Engineer
10  Paula          55   F  Housewife
11  Mary           30   F  Interpreter
12  Jacky          72   F  Engineer
13  Lora           30   F  Nurse
14
15  OUTPUT RANGE
16  FIRST NAME    AGE  SEX OCCUPATION
17  Adam           31   M  Engineer
18  Bob            32   M  Engineer
19  Jacky          72   F  Engineer
20
01-Jan-89  07:17 PM
```

```
A1: [W12] 'This database is being used to search for engineers or teachers.READY

         A       B    C      D              E          F         G
1   This database is being used to search for engineers or teachers.
2
3   FIRST NAME  AGE  SEX  OCCUPATION    INCOME                CRITERION RANGE
4   Adam        31   M    Engineer      $30,000               OCCUPATION
5   Andrea      36   F    Teacher       $31,000               Engineer
6   Moe         40   M    Officer       $40,000               Teacher
7   Bob         32   M    Engineer      $72,000
8   Paula       55   F    Housewife     $20,000
9   Mary        30   F    Interpreter   $19,000
10  Jacky       72   F    Engineer      $52,000
11  Lora        30   F    Nurse         $31,000
12
13
14  OUTPUT RANGE
15  FIRST NAME  AGE  SEX  OCCUPATION    INCOME
16  Adam        31   M    Engineer      $30,000
17  Andrea      36   F    Teacher       $31,000
18  Bob         32   M    Engineer      $72,000
19  Jacky       72   F    Engineer      $52,000
20
01-Jan-89  07:22 PM
```

Figure 7–6 Examples of Search with Either Criterion (Engineer or Teacher)

7-11 Search with Wild Cards

Lotus includes three wild card characters that can be used in the criterion range. Each has its own unique application. The three are the asterisk (*), the question mark (?), and the tilde (~). Placing an asterisk after a character means that you will retrieve that character *plus* any and all characters that follow it. For example, you would use *B* and an asterisk if you are interested in everyone who has a last name starting with B: Byan, Brown, Bandary, and so on.

The question mark will retrieve any character in one position. For example, ?anny will give you Fanny and Danny; ?ortland will give you Portland and sortland.

Finally, the tilde will retrieve all values *except* those that follow it. For example, ~engineer gives you every occupation listed except engineers. Figures 7–7, 7–8, and 7–9 show the effects of using these wild cards.

Figure 7–7 was generated as follows:

/Data, Query, Input A4..D11, Return, Criterion F5..F6, Return, Output A15..D20, Return, Extract

Figure 7–8 was generated as follows:

/Data, Query, Input A4..B11, Return, Criterion D5..D6, Return, Output A16..B20, Return, Extract

Figure 7–9 was generated as follows:

/Data, Query, Input A3..E11, Return, Criterion G4..G5, Return, Output A15..E25, Return, Extract

Figure 7–7 An Example of Wild Card * (Asterisk)

A1: [W12] 'This database is being searched for all records with last name   READY

	A	B	C	D	E	F	G
1	This database is being searched for all records with last name						
2	starting with B; the rest is not important.						
3							
4	FIRST NAME	LAST NAME		AGE	SEX	CRITERION RANGE	
5	Andrea	Byan		36	F	LAST NAME	
6	Moe	Byan		40	M	B*	
7	Adam	Alexander		32	M		
8	Paula	Bobby		55	F		
9	Jack	Jones		69	M		
10	Jacky	Brown		72	F		
11	Lora	Jones		30	F		
12							
13							
14	OUTPUT RANGE						
15	FIRST NAME	LAST NAME		AGE	SEX		
16	Andrea	Byan		36	F		
17	Moe	Byan		40	M		
18	Paula	Bobby		55	F		
19	Jacky	Brown		72	F		
20							

01-Jan-89 07:27 PM

Figure 7–8 An Example of Wild Card ? (Question Mark)

A1: [W25] 'This database was generated by using the wildcard "?".   READY

	A	B	C	D	E	F
1	This database was generated by using the wildcard "?".					
2						
3						
4	NAME	AGE		CRITERION RANGE		
5	Mary		30	NAME		
6	Sue		20	?anny		
7	Sunny		34			
8	Danny		34			
9	Fanny		34			
10	Jacky		39			
11	Adrienne		21			
12						
13						
14						
15	OUTPUT RANGE					
16	NAME	AGE				
17	Danny		34			
18	Fanny		34			
19						
20						

01-Jan-89 07:32 PM

7-12 Search with Multiple Criteria

Sometimes you may be interested in searching for records meeting multiple criteria. This is called an AND condition. For example, you may want to search for all the students who have a GPA of 3.6 or better *and* are MIS majors, or all the employees who have 10 years of experience and have a bachelor's degree and speak Spanish. An employee must meet all the criteria to be selected. The AND criteria must be in a horizontal line; that is, in a row.

Figure 7–11 illustrates an AND condition: all female engineers who make more than $50,000 and are less than 60 years old. We searched the database in Figure 7–10 to find the names that met all these criteria. Figure 14-11 was generated as follows:

/Data, Query, Input A4..F19, Return, Criterion I5..L6, Return, Output G11..L30, Return, Extract

As we mentioned earlier, you can include up to 32 fields in your criterion range. You can also combine AND and OR conditions as long as you are forming a rectangle in your Criterion range.

Figure 7–12 was searched to give the results in Figure 7–13. Figure 7–13 was generated as follows:

/Data, Query, Input, A4..F19, Return, Criterion I5..L8, Return, Output, G11..L30, Return, Extract

In the first row of the criterion range we are looking for whoever meets the following four criteria: Age < 60, Sex = F, Occupation = Engineer, Income > $50,000. As you see, there is only one candidate who meets all criteria, Allison Alexander.

In the second row of the criterion range, we are looking for candidates who meet the following criteria: Age > 90, Sex = Either, Occupation = Teacher, Income = Any. Only one candidate meets all these criteria, Lora Jones.

In the third line of criteria we are looking for any candidate who is a student; sex, age, and income are not important.

As you see, many of these criteria can be combined with the OR and AND conditions. Remember, if you leave a criterion empty in the criterion range, any data item can fill that range (any profession, any sex, etc.).

Another interesting search would be to apply AND/OR choices to one particular field. In Figure 7–14, we searched for individuals who are between the ages of 30 and 40. The figure was generated as follows:

/Data, Query, Input, A3..B18, Return, Criterion, E4..E5, Return Output, E9..F18, Return, Extract

In Figure 7–15, we searched for individuals who are younger than 10 or older than 70. The figure was generated as follows:

/Data, Query, Input, A3..B18, Return, Criterion, E4..E5, Return, Output, E9..F18, Return, Extract

7-13 Extract vs. Unique Options

Sometimes there are duplicate records in the database. Let us say you would like to generate a mailing list for a series of business organizations and you want to send

Figure 7–9 An Example of Wild Card ~ (Tilde)

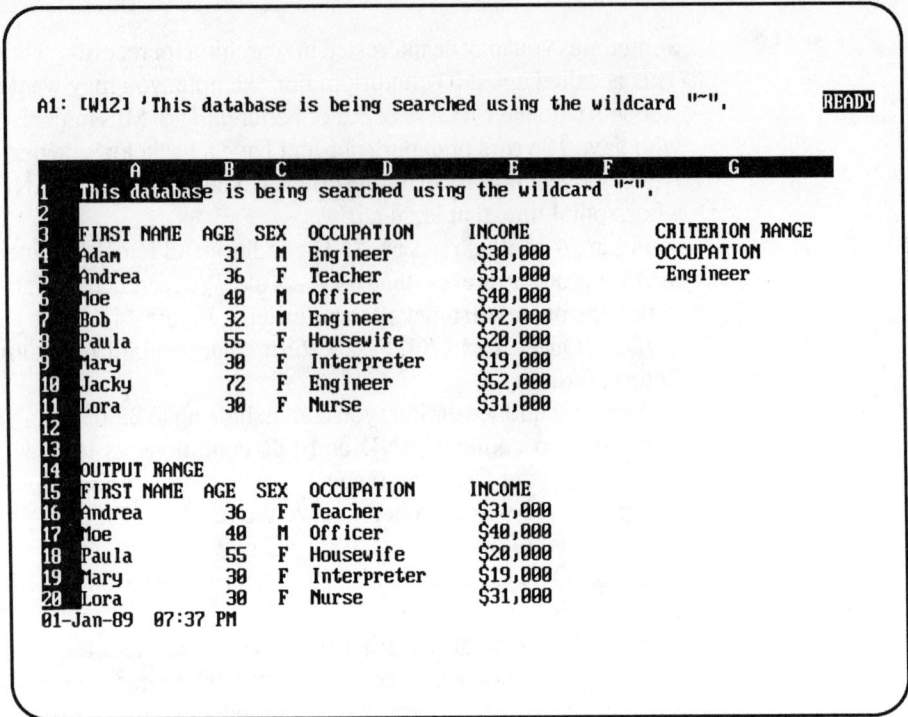

```
A1: [W12] 'This database is being searched using the wildcard "~".         READY


        A     B    C     D           E          F         G
1  This database is being searched using the wildcard "~".
2
3  FIRST NAME AGE  SEX  OCCUPATION    INCOME             CRITERION RANGE
4  Adam       31   M    Engineer      $30,000            OCCUPATION
5  Andrea     36   F    Teacher       $31,000            ~Engineer
6  Moe        40   M    Officer       $40,000
7  Bob        32   M    Engineer      $72,000
8  Paula      55   F    Housewife     $20,000
9  Mary       30   F    Interpreter   $19,000
10 Jacky      72   F    Engineer      $52,000
11 Lora       30   F    Nurse         $31,000
12
13
14 OUTPUT RANGE
15 FIRST NAME AGE  SEX  OCCUPATION    INCOME
16 Andrea     36   F    Teacher       $31,000
17 Moe        40   M    Officer       $40,000
18 Paula      55   F    Housewife     $20,000
19 Mary       30   F    Interpreter   $19,000
20 Lora       30   F    Nurse         $31,000
01-Jan-89  07:37 PM
```

Figure 7–10 Database Used for Multiple Criteria Search

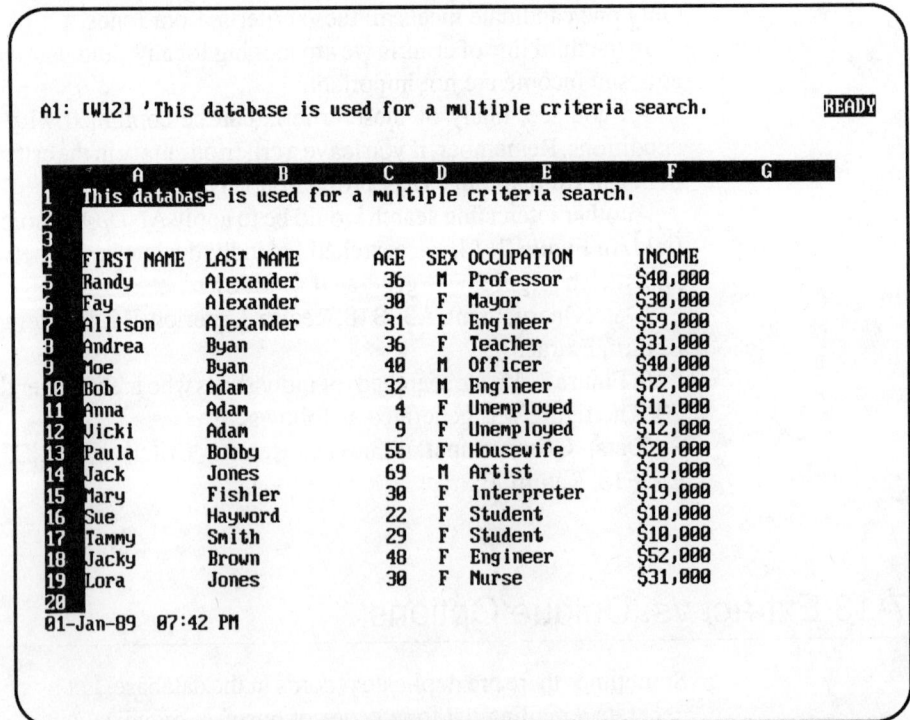

```
A1: [W12] 'This database is used for a multiple criteria search.           READY


        A          B           C    D    E           F         G
1  This database is used for a multiple criteria search.
2
3
4  FIRST NAME  LAST NAME     AGE  SEX OCCUPATION     INCOME
5  Randy       Alexander     36   M   Professor      $40,000
6  Fay         Alexander     30   F   Mayor          $30,000
7  Allison     Alexander     31   F   Engineer       $59,000
8  Andrea      Byan          36   F   Teacher        $31,000
9  Moe         Byan          40   M   Officer        $40,000
10 Bob         Adam          32   M   Engineer       $72,000
11 Anna        Adam          4    F   Unemployed     $11,000
12 Vicki       Adam          9    F   Unemployed     $12,000
13 Paula       Bobby         55   F   Housewife      $20,000
14 Jack        Jones         69   M   Artist         $19,000
15 Mary        Fishler       30   F   Interpreter    $19,000
16 Sue         Hayword       22   F   Student        $10,000
17 Tammy       Smith         29   F   Student        $10,000
18 Jacky       Brown         48   F   Engineer       $52,000
19 Lora        Jones         30   F   Nurse          $31,000
20
01-Jan-89  07:42 PM
```

Figure 7–11 An Example of Multiple Criteria (AND Option)

```
G1: [W12] 'This is the result of the multiple search done on Figure 7-10.   READY


          G        H         I      J        K             L
1    This is the result of the multiple search done on Figure 7-10.
2
3
4                          CRITERION RANGE
5                          AGE   SEX  OCCUPATION     INCOME
6                          +C5<60 F    Engineer      +F5>50000
7
8
9
10   OUTPUT RANGE
11   FIRST NAME  LAST NAME          AGE  SEX OCCUPATION      INCOME
12   Allison     Alexander           31   F  Engineer       $59,000
13   Jacky       Brown               48   F  Engineer       $52,000
14
15
16
17
18
19
20
01-Jan-89  07:47 PM
```

Figure 7–12 Sample Worksheet for Multiple Search

```
A1: [W12] 'This database is used for a multiple criteria search.         READY


          A         B         C    D        E             F        G
1    This database is used for a multiple criteria search.
2
3
4    FIRST NAME  LAST NAME          AGE  SEX OCCUPATION      INCOME
5    Randy       Alexander           36   M  Professor      $40,000
6    Fay         Alexander           30   F  Mayor          $30,000
7    Allison     Alexander           31   F  Engineer       $59,000
8    Andrea      Byan                36   F  Teacher        $31,000
9    Moe         Byan                40   M  Officer        $40,000
10   Bob         Adam                32   M  Engineer       $72,000
11   Anna        Adam                 4   F  Unemployed     $11,000
12   Vicki       Adam                 9   F  Unemployed     $12,000
13   Paula       Bobby               55   F  Housewife      $20,000
14   Jack        Jones               69   M  Artist         $19,000
15   Mary        Fishler             30   F  Interpreter    $19,000
16   Sue         Hayword             22   F  Student        $10,000
17   Tammy       Smith               29   F  Student        $10,000
18   Jacky       Brown              100   F  Engineer       $52,000
19   Lora        Jones               99   F  Teacher        $31,000
20
01-Jan-89  07:52 PM
```

Figure 7–13 An Example of a Multiple Search

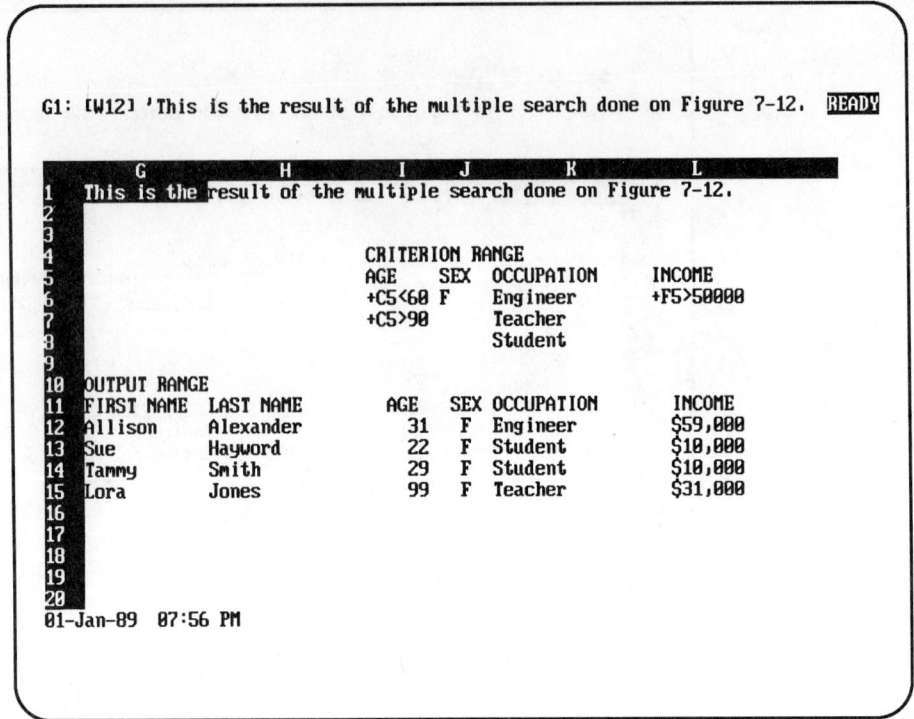

```
G1: [W12] 'This is the result of the multiple search done on Figure 7-12.     READY

        G        H        I    J    K        L
1    This is the result of the multiple search done on Figure 7-12.
2
3
4                          CRITERION RANGE
5                          AGE      SEX  OCCUPATION      INCOME
6                          +C5<60   F    Engineer        +F5>50000
7                          +C5>90        Teacher
8                                        Student
9
10   OUTPUT RANGE
11   FIRST NAME  LAST NAME          AGE  SEX  OCCUPATION      INCOME
12   Allison     Alexander           31  F    Engineer        $59,000
13   Sue         Hayword             22  F    Student         $10,000
14   Tammy       Smith               29  F    Student         $10,000
15   Lora        Jones               99  F    Teacher         $31,000
16
17
18
19
20
01-Jan-89   07:56 PM
```

Figure 7–14 Search with AND within One Field

```
A1: [W12]                                                           READY

        A        B  C  D        E          F      G        H
1                  SAMPLE DATABASE
2
3    FIRST NAME  AGE            CRITERION RANGE
4    Randy        36            AGE
5    Fay          30            +B4>30#AND#B4<40
6    Adam         31
7    Andrea       36
8    Moe          40            OUTPUT RANGE
9    Bob          32            FIRST NAME      AGE
10   Anna          4            Randy           36
11   Vicki         9            Adam            31
12   Paula        55            Andrea          36
13   Jack         69            Bob             32
14   Mary         30
15   Sue          22
16   Tammy        29
17   Jacky        72
18   Lora         30
19
20
01-Jan-88   08:03 PM                                              NUM
```

```
A1: [W12]                                                          READY

         A        B   C   D          E            F      G      H
1                 SAMPLE DATABASE
2
3    FIRST NAME   AGE            CRITERION RANGE
4    Randy        36             AGE
5    Fay          30             +B4<10#OR#+B4>70
6    Adam         31
7    Andrea       36
8    Moe          40             OUTPUT RANGE
9    Bob          32             FIRST NAME           AGE
10   Anna          4             Anna                  4
11   Vicki         9             Vicki                 9
12   Paula        55             Jacky                72
13   Jack         69
14   Mary         30
15   Sue          22
16   Tammy        29
17   Jacky        72
18   Lora         30
19
20
01-Jan-89   09:22 AM                                        NUM
```

Figure 7–15 Search with OR within One Field

a memo to each organization. As an example, you would like to send a memo to one university in each system; one memo to the Cal State system, one to the UC system, and so forth. In this case, the Extract option may not do the job if the organization is listed more than once in your database. If you use the Unique option, only one occurrence of each record will be selected.

Figure 7–16 shows a database used to compare the Extract and Unique options. Figure 7–17 compares the results of using these two options. This figure was generated as follows:

For the Extract option:

/Data, Query, Input A5..B20, Return, Criterion M18..N19, Return, Output G4..J21, Return, Extract

For the Unique option:

/Data, Query, Input A5..B20, Return, Criterion M18..N19, Return, Output K4..N16, Return, Unique

Remember, when the Unique option is used the entire record must be unique, not just one or more fields.

7-14 Delete Option

Besides using the /Worksheet and /Range commands for deleting a portion of your database, you can use the Delete option. Figure 7–19 was generated by using the

Figure 7–16 Database Used for Extract and Unique Options

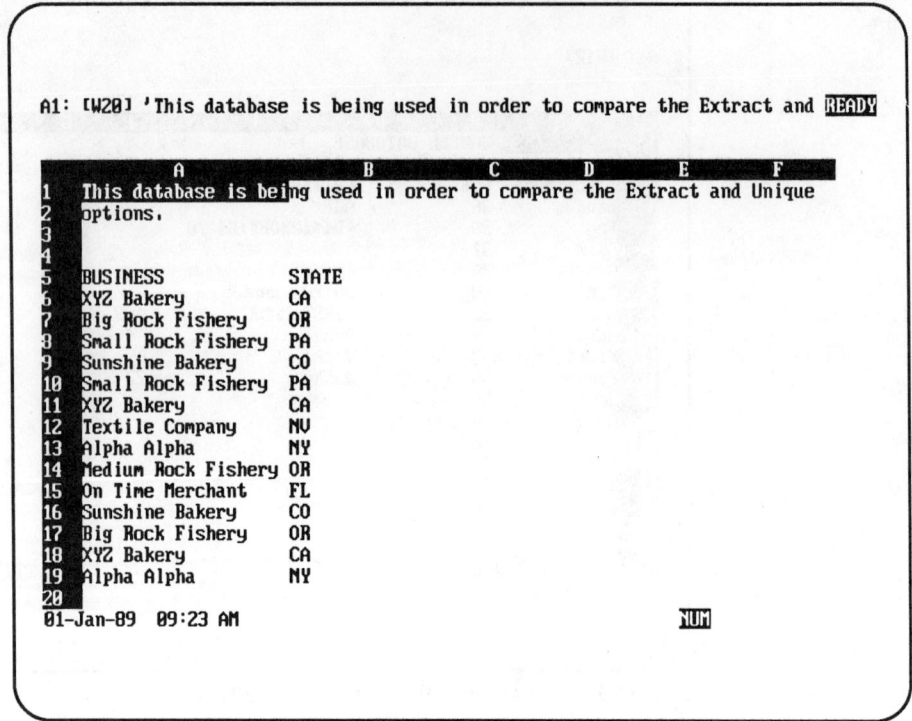

```
A1: [W20] 'This database is being used in order to compare the Extract and READY

            A            B         C         D         E         F
1  This database is being used in order to compare the Extract and Unique
2  options.
3
4
5  BUSINESS          STATE
6  XYZ Bakery        CA
7  Big Rock Fishery  OR
8  Small Rock Fishery PA
9  Sunshine Bakery   CO
10 Small Rock Fishery PA
11 XYZ Bakery        CA
12 Textile Company   NV
13 Alpha Alpha       NY
14 Medium Rock Fishery OR
15 On Time Merchant  FL
16 Sunshine Bakery   CO
17 Big Rock Fishery  OR
18 XYZ Bakery        CA
19 Alpha Alpha       NY
20
01-Jan-89  09:23 AM                                          NUM
```

Figure 7–17 Comparison of Extract and Unique Options

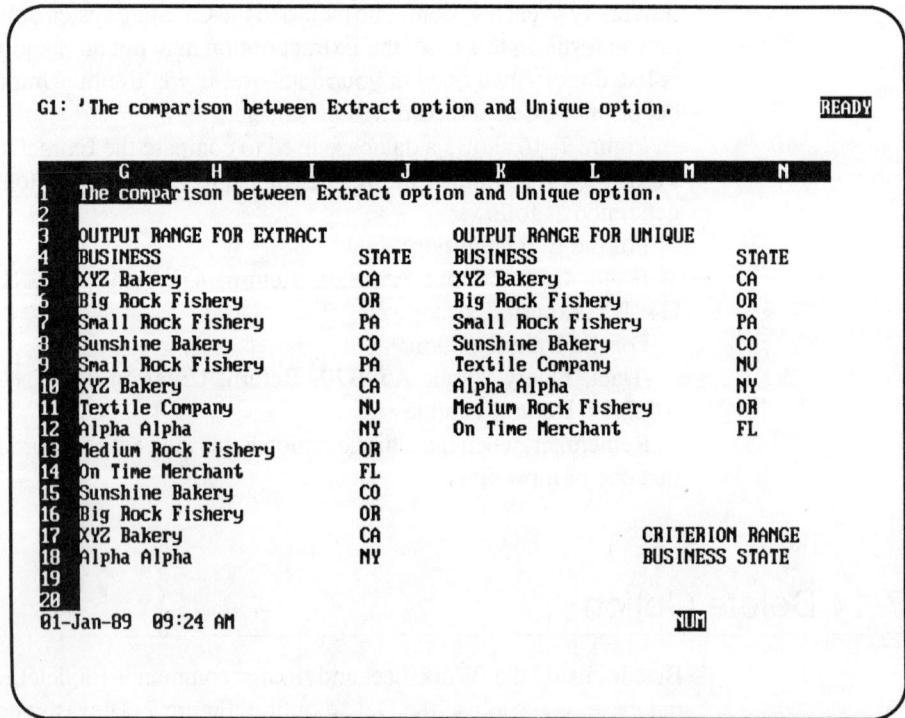

```
G1: 'The comparison between Extract option and Unique option.            READY

            G            H         I         J         K         L         M         N
1  The comparison between Extract option and Unique option.
2
3  OUTPUT RANGE FOR EXTRACT           OUTPUT RANGE FOR UNIQUE
4  BUSINESS          STATE           BUSINESS          STATE
5  XYZ Bakery        CA              XYZ Bakery        CA
6  Big Rock Fishery  OR              Big Rock Fishery  OR
7  Small Rock Fishery PA             Small Rock Fishery PA
8  Sunshine Bakery   CO              Sunshine Bakery   CO
9  Small Rock Fishery PA             Textile Company   NV
10 XYZ Bakery        CA              Alpha Alpha       NY
11 Textile Company   NV              Medium Rock Fishery OR
12 Alpha Alpha       NY              On Time Merchant  FL
13 Medium Rock Fishery OR
14 On Time Merchant  FL
15 Sunshine Bakery   CO
16 Big Rock Fishery  OR
17 XYZ Bakery        CA                                CRITERION RANGE
18 Alpha Alpha       NY                                BUSINESS STATE
19
20
01-Jan-89  09:24 AM                                          NUM
```

Figure 7–18 Database Used for the Delete Option

```
A1: [W12]                                                                    READY

           A              B          C   D      E                F          G
1                      MY FIRST DATABASE
2
3     FIRST NAME    LAST NAME       AGE  SEX OCCUPATION      INCOME
4     Randy         Alexander        36   M  Professor       $40,000
5     Fay           Alexander        30   F  Mayor           $30,000
6     Adam          Alexander        31   M  Engineer        $30,000
7     Andrea        Byan             36   F  Teacher         $31,000
8     Moe           Byan             40   M  Officer         $40,000
9     Bob           Adam             32   M  Engineer        $72,000
10    Anna          Adam              4   F  Unemployed      $11,000
11    Vicki         Adam              9   F  Unemployed      $12,000
12    Paula         Bobby            55   F  Housewife       $20,000
13    Jack          Jones            69   M  Artist          $19,000
14    Mary          Fishler          30   F  Interpreter     $19,000
15    Sue           Hayword          22   F  Student         $10,000
16    Tammy         Smith            29   F  Student         $10,000
17    Jacky         Brown            72   F  Engineer        $52,000
18    Lora          Jones            30   F  Nurse           $31,000
19                  OCCUPATION
20                  Engineer
01-Jan-89   09:25 AM                                              NUM
```

Figure 7–19 An Example of the Delete Option

```
A1: [W12]                                                                    READY

           A              B          C   D      E                F          G
1                      MY FIRST DATABASE AFTER DELETION OF ALL THE ENGINEERS
2
3     FIRST NAME    LAST NAME       AGE  SEX OCCUPATION      INCOME
4     Randy         Alexander        36   M  Professor       $40,000
5     Fay           Alexander        30   F  Mayor           $30,000
6     Andrea        Byan             36   F  Teacher         $31,000
7     Moe           Byan             40   M  Officer         $40,000
8     Anna          Adam              4   F  Unemployed      $11,000
9     Vicki         Adam              9   F  Unemployed      $12,000
10    Paula         Bobby            55   F  Housewife       $20,000
11    Jack          Jones            69   M  Artist          $19,000
12    Mary          Fishler          30   F  Interpreter     $19,000
13    Sue           Hayword          22   F  Student         $10,000
14    Tammy         Smith            29   F  Student         $10,000
15    Lora          Jones            30   F  Nurse           $31,000
16
17
18
19                  OCCUPATION
20                  Engineer
01-Jan-89   09:26 AM                                              NUM
```

database in Figure 7–18 and deleting all the engineers. Figure 7–19 was generated as follows:

/Data, Query, Input A3..F18, Return, Criterion B19..B20, Return, Delete, Delete

This command should be used carefully. You may find it useful to make a copy of the database before executing this command.

Summary

This chapter covered the rudiments of database operations and creation, update, sort and search procedures. Having the Lotus database in RAM makes the processing speed extremely fast. For this reason, a Lotus database is an impressive tool for business database applications. Chapter 8 will discuss advanced database operations in detail.

Review Questions

1. What is a database?
2. How do you create a database using Lotus?
3. What is the difference between numeric and nonnumeric data in a database?
4.* How do you erase a record in a database?
5. How do you erase a field in a database?
6. How many fields can you have in your database?
7. How many records can you have in your database?
8. How do you perform editing in your database?
9. How do you sort your database?
10.* What is the difference between the primary-key and secondary-key options?
11. How many ways can you sort your database?
12.* How many ways can you search your database?
13. What is the difference between the AND condition and the OR condition in the criterion range?
14. How many wild cards are available? What is the unique application of each wild card?
15.* What is the difference between the Extract option and the Unique option?
16.* How many fields can be included in your criterion range for an AND search?
17. What is the difference between a sort and a search range?
18. Generate the following database:

First Name	Last Name	Major	Age	Sex	GPA
Cora	Barnes	CS	22	F	3.20
Sue	Jones	MIS	29	F	2.80
Bobby	Trana	CS	30	F	3.70
Tamy	Smith	Marketing	22	F	3.85
John	Porsche	Management	36	M	3.60
Brian	Raban	Accounting	19	M	2.20
Adam	Vigen	MIS	21	M	3.70

First Name	Last Name	Major	Age	Sex	GPA
Clark	Standard	CS	28	M	3.00
Stanley	Jones	Personnel	24	M	2.90
Harry	Mohan	Management	26	M	2.75

a. Add two more students to this list.
b. Sort this list by GPA.
c. Sort this list by age.
d. Sort first by sex, then by age.
e. Extract all MIS majors.
f. Extract all MIS majors with GPA > 3.7.
g. Extract either MIS or accounting majors.
h. Extract students with age > 25 and GPA > 3.50 and who are female.
i. Extract students who are between 20 and 30.
j. Extract students who are either younger than 20 or older than 30.

Misconceptions and Solutions

M — If you try to sort a worksheet in order to generate a sorted worksheet, but leave out a portion of the worksheet in your data range, there is no way to return to the original database.

S — Either save the original database in a file or make sure that you have included the entire database in your sort range.

M — You have used the Extract option, but not all the appropriate data has been extracted.

S — Check that your output range is large enough.

Comprehensive Lab Assignment

Retrieve CHAPT5 and perform the following:

1. Sort the existing database by age.
2. Sort the existing database by total scores of each student.
3. Sort the existing database by sex and major.
4. Extract all the MIS majors.
5. Extract all the MIS majors who are female.
6. Extract all the MIS majors who are female and are graduate students.
7. Extract all the students who have a total score of greater than 92.
8. Extract all the students who are MIS or CS majors.
9. Using the Unique option, print one representative of each major.
10. Save this worksheet under CHAPT7.
11. Using the Delete option, delete all the students who are majoring in CS and are freshmen.

8

Database Operations/Part Two: Lotus as a Sophisticated Database

8-1 Introduction

In this chapter we will study some of the sophisticated operations performed by the Lotus database functions, including statistical functions. As you will see, these functions provide a lot of flexibility. We will explain table building using the /Data Fill command, what-if analysis performed by /Data Table 1 and /Data Table 2, and distribution analysis using the /Data Distribution command.

/Data Matrix and /Data Regression will be discussed at the end of this chapter. With these two commands, you can use the tremendous power of Lotus. A matrix of up to 90 rows by 90 columns can be easily inverted. This means that a 90 by 90 system of linear equations can be solved. Using /Data Regression, Lotus can handle a multiple linear regression of up to 16 variables. A dependent variable, such as income, can be predicted based on several independent variables (up to 16), such as education, number of years of experience, or field of study. /Data Matrix and /Data Regression can help you to develop fairly sophisticated forecasting models.

8-2 Database Statistical Functions

The seven statistical functions you saw in Chapter 4 can be used with database data with a minor variation. A database statistical function follows this format:

(@Dfunction name(database range, offset value, criterion range))

The database range or input range is usually the entire database or a selected portion, and the offset value defines which column of the database is under investigation.

This value starts from zero and goes to N-1, where N is the number of columns in a database. So if the offset value is 2, it means you are interested in column 3 of the database or field 3. If it is 10, it means you are interested in column 11. The criterion range must have a field heading. Below it you can define any criteria that you may be interested in.

There are seven database statistical functions: @DAVG, @DCOUNT, @DMAX, @DMIN, @DSTD, @DSUM, and @DVAR. These functions provide more flexibility than their statistical counterparts. By just changing the criterion range, you can perform all sorts of analyses. Figures 8–1 and 8–2 show some examples of database statistical functions.

In Figure 8–1, the database range is A3..C18; the offset value is 1, which means column 2 is under investigation; and the criterion range is H19..H20. In this example we are only interested in individuals who are older than 10 years. (In cell H20, we used the Text format in order to show the actual content of this cell.)

In Figure 8–2 we used the previous worksheet (Figure 8–1), but we changed a couple of the criterion ranges. This demonstrates the flexibility provided by database statistical functions. You can include or exclude any portion of the database just by changing the criterion range.

8-3 Table Building Using the /Data Fill Command

You can use the /Data Fill command to build tables. All you need is to define a range, which becomes the table that you wish to build, then define the start, step, and stop values. These values will be filled in the table from top to bottom and from left to right. If you do not specify any value and press the **Return** key at the prompt, Lotus will use default values for start (0), step (1) and stop (8191).

Table building will continue until either the range is filled or the stop value has been reached. Any of the three values can be a formula if the formula is defined at the time that it is needed by /Data Fill. An excellent application of the /Data Fill command is to return a sorted database to its original unsorted form. To do this, you can either use the /Data Fill Command in order to number all the records in the database into an adjacent column or just number them by entering a sequence number. When the entire database is sorted, this column will be sorted as well. To return the database to its original form, choose this column as the primary key and sort the database again. You will see the original database. Figures 8–3 and 8–4 show some examples of the /Data Fill command.

In the upper portion of Figure 8–3, we defined a high value for stop (5,000), but the table building was stopped as soon as range A1..D1 was filled. In the lower portion of Figure 8–3, table building stopped when the stop value was reached (19,000), and the specified table was not filled.

In Figure 8–4, we created a simple database in cells A3..C8. We made a copy of the database in cells A11..C16 and this database was sorted in ascending order.

The sequence numbers are no longer ordered. To return this database to its original form, we made a copy of it in cells E11..G16 and sorted this database using the sequence number field as the primary key, returning the database back to its original form.

Figure 8–1 Database Statistical Functions

```
A1: [W10]                                                                READY


        A       B    C        D              E          F        G        H
 1                            @DAVG(A3..C18,1,H19..H20)          39.30461
 2                            @DCOUNT(A3..C18,1,H19..H20)        13
 3  FIRST NAME AGE  SEX       @DMAX(A3..C18,1,H19..H20)          72
 4  Randy      36   M         @DMIN(A3..C18,1,H19..H20)          22
 5  Fay        30   M         @DSTD(A3..C18,1,H19..H20)          15.20899
 6  Adam       31   F         @DSUM(A3..C18,1,H19..H20)          512
 7  Andrea     36   F         @DVAR(A3..C18,1,H19..H20)          231.3136
 8  Moe        40   M
 9  Bob        32   M
10  Anna        4   F
11  Vicki       9   F
12  Paula      55   F
13  Jack       69   M
14  Mary       30   F
15  Sue        22   F
16  Tammy      29   F
17  Jacky      72   F
18  Lora       30   F                                           CRITERION RANGE
19                                                                      AGE
20                                                                     +B4>10
01-Jan-89  09:27 AM                                                NUM
```

Figure 8–2 Database Statistical Functions with a Different Criterion Range

```
A1: [W10]                                                                READY


        A       B    C        D              E          F        G        H
 1                            @DAVG(A3..C18,1,H19..H20)          39.30461
 2                            @DCOUNT(A3..C18,1,H19..H20)        13
 3  FIRST NAME AGE  SEX       @DMAX(A3..C18,1,D18..D19)          72
 4  Randy      36   M         @DMIN(A3..C18,1,D18..D19)          55
 5  Fay        30   F         @DSTD(A3..C18,1,H19..H20)          15.20899
 6  Adam       31   M         @DSUM(A3..C18,1,E18..E19)          72
 7  Andrea     36   F         @DVAR(A3..C18,1,H19..H20)          231.3136
 8  Moe        40   M
 9  Bob        32   M
10  Anna        4   F
11  Vicki       9   F
12  Paula      55   F
13  Jack       69   M
14  Mary       30   F
15  Sue        22   F
16  Tammy      29   F
17  Jacky      72   F                        CRITERION RANGE
18  Lora       30   F   AGE                  AGE
19                      +B4>50               +B4>70                        AGE
20                                                                        +B4>10
01-Jan-89  09:28 AM
```

Figure 8–3 /Data Fill Command

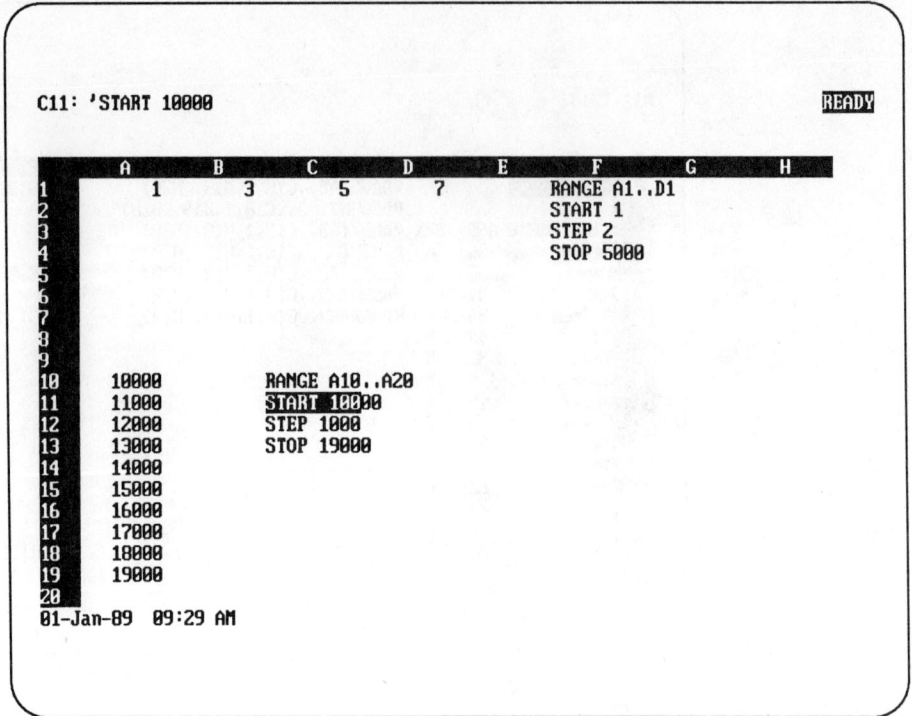

```
C11: 'START 10000                                                    READY

        A       B       C       D       E       F       G       H
1       1       3       5       7               RANGE A1..D1
2                                               START 1
3                                               STEP 2
4                                               STOP 5000
5
6
7
8
9
10      10000                   RANGE A10..A20
11      11000                   START 10000
12      12000                   STEP 1000
13      13000                   STOP 19000
14      14000
15      15000
16      16000
17      17000
18      18000
19      19000
20
01-Jan-89  09:29 AM
```

Figure 8–4 /Data Fill Command for Restoring a Sorted Database

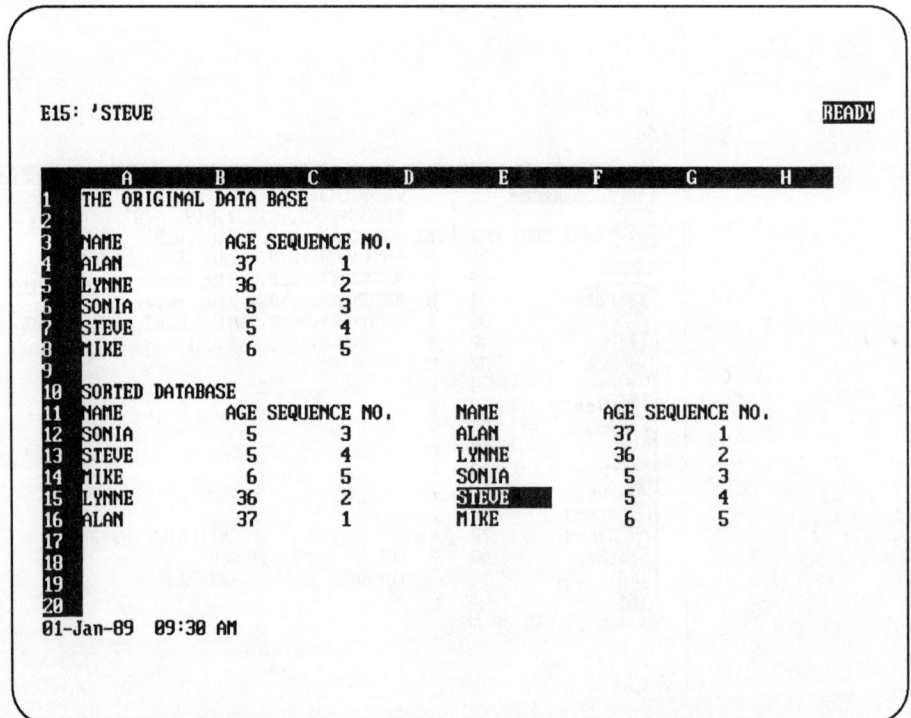

```
E15: 'STEVE                                                          READY

        A       B       C       D       E       F       G       H
1   THE ORIGINAL DATA BASE
2
3   NAME        AGE SEQUENCE NO.
4   ALAN         37     1
5   LYNNE        36     2
6   SONIA         5     3
7   STEVE         5     4
8   MIKE          6     5
9
10  SORTED DATABASE
11  NAME        AGE SEQUENCE NO.    NAME        AGE SEQUENCE NO.
12  SONIA         5     3           ALAN         37     1
13  STEVE         5     4           LYNNE        36     2
14  MIKE          6     5           SONIA         5     3
15  LYNNE        36     2           STEVE         5     4
16  ALAN         37     1           MIKE          6     5
17
18
19
20
01-Jan-89  09:30 AM
```

8-4 What-If Analysis Using /Data Table 1

The /Data Table 1 command can be used to determine the effect of one variable on a formula or an entire worksheet. There are many areas where this command can be useful; for example, the effect of different interest rates on an IRA plan, the effect of different interest rates on a loan, or the effect of different commission percentages on the total commission generated by a salesperson.

To use /Data Table 1, you must first establish a table range. The table range can be anywhere in the worksheet. In Figure 8–5, C4..E15 is the table range. You must choose an empty cell outside the table range as the input cell. The address of this cell will be used to change values in a formula. In our example, the input cell is A5. Now fill out the changing values in a column; in our case, cells C5..C15. Above and to the right of these values is our formula, here the future value, @FV(2000,A5,20). This is the future value of a $2,000 IRA plan for 20 years with a variable interest rate. This formula is in cell D4. The same formula was also copied to cell E4, but we have changed the number of years to 30. Remember, the intersection of these values (interest rates) and the formula is empty. This empty cell will be used by /Data Table 2.

As soon as the parameters are defined, the entire future value will be calculated for different interest rates and for two different years. Figure 8–5 shows one application of this command. If you change some of the input values, press F8 while in READY mode and the entire table will be recalculated. As you can see, this table can be a lot more complicated. You can do this calculation for several annuity periods. Simply define these periods and leave the rest of it to Lotus' amazing power and accuracy.

8-5 /Data Table 1 Using Database Data

Database statistical functions can be used as formulas with the /Data Table 1 and /Data Table 2 commands. The procedure is straightforward. In Figure 8–6, we used the database to the left of the screen as our input range (A3..B18). The offset value is 1, meaning column 2 (income) is under investigation and the criterion range has been set up in cells C10..C11. As before, this range includes the field title and the specific criteria are below it. Since we have left cell C11 empty, this means any occupation can be entered here. Cell C11 is used also as the input cell for /Data Table 1.

In /Data Table 1, the input range is D3..F6. The entire table range includes three occupations in the column and two formulas in the row. The input cell is C11. Now Lotus matches any of these three occupations with the original database and calculates the average salary and standard deviation of these salaries.

8-6 What-If Analysis Using /Data Table 2

In /Data Table 2 the effects of two variables over the entire worksheet or a specified range can be calculated. Let us walk through an example. Sunrise Electronic Firm has designed a formula for calculating the total salary of its employees, based on the

Figure 8–5 /Data Table 1 Showing the Effects of Different Interest Rates for Two Different IRA Plans

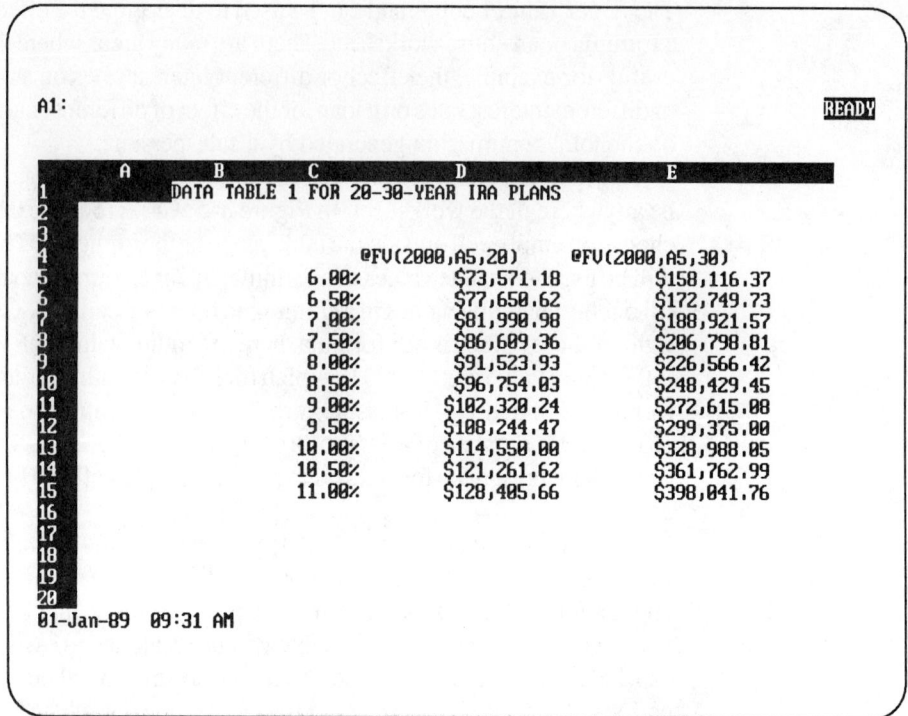

```
A1:                                                              READY

       A        B        C            D                E
1              DATA TABLE 1 FOR 20-30-YEAR IRA PLANS
2
3
4                              @FV(2000,A5,20)     @FV(2000,A5,30)
5                      6.00%     $73,571.18          $158,116.37
6                      6.50%     $77,650.62          $172,749.73
7                      7.00%     $81,990.98          $188,921.57
8                      7.50%     $86,609.36          $206,798.81
9                      8.00%     $91,523.93          $226,566.42
10                     8.50%     $96,754.03          $248,429.45
11                     9.00%    $102,320.24          $272,615.08
12                     9.50%    $108,244.47          $299,375.00
13                    10.00%    $114,550.00          $328,988.85
14                    10.50%    $121,261.62          $361,762.99
15                    11.00%    $128,405.66          $398,041.76
16
17
18
19
20
01-Jan-89   09:31 AM
```

Figure 8–6 Using Data Table 1 with Database Data

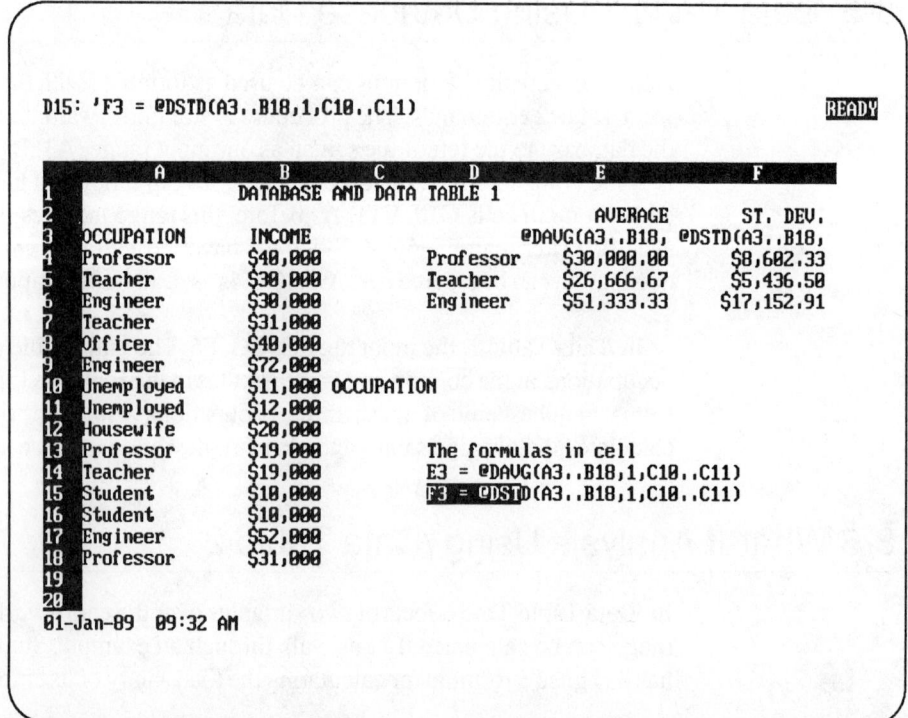

```
D15: 'F3 = @DSTD(A3..B18,1,C10..C11)                          READY

       A          B        C        D          E            F
1              DATABASE AND DATA TABLE 1
2                                            AVERAGE       ST. DEV.
3   OCCUPATION    INCOME               @DAVG(A3..B18, @DSTD(A3..B18,
4   Professor     $40,000    Professor      $30,000.00      $8,602.33
5   Teacher       $30,000    Teacher        $26,666.67      $5,436.50
6   Engineer      $30,000    Engineer       $51,333.33     $17,152.91
7   Teacher       $31,000
8   Officer       $40,000
9   Engineer      $72,000
10  Unemployed    $11,000 OCCUPATION
11  Unemployed    $12,000
12  Housewife     $20,000
13  Professor     $19,000    The formulas in cell
14  Teacher       $19,000    E3 = @DAVG(A3..B18,1,C10..C11)
15  Student       $10,000    F3 = @DSTD(A3..B18,1,C10..C11)
16  Student       $10,000
17  Engineer      $52,000
18  Professor     $31,000
19
20
01-Jan-89   09:32 AM
```

years of education (high school diploma, BS, MS, PhD) and the number of years of experience (1 to 15 years). In any case, $1,000 would be the base salary. The formula is 1000 + A1*50+B1*75, where A1 is the number of years of experience and B1 is the number of years of education. These are the input cells. For example, an employee with 5 years of experience and 12 years of education will make 1000+5*50+12*75 = $2150.

In Figure 8–7, we have used /Data Table 2 to calculate the entire table for the Sunrise Electronics Firm. The table range is D3..H18. Input cell 1 is A5 (years of experience), input cell 2 is B5 (years of education). Remember, the formula 1000+A5*50+B5*75 was copied into cell D3, the intersection of row 3 (years of education) and column D (years of experience).

You can change any of these values and press F8. The entire table will be recalculated immediately.

8-7 /Data Table 2 Using Database Data

/Data Table 2, like /Data Table 1, can be used effectively with database statistical functions. To show this we have collected a summary of a large survey in Figure 8–8. A group of professors in different disciplines were surveyed in different states. We are interested in finding out the average salary of each type of professor in three different states.

The table range is F4..I7, which includes three types of professors (CS, ACC, MIS, the column) in three states (OR, CA, ND, the row). Input cell 1 is D6, which will be either CS (computer science), ACC (accounting), or MIS (management information systems). Input cell 2 is E6, which will be either OR (Oregon), CA (California), or ND (North Dakota). The criterion range is defined in cells D5..E6. Cell F4, the intersection of row and column, contains the formula @DAVG(A3..C18,0,D5..E6).

Lotus searches for a CS professor in the state of Oregon (there are three of them) and calculates the average salary; ($31,000+$41,000+$39,000)/3 = $37,000. In California there is only one with a salary of $40,000; and so forth. We used Text Format in cell F4 to show you the actual formula used for our calculations.

8-8 Distribution Analysis Using the /Data Distribution Command

There are many cases where you may be interested in classifying a series of data into an orderly group, for example, classifying the salary of all the employees of Jack's Manufacturing into ten groups, or classifying your customers in nine sales groups. The /Data Distribution command will perform these types of analysis for you.

To use this command, define the range of values you would like to classify. Then select two empty columns. The first one is used for your bin range in ascending order, for example, salaries of 10,000, 12,000, 15,000, 18,000, etc. The empty column adjacent to the bin range will be used by Lotus to provide the frequency distribution. Figure 8–9 shows an example of the /Data Distribution command.

In this figure, the value range is B4..B17 and the bin range is D4..D8 (we have organized salaries into five groups in ascending order). As you see, the first number under the frequency is 6. This means there are six individuals whose income is

```
A1: [W9] 'DATA TABLE 2 TO CALCULATE SALARY BASED ON EDUCATION AND EXPERIENC READY

        A     B C       D            E      F      G      H
1    DATA TABLE 2 TO CALCULATE SALARY BASED ON EDUCATION AND EXPERIENCE
2                                   YEARS OF EDUCATION
3                   1000+A5*50+B5*75    12     16     18     21
4    INPUT 1   INPUT 2          1     1950   2250   2400   2625
5                               2     2000   2300   2450   2675
6                               3     2050   2350   2500   2725
7                               4     2100   2400   2550   2775
8                               5     2150   2450   2600   2825
9    YEARS OF EXPERIE           6     2200   2500   2650   2875
10                              7     2250   2550   2700   2925
11                              8     2300   2600   2750   2975
12                              9     2350   2650   2800   3025
13                             10     2400   2700   2850   3075
14                             11     2450   2750   2900   3125
15                             12     2500   2800   2950   3175
16                             13     2550   2850   3000   3225
17                             14     2600   2900   3050   3275
18                             15     2650   2950   3100   3325
19
20
     01-Jan-89   10:23 AM
```

Figure 8–7 /Data Table 2 Showing the Effect of Years of Experience and Education on Salary

between $0 and $20,000. There are four individuals whose income is between $20,001 and $40,000; and so on. The last frequency value is 0. This means nobody is making more than $100,000.

8-9 Inverting a Matrix Using the /Data Matrix Invert Command

Inverting a matrix that can be used in solving a system of linear equations is a time-consuming and complex task. Lotus provides an easy solution. The inverse of a matrix is a matrix which, if multiplied by the original matrix, will create an identity matrix. An *identity matrix* is one that has a diagonal of ones and the rest of the matrix filled by zeros. Figure 8–10 shows an original matrix, its inverse, and the result of the multiplication of the original matrix by its inverse. As you see, the result is an identity matrix. All the nonzero numbers are indeed very close to zero. If you format this matrix with two decimals, you will see the zeros.

To generate this result first we enter the original matrix in range B4..D6, then invoke the /Data Matrix Invert command. The range chosen was B4..D6, the output range was B9..D11. To verify this result we multiplied the original matrix by its inverse. The result is an identity matrix.

8-10 Matrix Addition, Subtraction, and Multiplication

Matrix addition and subtraction can be done by using /File Combine Add and /File

Figure 8-8 /Data Table 2 Using Database Data to Calculate the Average Salary of Three Different Types of Professors in Three Different States

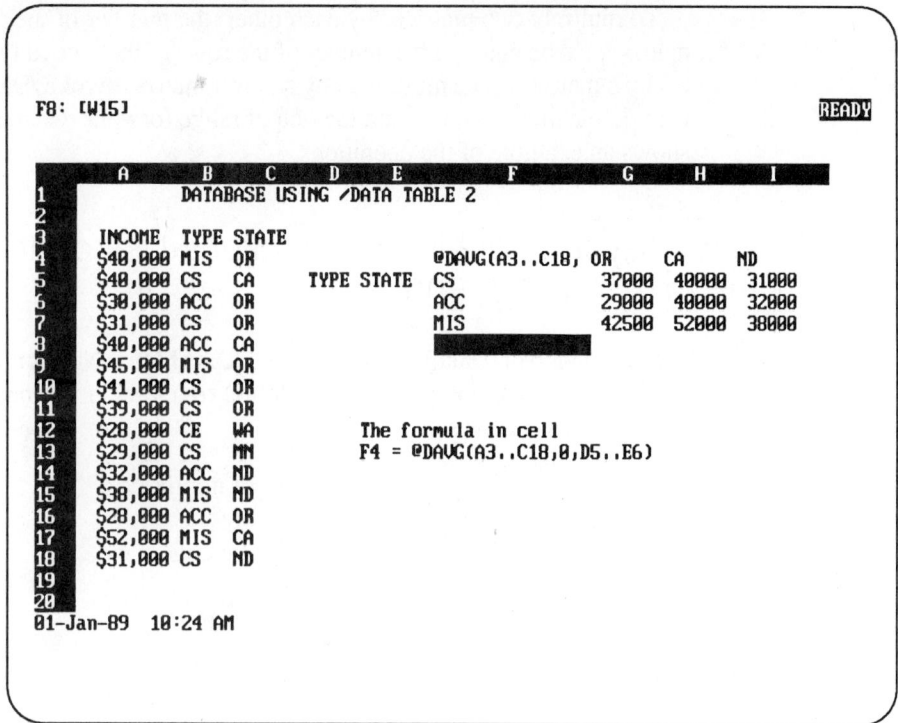

```
F8: [W15]                                                              READY

          A        B    C     D      E        F          G      H      I
1                   DATABASE USING /DATA TABLE 2
2
3        INCOME   TYPE STATE
4        $40,000  MIS  OR                      @DAVG(A3..C18, OR    CA     ND
5        $40,000  CS   CA     TYPE STATE       CS         37000  40000  31000
6        $30,000  ACC  OR                      ACC        29000  40000  32000
7        $31,000  CS   OR                      MIS        42500  52000  38000
8        $40,000  ACC  CA
9        $45,000  MIS  OR
10       $41,000  CS   OR
11       $39,000  CS   OR
12       $28,000  CE   WA          The formula in cell
13       $29,000  CS   MN          F4 = @DAVG(A3..C18,0,D5..E6)
14       $32,000  ACC  ND
15       $38,000  MIS  ND
16       $28,000  ACC  OR
17       $52,000  MIS  CA
18       $31,000  CS   ND
19
20
01-Jan-89  10:24 AM
```

Figure 8-9 An Example of /Data Distribution

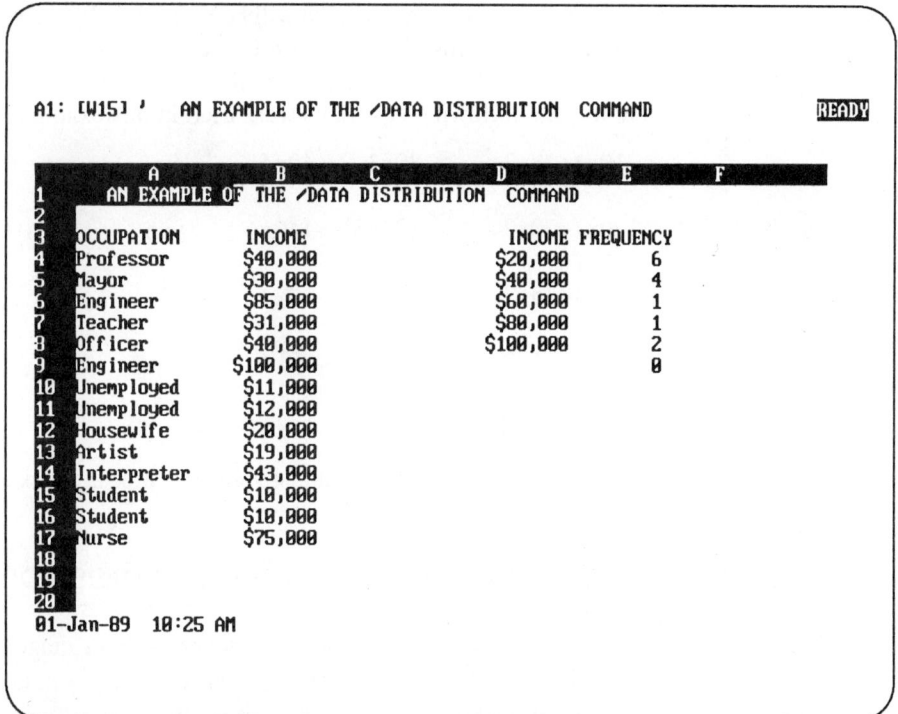

```
A1: [W15] '    AN EXAMPLE OF THE /DATA DISTRIBUTION  COMMAND              READY

          A             B          C          D         E       F
1        AN EXAMPLE OF THE /DATA DISTRIBUTION  COMMAND
2
3        OCCUPATION     INCOME                INCOME FREQUENCY
4        Professor      $40,000               $20,000      6
5        Mayor          $30,000               $40,000      4
6        Engineer       $85,000               $60,000      1
7        Teacher        $31,000               $80,000      1
8        Officer        $40,000              $100,000      2
9        Engineer      $100,000                            0
10       Unemployed     $11,000
11       Unemployed     $12,000
12       Housewife      $20,000
13       Artist         $19,000
14       Interpreter    $43,000
15       Student        $10,000
16       Student        $10,000
17       Nurse          $75,000
18
19
20
01-Jan-89  10:25 AM
```

Combine Subtract. For matrix multiplication, Lotus provides an additional facility under /Data Matrix Multiply.

To multiply two matrices by each other, the number of the columns of the first matrix must be equal to the number of the rows of the second matrix. For example, a 5 by 5 matrix can be multiplied by a 5 by 1 matrix. Invoke /Data Matrix Multiply, then define the data range and the output range for your two matrices. Figure 8–11 shows an example of the operations.

8-11 Solving a System of Linear Equations Using the Lotus /Data Matrix Command

A combination of /Data Matrix Invert and /Data Matrix Multiply can be used to solve a system of linear equations. The solution to a system of linear equations with n variables is as follows:

$$
\begin{bmatrix} X1 \\ X2 \\ X3 \\ X4 \\ \cdot \\ \cdot \\ \cdot \\ Xn \end{bmatrix}
=
\begin{bmatrix} \text{inverse of matrix} \\ \text{of} \\ \text{Coefficients} \end{bmatrix}
*
\begin{bmatrix} b1 \\ b2 \\ b3 \\ b4 \\ \cdot \\ \cdot \\ \cdot \\ bn \end{bmatrix}
$$

where X1, X2, ... Xn are the number of unknowns and b1, b2, ... bn are the righthand side of equations 1, 2, 3, ... n. Therefore to solve a system of linear equations, the inverse of the matrix of coefficients will be multiplied by the array of the righthand side. The result of this multiplication is the solution to the system of the linear equations. Figure 8–12 shows an example using Lotus to solve a system of linear equations. The following equations were used in this example:

-10x1+18x2+	30x3	-40x4	+12x5	=	10
120x1+30x2+	100x3	-140x4	-10x5	=	100
25x1+15x2+	10x3	-20x4	-5x5	=	25
38x1+16x2+	24x3	-30x4	-8x5	=	40
20x1+10x2+	40x3	-10x4	+20x5	=	60

The answers for x1, x2, x3, x4 and x5 are presented at the bottom of Figure 8–12.

8-12 Regression Analysis Using the /Data Regression Command

Simple linear regression is a tool used for either medium-range (less than two years) or long-range forecasting (two years or more). The formula for a simple linear regression is as follows:

Figure 8–10 Calculation of the Inverse of a Matrix

```
B16: 1                                                              READY

      A       B         C          D        E        F       G        H
1
2
3                       THE ORIGINAL MATRIX
4             8         2          4
5            15        -3          9
6             1         1          0
7
8                       THE INVERSE MATRIX
9          -0.5 0.222222 1.666666
10          0.5 -0.22222 -0.66666
11            1 -0.33333       -3
12
13
14      MULTIPLICATION OF THE ORIGINAL BY INVERSE
15
16             1 5.6E-17  8.9E-16
17             0        1  1.3E-15
18             0        0        1
19
20
01-Jan-89   10:26 AM
```

Figure 8–11 Matrix Multiplication

```
A20:                                                               READY

      A       B         C          D        E        F       G        H
1         THE FIRST MATRIX
2             1         2          3        4        5
3            12        14         16       18       20
4            11        12         13       14       15
5            40       42.5        45      47.5      50
6            42        44         46       48       50
7         THE SECOND MATRIX
8             1         2          3        4        5
9             6         7          8        9       10
10           22        24         26       28       30
11           80         5         10       11       29
12          100        110       115       60      200
13        THE MULTIPLICATION OF THE FIRST BY THE SECOND MATRIX
14          899        658        712      450     1231
15         3888       2796       3044     2020     5202
16         2989       2138       2332     1570     3971
17        10085       7195       7855     5325    13352.5
18        10158       7236       7904     5380    13422
19
20
01-Jan-89   10:27 AM
```

```
A1:                                                            READY

       A         B        C        D        E        F        G        H
1            MATRIX OF COEFFICIENTS
2        -10       10       30      -40       12
3       120       30      100     -140      -10
4        25       15       10      -20       -5
5        38       16       24      -30       -8
6        20       10       40      -10       20
7   RIGHTHAND SIDE ARRAY           THE INVERSE OF COEFFICIENTS MATRIX
8        10                   -0.02332 0.000480 0.056255 -0.05006 0.012270
9       100                    0.017492 -0.01831 0.051286 0.026682 0.003040
10       25                    0.013119 -0.01265 -0.12457 0.123272 0.003967
11       40                   -0.00583 -0.01418 -0.04028 0.063569 0.011763
12       60                   -0.01457 0.018887 0.147116 -0.17803 0.033755
13
14            THE RESULTS
15  0.754595         X1
16  0.923104         X2
17  0.920649         X3
18  0.764735         X4
19  0.324882         X5
20
01-Jan-89   10:28 AM
```

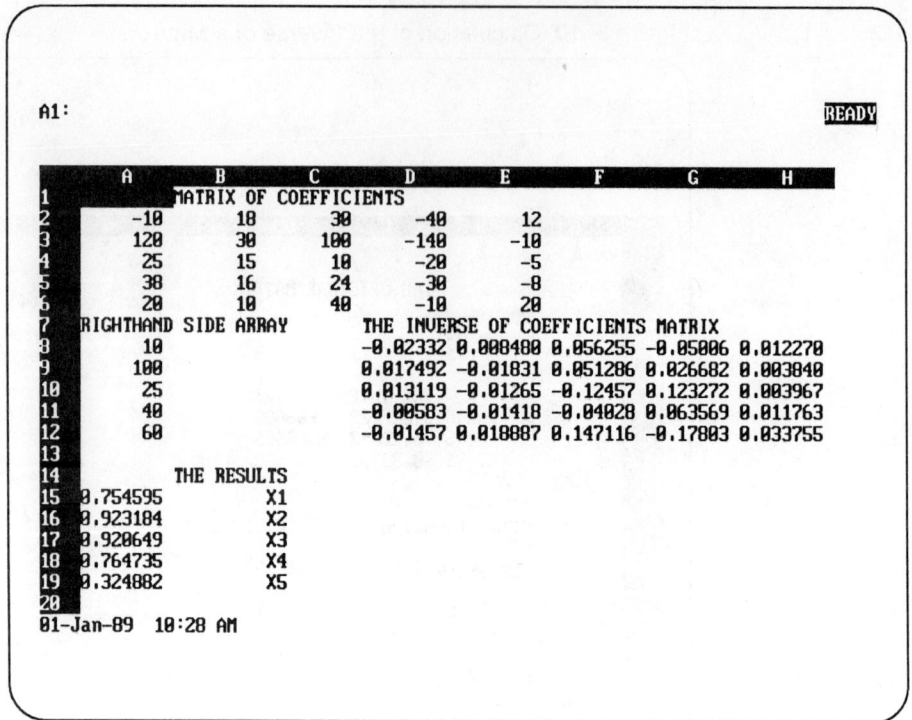

Figure 8–12 Solving a System of Linear Equations

$Y = A + BX$ (equation for a straight line)

where Y is the dependent variable, such as income, total sales, total costs; X is the independent variable, such as education, advertising budget, fixed cost; A is the intercept; and B is the slope of the line.

In order to apply this model to forecasting problems, values for A and B must be estimated. One way of estimating these values is by using the least squares method.

The least squares method estimates the values of A and B in such a way that the mean squared deviation between actual and predicted values is as small as possible. The following two formulas will be used to satisfy the requirements of the least squares method:

$$B = \frac{N\Sigma XY - \Sigma X\Sigma Y}{N\Sigma X^2 - (\Sigma X)^2}$$

$$A = \frac{\Sigma Y}{N} - \frac{B\,\Sigma X}{N}$$

To measure the strength of the relative association between two variables we use the *correlation coefficient*. The correlation coefficient, r, can vary from -1 to +1; r = 0 indicates no correlation, r = -1 indicates perfect negative correlation, and r = +1 indicates perfect positive correlation.

The formula for the correlation coefficient is as follows:

$$r = \frac{N\Sigma XY - \Sigma X\Sigma Y}{\sqrt{[N\Sigma X^2 - (\Sigma X)^2][N\Sigma Y^2 - (\Sigma Y)^2]}}$$

The square of the correlation coefficient is called the *coefficient of determination*. The coefficient of determination is the ratio of the sum of explained variation over the sum of total variation. The following formula indicates this:

$$r^2 = \frac{[N\Sigma XY - \Sigma X\Sigma Y]^2}{[N\Sigma X^2 - (\Sigma X)^2][N\Sigma Y^2 - (\Sigma Y)^2]}$$

This ratio shows how well a regression line can define the total variation in a series of data points. This ratio varies from 0 to 1; 0 means that the regression line does not explain any variation in the data points and 1 means that total variation is perfectly explained by the regression line.

Let us say you have an equation of Y = 10,000 + 250X, where Y is the total sales and X is the amount of advertising. This equation indicates that if you do not advertise at all, your estimated total sales would be $10,000. For every one dollar of advertising, your estimated total sales would increase by $250.

Figure 8–13 shows an example of simple linear regression for total sales and advertising for Pacific Rain Glass Company. This forecast is based on the past 12 years of available data. To generate this forecast, invoke the /Data Regression command. For the X range, independent variable, we have data in cells C5..C16. For the Y dependent variable we have data in cells B5..B16. For the output range we chose E1 (only the left corner). We chose the intercept to be calculated. Then choose Go and you will see the result. As you see the final equation is:

Y = -247,600 + 20.04091x

Also, as R squared shows, there is a high correlation between the amount of advertising and the total sales (0.840304).

8-13 Multiple Linear Regression Using Lotus

Simple regression finds the relationship between two variables. Lotus has provided you with the ability to include up to 16 independent variables. Naturally a multiple regression can be more comprehensive and more accurate information can be revealed. In Figure 8–14 we have demonstrated an example of a multiple regression.

In this analysis, the independent variables are a salesperson's age, high school GPA, and number of years' selling experience. The dependent variable is the total sales generated by the salespeople.

In this example the /Data Regression command was invoked. For the X range we defined B5..D14, for the Y range, we defined A5..A14, and the output range starts at cell F3. You need only one empty cell. Lotus will provide you with all the calculated results.

Figure 8–13 Simple Regression

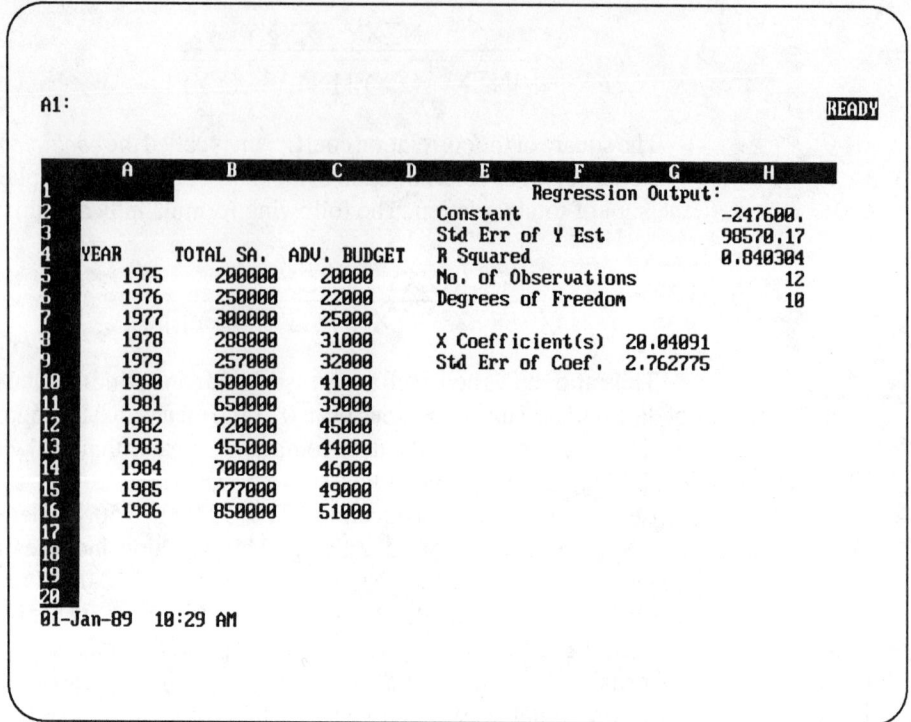

```
A1:                                                                          READY

        A           B           C       D       E       F       G       H
1                                                        Regression Output:
2                                               Constant                -247600.
3                                               Std Err of Y Est        98570.17
4   YEAR        TOTAL SA.    ADV. BUDGET        R Squared               0.840304
5       1975       200000       20000           No. of Observations           12
6       1976       250000       22000           Degrees of Freedom            10
7       1977       300000       25000
8       1978       280000       31000           X Coefficient(s)    20.04091
9       1979       257000       32000           Std Err of Coef.    2.762775
10      1980       500000       41000
11      1981       650000       39000
12      1982       720000       45000
13      1983       455000       44000
14      1984       700000       46000
15      1985       777000       49000
16      1986       850000       51000
17
18
19
20
01-Jan-89   10:29 AM
```

Figure 8–14 Multiple Regression

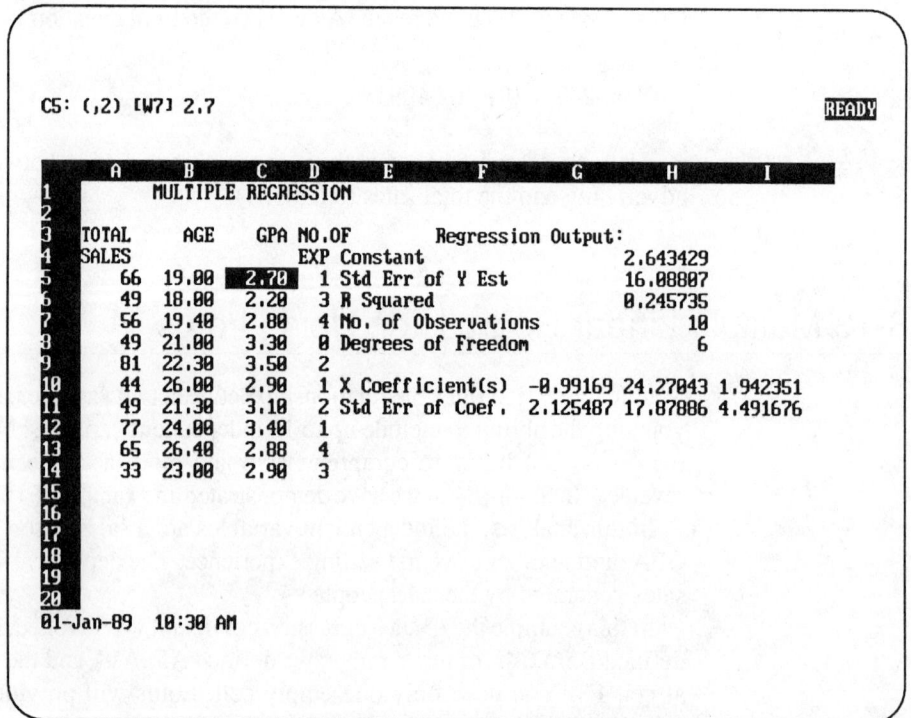

```
C5: (,2) [W7] 2.7                                                            READY

        A       B       C       D       E       F       G       H       I
1               MULTIPLE REGRESSION
2
3   TOTAL       AGE     GPA  NO.OF           Regression Output:
4   SALES                    EXP  Constant                    2.643429
5       66     19.00    2.70   1 Std Err of Y Est            16.08807
6       49     18.00    2.20   3 R Squared                   0.245735
7       56     19.40    2.80   4 No. of Observations              10
8       49     21.00    3.30   0 Degrees of Freedom               6
9       81     22.30    3.50   2
10      44     26.00    2.90   1 X Coefficient(s)  -0.99169 24.27043 1.942351
11      49     21.30    3.10   2 Std Err of Coef.  2.125487 17.87886 4.491676
12      77     24.00    3.40   1
13      65     26.40    2.80   4
14      33     23.00    2.90   3
15
16
17
18
19
20
01-Jan-89   10:30 AM
```

Even though Lotus can perform all these calculations, it cannot report some very important statistical measures, such as a t-test, Durbin-Watson test, and so on. We believe these are some of the limitations of this otherwise very powerful command.

Summary

In this chapter we have covered some of the advanced operations performed by a Lotus database: database statistical functions, table building using /Data Fill, sophisticated what-if analysis using /Data Table 1 and /Data Table 2, and /Data Distribution. At the end of this chapter, we spent some time on /Data Matrix and /Data Regression commands. These two sets of commands are extremely powerful since Lotus can solve a system of linear equations with up to 90 variables. Multiple linear regression in Lotus is also capable of handling up to 16 independent variables.

Review Questions

1. How many database statistical functions does Lotus have?
2. What is the major difference between these database functions and their statistical counterparts?
3. What are two applications of the /Data Fill command?
4. What are the default values for the /Data Fill command?
5.* When does table building in the /Data Fill command stop?
6. Why and how can /Data Table 1 and /Data Table 2 be used as a DSS tool?
7. Give two applications of /Data Table 1 and /Data Table 2.
8.* When you use a database with /Data Table 1 or /Data Table 2, are the input cell and criterion range the same?
9. What are some of the applications of the /Data Distribution command?
10. Why must bin range in data distribution be in ascending order?
11.* What will happen in /Data Distribution if one of your data items does not fall within the bin range?
12. How do you invert a matrix?
13. Do all matrices have an inverse?
14. How do you multiply two matrices?
15.* Can you multiply any two matrices?
16. How do you solve a system of linear equations?
17.* What is the righthand side array?
18.* What are some limitations of the /Data Regression command?
19. What statistics are generated by the /Data Regression command?
20. Using the /Data Fill command, build a table with the following values: Start value = 10, step value = 5, and stop value = 200.
21. Generate an example of your own using /Data Table 1.
22. Generate an example of your own using /Data Table 2.
23. Using the /Data Distribution command, classify the following sales data into six groups. The interval between each group is 20,000.

100,000, 150,000, 135,000, 200,000, 164,000, 169,000, 220,000, 300,000, 250,000

24. Using the /Data Matrix Invert command, invert the following matrix:

5 -5 15
10 -7 -3
6 -3 -3

25. Using the /Data Matrix command, solve the following system of linear equations:

5x1	-5x2	+15x3	=	5
10x1	-7x2	-3x3	=	0
6x1	-3x2	-3x3	=	0

26. Following are sales data for the past seven years for Cotton Textile Firm. Using /Data Regression, generate a forecast for total sales for 1988:

1981	100,000
1982	130,000
1983	175,000
1984	155,000
1985	200,000
1986	250,000
1987	300,000

Misconception and Solution

M — If the protection facility is on, /Data Table operations may not generate a correct answer.

S — Before performing any /Data Table operations, use either /Worksheet Global Protection Enable or /Range Unprotected on input cell(s), then perform /Data Table operations.

Comprehensive Lab Assignment

Retreive CHAPT5 and perform the following:

1. Using /Data Fill, number all students from 1 to 10 in column K.
2. Sort this new database by age.
3. Using column K as the key, return the worksheet to its original shape.
4. Using database statistical functions, generate the seven statistics for male and female students.
5. Using /Data Regression, calculate the R^2 between the total scores and the student's age. In this case, we assume age as the independent and total scores as the dependent variable. Is there any correlation between these two variables?
6. Using /Data Distribution, generate a distribution analysis for the total scores.
7. Save this final worksheet under CHAPT8.

9

**Macros/Part One:
Typing Alternatives**

9-1 Introduction

In this chapter we will discuss the principles of macro design and use. We will provide guidelines for naming, debugging, and documenting macros, and we will introduce more than 50 of the most commonly used macros. In Chapters 10 and 11 we introduce advanced features of macro operation.

9-2 What Is a Macro?

In simple terms, a *macro* is a collection of a series of keystrokes. As you have learned, everything in Lotus is a series of keystrokes, therefore everything in Lotus can be done by using a macro. Let us assume that you have to type the following statement in many different locations of your worksheet:

THE TOTAL COSTS OF PRODUCTION FOR THIS PERIOD

You have two alternatives. Either type this statement over and over, or create a macro. Whenever you are doing something repeatedly, think of using macros. They increase the speed and accuracy of operations, since they repeat the same sequence over and over.

9-3 Your First Macro

The first question asked by new macro users is, where do we put a macro? You can put a macro in any of the empty cells in your worksheet. It is a good practice to put a macro in a location that is easy to reach but where it will not get in your way. Most users put their macros in column AA. This is twenty-six columns to the right, close enough for easy access. Let us move the cursor to column AB1 (save AA1 for the macro name) and type the label:

THE TOTAL COSTS OF PRODUCTION FOR THIS PERIOD

The next task is to name the macro. A macro name can be any letter of the alphabet. It does not matter if it is uppercase or lowercase. The name must start with a backslash (\). You must also enter the name as a label. This means you must use one of the label prefixes (, or " or ^). If you do not use a prefix, the letter used for the macro name will be repeated, which you do not want. Next, you should name the location in which the macro is residing. Use /Range Name Create and name your macro \A. To name a macro, you can also use /Range Name Label Right (assuming the cursor is to the left of the macro, at the name cell). Figure 9–1 shows your first macro.

The next question is, how do you execute this macro? It can be executed from any location in the worksheet. Move the cursor to cell A1, hold down the **Alt** key (macro key), and at the same time, type A (the name of your macro). You will see THE TOTAL COSTS OF PRODUCTION FOR THIS PERIOD appear at the top of the screen in the control panel. Just hit the **Return** key in order to enter this label into cell A1.

Can you include *Return* in your macro? The answer is yes. Each key on your keyboard has a representative in macro design. Table 9–1 shows all key representations and certain commands. As you can see in this table, the representative for Return is the tilde (~). Move to cell AB1 and edit the content of this cell by pressing F2. Add a tilde to the end of the label. Now the content of cell AB1 is as follows:

THE TOTAL COSTS OF PRODUCTION FOR THIS PERIOD~

Now move the cursor to cell A2 and invoke your macro. Hold down the **Alt** key and type A. You will see that the label enters directly to cell A2.

Which cell is the address for naming your macro? All you need to do is to use the first cell as the address for the range. In this case cell AB1 is the beginning of the range. However, if you want to provide the entire range address, AB1..AF1, you may.

9-4 Your Second Macro

Your first macro only included a label. You can use a macro to automate a command or a series of commands. In order to do this, you must first record all the steps that you follow for performing a command. Let us assume you are interested in formatting 20000 with the Currency format and two decimal places. Let us record the steps involved:

- / (call the menu)
- R (invoke range)
- F (invoke format)
- C (invoke currency)
- 2 (2 decimal places)
- Return (to enter 2)
- Return (to enter the correct cell as the desired range to be formatted)

Table 9–1 Keyboard Representatives*

DESCRIPTION	MACRO KEY
ABS	{ABS}
BACKSPACE	{BACKSPACE} or {BS}
BIG LEFT (move to left one screen)	{BIGLEFT}
BIG RIGHT (move to right one screen)	{BIGRIGHT}
CALC	{CALC}
DELETE (you must use only in EDIT mode)	{DELETE} or {DEL}
DOWN	{DOWN}
EDIT	{EDIT}
END	{END}
ESCAPE	{ESCAPE} or {ESC}
GOTO	{GOTO}
GRAPH	{GRAPH}
HOME	{HOME}
LEFT	{LEFT}
NAME	{NAME}
PAGE DOWN	{PGDN}
PAGE UP	{PGUP}
QUERY	{QUERY}
RETURN (tilde)	~
RIGHT	{RIGHT}
TABLE	{TABLE}
To have braces appear as {and}	{{}and{}}
To have tilde appear as ~	{~}
UP	{UP}
WINDOW	{WINDOW}

* In order to specify two or more consecutive uses of the same key, you can always include a repetition factor within the braces. For example:

DOWN 6	tells Lotus to move the cursor six cells down
UP 2	tells Lotus to move the cursor two cells up

First, we set the column width to 12, now move the cursor to cell AA3 and enter \B (as label with apostrophe). In cell AB3 enter /RFC2~~ (as label with apostrophe). Using /Range Name Create, name cell AB3 as \B.

Now move the cursor to cell AA10, which contains number 20000, and invoke your B macro. Your number is formatted. Figure 9–2 shows this process.

9-5 An Interactive Macro

In your second macro, the number which was formatted was predefined. It is possible to include a question mark (?) within your macro in order to make it interactive. This means that when you execute your macro the process stops when it encounters the question mark until you enter a number, then the process continues. Let us start with an empty worksheet. Move the cursor to column AB1 and type the following:

YOU TELL ME A NUMBER~
{DOWN}

Figure 9–1 Your First Macro

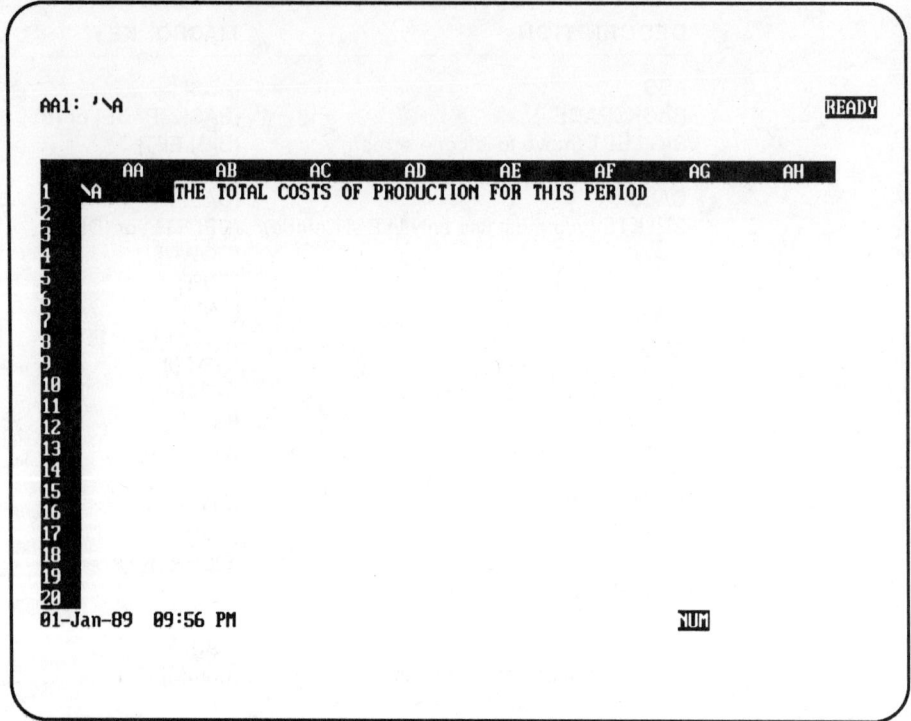

Figure 9–2 Your Second Macro

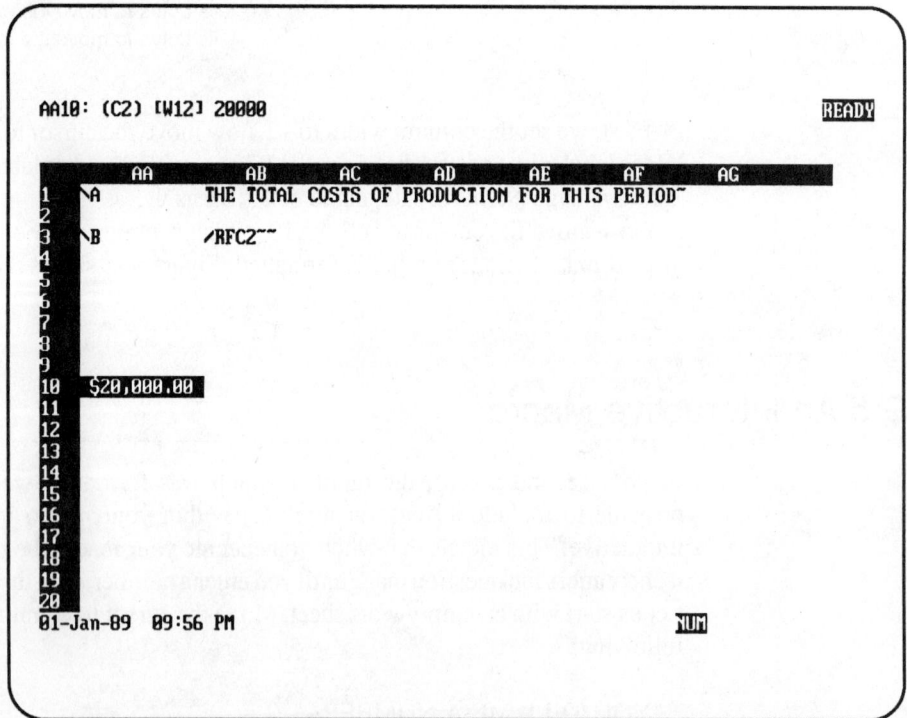

{?}~
/RFC2~~

Name this macro \C. Remember, only cell AB1 needs to be indicated as the range since the macro will execute all rows until an empty row is encountered. Now move the cursor to cell AA6 and invoke the macro. As you see, the label YOU TELL ME A NUMBER appears in cell AA6 and CMD is displayed at the bottom of the screen, meaning the macro is in progress. The macro waits for you to enter a number. Type 36000 and hit **Return**. Your number is formatted. We have set column width to 12. So the question mark within the braces in the macro makes the macro interactive. Figure 9–3 shows this process.

We can enhance the macro by including W(worksheet)C(column)S(set-width) {?} or /WCS{?}~. In this case, the column width is set by the user. We could also include a question mark in place of the number of decimal places. Figure 9–4 shows these variations of our original macro.

To stop a macro, press the **Ctrl** and **Break** keys together.

9-6 How Is a Macro Executed?

As you have seen so far, a macro is a column of keystrokes. The number of keystrokes can be as many as 240. The macro is executed from left to right and top to bottom. As soon as the macro encounters a blank cell, it halts execution. Therefore, if you are putting more than one macro in a worksheet, make sure there is at least one empty line between each macro.

It is also a good idea to document your macro. Since the name of your macro is only one letter there is no way to remember what each macro does. So to the right of the macro, after leaving one empty cell, always indicate briefly what task a particular macro performs. In Figure 9–5 we show an example of a macro. In column AA1, the letter G is the name of the macro. We call this name *documentation*. In column AB1 is the macro itself. And finally, in column AD1 we have mentioned the function of the macro. We call this function *documentation* also.

9-7 Debugging Your Macro

Macros are executed extremely fast. There is always the possibility of making mistakes. Lotus provides a facility for debugging your macro. You can process your macro step by step as follows:

1. Press the **Alt** key and the **F2** key at the same time. Now the status indicator shows STEP.
2. Invoke your macro. Now the status indicator shows SST (single step). 1-2-3 pauses after the execution of each keystroke. To continue, press any key.
3. If you see anything wrong, press the **Ctrl** and **Break** keys at the same time to abort the execution of the macro.
4. By editing, correct your mistake(s).

If you continue hitting a key until the macro is fully executed, SST changes to

Figure 9–3 An Example of an Interactive Macro

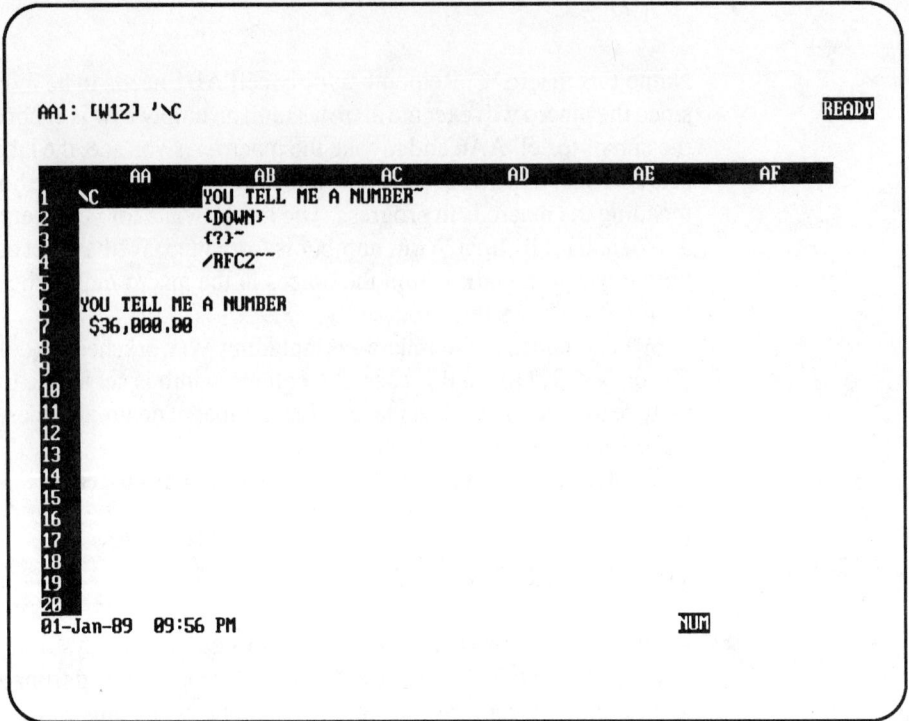

```
AA1: [W12] '\C                                                              READY

          AA              AB              AC         AD         AE         AF
1    \C              YOU TELL ME A NUMBER~
2                    {DOWN}
3                    {?}~
4                    /RFC2~~
5
6   YOU TELL ME A NUMBER
7    $36,000.00
8
9
10
11
12
13
14
15
16
17
18
19
20
01-Jan-89   09:56 PM                                          NUM
```

Figure 9–4 More Complicated Interactive Macro

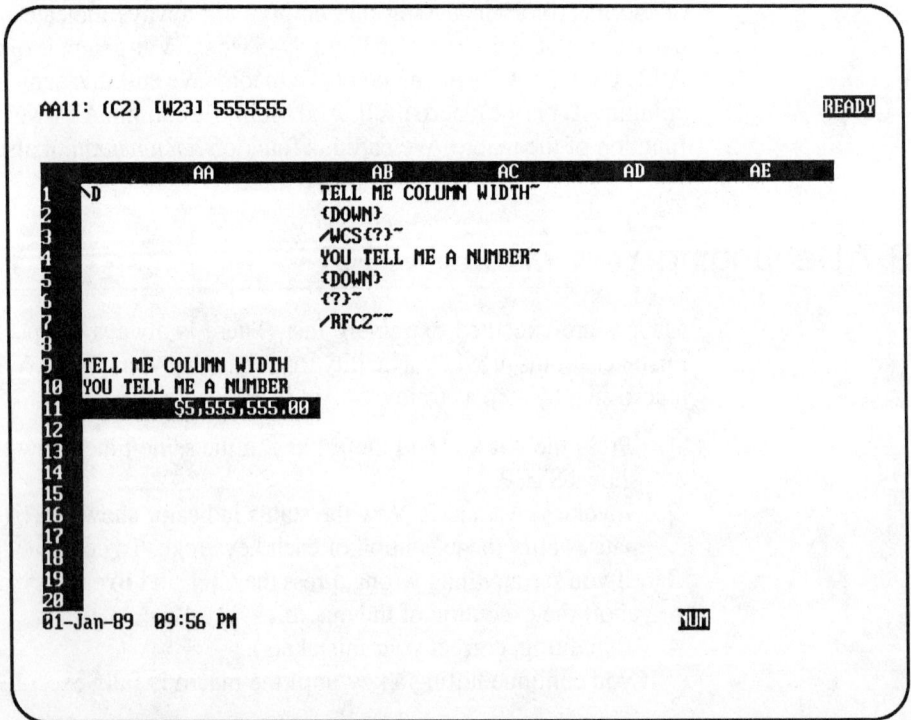

```
AA11: (C2) [W23] 5555555                                                    READY

          AA              AB              AC         AD         AE
1    \D              TELL ME COLUMN WIDTH~
2                    {DOWN}
3                    /WCS{?}~
4                    YOU TELL ME A NUMBER~
5                    {DOWN}
6                    {?}~
7                    /RFC2~~
8
9   TELL ME COLUMN WIDTH
10  YOU TELL ME A NUMBER
11             $5,555,555.00
12
13
14
15
16
17
18
19
20
01-Jan-89   09:56 PM                                          NUM
```

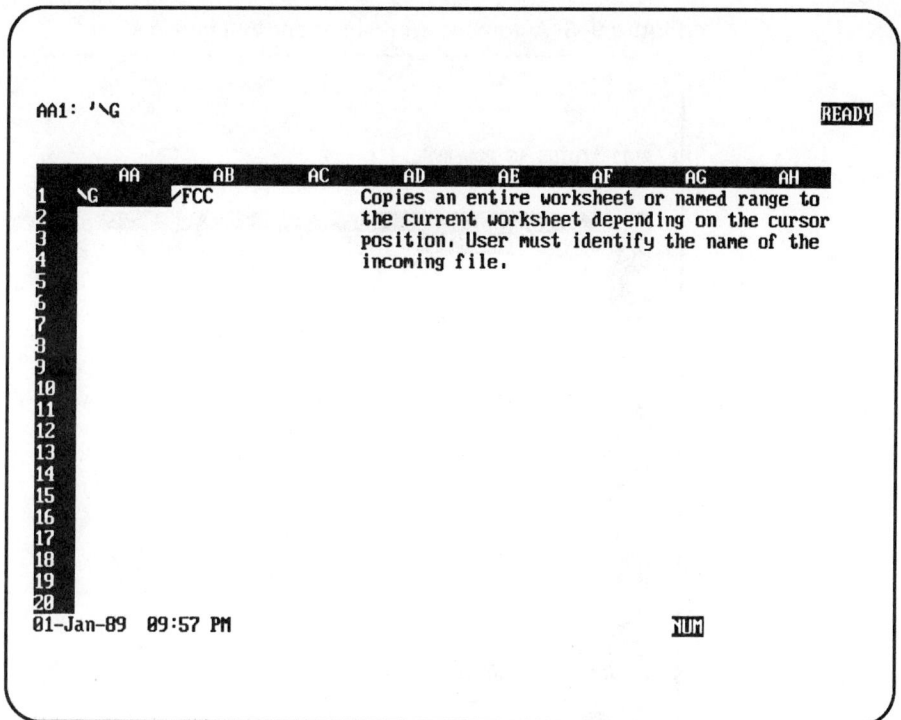

```
AA1: ' \G                                                              READY

        AA        AB        AC        AD        AE        AF        AG        AH
1   \G        /FCC                Copies an entire worksheet or named range to
2                                 the current worksheet depending on the cursor
3                                 position. User must identify the name of the
4                                 incoming file.
5
6
7
8
9
10
11
12
13
14
15
16
17
18
19
20
01-Jan-89   09:57 PM                                            NUM
```

Figure 9–5 An Example of a Documented Macro

STEP, which means the macro is fully executed. To get out of the STEP mode, press **Alt** and **F2** together. The STEP indicator will disappear.

9-8 An Automatic Macro

If you name your macro Zero (\0), it will automatically execute when the worksheet that includes it is loaded. This is very useful for designing menus. If you save the worksheet that includes the \0 macro as AUTO123.WK1, this worksheet will be automatically loaded to RAM as soon as you get the system started. A combination of AUTO123.WK1 and the \0 macro can be used for any application involving first-time computer users, giving them easy access to the system. It is also handy for commonly used worksheets. Figure 9–6 shows the \0 macro.

9-9 Creating a Macro Library

When you get used to designing and using macros, you may want to use some of them from worksheet to worksheet. If you put all your macros in a remote location of your worksheet, such as column AA, and if you document them properly, you can use them over and over again. However, if you transfer your macros to a different worksheet, you must rename them. Chapter 10 will show you a macro for naming other macros. Figures 9–7 to 9–9 present some of the most commonly used macros. Figure 9–10 presents key representative macros.

Figure 9–6 Automatic Worksheet and Automatic Macro

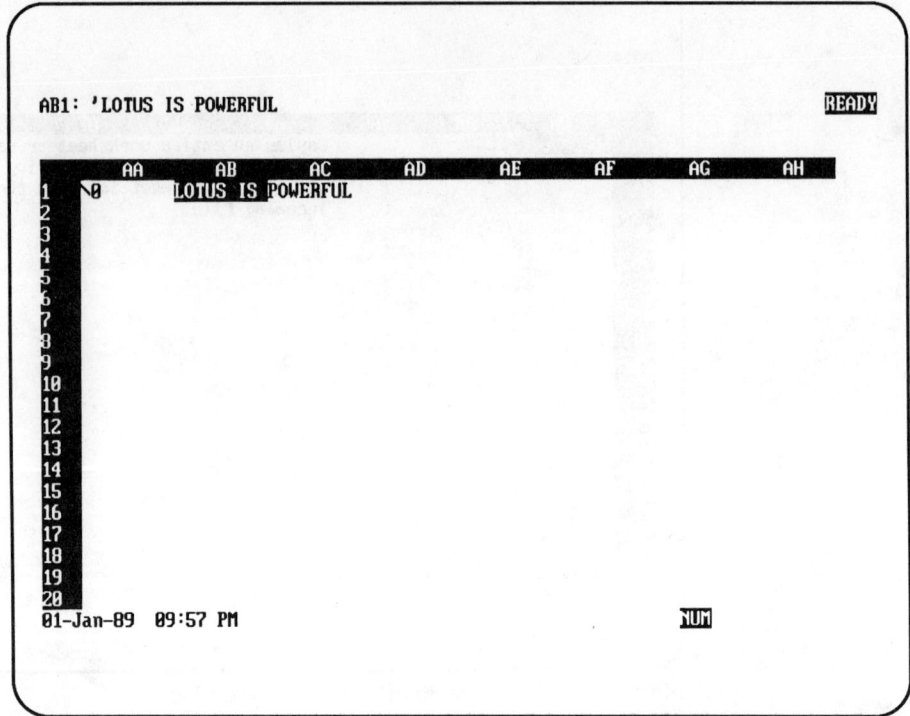

```
AB1: 'LOTUS IS POWERFUL                                           READY

         AA      AB      AC      AD      AE      AF      AG      AH
1    \0      LOTUS IS POWERFUL
2
3
4
5
6
7
8
9
10
11
12
13
14
15
16
17
18
19
20
01-Jan-89   09:57 PM                                        NUM
```

Figure 9–7 Commonly Used Macros Part 1

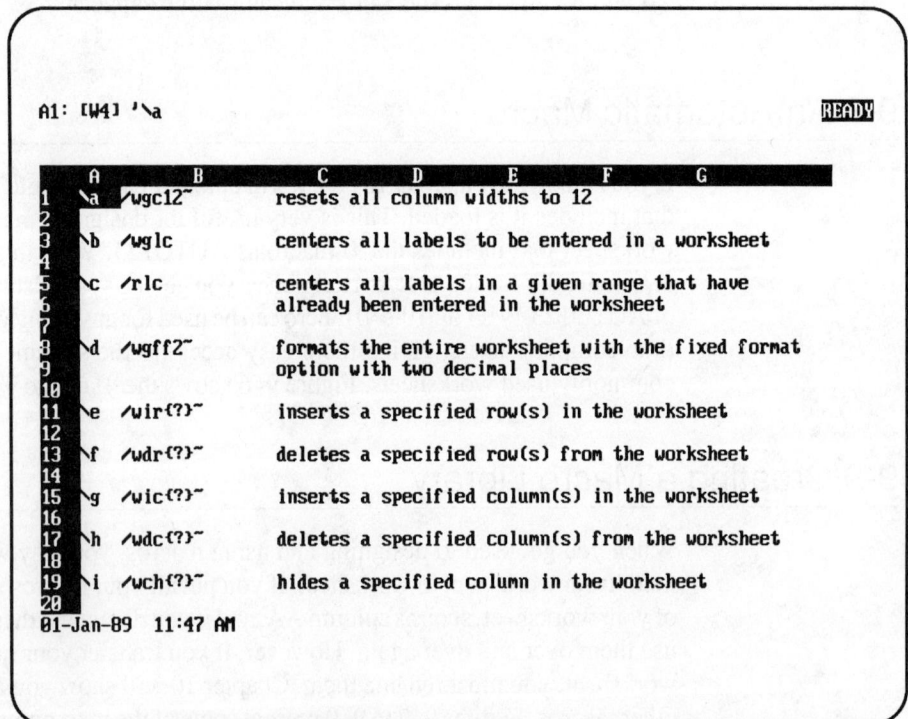

```
A1: [W4] '\a                                                      READY

     A      B          C        D       E       F       G
1   \a  /wgc12~        resets all column widths to 12
2
3   \b  /wglc          centers all labels to be entered in a worksheet
4
5   \c  /rlc           centers all labels in a given range that have
6                      already been entered in the worksheet
7
8   \d  /wgff2~        formats the entire worksheet with the fixed format
9                      option with two decimal places
10
11  \e  /wir{?}~       inserts a specified row(s) in the worksheet
12
13  \f  /wdr{?}~       deletes a specified row(s) from the worksheet
14
15  \g  /wic{?}~       inserts a specified column(s) in the worksheet
16
17  \h  /wdc{?}~       deletes a specified column(s) from the worksheet
18
19  \i  /wch{?}~       hides a specified column in the worksheet
20
01-Jan-89   11:47 AM
```

Figure 9–7 (Continued)

```
A21: [W4] '\j                                                    READY

        A       B          C       D       E       F       G
21  \j  /wcd{?}~          reveals (displays) a hidden column in the worksheet
22
23  \k  /wey              erases the entire worksheet
24
25  \l  /ru               selectively unprotects a specified range of cells
26
27  \m  /rp               protects a specified range of cells from modification
28
29  \n  /wgzy             suppresses the display of cells that have a numeric
30                        value of zero
31
32  \o  /wwv              splits the screen vertically where the cursor is
33                        positioned
34
35  \p  /wwh              splits the screen horizontally where the cursor is
36                        positioned
37
38  \q  /wtb              freezes all cells to the left and above the cursor
39                        so the cells cannot move off the screen
40
01-Jan-89  11:48 AM
```

Figure 9–7 (Continued)

```
A41: [W4] '\r                                                    READY

        A       B            C       D       E       F       G
41  \r  /wgrm             changes the worksheet from the standard automatic
42                        recalculation to manual recalculation
43
44  \s  /rnc{?}~{?}~      allows the user to specify a name for any range
45
46  \t  /re{?}~           erases a specified range
47
48  \u  /rfc0~{?}~        formats a specified range with the currency format
49                        option and zero decimal places
50
51  \v  @TODAY~           formats today's date with the long international date
52      /rfd4~            format
53
54  \w  /rfdt2{?}~        formats a specified range with the #2 time option
55
56  \x  /rf,2~{?}~        formats a specified range with the comma format
57                        option and two decimal places
58
59  \y  /rfh{?}~          hides a specified range
60
01-Jan-89  11:48 AM
```

Figure 9–7 (Continued)

```
A61: [W4] '\z                                                              READY

      A       B          C       D        E       F        G
61  \z  /rft{?}~          formats a specified range with the text format option
62
63
64
65
66
67
68
69
70
71
72
73
74
75
76
77
78
79
80
01-Jan-89   11:48 AM
```

Figure 9–8 Commonly Used Macros Part 2

```
A1: [W5] '\a                                                               READY

      A       B            C       D        E       F        G
1   \a  /rfp2~{?}~          formats a specified range with the percent
2                           format option and two decimal places
3
4   \b  /rfr{?}~            resets the format of the specified range to
5                           the global default setting
6
7   \c  /fr{?}~             retrieves a specified file back to the main memory
8                           from a data disk
9
10  \d  /fs{?}~             saves an entire worksheet on a data disk under
11                          a specified name
12
13  \e  /fxv{?}~{?}~r~      extracts a portion of a worksheet with Values
14                          option and stores the result in a given file
15
16  \f  /fxf{?}~{?}~r~      extracts a portion of a worksheet with Formulas
17                          option and stores the result in a given file
18
19  \g  /fcce~{?}~          copies an entire file to the current worksheet
20                          depending on cursor position
01-Jan-89   11:48 AM
```

Figure 9–8 (Continued)

```
A21: [W5]                                                              READY

        A         B            C        D        E        F        G
21
22   \h   /fcae{?}~          takes the values from an entire file and adds
23                           those values to the corresponding cells in the
24                           current worksheet
25
26   \i   /few{?}~y          deletes a specified worksheet file from a data
27                           disk
28
29   \j   /gtba{?}~v         sets up and views a bar graph with one data
30                           range
31
32   \k   /gtpa{?}~x{?}~otf{?}~qv   sets up and views a pie chart with
33                                  two data ranges and one title
34
35   \l   /gtla{?}~x{?}~otx{?}~ty{?}~qv   sets up and views a line graph
36                                        with two data ranges and a
37                                        title for the x- and y-axis
38
39   \m   /gotx{?}~ty{?}~qv   enters a title for the x-axis and the y-axis
40                            on a specified graph and views the graph
01-Jan-89  11:48 AM
```

Figure 9–8 (Continued)

```
A41: [W5]                                                              READY

        A         B            C        D        E        F        G
41
42   \n   /gosxml{?}~u{?}~qqv   overrides the automatic scale and allows
43                              the user to rescale the x-axis manually
44                              and view the changes
45
46   \o   /gnc{?}~q          names a current graph and saves all the
47                           current parameters defining that graph
48
49   \p   /gnu{?}~q          recalls a graph you have previously named and
50                           saved
51
52   \q   /gnd{?}~q          deletes a single graph name and its parameters
53                           from the worksheet
54
55   \r   /gola{?}~qq        enters a legend below the x-axis
56
57   \s   /gofgsqqv          formats all the graph lines of a graph with
58                           the symbols option and views it
59
60   \t   /dsd{?}~p{?}~g     sorts an entire database or specified data-
01-Jan-89  11:48 AM
```

Figure 9–8 (Continued)

```
A61: [W5]                                                              READY

      A          B              C      D        E      F      G
61                              range according to a primary key field
62
63   \u    /dsd{?}~p{?}~s{?}~g   sorts an entire database or specified
64                               datarange according to primary and
65                               secondary key fields
66
67   \v    /dqi{?}~c{?}~o{?}~e   searches a database and extracts a por-
68                               tion of the database to an output range
69                               based on a specified criterion range
70
71   \w    /dqi{?}~c{?}~o{?}~u   searches a database and extracts a
72                               unique portion of the database to an
73                               output range based on a specified
74                               criterion range. Duplicate records will
75                               not be chosen.
76
77   \x    /pf{?}~r{?}~gq        specifies the range of cells to be printed
78                               into a file
79
80   \y    /ppcrq                clears and resets print range
01-Jan-89  11:49 AM
```

Figure 9–8 (Continued)

```
A81: [W5]                                                              READY

      A          B              C      D        E      F      G
81
82   \z    /ppomr{?}~ml{?}~qq    resets the left and right margins
83
84
85
86
87
88
89
90
91
92
93
94
95
96
97
98
99
100
01-Jan-89  11:49 AM
```

Figure 9–9 Commonly Used Macros Part 3

```
AA1: '\a                                                              READY

         AA      AB        AC       AD      AE      AF      AG      AH
1    \a      /wgc20~
2            /rlla1..a7~
3                                         These three macros increase the
4    \b      /wgc20~                      column width (globally) to 20 and
5            /rlra1..a7~                   then left-justifies (\a), right-
6                                         justifies (\b) and center-justifies
7    \c      /wgc20~                      (\c) the label in the range a1..a7.
8            /rlca1..a7~
9
10   \d      {goto}a15~                   This macro changes the date in
11           @NOW~                        cell a15 to today's date.
12           /rfd4~
13
14   \e      {goto}aa1~                   This macro loads a macro library.
15           /fcce{?}~
16
17   \f      /ppcrr                       This macro prints any portion of a
18           {?}~g                        worksheet specified by the user.
19
20
01-Jan-89   11:49 AM
```

Figure 9–10 Key Representative Macros

```
AA1: '\m                                                              READY

         AA      AB        AC       AD      AE      AF      AG      AH
1    \m      {home}
2            Payment{right}Interest{right}^Term{right}Future Value~
3            {down}{end}{left}
4            100{right}.05{right}5{right}@FV(a2,b2,c2)~
5            /rfc0~a2~
6            /rfp0~b2~                    This macro uses the table
7            {goto}b4~                    building function to deter-
8            Interest~{down}              mine the future value of
9            Rate~{right}{up}             a specific payment based on
10           Future~{down}                interest rates from 5% to
11           Value~{down}                 14%. The data is then
12           +d2~                         graphed. The payment amount
13           /dfb7..b16~.05~.01~.14~      changes to $200,the
14           /rfp0~b7..b16~               table is rebuilt and the
15           /dt1b6..c16~b2~              graph is redrawn.
16           /wcs12~                      After execution of the
17           /rfc2~c7..c16~               macro, the user can change
18           /gtlab7..b16~xc7..c16~vq     any of the values then
19           {goto}a2~                    press F9, the entire table
20           200~                         will be recalculated.
01-Jan-89   11:51 AM
```

Figure 9–10 (Continued)

```
AA21:                                                              READY

        AA      AB       AC      AD      AE      AF      AG      AH
21              {table}
22              {graph}
23
24
25
26    \n        {HOME}/fcceCH14-5~          This macro combines a file called
27              /dqia5..d13~cf6..f7~f       CH14-5, performs a query for
28              {down}{goto}f7~             people who are engineers,then
29              Professor~                  changes the criterion range to
30              {query}                     professor and "queries" again.
31
32
33
34
35
36
37
38
39
40
01-Jan-89   11:51 AM
```

Figure 9–10 (Continued)

```
AA41: '\o                                                          READY

        AA      AB       AC      AD      AE      AF      AG      AH
41    \o        {Home}/fcceCASHFLOW~
42              {goto}tax~
43              {edit}                      This macro combines the CASHFLOW
44              {backspace 3}               file, which contains a split screen.
45              {delete}                    The macro edits the tax rate to
46              5~                          change it from 40% to 50% on both
47              {window}                    sides of the window and then recal-
48              {edit}                      culates the entire worksheet.
49              {backspace 3}               This macro assumes there is a file
50              {delete}                    called CASHFLOW on the disk with
51              5~                          split screen. It also assumes there
52              {calc}                      is a range called tax with a value
53                                          of .40.
54
55
56
57
58
59
60
01-Jan-89   11:51 AM
```

Figure 9–10 (Continued)

```
AA61: '\p                                                              READY

        AA        AB        AC        AD        AE        AF        AG        AH
61   \p           {home}
62                This is home~
63                {WAIT @now+@time(0,0,3)}
64                {bigright}
65                You have just moved one screen to the right~
66                {WAIT @now+@time(0,0,3)}
67                {pgdn}
68                You have just moved one screen down~
69                {WAIT @now+@time(0,0,3)}
70                {bigleft}
71                You have just moved one screen to the left~
72                {WAIT @now+@time(0,0,3)}
73                {pgup}
74                You are back home!~
75
76
77                This macro guides the user around the worksheet
78                utilizing BIGLEFT, BIGRIGHT, PGDN, and PGUP.
79
80
01-Jan-89  11:51 AM
```

Figure 9–10 (Continued)

```
AA81:                                                                  READY

        AA        AB        AC        AD        AE        AF        AG        AH
81
82
83
84
85
86
87
88   \q           {HOME}/fcceSALES~          This macro combines a SALES file
89                {name}                     and creates a range named "totals"
90                {esc}                      and a range named "grandtot(als),"
91                {end}{down}                The cells in both ranges are made
92                /rnctotals~a20..h20~       absolute.
93                {abs}a20..h20~             This macro assumes there is a file
94                {end}{right}               called SALES on the disk.
95                /rncgrandtot~i11..i19~
96                {abs}i11..i19~
97
98
99
100
01-Jan-89  11:51 AM
```

Summary

This chapter has covered the principles of macro design and use, creation of a macro, documentation and invoking of a macro. We also discussed debugging a macro, the automatic macro and a self-booting worksheet, and presented a list of more than 50 commonly used macros. This should provide you with a good background for getting started with macros. In the next chapter we will discuss macro commands.

Review Questions

1. What is a macro?
2. What are some of the advantages of using a macro?
3. How do you name a macro?
4.* How do you invoke a macro?
5. How do you document a macro?
6.* What is the function of a \0 macro?
7. How many macros can you have in a worksheet?
8. What is a self-booting worksheet?
9.* What are some of the applications of a self-booting worksheet?
10. How do you debug a macro?
11. What is the STEP indicator?
12. What is the SST indicator?
13.* What is the CMD indicator?
14. How do you get out of STEP mode?
15.* How do you halt the execution of a macro?
16.* How many keystrokes can be included in a macro?
17. How is a macro executed?
18. Design a macro in order to generate a pie chart using the following data:

   Sue   2,000
   Sam   18,000
   Sara   15,000

19. Design a macro to load a file from a disk to a worksheet, then erase the worksheet.
20. Design a macro to print the following message, then exit from the Lotus worksheet:

   IT WAS A PRODUCTIVE SESSION!

21. Design an interactive macro that accepts any three numbers, then calculates their average.
22. Design a macro that accepts any number up to eight digits, then format them using the comma option with three decimal places.
23. Design a macro that prints any portion of a worksheet using default settings.

Misconception and Solution

M — Lotus handles macros and functions differently. Lotus does not adjust cell addresses when you use /Move, /Copy, /Worksheet Delete, or /Worksheet Insert. When your macro is using cell addresses after rearranging, it may no longer work.

S — To avoid this, use range names to refer to cells.

Comprehensive Lab Assignment

Retrieve CHAPT5 and perform the following:

1. Erase the current title of this worksheet.
2. Move the cursor to column AA1.
3. Generate a mcaro that automatically prints the old title for this worksheet.
4. Generate a macro that automatically formats all the test socres to a fixed format with two decimals.
5. Save this worksheet under CHAPT9.

10

Macros/Part Two: Advanced Commands

10-1 Introduction

As we discussed in the last chapter, macros are extremely handy for automating frequently used Lotus commands, such as repeatedly typing a label in a worksheet, or performing a long task requiring a series of keystrokes. In this chapter, we will teach you how to use advanced features of macro operation. We will explain the structure of an advanced macro command, then divide advanced macro commands into five groups. By using numerous examples we will highlight the real power of Lotus macros. In Chapter 11 we will demonstrate using Lotus macros as a high-level programming language.

10-2 The Structure of Advanced Macro Commands

All advanced macro commands follow a common structure:

{KEYWORD ARGUMENT1, ARGUMENT2, ...}

They must start with a left brace and end with a right brace. KEYWORD includes any valid Lotus advanced command, e.g., LET, BRANCH, INDICATE, and so on. ARGUMENT(S) are one or more of the following four groups:

1. *Address or location*. This includes the address of any of the cells within the entire worksheet. This can also include a range.

2. *Numeric value*. This includes any number, expression, or formula resulting in a specific value. The number can be in standard form (e.g., 5200) or in scientific notation (e.g., 2.002E+3).

3. *Condition*. Any valid logical operation can be used as an argument. The macro command will proceed based on the result of the logical operations.

4. *String*. Any sequence of characters up to 240 can be used as an argument for your advanced macro command.

Argument types can be either numeric or string. Some macro commands such as LET can hold either number or string. For example:

{LET R1, 2 + 3} or
{LET R1, 2 + 3: value} enters number 5 in cell R1
{LET R1, "2 + 3"} or
{LET F1, 2 + 3: String} enters string "2 + 3" in cell R1

Arguments must be separated by a comma (,) or a semicolon (;). There must be a blank space between the KEYWORD and the ARGUMENT. Arguments can be written in either uppercase or lowercase; it does not make a difference.

If you are using a label or a string and if your label contains one of the separators (, or ;), you must include the entire string within a double quotation:

{LET R28, "TYPE YOUR FIRST NAME; THEN YOUR LAST NAME"}

10-3 Valid and Invalid Macro Commands

If you do not follow the rules just mentioned, 1-2-3 will issue an error message. Following are some valid and invalid examples of LET as a macro command.

{LET Q1, 50}	Valid
{let Q2, 55}	Valid
{LET Q3, 2*G1+6*G9}	Valid
{LET Q4, 91	Invalid (second brace is missing)
{LETQ5,65}	Invalid (space is missing)
{LET Q697}	Invalid (separator is missing)
{Q7, 99}	Invalid (keyword is missing)

10-4 An Overview of Advanced Macro Commands

Macro commands have been divided into five groups based on the particular function performed by each group.

Group #1 —Data Manipulation Commands are used for changing the content and/or format of data in a particular location or locations of the worksheet.

Group #2 — Program Flow (branching and looping) Commands are used for controlling the flow of a macro, e.g., performing a loop (printing 200 checks), transferring the control (moving from one part of the macro to another part), and so on.

Group #3 — Testing Keyboard Operations Commands allow you to perform interactive programming with Lotus. For example, a macro pauses during execution, waiting for user input.

Group #4 — Screen Design and Control Commands will help you to change the appearance of the screen, both audibly and visually.

Group #5 — File Operations Commands will help you to perform file operations, such as data transfer between files, writing to a file, reading from a file, and so forth.

Table 10–1 illustrates the commands included in these five groups.

Table 10–1 Summary of Advanced Macro Commands

Command Name	Description
Group #1 - Data Manipulation	
{BLANK address}	Erases the content of a cell or cells
{CONTENTS target-location, source-location}	Places the content of one cell into another cell as label
{LET address, data}	Stores data in an address
{PUT address, column-number, row-number, number}	Stores a number in a specified address within a range
{RECALC address}	Recalculates a formula in a specified address, proceeding row by row
{RECALCCOL address}	Recalculates a formula in a specified address, proceeding column by column
Group #2 - Program Flow (branching and looping)	
{BRANCH address}	Continues macro execution at a specified address
{DEFINE address1: type1, address2: type2 ...}	Specifies address and defines data type
{DISPATCH address}	Branches to a target location which is specified in address
{FOR counter, start, stop, step, starting address}	Executes a macro for a specified number of times
{FORBREAK}	Cancels execution of a FOR loop
{IF condition}	Conditionally executes a macro
{ONERROR branch-address}	Branches to branch-address if an error occurs during macro execution
{QUIT}	Terminates macro execution
{RESTART}	Cancels a subroutine
{RETURN}	Returns from a macro subroutine
Group #3 - Testing Keyboard Operations	
{?}	Halts macro execution temporarily for user input
{BREAKOFF}	Disables the **Break** key during the macro execution
{BREAKON}	Restores the **Break** key
{GET address}	Pauses for the user to input a single character, then stores it in address
{GETLABEL prompt-string, address}	Pauses for the user to input a string, then stores it as a string in address
{GETNUMBER prompt-string, address}	Pauses for the user to input a number, then stores it as a number in address
{LOOK address}	Checks to see if the user has typed a character
{MENUBRANCH address}	Halts macro execution temporarily in order for the user to choose a menu item, then branches accordingly

Table 10–1 (Continued)

Command Name	Description
{MENUCALL address}	Halts the macro execution temporarily in order for the user to choose a menu item, then executes the corresponding macro as a subroutine
{WAIT time}	Waits for a specified amount of time
Group #4 - Screen Design and Control	
{BEEP number}	Causes computer's bell to sound
{INDICATE string}	Changes the mode indicator to string
{PANELOFF}	Suppresses display of the control panel during the execution of the macro
{PANELON}	Restores panel display
{WINDOWSOFF}	Freezes screen display
{WINDOWSON}	Restores normal screen display
Group #5 - File Operations	
{CLOSE}	Closes an open file (the file that was opened by {OPEN} command)
{FILESIZE address}	Determines the size of the file in bytes and puts it in address
{GETPOS address}	Determines correct position of file pointer and displays it in address
{OPEN filename, access-mode}	Opens a specific file for a specific access: reading, writing, or both
{READ bytecount, address}	Reads characters from a file into address
{READLN address}	Copies one line of data from an open file into address
{SETPOS file-position}	Sets a new position for file pointer (of an open file)
{WRITE string}	Copies string into an open file
{WRITELN string}	Copies a complete line into open file (this includes carriage-return, line-feed)

10-5 Data Manipulation Commands

These commands are used for changing the content and format of data in a worksheet. These commands include BLANK, CONTENTS, LET, PUT, RECALC, and RE-CALCCOL.

10–5–1 {BLANK address}

Erases the contents of a cell or cells in a worksheet. This command is equivalent to /Range Erase. For example, {BLANK G1..G5} will erase the contents of cells G1, G2, G3, G4 and G5.

10–5–2 {LET address, number, or string}

Stores a number or string in an address or location. {LET} can be used to generate a label or number entry. For example:

{LET R10, 2 + 3: value}   stores number 5
{LET R11, 2 + 3: string}   stores label 2 + 3

Figure 10–1 illustrates using the LET and BLANK commands.

10–5–3 {CONTENTS target-location, source-location}

This command is similar to LET. The only difference is that {LET} can store either a number or a string, but {CONTENTS} only stores LABEL data. A more elaborate format of this command is as follows:
{CONTENTS target-location, source-location, <width-number>, <format-number>}
The width-number and format-number are optional. If you specify format-number, you must also specify width-number. Table 10–2 contains a complete listing of the numeric format codes for the {CONTENTS} command.

One good use of this command is to use code 117 for text display of formulas for debugging. For example, if the content of H2 is 555.55, {CONTENTS H10,H2,17,36} places the 17-character label $555.550 (currency, three decimal places) in cell H10.

10–5–4 {PUT address, column-number, row-number, number or string}

Stores a number or a string in a specific location within a range. The difference between this command and the {LET} command is that {PUT} stores data in a particular column and row of a specified range. (Remember, column-number and row-number start from zero. {PUT A1..H20,0,5,BASIC} will put BASIC in A6 left-justified.) Figure 10–2 illustrates using the {PUT} and {CONTENTS} commands.

10–5–5 {RECALC address} and {RECALCCOL address}

RECALC recalculates a formula in a specified address, proceeding row by row. This macro command could also include condition and iteration-number as follows:
{RECALC address, <condition>, <iteration-number>}
For example, if your macro changes a value in cell C7 and you are interested in the value in cell B13, which depends on cell C7, macro {RECALC B13..C7} will do the job for you.

{RECALCCOL address, <condition>, <iteration-number>} will recalculate the formulas in a specified address, proceeding column by column. You should always remember to use {RECALC} for a formula that is located below and to the left of the cells that you are referring to. Use {RECALCCOL} if the formula is above and to the right of the cell which it refers. Use {CALC} if the formula is both above and to the left of cells whose values have changed.

If you use a condition and/or iteration number, the process of recalculation will stop regardless of which number is reached first. For example, the macro {RECALC NETPRESENT, (B5>5),12} will cause the NETPRESENT range to be calculated continuously until the value of cell B5 reaches 5 or the number of iterations equals 12. Figure 10–3 illustrates using RECALC and RECALCCOL.

Figure 10–1 Example of BLANK and LET Commands

```
AA1: '\h                                                                READY

         AA      AB        AC        AD       AE       AF       AG       AH
1    \h      {BLANK f1..f3}
2            {home}
3            What is your investment amount?~                     This macro
4            {goto}f1~                                            computes the
5            {?}~                                                 present value
6            {down}{left 5}                                       of a given
7            What is the annual interest rate in percent?~investment.
8            {goto}f2~                                            The macro
9            {?}~                                                 branches back
10           {down}{left 5}                                       to the start
11           What is the number of periods in year?~             so more than
12           {goto}f3~                                            one inquiry
13           {?}~                                                 can be made.
14           {down 2}{left 5}                                     Use CTRL-BREAK
15           The present value of your investment is~             to stop macro
16           {LET f5,@PV(f1,f2,f3)}                               execution.
17           {BRANCH \h}
18
19
20
01-Jan-89   11:51 AM
```

Figure 10–2 Example of CONTENTS and PUT Commands

```
AA1: '\g                                                                READY

         AA      AB        AC        AD       AE       AF       AG       AH
1    \g      {home}                                     This macro inputs a label,
2            {PUT a5..h10,2,0,John}                     the current date, and a
3            {PUT a5..h10,4,2,@NOW}                      numeric value within a
4            {PUT a5..h10,6,4,25000}                     specified range using the
5            {CONTENTS b15,c5}                           PUT command. These three
6            {CONTENTS d15,e7,12,121}                    entries are copied and
7            {CONTENTS f15,g9,12,34}                     formatted to a new location
8            {calc}~                                     using the CONTENTS command.
9
10
11
12
13
14
15
16
17
18
19
20
01-Jan-89   11:52 AM
```

Figure 10-3 Example of RECALC and RECALCCOL Commands

```
AA1: '\d                                                              READY

        AA      AB        AC        AD       AE       AF       AG       AH
1    \d        /wgrm
2              {goto}b20~
3              Please enter a number in each cell (b4..d6) and press RETURN~
4              /rub4..d6~
5              /rib4..d6~
6              {goto}f4~
7              +b4+c4+d4~{down}
8              +b5+c5+d5~{down}
9              +b6+c6+d6~{down 2}{left 2}        This macro has the user
10             +d4+d5+d6~{left}                  create a matrix and the
11             +c4+c5+c6~{left}                  macro provides the formulas
12             +b4+b5+b6~{down 2}                to sum the rows and
13             Enter a new number in {down}      columns. The user is then
14             cell b4, c5, and d6~              asked to change three
15             {goto}b4~                         entries, and the sums of
16             {?}~                              the rows and columns are
17             {goto}c5~                         recalculated using the
18             {?}~                              RECALC and RECALCCOL
19             {goto}d6~                         commands.
20             {?}~
01-Jan-89  11:52 AM                                      CALC
```

Figure 10-3 (Continued)

```
AA21:                                                                 READY

        AA      AB        AC        AD       AE       AF       AG       AH
21             {calc}
22             {RECALC b4..d6}
23             {RECALCCOL b4..d6}
24
25
26
27
28
29
30
31
32
33
34
35
36
37
38
39
40
01-Jan-89  11:52 AM                                      CALC
```

Table 10–2 Numeric Format Codes for the CONTENTS Command (the optional part)

CODE	FORMAT EQUIVALENT
1-15	Fixed, 0 to 15 decimal places
16-32	Scientific, 0 to 15 decimal places
33-47	Currency, 0 to 15 decimal places
48-63	% (percent), 0 to 15 decimal places
64-79	, (comma), 0 to 15 decimal places
112	+/- (horizontal bar graph)
113	General
114	D1 (DD-MMM-YY)
115	D2 (DD-MMM)
116	D3 (MMM-YY)
121	D4 (Full international)
122	D5 (Partial international)
119	D6 (HH:MM:SS AM/PM)
120	D7(HH: MM AM/PM)
123	D8 (Full international)
124	D9 (Partial international)
117	Text format
118	Hidden format
127	Default format display

10-6 Program Flow (Branching and Looping)

Program flow commands are used to perform loops and branches within a macro. They include BRANCH, DEFINE, DISPATCH, FOR, FORBREAK, IF, ONERROR, QUIT, RESTART and RETURN.

10–6–1 {BRANCH address}

Continues macro execution at a specified cell. The specified location or address can be either a single cell or a range. This command is the same as a GOTO command in BASIC. There is a difference between this command and the Lotus GOTO. The Lotus GOTO command moves the cell pointer. The command {BRANCH} transfers the control (or macro execution) to a specified location. Figure 10–4 illustrates an example of this command.

10–6–2 {DEFINE address1: type1, address2: type2, ...}

Specifies the location and arguments to be passed to a subroutine. This must be the first command in the subroutine. The default value for the argument is a string. There must be a match between the number of arguments in the subroutine and the DEFINE command. The following is one example of {DEFINE} and a subroutine:
SUB-GROSS-total H1, N1

DEFINE F1: value, N1: value
Figure 10–5 illustrates an example of this command.

10–6–3 {DISPATCH address}

Transfers macro execution to the location specified in the address. The difference between this command and {BRANCH} is that DISPATCH can execute instructions in several locations specified in the address. Figure 10–6 illustrates one example of this command.

10–6–4 {FOR counter, start, stop, step, starting address} and {FORBREAK}

FOR executes a macro for a certain number of times. This is equivalent to the FOR-NEXT loop in BASIC or the DO loop in FORTRAN. Other programming languages have something similar to this command. The counter keeps track of the number of times the macro has been executed. Start is the starting value stored in the counter location. Stop marks the end of the loop. Step tells the counter how to increment the counter. The starting address is the cell address or range in which the macro starts the execution. Lotus always checks the condition of start, stop, and step before executing the macro. The FORBREAK command cancels the execution of a FOR loop. If the value of step is 0, an endless loop will be generated (a loop that never stops). If the start value exceeds the stop value, the macro will not be executed at all. Figure 10–7 is an example of the FOR command. Figure 10–8 illustrates an example of FOR and FORBREAK.

10–6–5 {IF condition}, {QUIT}, and {ONERROR branch address}

IF executes a macro conditionally. This command is similar to the IF-THEN-ELSE command available in many programming languages. The instructions in the cell after the IF are the THEN part and those below the cell are the ELSE part. If the expression does not have a value of zero, 1-2-3 considers it true and the statement in the same cell (the cell that includes IF) will be executed, otherwise the statement in the cell below will be executed.

To protect the accurate execution of IF-THEN-ELSE clauses you may have to use {QUIT} and/or {ONERROR} commands. {ONERROR branch-address} branches to a specified address. You can also include a message in this command. {QUIT} terminates macro execution. Figure 10–9 illustrates the operation of these three commands.

10–6–6 {RESTART}

Cancels a subroutine (a series of instructions that perform a specific task) and clears the subroutine parameters. This is a useful command for canceling a series of commands if a particular condition does not exist. Figure 10–10 illustrates an application of this command.

10–6–7 {RETURN}

Returns control from a subroutine. This command is used either by a routine name or with a MENUCALL. {RETURN} instructs the macro to return to the cell

10–4 An Example of the BRANCH Command

```
AA1: '\p                                                          READY

        AA      AB       AC       AD       AE       AF       AG       AH
1    \p       {home}
2             What is your sex? Choose (M)ale or (F)emale {right 6}~
3             {GET sex}
4             {IF sex="F"}{BRANCH no_go}
5             {IF sex="M"}{BRANCH age_rtn}
6
7    age_rtn  {down 2}{LEFT 6}
8             How old are you? {right 2}~
9             {?}~
10            {IF c3<18}{BRANCH no_go}
11            {IF c3>35}{BRANCH no_go}
12            {BRANCH status}
13
14   status   {down 2}{left 2}
15            What is your marital status? Choose (M)arried or (S)ingle {righ
16            {GET marital}
17            {IF marital="M"}{BRANCH no_go}
18            {IF marital="S"}{goto}a15~
19            You qualify for overseas employment. HaHa!~
20
01-Jan-89  11:52 AM
```

Figure 10–4 (Continued)

```
AA21: 'no_go                                                      READY

        AA      AB       AC       AD       AE       AF       AG       AH
21   no_go    {goto}a15~
22            Sorry, you do not qualify for overseas employment.~
23
24
25
26
27            This macro checks to see if an employee meets the
28            requirements for an overseas position by using the
29            BRANCH command to move to various subroutines.
30            The requirements for overseas employment are:
31                      1. male
32                      2. between 18 and 35 years of age
33                      3. single
34
35
36
37
38
39
40
01-Jan-89  11:52 AM
```

Figure 10–5 An Example of the DEFINE Command

```
AB5: 'The amount of your paycheck this week is~                          READY

           AA        AB        AC        AD        AE        AF        AG        AH
1     \o          {GETNUMBER "how many hours did you work this week?:",aa12}
2                 {GETNUMBER "what is your hourly wage?:",aa13}
3                 {PAYROLL aa12,aa13}
4                 {goto}aa15~
5                 The amount of your paycheck this week is~
6                 {LET af15,ah13}
7                 /rfc2~af15~
8
9     PAYROLL     {DEFINE ah11:value,ah12:value}
10                {LET ah13,ah11*ah12}
11
12
13
14
15
16
17                This macro determines the amount of an employee's weekly
18                paycheck utilizing the DEFINE command and a PAYROLL
19                routine-name command.
20
01-Jan-89  11:52 AM
```

Figure 10–6 An Example of the DISPATCH Command

```
AA1: [W10] '\n                                                           READY

           AA        AB        AC        AD        AE        AF        AG
1     \n          {GETLABEL "Enter undergraduate or graduate (U or G):",code}
2                 {IF code="U"}{LET choice,"undergrad"}
3                 {IF code="G"}{LET choice,"grad"}
4                 {DISPATCH choice}
5
6     code        g
7
8     choice      grad
9
10    undergrad   {goto}a10~
11                You will need 120 units to graduate with a bachelor's degree~
12
13    grad        {goto}a10~
14                You will need 45 graduate units to obtain your master,s degree
15
16
17                This macro uses the DISPATCH command to branch indirectly
18                to a message based on the user's choice of a code.
19
20
01-Jan-89  11:53 AM
```

Figure 10–7 An Example of the FOR Command

```
AC8:                                                              READY

        AA      AB       AC      AD       AE       AF      AG       AH
1   \f        {FOR ab7,1,18,1,ab4}
2
3
4   name_rtn /rnc{?}~{?}~
5            {down 2}
6                                           This macro names 18 more macros.
7   counter                                 Place cursor on cell to be named.
8
9
10
11
12
13
14
15
16
17
18
19
20
01-Jan-89   11:53 AM
```

Figure 10–8 An Example of the FOR and FORBREAK Commands

```
AA1: [W9] '\b                                                    READY

        AA      AB       AC      AD       AE       AF      AG       AH
1   \b        {home}{goto}a18~
2             Please enter -999 if you would like to terminate this macro.~
3             {FOR i5,1,20,1,ab6}{goto}a6~
4             The number of students who passed the test is~
5
6             {home}
7             What is the test score?~/red1~
8             {goto}d1~
9             {?}~
10            {IF d1>59}{LET i6,i6+1}
11            {IF d1=-999}/mi6..i6~f6~/MI7..I7~F7~{branch ab13}
12
13            {IF f6<1}{goto}a6~No students passed the test.~{home}{quit}
14            {forbreak}
15
16            This macro allows the user to enter the test score results
17            for a maximum of twenty students and calculates how many of
18            these students received a passing grade (>60). If there are
19            less than 20 test scores to enter, the user inputs -999 as a
20            flag to stop the execution of the macro.
01-Jan-89   11:53 AM
```

Figure 10-9 An Example of the IF, ONERROR and QUIT Commands

```
AA1: '\a                                                          READY

         AA        AB        AC        AD        AE        AF        AG        AH
1    \a        {home}
2              John{down}
3              Mary{down}
4              Jack{down}
5              Sue{down}~
6              Do you want to save this file? Choose (Y)es or (N)o~
7              {GET answer}
8              {IF answer="N"}{QUIT}
9              {IF answer="Y"}{BRANCH subr_save}
10                                                      This macro enters a name
11   answer    y                                        file and then asks the
12                                                      user if the file is to be
13   subr_save{ONERROR full_msg}                        saved. If "no" the macro
14              /fsNAMES~                                quits. If "yes" the macro
15                                                      goes to the save subroutine
16   full_msg  {goto}a15~                               and tries to save the file.
17              Disk is full~{down}                     If the disk is full, or not
18              Replace data disk~{down}                ready  an error message is
19              Press RETURN to continue~{?}~           displayed and the user must
20              {BRANCH subr_save}                      replace the data disk
01-Jan-89  11:54 AM
```

Figure 10-10 An Example of the RESTART Command

```
AA1: '\t                                                          READY

         AA        AB        AC        AD        AE        AF        AG        AH
1    \t        {goto}ae2~
2              {SUBR_1}
3              {goto}ae3~
4              {SUBR_1}
5              {goto}ae4~
6              {SUBR_1}
7              {SUBR_2}
8              {goto}ae15~
9              If your macro works,
10             {down}
11             it should never print this line!~
12
13   SUBR_1    1000+ah1~
14             {LET ah1,1000+ah1}                       This macro uses the RESTART
15             /rv~~                                     command to prevent the
16             {RETURN}                                  macro from returning by the
17                                                      path it came. In this case,
18   SUBR_2    {goto}ae6~                               when ae6>=10000, the macro
19             +ae2+ae3+ae4~                            stops execution in SUBR_2
20             {IF ae6<10000}{BRANCH \t}                and the RETURN is ignored.
01-Jan-89  11:54 AM
```

```
AA21:                                                              READY

         AA      AB      AC      AD      AE      AF      AG      AH
21          {IF ae6>=10000}{RESTART}
22          {down 2}
23          You are finished!~
24          /reah1~
25          {RETURN}
26
27
28
29
30
31
32
33
34
35
36
37
38
39
40
         01-Jan-89  11:54 AM
```

Figure 10–10 (Continued)

immediately after the call location. By using several subroutines you will be able to break down a large problem into several smaller units or modules (see Figure 10–11).

Macro subroutines must be started with SUBR-. The routine name is a range. The routine name cannot be one of the Lotus reserved words such as NAME (see Table 9–1 in Chapter 9 for the listing of reserved words). If duplication occurs Lotus performs the subroutine, not the keystroke (or reserved word).

10-7 Testing Keyboard Operations

These commands are used for interactive programming. During the execution of these commands, 1-2-3 will pause and ask for user input. Commands include ?, BREAKOFF, BREAKON, GET, GETLABEL, GETNUMBER, LOOK, MENUBRANCH, MENUCALL, and WAIT.

10–7–1 {?}

Halts the execution of the macro temporarily and waits for user input. The {?} command is an alternative to GET, GETLABEL, GETNUMBER, LOOK, MENUBRANCH, and MENUCALL.

Figure 10–11 An Example of the RETURN Command

```
AA1: '\u                                                                    READY

         AA       AB        AC        AD        AE        AF        AG        AH
1    \u        {home}
2              What is the retail price?~
3              {goto}f1~
4              {?}~
5              /rfc2~~
6              {LET f12,f1}
7              {down 2}{left 5}
8              Is the item on sale? Choose (Y)es or (N)o~
9              {GET answer}
10             {IF answer="Y"}{subr_sale}
11             {goto}a12~
12             The final purchase price is~
13             {LET f12,f12+(f12*.06)}~
14             /rfc2~f12~
15
16   subr_sale{goto}a5~
17             Sale items are 20 percent off~
18             {LET f12,f1-(f1*.20)}
19             {down 2}
20             Does the price tag have a red star? Choose (Y)es or (N)o~
01-Jan-89  11:54 AM
```

Figure 10–11 (Continued)

```
AA21:                                                                       READY

         AA       AB        AC        AD        AE        AF        AG        AH
21            {GET response}
22            {IF response="Y"}{subr_star}
23            {LET f12,f12-g9}
24            {RETURN}
25
26   subr_star{goto}a9~
27            Red star tags get an additional 10 percent off~
28            {LET g9,f1*.10}~
29            {RETURN}
30
31   answer
32
33   response
34
35
36
37            This macro is an example of a nested loop which determines
38            the final purchase price of a retail item that may have
39            one, two or no discounts and has a 6% sales tax.
40
01-Jan-89  11:54 AM
```

10-7-2 {BREAKOFF} and {BREAKON}

Disables the BREAK key during macro execution. {BREAKON} restores the BREAK key. You must always remember that if your macro enters an endless loop and {BREAKOFF} is active you cannot stop the endless loop. The only solution is to stop the computer. The combination of these two commands is used for applications in which you want to show the execution of the entire macro without user interruption.

10-7-3 {WAIT time-serial-number}

Waits until the time-serial-number is up. You can halt a {WAIT} command by pressing the **Break** key, unless you have executed a {BREAKOFF} command. Figure 10-12 illustrates an application of BREAKOFF, BREAKON and WAIT.

10-7-4 {GET address}

Pauses for the user to input a single character, then stores it in an address. The single character can be either a standard typewriter key or a Lotus standard key (TABLE, QUERY, etc.). Figure 10-13 illustrates an example of this command.

10-7-5 {GETLABEL prompt, address} and {GETNUMBER, prompt, address}

GETLABEL pauses for the user to type a character string, then stores it as a label in the address. {GETNUMBER} does the same thing, but stores the data as a number. Your prompt (your message or statement) must be short enough to fit into the control panel. Also, if your prompt includes separators (commas or semicolons), you must enclose the prompt in quotation marks. Figure 10-14 illustrates an application of these two commands.

10-7-6 {LOOK address}

Checks to see if the user has typed a character. LOOK is similar to GET except that LOOK does not halt the macro execution. LOOK leaves the character in the type-ahead buffer for future use by GET, GETLABEL or GETNUMBER. Figure 10-15 illustrates an example of this command.

10-7-7 {MENUBRANCH address} and {MENUCALL address}

MENUBRANCH suspends the execution of the macro temporarily in order to allow the user to choose from a menu and then continues to the macro branch. The MENUCALL address does the same thing, but it executes the corresponding macro as a subroutine. Using MENUCALL you can design your own menu consisting of any of several commands. To establish a menu, remember the following:

1. You can have up to eight commands in your menu.
2. There are three lines available to you. Line one is the name of the command (menu item). Line two is a brief description of the menu item. Line three is the command summary (macro instruction), e.g., /WIC (/Worksheet Insert Column).
3. In your menu the starting character of each menu item must be unique,

Figure 10–12 An Example of BREAKOFF, BREAKON, and WAIT

```
AB19: 'halting macro execution during the eight-second pause.              READY

          AA          AB          AC        AD        AE        AF        AG
1    `c              {goto}instructions~
2                    {BREAKOFF}
3                    {WAIT @now+@time(0,0,8)}
4                    {BREAKON}
5                    {goto}aa15~
6                    {?}~
7                    {right 2}
8                    thank you!~
9
10   instructions    Please enter your Social Security number in the
11                   following format - XXXXXXXXX
12
13
14
15
16                   This macro gives the user eight seconds to read a set
17                   of instructions that requests a social security number be
18                   entered.   The BREAKOFF/ON commands prevent the user from
19                   halting macro execution during the eight-second pause.
20
01-Jan-89  11:55 AM
```

Figure 10–13 An Example of the GET Command

```
AA1: '\i                                                                   READY

          AA          AB          AC        AD        AE        AF        AG        AH
1    \i              {home}~
2                    /ree1..e3~
3                    Please enter the catalogue number~
4                    {goto}e1~
5                    {?}~                                          This macro simulates
6                    {down}{left 4}                                a catalogue order
7                    Quantity?~                                    process that has the
8                    {goto}e2~                                     user inputting infor-
9                    {?}~                                          mation about that
10                   {down}{left 4}                                order, and then asks
11                   Item price?~                                  if additional orders
12                   {goto}e3~                                     are to be placed.
13                   {?}~
14                   /rfc2~{down}~
15                   {down}{left 4}
16                   Total Price~{goto}e4~
17                   (e3*e2)~
18                   {down 3}{left 4}
19                   Do you have another order? Choose (Y)es or (N)o~
20                   {GET answer}
01-Jan-89  11:55 AM
```

Figure 10–13 (Continued)

```
AA21:                                                              READY

        AA        AB        AC        AD        AE        AF        AG        AH
21              {IF answer="Y"}{BRANCH \i}
22              {IF answer="N"}{down 2}'Thank you for your order!~
23
24
25 answer     y
26
27
28
29
30
31
32
33
34
35
36
37
38
39
40
01-Jan-89  11:55 AM
```

Figure 10–14 An Example of GETLABEL and GETNUMBER

```
AA1: '\k                                                          READY

        AA        AB        AC        AD        AE        AF        AG        AH
1  \k          {goto}a1~
2              {GETLABEL "What is the employee's name?:",a3}~
3              {GETNUMBER "How many hours did employee work?:",d3}~
4              {IF d3<=40}{BRANCH Regular}
5              {IF d3>40}{BRANCH Overtime}
6                                        This macro asks for the
7  Regular     {IF d3<=0}{BRANCH Error}  employee's name and the
8              {LET c5,+d3*10}~          number of hours worked and,
9              {goto}a5~                 calculates that employee's
10             Your pay is~              pay based on Regular or
11             /rfc2~c5~                 Overtime hours.  Regular
12                                        pay is $10 per hour and
13 Overtime    {LET c5,40*10+(d3-40)*15}~ Overtime is $15 per hour.
14             {goto}a5~                 If the employee inputs
15             Your pay is~              zero or negative hours, an
16             /rfc2~c5~                 error message is displayed.
17
18 Error       {goto}a15~
19             Your entry will not compute, please try again!~
20             {BRANCH \k}
01-Jan-89  11:57 AM
```

AA1: '\j   READY

```
         AA        AB        AC        AD        AE        AF        AG        AH
1    \j            {home}
2              please type your name when you hear the "beep"~
3              {WAIT @now+@time(0,0,5)}
4              {LOOK a15}
5              {IF a15<>""}{BRANCH message}
6              {BEEP 4}
7              {goto}d6~
8              {?}~
9
10   message  please wait for the beep!~
11
12
13
14
15             This macro has the user type his/her name at the
16             sound of the beep.  If the user tries to type a
17             name before the beep, a friendly message is displayed!
18
19
20
01-Jan-89  11:57 AM
```

Figure 10–15 An Example of the LOOK Command

otherwise 1-2-3 always chooses the first one. For example, do not use worksheet and window in the same menu.

4. You can extend the column width to any number between 1 and 240, inclusive.
5. Blank cells are not allowed between menu items.
6. The cell to the right of the final menu item must be empty.
7. Uppercase and lowercase are the same.
8. A menu item can be chosen by moving the cursor and pressing the **Return** key, or typing the first character of each command.
9. Pressing the **Escape** key will cancel a menu item.

Figure 10–16 illustrates an example of MENUCALL. Figure 10–17 illustrates an example of MENUBRANCH.

10-8 Screen Design and Control

These commands help you to design the look of the screen and the sound. They include BEEP, INDICATE, PANELOFF, PANELON, WINDOWSOFF, and WINDOWSON.

10–8–1 {BEEP <number>}

Activates the computer bell. The number argument is optional. This command is used to convey a signal to the user. The number can be either 1, 2, 3, or 4, to choose

Figure 10–16 An Example of MENUCALL

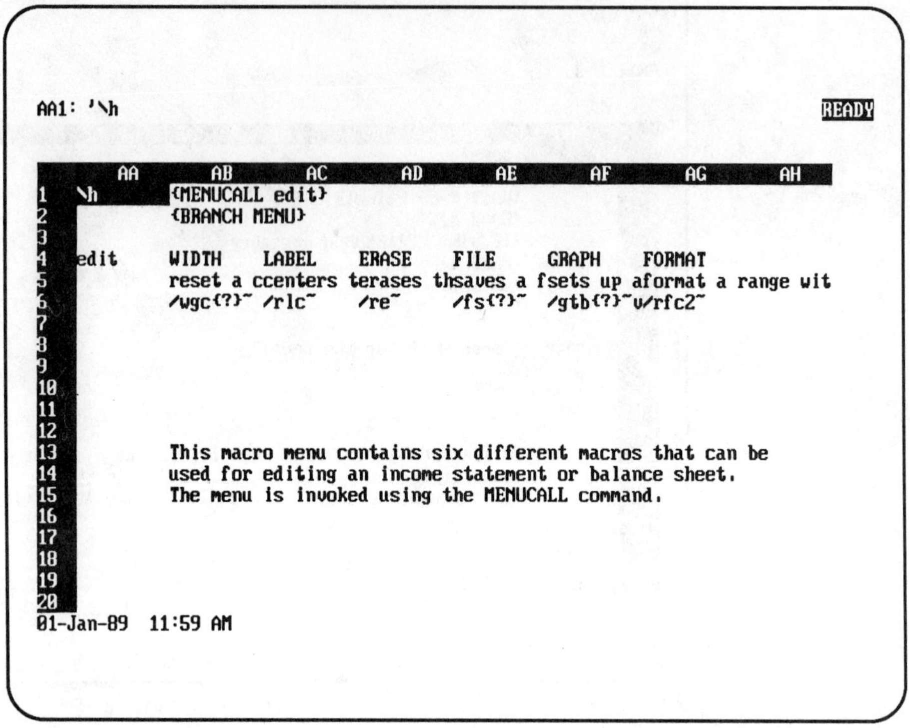

```
AA1: '\h                                                              READY

        AA      AB      AC       AD      AE      AF      AG      AH
   1   \h      {MENUCALL edit}
   2           {BRANCH MENU}
   3
   4   edit    WIDTH   LABEL    ERASE   FILE    GRAPH   FORMAT
   5           reset a ccenters terases thsaves a fsets up aformat a range wit
   6           /wgc{?}~ /rlc~    /re~    /fs{?}~ /gtb{?}~w/rfc2~
   7
   8
   9
  10
  11
  12
  13           This macro menu contains six different macros that can be
  14           used for editing an income statement or balance sheet.
  15           The menu is invoked using the MENUCALL command.
  16
  17
  18
  19
  20
  01-Jan-89   11:59 AM
```

Figure 10–17 An Example of MENUBRANCH

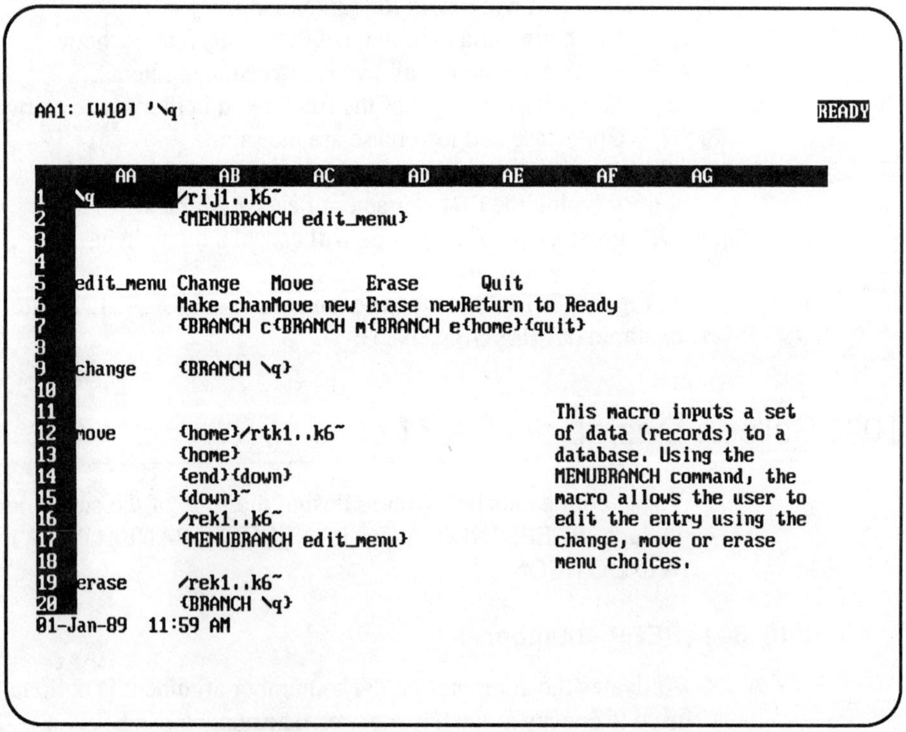

```
AA1: [W10] '\q                                                       READY

        AA       AB      AC      AD      AE      AF      AG
   1   \q       /rij1..k6~
   2            {MENUBRANCH edit_menu}
   3
   4
   5   edit_menu Change  Move    Erase    Quit
   6            Make chanMove new Erase newReturn to Ready
   7            {BRANCH c{BRANCH m{BRANCH e{home}{quit}
   8
   9   change   {BRANCH \q}
  10
  11                                      This macro inputs a set
  12   move     {home}/rtk1..k6~          of data (records) to a
  13            {home}                     database. Using the
  14            {end}{down}                MENUBRANCH command, the
  15            {down}~                    macro allows the user to
  16            /rek1..k6~                 edit the entry using the
  17            {MENUBRANCH edit_menu}     change, move or erase
  18                                       menu choices.
  19   erase    /rek1..k6~
  20            {BRANCH \q}
  01-Jan-89   11:59 AM
```

four different tones. The default value is one. Figure 10–18 illustrates an application of this command.

10–8–2 {INDICATE <string>}

Changes the mode indicator in the upper right corner of the screen. When INDI-CATE is activated the only way to deactivate it is to use another INDICATE command. The default value of string is the READY mode. To remove the mode indicator from the control panel you can use {INDICATE " "}. Figure 10–19 illustrates an example of this command.

10–8–3 {PANELOFF} and {PANELON}

PANELOFF suppresses redrawing (display) of the control panel during the execution of the macro. {PANELON} restores the setting. {PANELOFF} is very useful when the macro is executing Lotus menu commands. Figure 10–20 illustrates an example of these commands.

10–8–4 {WINDOWSOFF} and {WINDOWSON}

WINDOWSOFF freezes the screen display (except for the control panel). {WIN-DOWSON} restores the normal setting. Using WINDOWSOFF will speed up the execution time of a macro since it does not do any redrawing; this is especially useful for long macros. These two commands are similar to PANELOFF and PANELON. Figure 10–21 illustrates an example of these two commands.

10-9 File Operations

The commands in this group enable you to perform file operations. These commands include CLOSE, FILESIZE, GETPOS, OPEN, READ, READLN, SETPOS, WRITE and WRITELN. These are designed only for ASCII files. (For more information on ASCII files, see Appendix C.)

10–9–1 {CLOSE}

Closes a file that was opened with the {OPEN} command.

10–9–2 {FILESIZE address}

Counts the number of bytes (characters) in an open file and then stores the result in address. The address is a cell or a range name.

10–9–3 {GETPOS address}

Determines the present position of the file pointer and displays the result in the address. Naturally the file must be opened first. Remember, the first position in a file is 0 (zero), not 1 (one).

Figure 10–18 An Example of the BEEP Command

```
AA1: '\f                                                                    READY

        AA        AB        AC        AD        AE        AF        AG        AH
1    \f        {goto}a1~                        This macro fills the screen with
2              @RAND~                           random numbers (between 0 and 1)
3              /ca1..a1~a1..h20~                and "beeps" when the macro has
4              {BEEP 3}                         been completed.
5
6
7
8
9
10
11
12
13
14
15
16
17
18
19
20   '
01-Jan-89   12:00 PM
```

Figure 10–19 An Example of the INDICATE Command

```
AB15: 'the box in the upper righthand corner indicates "GO."                 READY

        AA        AB        AC        AD        AE        AF        AG        AH
1    \s        {home}
2              When the box in the upper righthand corner
3              {down}
4              indicates "Go", please enter your last name~
5              {WAIT @now+@time(0,0,5)}
6              {INDICATE Go}
7              {goto}c10~
8              /wcs15~
9              {?}~
10             {INDICATE}
11
12
13
14             This macro asks the user to enter a last name when
15             the box in the upper righthand corner indicates "GO,"
16             The second INDICATE command changes the box back to
17             the READY mode.
18
19
20
01-Jan-89   12:00 PM
```

Figure 10–20 An Example of PANELOFF and PANELON

```
AA1: '\e                                                              READY

            AA          AB          AC          AD          AE          AF
1    \e        /wgc12~
2              {home}
3              Enter 5000 in cell a5~
4              {goto}a5~
5              {?}~
6              {PANELOFF}
7              /ca5~b5..f5~
8              /rfc2~a5..f5~
9              {PANELON}
10
11
12             This macro sets the width of all columns to 12
13             and prompts the user to input 5000 in cell a5.
14             The redrawing of the control panel is then frozen
15             by the PANELOFF command while the macro copies
16             the contents of cell a5 to cells b5, c5, d5, e5 and
17             f5 and formats all six cells with the currency format
18             option to two decimal places.
19
20
01-Jan-89   12:00 PM
```

Figure 10–21 An Example of WINDOWSOFF and WINDOWSON

```
AF11: 'the WINDOWSOFF and                                             READY

            AA          AB          AC          AD          AE          AF          AG
1    \r        {WINDOWSOFF}
2              {PANELON}
3              /wgc10~
4              {goto}d1~
5              January{right}                           This macro sets up
6              June{right}                              a portion of an
7              September{right}                         income statement
8              December~                                for four quarters.
9              /rlcd1..i1~                              While the commands
10             {goto}a5~                                are being executed,
11             Sales{down}                              the WINDOWSOFF and
12             Cost of Goods Sold{down}                 PANELOFF command
13             Gross Profit{down}                       freezes the lower
14             Expenses{down}NetIncome~                 part of the screen.
15             /rfc2~d5..i9~
16             {home}
17             {WINDOWSON}
18             {PANELON}
19
20
01-Jan-89   12:00 PM
```

10–9–4 {OPEN filename, access-mode}

Opens a selected file for reading, writing, or both. The file must be in the current directory. The file name should specify a drive location and subdirectory path if needed. There are three types of access modes:

1. R (Read) allows only the read option for READ and READLN commands.
2. W (Write) allows WRITE and WRITELN commands. This option also allows READ and READLN commands. This access is for a new file.
3. M (Modify) allows READ, READLN, WRITE, and WRITELN commands. This access is for an existing file.

10–9–5 {READ bytecount, address}

Reads characters from an open file into an address. If the bytecount is larger than the number of characters left in the file, Lotus reads the remaining characters. The bytecount must be between 0 and 240. A negative bytecount is equivalent to the maximum positive bytecount of 240.

10–9–6 {READLN address}

Copies an entire line of characters from an open file into an address. This command starts reading from the present position of the file pointer and ends with a carriage return, line feed.

10–9–7 {SETPOS file-position}

Sets a new position for the file pointer in a specified open file. File-position is a number. The first character in the file is always at position 0, the second character at position 1, and so forth. If you specify a large number, you may pass the end of the file.

10–9–8 {WRITE string}

Copies a series of characters into an open file. This macro command copies from the worksheet to the current position of the file pointer in a file that has been opened with either Write or Modify.

10–9–9 {WRITELN}

This command does the same thing as WRITE, except that it adds a carriage-return line feed to the end of the string in the file.

Figures 10–22 through 10–25 show some simple macros to illustrate file operations.

Figure 10–22 Example of OPEN, WRITELN, WRITE, and CLOSE

```
AB17: 'into ASCII files.                                           READY

        AA        AB        AC        AD        AE        AF        AG        AH
1    \a        {OPEN MYFILE.WK1,W}
2              {WRITELN This is a sample file}
3              {WRITE This file has been saved under MYFILE}
4              ~{CLOSE}
5
6
7
8              This macro opens a file called MYFILE with
9              the Write access mode. The WRITELN command
10             writes a string of text to the file and
11             places a carriage-return, line-feed sequence
12             after the last character.  The WRITE command
13             writes another string of characters to the
14             file and then the file is closed.  Through
15             regular /File Retrieve, you cannot see the
16             contents of this file because it only writes
17             into ASCII files.
18
19
20
01-Jan-89   12:00 PM
```

Figure 10–23 Example of FILESIZE

```
AA1: '\b                                                           READY

        AA        AB        AC        AD        AE        AF        AG        AH
1    \b        {OPEN MYFILE.WK1,R}         This macro opens a file called
2              {FILESIZE bytes}            MYFILE.WK1.  It is opened with Read
3              ~{CLOSE}                    access mode.  This file was
4                                          generated and saved under this name.
5                                          We have presented a copy of this
6                                          file at the bottom of this work-
7                                          sheet. We executed this macro and
8                                          received the number 1470 in cell
9                                          AA15 which is named bytes.
10
11
12
13
14
15     1470
16
17
18   This is a sample file
19   This file has been saved under MYFILE
20
01-Jan-89   12:01 PM
```

Figure 10–24 Example of READ and SETPOS

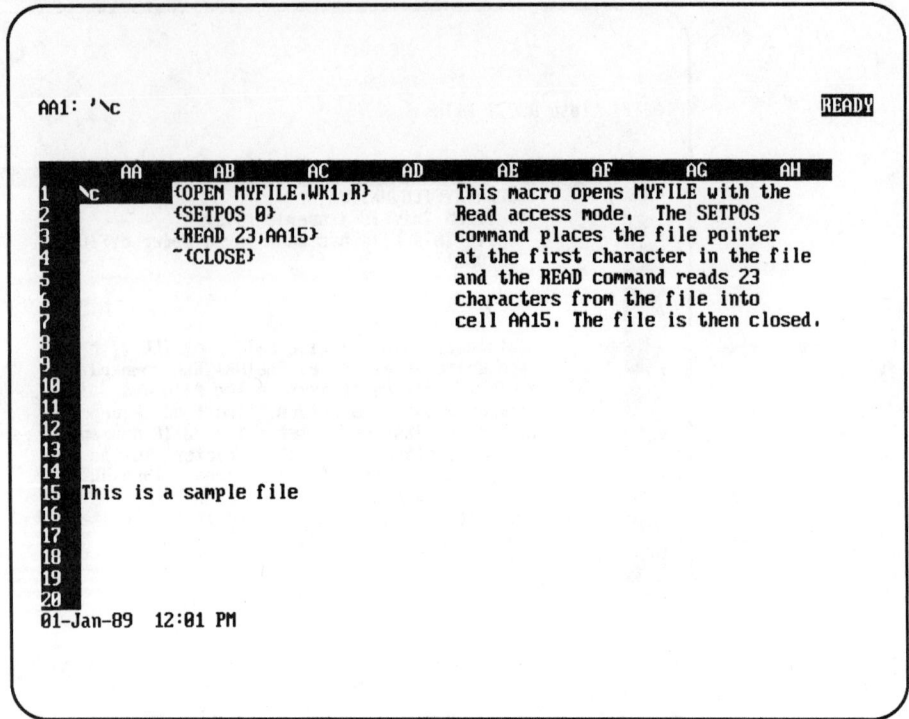

```
AA1: '\c                                                              READY

         AA      AB        AC      AD      AE      AF      AG      AH
1     \c        {OPEN MYFILE.WK1,R}          This macro opens MYFILE with the
2               {SETPOS 0}                   Read access mode.  The SETPOS
3               {READ 23,AA15}               command places the file pointer
4               ~{CLOSE}                     at the first character in the file
5                                            and the READ command reads 23
6                                            characters from the file into
7                                            cell AA15. The file is then closed.
8
9
10
11
12
13
14
15    This is a sample file
16
17
18
19
20
01-Jan-89   12:01 PM
```

Figure 10–25 Example of GETPOS and READLN

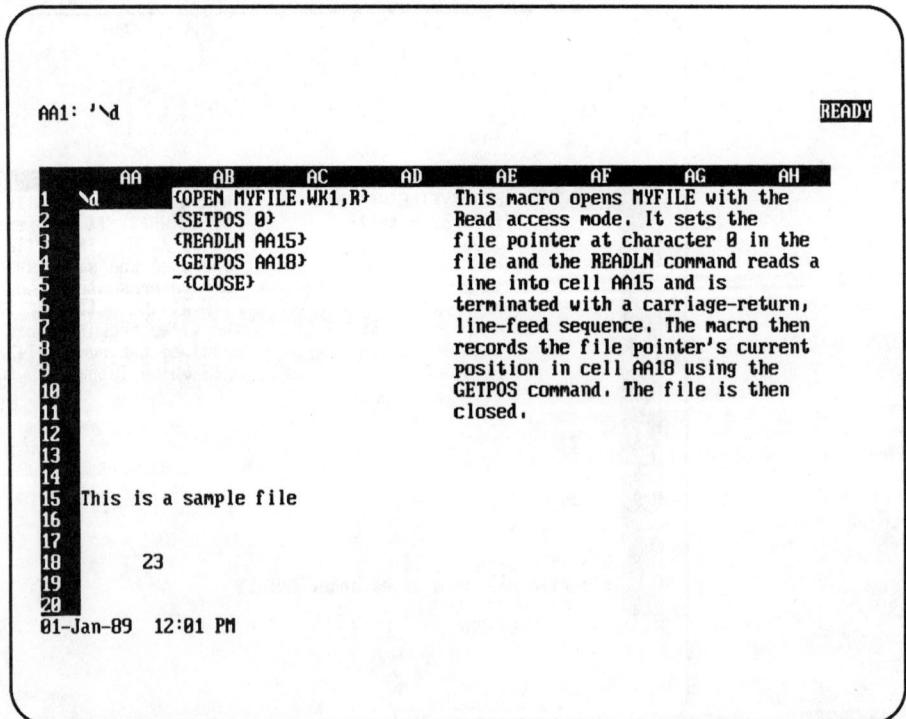

```
AA1: '\d                                                              READY

         AA      AB        AC      AD      AE      AF      AG      AH
1     \d        {OPEN MYFILE.WK1,R}          This macro opens MYFILE with the
2               {SETPOS 0}                   Read access mode. It sets the
3               {READLN AA15}                file pointer at character 0 in the
4               {GETPOS AA18}                file and the READLN command reads a
5               ~{CLOSE}                     line into cell AA15 and is
6                                            terminated with a carriage-return,
7                                            line-feed sequence. The macro then
8                                            records the file pointer's current
9                                            position in cell AA18 using the
10                                           GETPOS command. The file is then
11                                           closed.
12
13
14
15    This is a sample file
16
17
18         23
19
20
01-Jan-89   12:01 PM
```

Summary

The Lotus advanced macro commands have been divided into five groups. Each group has been designed to perform a unique task: data manipulation, program flow, testing keyboard operations, screen design and control, and file operations. Lotus advanced commands also serve as a high-level programming language, closely paralleling other high-level programming languages. In Chapter 11 we will utilize these advanced commands in some simple programming assignments.

Review Questions

1.   What is a Lotus advanced command?
2.   What is the structure of an advanced command?
3.* Is an argument needed for all the advanced commands?
4.* How many different types of arguments do we have in an advanced command?
5.   How many different groups of macro commands do we have?
6.   Give one command as an example of each group.
7.* What is the equivalent of BLANK in a nonmacro setting (in worksheet or range commands)?
8.   What is the difference between CONTENTS and LET?
9.   Does LET hold numeric values, nonnumeric values, or both?
10.   What is the difference between DISPATCH and BRANCH?
11.* If Start in the FOR command is larger than Stop, what will happen?
12.* Does **Return** need an argument?
13.   What is the application of the LOOK command?
14.   How do you design your own menu?
15.   How many lines can you have in a menu?
16.* Why must all the commands in your menu be unique (the starting point must be unique)?
17.   How many commands are included in the file operations group?
18.   What is the difference between the READLN and READ commands?
19.   Why must a file be opened before you invoke a command?
20.* How many different access modes do we have?
21.   Using the FOR advanced command, design an macro that prints "LOTUS IS EASY TO LEARN" 20 times.
22.   Using the MENUCALL advanced command, design a menu with four options:

    a.   Extend a column length to any number between 1 and 240 characters.
    b.   Center any label typed from the keyboard.
    c.   Erase any range specified by the user.
    d.   Format any number in Currency with two decimal places.

23.   Using the INDICATE advanced command, design a macro to turn the mode indicator to "Bye."
24.   Using BRANCH and other advanced commands, design a macro to select

students for a dean's scholarship if they meet the following criteria:

MIS major
GPA > 3.70
Age < 21
Single

25.   Using Figure 10–16, add two more options to this menu.

Misconceptions and Solutions

M — A subroutine name can be any name except reserved Lotus words. If there is a duplicate, Lotus performs the subroutine, not the reserved word.

S — All Lotus reserved words are in Table 9–1. Try not to use any of these as subroutine names.

M — If macro command BREAKOFF is in effect and the macro goes into an endless loop, there is no way to get back to the 1-2-3 command mode.

S — To stop this you have to reset your computer (turn the computer off).

M — In sequential file processing, when you use the OPEN command accompanied with the access mode to open a file you may get an error message.

S — You must use the file extension with the file name.

M — In sequential file processing, Lotus does not prevent you from putting the file pointer past the end of the file.

S — You must use the FILESIZE command to determine the number of the last character in the file.

M — The BRANCH macro command and GOTO both cause branching to different locations not followed in the normal program sequence.

S — Use GOTO only if you want to move the cell pointer. Use BRANCH if you want to transfer the macro execution to a different location that is not the normal program sequence.

M — Entering a series of numbers into a worksheet can be a time-consuming process. You can either use the upper part of the keyboard or you can use the numeric pad after pressing the **Num Lock** key. Both of these processes can be slow.

S — Design a simple macro that accepts a numeric value and moves the cursor down continuously. The following is this macro:

```
AA          AB              AC              . . .
\A          {?}
            {DOWN}
            {BRANCH \A}
```

(To stop this macro you must press **Ctrl** and **Break** keys simultaneously.)

Comprehensive Lab Assignment

Retrieve CHAPT5 and perform the following:

1. Design a menu macro that includes three options:

   Statistics   Graph   Quit

   The Statistics options should tell us the name of the students with the highest and lowest scores. The Graph option should give a choice of a line graph of total scores or the bar graph of the total of the three test scores.

2. Design a menu macro that provides six Sort options and a Quit option on the existing worksheet:

   Name   Major   Sex   Standing   Age   Total Score   Quit

3. Save the current worksheet under CHAPT10.

4. Design an interactive macro that asks the user if he/she wants to save the worksheet under CHAPT10. If the answer is Yes, it saves the worksheet, erases the worksheet, and exits from Lotus.

11

Macros/Part Three: Using Lotus Macros as a Super Programming Language

11-1 Introduction

In this chapter we are wrapping up our discussion of macros. We will present a quick review of the program development life cycle. Modular programming and structured programming also will be briefly discussed. We put a heavy emphasis on program documentation and the types of documentation. We will also compare Lotus macros with a typical high-level programming language.

After this brief presentation we will introduce you to several short programs using Lotus as a programming language. This chapter should provide you with a good background for further investigations into Lotus as a super programming language.

11-2 Steps in the Program Development Life Cycle

The purpose of this chapter is not to teach you how to program. There are several excellent texts available which teach the subject of programming thoroughly. In this chapter, we are trying to provide you with a quick overview of programming and the program development life cycle.

In order to use Lotus as a programming language you should follow these steps:

Step 1 Problem Definition. You should carefully define the nature and scope of the problem which you intend to use Lotus to solve. On a broader scale, you may have to perform an output analysis first. This means that you clearly define all the outputs or answers to the questions you intend to receive from your macro program. A clear definition of the problem and the output specifications may help you to achieve a solution faster.

A typical problem would be a payroll problem. Your program should be able to print accurate monthly, biweekly, and weekly paychecks for a group of employees. The paycheck is the output of the program. Naturally, some input data is needed in order to print a paycheck. In the simplest case, you need the number of hours a particular employee works, his/her pay rate, overtime rate, deductions, and so forth.

Step 2 Logic Design. In programming terminology, before you attempt to write a program, you must first define how you will reach your solution. For example, if an employee has worked more than 40 hours, what do you do? If the employee has worked less than 40 hours, what do you do? There are many tools to use in clarifying the logic of your program. The flowchart (the most commonly used tool), structure chart, pseudocode, or Nassi-Shneiderman chart are some of the techniques available. If you use these tools, you are safeguarding against logical errors, those that create erroneous results in your program – your program runs but the results are not correct. Other errors you may see are called syntax errors. These include using the wrong keyword or the wrong grammar. The correction of syntactical errors is usually easier than the correction of logical errors.

Using logic design tools such as a flowchart or pseudocode should assist you in minimizing or eliminating errors, especially logical errors. After you design your logic and walk through it to make sure it is working, you move to the next step.

Step 3 Coding. After designing your logic and checking it manually, you are ready to code it. Chapters 9 and 10 taught you how to use Lotus as a programming language.

The best approach for coding your program is a modular approach. This means entering the program as a series of smaller independent blocks. Test these blocks and document them; if one works, begin the next block. We will talk more about modular programming later in this chapter.

Step 4 Execution and Debugging. Usually your program will not run the first time, or it runs partially, or it may run completely but generate the wrong answers. In each case there is a bug (error) in your program. As we discussed in Chapter 9, you can debug each individual macro. To make sure that the entire program is working, you should use some simple data and run it through your program. You can then be pretty sure that your program is working correctly.

Step 5 Documentation. In order to make your program self-explanatory for other people and for your own future reference, you should document it. Documentation can be internal or external. Internal documentation may include a series of statements within your macro to explain its function.

Internal documentation can be three types. Type one is called program documentation. This may include a few lines of explanation at the beginning of the program to describe its function. Type two is called module documentation. This type describes the function of a particular module. Type three is called line documentation or segment documentation. This type of documentation explains lines or segments of a module.

External documentation may include a flowchart, pseudocode, structure chart, or program listing. Comprehensive external documentation may serve as a user's guide or user's manual for future reference. Both internal and external documentation are important and you should get in the habit of using them.

11-3 Modular Programming

Problems you may encounter in real-life situations are usually large and complex. To solve the entire problem in one shot may not be a feasible option. Modular programming methodology advocates the breakdown of a large project into several smaller ones. Solve each small module, then put them together in order to generate the answer to the entire problem. Modular programming has several unique advantages:

1. It is easier to understand.
2. It is easier to code.
3. It is easier to debug.
4. It is easier to document.
5. It is easier to modify.

In order to implement each module in Lotus, use a subroutine. In programming terminology, a subroutine is a series of instructions that performs a particular task. Any large problem can be broken down into a series of subroutines.

11-4 Structured Programming

Since the early 1970s a new methodology has become very common in a programming environment. This new methodology advocates GOTO-less programming. The intention is to eliminate the use of GOTO statements in your program. Proponents of this methodology believe GOTO statements make the program complex and difficult to debug or modify.

In structured programming, four structures are used for performing any tasks. These include sequence, selection, iteration, and CASE structures.

The sequence structure means going from step 1 to step 2 to step 3. There is no looping or branching involved here.

The selection structure is used whenever you have to choose between two options, e.g., regular routine or overtime routine, high commission or low commission.

The iteration structure indicates a loop for a specific task; for example, 100 times printing 100 different checks or 200 times calculating the commissions for a group of salespeople.

The CASE structure is used when you choose from more than two options; for example, selection of a commission formula from 15 different routines. Table 11–1 illustrates the equivalent of these structures in Lotus. The remaining part of this chapter presents some simple macro programs.

Table 11–1 Structured Programming and Lotus

NAME OF THE STRUCTURE	PROGRAMMING EQUIVALENT	LOTUS MACRO EQUIVALENT
Sequence	LET A+10 B=25	LET, PUT, BLANK, CONTENTS, etc.
Selection	IF-THEN IF-THEN-ELSE	IF, BRANCH, etc. DISPATCH, etc.
Iteration	FOR-NEXT DO-WHILE DO-UNTIL DO-CONTINUE REPEAT-UNTIL	FOR, etc.
CASE	CASE expression OF	BRANCH, DISPATCH, etc.

11-5 Program 1 — Area and Circumference of a Circle

Our first example calculates the area and circumference of a circle. The program is in interactive mode. The user inputs the radius and the program calculates the area and the circumference of a particular circle. This is illustrated in Figure 11–1.

11-6 Program 2 — Arithmetic Operations with Two Numbers

Example two illustrates a simple program; shown in Figure 11–2. The user inputs two numbers and then the program calculates their sum, their difference, their product, and their quotient.

11-7 Program 3 — Average Score of Five Numbers

In Figure 11–3, if we input five different scores, the program calculates their average.

11-8 Program 4 — Checking the Sign of a Number

Example four, in Figure 11–4, inputs a number with any sign. Then the program examines the number to see if it is positive, negative, or zero. The appropriate message is printed and the program waits for six seconds, erases the previous message, and asks for a new number. To stop this program, type N (for No).

11-9 Program 5 — Random Numbers Generation between Zero and One

Program 5, shown in Figure 11–5, generates as many random numbers as the user specifies. These random numbers are between zero and one.

Figure 11–1 Area and Circumference of a Circle

```
AA1: '\b                                                            READY

       AA        AB        AC        AD        AE        AF        AG        AH
1  \b        {home}
2            what is the radius of your circle?~
3            {goto}f1~                                      This macro accepts
4            {?}~                                           the radius of a
5            {goto}a3~                                      circle from the
6            the area of your circle is~                    terminal and
7            {let f3,@pi*f1^2}~                             computes the area
8            {goto}a5~                                       and the circum-
9            the circumference of your circle is~           ference of that
10           {let f5,2*f1*@pi}~                             circle.
11           {quit}
12
13
14
15
16
17
18
19
20
01-Jan-89   12:01 PM
```

Figure 11–2 Arithmetic Operations with Two Numbers

```
AA1: '\i                                                            READY

       AA        AB        AC        AD        AE        AF        AG        AH
1  \i        {home}
2            Give me two numbers and I will add, subtract,
3            {down}
4            multiply and divide them.~
5            {goto}a5~
6            What is your first number?~
7            {goto}d5~
8            {?}~
9            {down}{left 3}
10           What is your second number?~
11           {goto}d6~                                      This macro accepts two
12           {?}~                                           numbers given by the user
13           {goto}a10~                                     and finds their sum,
14           Their sum is~                                  difference, product,
15           {goto}d10~                                     and quotient.
16           @sum(d5,d6)
17           {down 2}{left 3}
18           Their difference is~
19           {goto}d12~
20           +d5-d6~
01-Jan-89   12:02 PM
```

Figure 11–2 (Continued)

```
AA21:                                                                 READY

        AA      AB      AC      AD      AE      AF      AG      AH
21             {down 2}{left 3}
22             Their product is~
23             {goto}d14~
24             +d5*d6~
25             {down 2}{left 3}
26             Their quotient is~
27             {goto}d16~
28             +d5/d6~
29
30
31
32
33
34
35
36
37
38
39
40
01-Jan-89  12:02 PM
```

Figure 11–3 Average Scores of Five Numbers

```
AA1: '\c                                                              READY

        AA      AB      AC      AD      AE      AF      AG      AH
1   \c         {home}
2              What is your first test score?~
3              {goto}e1~
4              {?}~
5              {down}{left 4}
6              What is your second test score?~
7              {goto}e2~
8              {?}~
9              {down}{left 4}
10             What is your third test score?~             This macro calculates
11             {goto}e3~                                   the average score
12             {?}~                                        from five test scores
13             {down}{left 4}
14             What is your fourth test score?~
15             {goto}e4~
16             {?}~
17             {down}{left 4}
18             What is your fifth test score?~
19             {goto}e5~
20             {?}~
01-Jan-89  12:02 PM
```

Figure 11-3 (Continued)

```
AA21:                                                              READY

        AA       AB        AC        AD        AE        AF        AG        AH
21  ┐         {down 2}{left 4}
22  │         Your average score is~
23  │         {goto}e7~
24  │         (+E1+E2+E3+E4+E5)/5~
25  │
26  │
27  │
28  │
29  │
30  │
31  │
32  │
33  │
34  │
35  │
36  │
37  │
38  │
39  │
40  ┘
01-Jan-89   12:03 PM
```

Figure 11-4 Checking the Sign of a Number

```
AA1: '\a                                                           READY

        AA       AB        AC        AD        AE        AF        AG        AH
1   \a        {home}
2   │         What is your number?~
3   │         {goto}d1~
4   │         {?}~                                      This macro inputs
5   │         {goto}a3~                                 any number from
6   │         {IF d1>0} Your number is positive~        the keyboard and
7   │         {IF d1<0} Your number is negative~        will tell you
8   │         {IF d1=0} Your number is zero~            whether the number
9   │         {goto}a10~                                is positive,
10  │         Do you want to try again? Choose (Y)es or (N)negative or zero.
11  │         {GET answer}
12  │         {IF answer="Y"}{branch \a}
13  │
14  │
15  │
16  │
17  │
18  │
19  │
20  ┘
01-Jan-89   12:03 PM
```

```
AA1: '\k                                                              READY

         AA       AB      AC      AD      AE      AF      AG      AH
1    \k       {home}
2             this macro will generate as many random numbers as you specify~
3             {down 3}
4             how many random numbers do you want?~
5             {goto}e4~
6             {?}~
7             {goto}a6~
8             {FOR ab15,1,e4,1,ab10}           This macro will
9                                              generate as many
10   rand_num @RAND                            random numbers as
11            {down}                           the user specifies.
12                                             The random numbers
13                                             are between zero
14                                             and one.
15   counter
16
17
18
19
20
     01-Jan-89  12:03 PM
```

Figure 11–5 Random Number Generation between Zero and One

11-10 Program 6 — Random Numbers Generation between Specific Limits

In the business world random numbers have many different applications, in the production process, in acceptance or rejection of a shipment, in process control, and so forth. In many cases the user may be interested in a random number which is within a certain limit. For example, you are interested in choosing a random number between 1 and 1,000. If this is the case, you have to do some modification of the @RAND function in order to generate a specific random number. The process is very simple.

1. Define your upper limit (in the above example, 1,000), U.
2. Define your lower limit (in the above example, 1), L.
3. Define the difference between the upper and lower limits (in the above example, 999), U-L.

The formula is (upper limit – lower limit + 1), multiply by the @RAND function, then add the lower limit. In order to generate only an integer portion of the number, you must use the @INT function. The whole formula is @INT((U –L+1)* @RAND+L). Figure 11–6 illustrates this process.

11-11 Program 7 — Many Random Numbers in Any Range

Program 7, shown in Figure 11–7, is an extension of program 6. This program follows the same pattern, but the user can define as many random numbers as he/she is interested in, and in any range.

11-12 Program 8 — Break-Even Analysis

There are many times when a businessperson is interested in calculating the break-even point of the operation. The break-even point is a production point at which there is no loss and no gain, i.e., the total revenue is equal to the total costs. To calculate the break-even point, the following items are needed:

1. FC — Total fixed costs or overhead such as rent and electricity.
2. VC — Variable costs per unit such as raw material and labor.
3. SP — Unit selling price.

The break-even point will be calculated by dividing (FC) by (SP-VC). The difference between SP and VC is called the contribution margin. For example, if FC = 500, VC = 10, SP = 15, the break-even point = 100 units. This means if you sell

Figure 11–6 Random Numbers between Specific Limits

```
AB14: 'Your random number is~                                        READY

        AA      AB        AC      AD       AE      AF       AG      AH
1    \j          {home}
2               This macro will generate one random number~
3               {down}
4               between a specified upper and lower bound~
5               {down 2}
6               What is your upper bound number?~
7               {goto}e4~
8               {?}~                                   This macro
9               {down}{left 4}                         generates one
10              What is your lower bound number?~      random number
11              {goto}e5~                               between a
12              {?}~                                    specified upper
13              {down 2}{left 4}                        and lower bound.
14              Your random number is~
15              {goto}e7~
16              @INT((+e4-e5+1)*@RAND+e5)~
17
18
19
20
01-Jan-89   12:03 PM
```

Figure 11–7 Many Random Numbers in Any Range

```
AB4: 'between a given upper and lower bound~                          READY

        AA      AB      AC      AD      AE      AF      AG      AH
1    \m         {home}
2            This macro will generate as many random numbers as you want~
3            {down}
4            between a given upper and lower bound~
5            {down 3}
6            How many random numbers do you want?~
7            {goto}e5~
8            {?}~
9            {down}{left 4}
10           What is your upper bound?~        This macro will generate
11           {goto}e6~                         as many random numbers
12           {?}~                              as the user specifies
13           {down}{left 4}                    between a specified upper
14           What is your lower bound?~        and lower bound.
15           {goto}e7~
16           {?}~
17           {goto}a10~
18           {FOR ab23,1,e5,1,ab20}
19
20   rand_num @INT((+e6-e7+1)*@RAND+e7)~
01-Jan-89  12:03 PM
```

Figure 11–7 (Continued)

```
AB24:                                                                READY

        AA      AB      AC      AD      AE      AF      AG      AH
21           {down}
22
23   counter         11
24
25
26
27
28
29
30
31
32
33
34
35
36
37
38
39
40
01-Jan-89  12:03 PM
```

less than 100 units, you are losing money; if you sell 100 units, no loss, no gain; if you sell more than 100 units, you are making a profit.

This simple formula can be very helpful when performing what-if analysis. You may ask yourself if the variable cost increases by one dollar, what would be the effect on the break-even point? Or if you reduce the selling price by one dollar, what would be the effect? Figure 11–8 illustrates this calculation in an interactive mode.

11-13 Program 9 — Economic Order Quantity

How much to order and when to order is a major concern for many businesses. Ordering large quantities may increase the cost of capital (tying up money, warehouse space, etc.). At the same time, ordering very small quantities may increase the ordering cost, cost of losing customers, and so on. A model known as the Economic Order Quantity (EOQ) has been utilized by many businesses for minimizing inventory cost. The outcome of this model is the optimum order quantity or the number of units to be ordered that will minimize the business's total inventory costs. This model utilizes the following formula and variables:

$$EOQ = \sqrt{\frac{2*A*B}{C*P}}$$

where A =   annual inventory requirements (annual sales)

B =   cost of placing an order (ordering cost)

C =   single unit cost (sales price)

P =   percentage of inventory value allotted for carrying costs

EOQ =   number of units to order that will minimize the business's total inventory cost.

This formula makes it possible for the user to compute the EOQ for many products with different selling prices and annual sales. Figure 11–9 illustrates this process in an interactive mode.

11-14 Program 10 — Tabulation Analysis

Program 10 is a simple example that keeps track of entries with different code numbers. The user can enter codes 1, 2, 3 and the program keeps track of how many units of each code has been entered. If the user responds with a code that is not 1, 2, or 3, Lotus will beep. The program will also provide a percentage tabulation result. Figure 11–10 shows this example.

Figure 11–8 Break-Even Analysis

```
AA1: '\g                                                           READY

          AA        AB        AC        AD        AE        AF        AG        AH
1    \g        {home}
2              What is the total fixed cost?~
3              {goto}f1~
4              {?}~
5              {down}{left 5}
6              What are the variable costs per unit?~
7              {goto}f2~                              This macro
8              {?}~                                   determines the
9              {down}{left 5}                         break-even point
10             What is the unit selling price?~       in units for a
11             {goto}f3~                              product based on
12             {?}~                                   the unit selling
13             {down 2}{left 5}                       price and the
14             The unit contribution to overhead is~  known production
15             {goto}f5~                              costs.
16             +f3-f2~
17             {down}{left 5}
18             The break-even point in units is~
19             {goto}f6~
20             +f1/f5~
01-Jan-89   12:04 PM
```

Figure 11–9 Economic Order Quantity

```
AA1: '\h                                                           READY

          AA        AB        AC        AD        AE        AF        AG        AH
1    \h        {home}
2              What is the single unit cost?~
3              {goto}g1~
4              {?}~
5              {down 2}{left 6}
6              What are the number of units sold annually?~
7              {goto}g3~
8              {?}~
9              {down 2}{left 6}
10             What is the cost of placing and handling an order?~
11             {goto}g5~
12             {?}~
13             {down 2}{left 6}
14             What is the percentage of inventory value allotted~
15             {down}
16             to carrying costs? (please answer using decimal)~
17             {goto}g8~
18             {?}~
19             {down 2}{left 6}
20             The economic order quanitity (EOQ) is~
01-Jan-89   12:04 PM
```

Figure 11–9 (Continued)

```
AA21:                                                                    READY

           AA       AB       AC       AD       AE       AF       AG       AH
21         {LET g10,@ROUND(@SQRT(2*g3*g5/(g8*g1)),0)}~
22
23
24
25
26
27              This macro determines the economic order quantity
28              that will minimize total inventory costs.
29
30
31
32
33
34
35
36
37
38
39
40
01-Jan-89   12:04 PM
```

Figure 11–10 Tabulation Analysis

```
AA1: '\j                                                                 READY

           AA       AB       AC       AD       AE       AF       AG       AH
1    \j         {home}
2               /rea6..e8~
3               This macro keeps totals for Republicans, Democrats and Others~
4               {down}
5               Republicans = 1~
6               {down}
7               Democrats = 2~
8               {down}
9               Others = 3~
10   \P         {goto}a6~
11              Please enter the code number~
12              {goto}e6~/RE~
13              {?}~
14              {IF e6=1}{BRANCH Rep_tot}
15              {IF e6=2}{BRANCH Dem_tot}
16              {IF e6=3}{BRANCH Other}
17              {down}{left 4}
18              You have not entered a proper code number, please try again~
19              {BEEP 2}
20              {WAIT @now+@time(0,0,10)}~/RE~
01-Jan-89   12:05 PM
```

Figure 11-10 (Continued)

```
AA21:                                                                    READY

        AA       AB        AC        AD        AE        AF        AG        AH
21               {BRANCH \P}                             This macro uses branching
22                                                       routines to keep track of
23  Rep_tot  {LET i10,i10+1}                             the total number of
24           {BRANCH Gr_tot}                             Republicans, Democrats,
25                                                       and Others.  It then
26  Dem_tot  {LET i11,i11+1}                             converts the total for
27           {BRANCH Gr_tot}                             each category to a
28                                                       percentage of the grand
29  Other    {LET i12,i12+1}                             total.
30           {BRANCH Gr_tot}
31
32  Gr_tot   {goto}a8~
33           Do you have another entry? Choose (Y)es or (N)o~
34           {GET answer}/RE~
35           {IF answer="Y"}{BRANCH \P}
36           {goto}a10~
37           The total number of Republicans is~/mi10..i10~e10~
38           {down}
39           The total number of Democrats is~/mi11..i11~e11~
40           {down}
01-Jan-89  12:05 PM
```

Figure 11-10 (Continued)

```
AA41:                                                                    READY

        AA       AB        AC        AD        AE        AF        AG        AH
41               The total number of Others is~/mi12..i12~e12~
42               {down 2}
43               The percentage of Republicans is~
44               {goto}e14~
45               +e10/(+e10+e11+e12)~
46               /rfp2~e14~
47               {down}{left 4}
48               The percentage of Democrats is~
49               {goto}e15~
50               +e11/(+e10+e11+e12)~
51               /rfp2~e15~
52               {down}{left 4}
53               The percentage of Others is~
54               {goto}e16~
55               +e12/(+e10+e11+e12)~
56               /rfp2~e16~
57
58  answer   N
59
60
01-Jan-89  12:05 PM
```

11-15 Programs 11, 12, and 13 — Depreciation Assessment

As you saw in Chapter 4, Lotus provides functions for three depreciation calculations: straight line, sum-of-the-years digits depreciation, and double-declining balance. Figures 11–11, 11–12, and 11–13 illustrate the macro version of these functions.

```
AA1: '\d                                                            READY

        AA       AB       AC       AD       AE       AF       AG       AH
1    \d       {home}
2             What is the cost?~                       This macro calculates
3             {goto}e1~                                straight-line depreciation
4             {?}~                                     based on the cost, the
5             {down}{left 4}                           salvage value, and the
6             What is the salvage value?~              economic life of a
7             {goto}e2~                                given asset.
8             {?}~
9             {down}{left 4}
10            What is the economic life (in year)?~
11            {goto}e3~
12            {?}~
13            {down}{down}{left 4}
14            Straight-line depreciation is~
15            {goto}e5~
16            @SLN(e1,e2,e3)~
17            {quit}
18
19
20
01-Jan-89  12:05 PM
```

Figure 11–11 Straight-Line Depreciation

Figure 11–12 Sum-of-the-Years Digits Depreciation

```
AB10: 'What is the economic life (in year)?~                           READY

        AA        AB        AC        AD        AE        AF        AG        AH
1    \f        {home}
2              What is the cost?~
3              {goto}f1~
4              {?}~
5              {down}{left 5}
6              What is the salvage value?~
7              {goto}f2~
8              {?}~
9              {down}{left 5}                        This macro calculates
10             What is the economic life (in year)?sum-of-the-years'digits
11             {goto}f3~                             depreciation based on the
12             {?}~                                  cost, the salvage value,
13             {down 3}{left 5}                      and the economic life
14             {LET a7,Period}                       of a given asset.
15             {LET c7,SYD depreciation}
16             {goto}a9~
17             {FOR h1,1,f3,1,ab19}
18
19   calc_rtn  +h1~
20             /rv~~
01-Jan-89  10:31 AM
```

Figure 11–12 (Continued)

```
AB30:                                                                 READY

        AA        AB        AC        AD        AE        AF        AG        AH
21             {right 2}
22             @SYD(f1,f2,f3,h1)~
23             /rv~~
24             {down}{left 2}
25
26
27
28
29
30
31
32
33
34
35
36
37
38
39
40
01-Jan-89  10:32 AM
```

Figure 11–13 Double-Declining-Balance Depreciation

```
AA1: '\e                                                                    READY

         AA       AB        AC       AD       AE       AF       AG       AH
1    \e          {home}
2               What is the cost?~
3               {goto}e1~
4               {?}~
5               {down}{left 4}
6               What is the salvage value?~
7               {goto}e2~
8               {?}~                           This macro calculates
9               {down}{left 4}                 double-declining-balance
10              What is the economic life?~    depreciation based on the
11              {goto}e3~                      cost, the salvage value,
12              {?}~                           and the economic life
13              {down}{left 4}                 of a given asset.
14              {LET a7,Period}
15              {LET c7,DDB depreciation}
16              {goto}a9~
17              {FOR h1,1,e3,1,ab19}
18
19   calc_rtn +h1~
20              /rv~~
01-Jan-89  11:22 AM
```

Figure 11–13 (Continued)

```
AA21:                                                                       READY

         AA       AB        AC       AD       AE       AF       AG       AH
21              {right 2}
22              @DDB(e1,e2,e3,h1)~
23              /rv~~
24              {down}{left 2}
25
26
27
28
29
30
31
32
33
34
35
36
37
38
39
40
01-Jan-89  11:23 AM
```

Summary

In this chapter we have seen that Lotus macros can be used as a super programming language. Basic structures such as sequence, selection, iteration, and CASE can be performed by macros. We reviewed the principles of programming and the program development life cycle. Several simple examples highlighted the application of Lotus macros as a programming language. In the next two chapters you will see more diverse applications of Lotus macros.

Review Questions

1. What is a program development life cycle?
2. Why is problem definition so important?
3. Why is program documentation important?
4.* How many types of documentation do we have?
5. What is the difference between external and internal documentation?
6. What are some of the tools for external documentation?
7.* Logic design methodology is useful for eliminating and reducing one type of error. What kind of error?
8. What is modular programming?
9. What are some of the advantages of modular programming?
10. What is structured programming?
11.* Why has structured programming become so popular?
12. Can Lotus be used as a full-fledged structured programming language? If yes, why? If no, why not?
13.* Why do we use random numbers?
14. What are some of the business applications of random numbers?
15. What is the break-even point? How is it calculated?
16. What is EOQ? How is it calculated?
17.* What is nested subroutine? What are some uses of this type of subroutine?
18.* What are some of the advantages of using macros to calculate depreciation methods?
19. Extend the macro presented in Figure 11–10 in order to generate a bar graph from 10 sets of data; for example, three of code 1, five of code 2, and two of code 3.
20. Design a macro that accepts grades A-F, then calculates a G.P.A. Also, your program should print the following message:

Excellent	for G.P.A. >= 3.8
Good	for G.P.A. >= 3.5
Average	for G.P.A. >= 2.5
In trouble	for G.P.A. <= 2.0

21. Design a macro to generate a mailing list. The output should include three lines as follows:

    First Name   Last Name
    Street Address
    City, State, Zip

    Your macro must accept any number of data items, then generate a mailing label.

12

Lotus Applications in Specific Disciplines/Part One

12-1 Introduction

As you have seen throughout this book, Lotus can perform an unlimited number of applications. In Chapters 12 and 13 we would like to show you some more specific applications using Lotus macros. This chapter includes five applications in the areas of production, finance, capital budgeting, accounting, and forecasting. These applications are more suited to a business environment. The applications presented in Chapter 13 are more diverse.

12-2 Production Analysis

Suppliers of perishable products and those in service businesses face a serious question: How much to supply in order to satisfy demand but not to oversupply? Spoilage or extra service is a problem. One method for minimizing the cost of oversupply and/or undersupply is known as expected opportunity loss. The following example explains the way this method works.

The manager of Always-Open Rental Car Company is faced with the question of how many rental cars to make available for customers. Oversupply and undersupply is a problem. Past experience shows that the number of rental cars demanded ranges from 15 to 21 with the following probabilities:

15	.12
16	.12
17	.10

18	.08
19	.20
20	.25
21	.13

How many cars should the Always-Open Rental Car Company make available in order to minimize the supply cost? The cost of renting a car for this company is $20 and customers pay $28 for renting a car.

The following table is known as the opportunity loss table. Whenever the supply is equal to demand there is no opportunity loss. Each unit of oversupply will cost the company $20. Each unit of undersupply will have an $8 opportunity cost (the company could have been able to make this much profit).

Opportunity Loss Table for Always-Open Rental Car Company

NUMBER OF RENTAL CARS DEMANDED	PROBABILITY OF PAST DEMAND	NUMBER OF RENTAL CARS SUPPLIED						
		15	16	17	18	19	20	21
15	.12	0	20	40	60	80	100	120
16	.12	8	0	20	40	60	80	100
17	.10	16	8	0	20	40	60	80
18	.08	24	16	8	0	20	40	60
19	.20	32	24	16	8	0	20	40
20	.25	40	32	24	16	8	0	20
21	.13	48	40	32	24	16	8	0

The expected opportunity loss of supplying 15 cars is $27.12, as follows: 0(12) + 8(.12) + 16(.10) + 24(.08) + 32(.20) + 40(.25) + 48(.13) = 27.12 The expected opportunity loss for the other units of supply is as follows:

15	27.12
16	22.48
17	21.20
18	22.72
19	26.48
20	35.84
21	52.20

As we see, supplying 17 cars has the minimum opportunity cost.

We have developed a macro-based program to calculate the opportunity loss for various levels of demand. The macro can plot a graph if your computer has graphics capability. Figure 12–1 shows the documentation, the macro-based program, and the execution of the program.

12-3 Financial Analysis

To measure the financial strength of a company many analysts use financial statement analysis. In order to perform this task a series of ratios are computed and compared with those of other companies in the same industry or with the past years of the company itself. However, ratio analysis for determining a company's financial strength can be misleading. These ratios can be manipulated in order not to reflect a company's actual financial situation. But if these ratios are calculated periodically in a straightforward manner, they can be a good basis for further financial investigation. Some of the most commonly used ratios are as follows:

Return on investment:

R = I/E, where:
R = return on investment
I = net income
E = owners' equity

Earnings per share:

G = I/S, where:
G = earnings per share
I = net income
S = number of shares outstanding

Figure 12-1 Documentation for Opportunity Loss Table

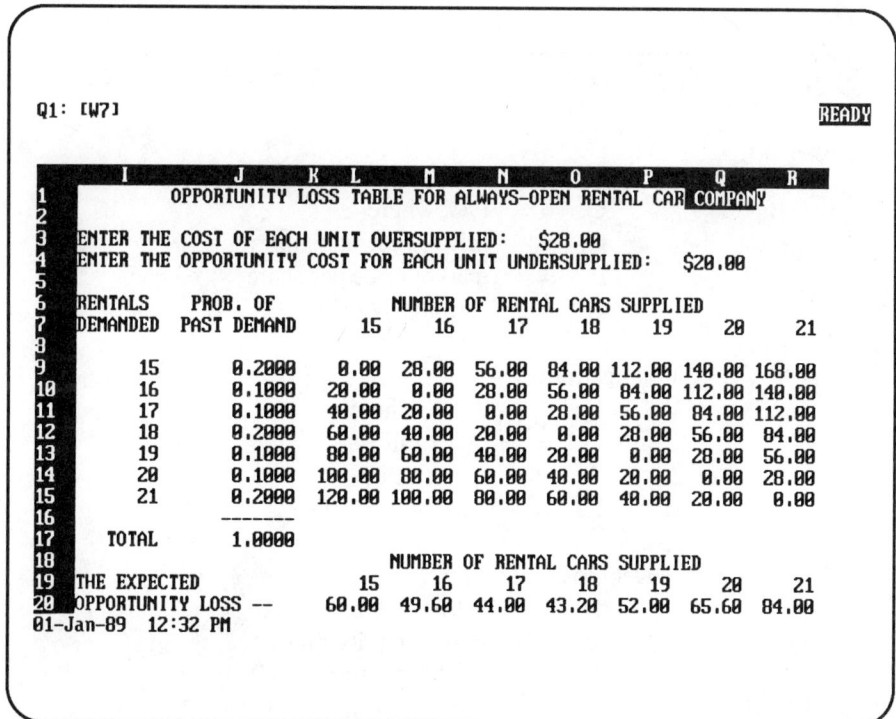

```
Q1: [W7]                                                                    READY


          I       J       K   L       M       N       O       P       Q       R
1                OPPORTUNITY LOSS TABLE FOR ALWAYS-OPEN RENTAL CAR COMPANY
2
3  ENTER THE COST OF EACH UNIT OVERSUPPLIED:     $20.00
4  ENTER THE OPPORTUNITY COST FOR EACH UNIT UNDERSUPPLIED:    $20.00
5
6  RENTALS   PROB. OF          NUMBER OF RENTAL CARS SUPPLIED
7  DEMANDED  PAST DEMAND    15      16      17      18      19      20      21
8
9      15      0.2000     0.00   28.00   56.00   84.00  112.00  140.00  168.00
10     16      0.1000    20.00    0.00   28.00   56.00   84.00  112.00  140.00
11     17      0.1000    40.00   20.00    0.00   28.00   56.00   84.00  112.00
12     18      0.2000    60.00   40.00   20.00    0.00   28.00   56.00   84.00
13     19      0.1000    80.00   60.00   40.00   20.00    0.00   28.00   56.00
14     20      0.1000   100.00   80.00   60.00   40.00   20.00    0.00   28.00
15     21      0.2000   120.00  100.00   80.00   60.00   40.00   20.00    0.00
16              -------
17   TOTAL     1.0000
18                                NUMBER OF RENTAL CARS SUPPLIED
19 THE EXPECTED            15      16      17      18      19      20      21
20 OPPORTUNITY LOSS --   60.00   49.60   44.00   43.20   52.00   65.60   84.00
01-Jan-89  12:32 PM
```

```
\C    |PANELOFF||GOTO|INAREA~|GOTO|OVER~  *--- To enter the data ---*
      |GETNUMBER "Enter the cost of oversupplied: ",OVER|
      |GOTO|UNDER~
      |GETNUMBER "Enter the Opp. cost of undersupplied: ",UNDER|
      |GOTO|LOWER~
      |GETNUMBER "Enter the minimum car demanded: ",LOWER|
      |GOTO|PROB15~/re.|down 6|~
PROBAB/RETEMP~        *--- Entering the probability for each event ---*
      |MENUCALL WARN|
      |GETNUMBER "Enter the probability of the cars demanded: ",PROB15|
      |DOWN||LET TEMP,TEMP+PROB15|~
      |GETNUMBER "Enter the probability of the cars demanded: ",PROB16|
      |DOWN||LET TEMP,TEMP+PROB16|~
      |GETNUMBER "Enter the probability of the cars demanded: ",PROB17|
      |DOWN||LET TEMP,TEMP+PROB17|~
      |GETNUMBER "Enter the probability of the cars demanded: ",PROB18|
      |DOWN||LET TEMP,TEMP+PROB18|~
      |GETNUMBER "Enter the probability of the cars demanded: ",PROB19|
      |DOWN||LET TEMP,TEMP+PROB19|~
      |GETNUMBER "Enter the probability of the cars demanded: ",PROB20|
      |DOWN||LET TEMP,TEMP+PROB20|~
      |GETNUMBER "Enter the probability of the cars demanded: ",PROB21|
      |LET TEMP,TEMP+PROB21|~|GOTO|PROB15~|PANELON|
      |IF TEMP=1||BRANCH RESULT|
      |GETLABEL "The total prob.<>1, please hit <RET> and reenter.",JUNK|
      |GOTO|PROB15~|BRANCH PROBAB|~

JUNK2         *--- Temporary storage ---*

JUNK  Y       *--- Temporary storage ---*

RESULT|GOTO|OUTPUT~      *--- Arrange the result and draw the graph ---*
      /DSDDATA~PPRIMARY~A~G~|GOTO|BEST~
      |GETLABEL "Enter `Y' or `y' to see the graph: ",JUNK|
      |IF JUNK<>"Y"||QUIT|~
      |IF JUNK<>"y"||QUIT|~
      /GRGTLXXAXIS~AVALUE~
      OSYFCO~QTFTHE OPPORTUNITY LOSS GRAPH~
      TXCARS SUPPLIED~TYTHE EXPECTED OPPORTUNITY LOSS~QQ
      |GETLABEL "Hit <RET> & F10 keys to see the graph. ",JUNK2|

WARN  Now enter the probability of each event and watch out for the total.
      Make sure it is not more than 1. Hit <Return>
              *--- Warning label for entering the probability ---*
```

Figure 12–1 (Continued) Macro-Based Program for Opportunity Loss Analysis

Price to earnings ratio:

C = P/G, where

C = price to earnings ratio

P = market price per share

G = earnings per share

Quick ratio:

Q = $A/L1$, where

Q = quick ratio

A = quick assets

$L1$ = current liabilities

Debt to equity ratio:

D = $L2/E$, where:

D = debt to equity ratio

$L2$ = total liabilities

E = owner's equity

Figure 12–1 Execution of Macro-Based Program for Opportunity Loss Analysis

```
**********************************************************************
                          DOCUMENTATION
**********************************************************************
THE PURPOSE OF THIS PROGRAM:
     To calculate the opportunity cost of over- and undersupplying
     rental cars for a fictitious car rental company.  It will calculate
     the opportunity cost and give the result according to the lowest
     opportunity cost.  It will also draw the opportunity cost graph.

INSTRUCTIONS:
  1. The macro for this program can be activated by pressing <ALT> and C
     keys simultaneously.

  2. You will be asked to enter several inputs while running the
     program.

  3. The first input is the cost of oversupplying per car, followed by
     the opportunity cost of undersupplying per car. Then you will be
     asked to enter the minimum number of rental cars demanded, then the
     probability for each demand. For example, if the probability of a
     certain number of cars is 12%, enter the probability as 0.12.

  4. If you made any mistakes, hit <CTRL> and <BREAK> keys
     simultaneously.  Hit <ESC> keys and follow step 1 to start again.

LIMITATIONS:
  1. The range of the cars calculated is limited to the [(minimum
     demanded) + additional 6 cars].

  2. You are not allowed to make any changes to the table.
```

Figure 12–1 (Continued)

```
Q21: (F2) [W7]                                                    READY

        I         J        K   L      M      N     O    P     Q     R
21
22 BELOW IS THE TABLE FOR THE OPPORTUNITY LOSS TABLE FOR THE CARS SUPPLIED
23 ARRANGED ACCORDING TO THE LOWEST OPPORTUNITY LOSS
24
25      CARS       OPPOR.
26   SUPPLIED       COST
27         18      $43.20    <------ The optimal solution
28         17      $44.00
29         16      $49.60
30         19      $52.00
31         15      $60.00
32         20      $65.60
33         21      $84.00
34
35
36
37
38
39
40
01-Jan-89   12:33 PM
```

We have developed a macro-based program to calculate seven of these ratios. The program is fully interactive. Figure 12–2 shows the documentation, the macro-based program, and the actual execution of the macro-based program.

12-4 Capital Budgeting Analysis

Many financial analyses are classified under the capital budgeting domain. Present value, future value, internal rate of return, and return on investment are some of the most important techniques used in capital budgeting analysis. To show a simple

Figure 12–2 Documentation for Macro-Based Financial Analysis Program

```
***********************************************************************
                            DOCUMENTATION
***********************************************************************
THE PURPOSE OF THE PROGRAM:
     This program will produce a balance sheet and an income statement
     and calculate the financial ratios for a fictitious company after
     the user has entered the values for the different variables upon
     request.

INSTRUCTIONS:
  1. The macro for this program can be activated by pressing <ALT> and
     A keys simultaneously.

  2. The user will be asked to input the values while the program is
     executing.

  3. The first section will ask the inputs for the company's assets. The
     inputs are: CASH, ACCOUNTS RECEIVABLE, INVENTORY, LONG-TERM
     INVESTMENTS, PLANT & EQUIPMENT, and ACCUMULATED DEPRECIATION.

  4. The second section will ask the inputs for the company's
     liabilities and owners' equity. The inputs are: ACCOUNTS
     PAYABLE, TAXES PAYABLE, BONDS PAYABLE, COMMON STOCK, and RETAINED
     EARNINGS.

  5. The program will check the balance of the balance sheet.  It will
     alert the user if the balance sheet is not balanced.

  6. The third section will ask the inputs for the company's income
     statement. It will calculate the company's income. The inputs
     are: SALES, COST OF GOODS SOLD, SELLING EXPENSES, ADMINISTRATIVE
     EXPENSES, INTEREST EXPENSES, and CORPORATE TAX LEVEL.

  7. The fourth section is where all the financial ratios are. They are:
     A. EARNINGS PER SHARE    = Net Income / (Common Stock / Par Value).
     B. PRICE-EARNINGS RATIO  = Stock Price / Earnings Per Share.
     C. RETURN ON ASSETS      = (Net Inc.+(Int.Exp.*(1-Income Tax)))/
                                Total Assets.
     D. QUICK RATIO           = (Current Asset - Inventory)/Current
                                Liabilities.
     E. CURRENT RATIO         = Current Assets/Current Liabilities.
     F. DEBT TO EQUITY RATIO  = (Current Liabilities + Bonds)/Total
                                Stockholders' Equity.
     G. RETURN ON INVESTMENT  = Net Income / Stockholders' Equity.

  8. When you are done entering all the inputs, a menu will appear. Use
     the cursor keys to make the selection and hit <RETURN>.

  9. If you made any mistakes while entering the inputs, hit <CTRL>
     and <BREAK> keys simultaneously followed by <ESC>.  Repeat
     step 1 to start again.

LIMITATIONS:
  1. The user may not change the format of the balance sheet and income
     statement because it is predefined.
```

```
\A   |GOTO|BALANCE~|GOTO|CASH~          *--- To enter the input to Balance Sheet ---*
     |GETNUMBER "Enter the cash amount: ",CASH||DOWN|
     |GETNUMBER "Enter the amount acc. receivable: ",ACC.REC||DOWN|
     |GETNUMBER "Enter the amount on Inventory: ",INV||GOTO|LT.INV~
     |GETNUMBER "Enter the amount of Long Term Investment: ",LT.INV|
     |GOTO|PLANT~
     |GETNUMBER "Enter the amount of Plant & Equipment: ",PLANT|
     |GOTO|DEPRE~
     |GETNUMBER "Enter the amount of Depreciation: ",DEPRE||GOTO|TOT.AS.~
     /reOFF~|LET OFF,OFF+TOT.AS.|~
     |GETLABEL "Hit <RETURN> key to go to the LIABILITIES section",JUNK|
     |PGDN||GOTO|ACC.PAY~          *--- Liabilities & Owners' Equities Section ---*
     |GETNUMBER "Enter the amount of Account Payable: ",ACC.PAY|
     |LET OFF,OFF-ACC.PAY|~
     |GOTO|TAX.PAY~
     |GETNUMBER "Enter the amount of Taxes Payable: ",TAX.PAY|
     |LET OFF,OFF-TAX.PAY|~
     |GOTO|BONDS~
     |GETNUMBER "Enter the amount of Bonds Payables: ",BONDS|
     |LET OFF,OFF-BONDS|~
     |GOTO|STOCK~
     |GETNUMBER "Enter the amount of Common Stock: ",STOCK|
     |LET OFF,OFF-STOCK|~
     |GOTO|RET.EARN~
     |GETNUMBER "Enter the amount of Retained Earnings: ",RET.EARN|
     |LET OFF,OFF-RET.EARN|~
     |GOTO|TOT.EQ~|IF (TOT.AS.-TOT.EQ)>0||BRANCH NO|~
     |IF (TOT.EQ-TOT.AS.)>0||BRANCH NOT|
     |GETLABEL "Hit <RET> to go to the INCOME STATEMENT. ",JUNK|
     |GOTO|R1~|GOTO|SALES~          *--- Income Statement Section ---*
     |GETNUMBER "Enter the amount Sales: ",SALES||GOTO|COGS~
     |GETNUMBER "Enter the amount of Cost Of Goods Sold: ",COGS|
     |GOTO|SELL.EXP~
     |GETNUMBER "Enter the amount of Selling Expenses: ",SELL.EXP|
     |GOTO|AD.EXP.~
     |GETNUMBER "Enter the amount of Advertising Expenses: ",AD.EXP.|
     |GOTO|INT.EXP~
     |GETNUMBER "Enter the amount of Interest Expenses: ",INT.EXP|
     |GOTO|TAX~
     |GETNUMBER "Enter the corporate tax level (in percent): ",TAX||GOTO|NI~
     |GETLABEL "Hit <RET> to go to the calculated RATIOS. ",JUNK|
     |GOTO|Z1~|GOTO|ST.PRICE~          *--- Financial Ratios ---*
     |GETNUMBER "Enter the price of the stock:",ST.PRICE|~
     |GETLABEL "Hit <RETURN> key to get the menu.",JUNK|
     |GETLABEL "Use the cursor keys to make your choice and hit <RETURN>.",JUNK|
O    |MENUBRANCH MENU|

MENUAssets          Liabilities      Income Statement     Financial Ratios     Quit
     View Total AsseView Total LiabilitiView Income StatemenView Financial RatioTo QUIT the program.
     |GOTO|INPUT~     |GOTO|SECOND~     |GOTO|INC~          |GOTO|z1~          |QUIT|
     |BRANCH O|       |BRANCH O|        |BRANCH O|          |BRANCH O|

               *--- Menu for the result ---*
junk

NO   |BEEP 3|~
     |GETLABEL "TOTAL ASSETS is more than TOTAL LIABILITIES & OWNERS' EQUITIES.",JUNK|
     |BRANCH \A|~

NOT  |BEEP 3|~
     |GETLABEL "TOTAL LIABILITIES & OWNERS' EQUITIES is more than TOTAL ASSETS.",JUNK|
     |BRANCH \A|~
```

Figure 12–2 (Continued) Macro-Based Program Performing Financial Analysis

Figure 12–2 (Continued) Execution of Macro-Based Financial Analysis Program

```
Q1: [W3]                                                          READY

      I   J   K       L       M       N       O       P       Q
1
2                           BALANCE SHEET
3    ================================================================
4                             ASSETS                        19XX
5    CURRENT ASSETS:
6        CASH ........................................... $4,309,000
7        ACCOUNTS RECEIVABLE ............................  2,070,000
8        INVENTORY .....................................    580,000
9                                                        -----------
10           TOTAL CURRENT ASSETS .......................  6,959,000
11
12   LONG-TERM INVESTMENT ..............................    500,400
13   PLANT & EQUIPMENT .....................     400,500
14   LESS: ACCUMULATED DEPRECIATION ........      58,000
15                                            -----------
16   NET PLANT & EQUIPMENT .............................    342,500
17                                                        -----------
18   TOTAL ASSETS ...................................... $7,859,900
19                                                        ===========
20
01-Jan-89   12:33 PM
```

Figure 12–2 (Continued)

```
Q21: [W3]                                                         READY

      I   J   K       L       M       N       O       P       Q
21
22              CURRENT LIABILITIES AND OWNERS' EQUITY
23   ================================================================
24   CURRENT LIABILITIES
25       ACCOUNTS PAYABLE .............................. $4,000,500
26       TAXES PAYABLE .................................  2,000,500
27                                                       ------------
28           TOTAL CURRENT LIABILITIES ..................  6,001,000
29   BONDS PAYABLE .....................................    550,000
30
31   STOCKHOLDERS' EQUITY
32       COMMON STOCK,  $15.00 par value ..........   150,000
33       RETAINED EARNINGS ...................... 1,158,900
34                                                -----------
35           TOTAL STOCKHOLDERS' EQUITY .............  1,308,900
36                                                       ------------
37   TOTAL LIABILITIES & STOCKHOLDERS' EQUITY .......... $7,859,900
38                                                       ============
39       This balance sheet is off by          $0
40
01-Jan-89   12:34 PM
```

Figure 12–2 (Continued)

```
R1: [W4]                                                              READY

        R   S      T        U              V            W          X      Y
1                              INCOME STATEMENT
2       ===========================================================
3                                              19XX
4       SALES .........................................  $7,800,000
5       COST OF GOODS SOLD ............................   1,500,000
6                                                        ----------
7       GROSS MARGIN ..................................   6,300,000
8       OPERATING EXPENSES
9            SELLING EXPENSES ...............    900,500
10           ADMINISTRATIVE EXPENSES ........  1,250,000
11                                             ----------
12           TOTAL OPERATING EXPENSES ..................   2,150,500
13                                                        ----------
14      NET OPERATING INCOME  .........................   4,149,500
15      INTEREST EXPENSES .............................      15,000
16                                                        ----------
17      NET INCOME BEFORE TAXES .......................   4,134,500
18      INCOME TAXES AT    46% ........................   2,232,630
19                                                        ==========
20      NET INCOME ....................................  $1,901,870
01-Jan-89  12:34 PM
```

Figure 12–2 (Continued)

```
AH1: \=                                                               READY

        Z      AA     AB    AC    AD     AE     AF     AG       AH
1       ============================================================
2                          FINANCIAL RATIOS
3       ============================================================
4
5            1. EARNINGS PER SHARE .........................  $190.19
6
7            2. PRICE-EARNINGS RATIO
8               ASSUMING STOCK MARKET PRICE AT $29 .........   0.1525
9
10           3. RETURN ON ASSETS ...........................   0.2430
11
12           4. QUICK RATIO ................................   1.0630
13
14           5. CURRENT RATIO ..............................   1.1596
15
16           6. DEBT TO EQUITY RATIO .......................   5.0050
17
18           7. RETURN ON INVESTMENT .......................   1.4530
19
20
01-Jan-89  12:35 PM
```

example, we have developed a macro-based program designed to calculate net present value (NPV), internal rate of return (IRR), and the profitability index (PI). Figure 12–3 shows the documentation, the macro-based program, and the execution of this macro-based program.

Figure 12–3 Documentation for Capital Budgeting Problems

```
*********************************************************************
                          DOCUMENTATION
*********************************************************************
THE PURPOSE OF THE PROGRAM:
     To calculate the NPV, IRR, and PI of a proposed project of
     replacing an old machine with a new automated machine.  The old
     machine is currently operated by a worker. The new machine
     requires no worker to operate it.

INSTRUCTIONS:
     1. To activate the macro for this program, press <ALT> and Q keys
        simultaneously.

     2. You will be asked to enter the inputs while running the program.

     3. The first part of the program will ask the information on the old
        equipment: all the costs associated with the old equipment, the
        original price, the expected salvage value, the expected life
        (from beginning), and the current age of the equipment. The
        corporate tax level and the required rate of return are asked in
        this module.

     4. The second part will ask for the information on the new proposed
        equipment. It will ask for the costs of the machine, delivered
        and installed. It will also ask for the expected economic life
        of the machine and expected salvage value after 10 years of
        service.

     5. The third part will show the initial cash outlay for the project.

     6. The fourth part will show the calculation of the cash flow for the
        project. It will calculate all the savings deducted by the costs
        and taxes giving the annual cash flow after taxes.

     7. The last part will show the yearly cash flow, the calculated net
        present value, profitability index, and internal rate of return.
        The conclusion will be given depending on the NPV, IRR and PI.
        The formula used:
        NPV = @NPV(Com. Req. Rate of Return, CashFlow) - Initial
              Cash outflow
        PI  = NPV / ABS(Initial Cash outflow)
        IRR = @IRR (Com. Req. Rate of Return, Cash inflow +
              Initial Cash outflow)

     8. If you make a mistake, hit <CTRL> & <BREAK> keys simultaneously
        to stop the program. To start all over again, hit <ESC> and
        follow step 1.

LIMITATIONS:
     1. The tables are predefined, so you have to follow the instructions
        while running the program.

     2. The cash flow will be calculated for only 10 years.

     3. Depreciation is calculated using the straight-line method.

     4. You are not allowed to make any changes to the table.
```

```
\Q  {GOTO}INPUT~{PANELOFF}                    *--- The Current Situation Data ---*
    {GETLABEL "Hit <RETURN> key and enter the current situation data.",JUNK}{GOTO}CSSALARY~
    {GETNUMBER "Enter the salary of the worker (per annum): ",CSSALARY}
    {DOWN}
    {GETNUMBER "Enter the overtime pay (per annum): ",CSO/TIME}
    {DOWN}
    {GETNUMBER "Enter the fringe benefits (insur.,paid vacation, etc. per annum): ",CSBENEFIT}
    {DOWN}
    {GETNUMBER "Enter the cost of defects (per annum) caused by the machine: ",CSDEFECT}
    {DOWN}
    {GETNUMBER "Enter the original price of the machine: ",CSPRICE}
    {DOWN}
    {GETNUMBER "What's the expected life (from beginning) of the old machine: ",CSLIFE}
    {DOWN}
    {GETNUMBER "Enter the expected salvage value of the machine: ",CSSALVAGE}
    {DOWN}
    {GETNUMBER "How old is the machine: ",CSAGE}
    {DOWN 2}
    {GETNUMBER "What's the current book value of old machine: ",CSCURSALVAGE}
    {DOWN}
    {GETNUMBER "Enter the annual maintenance: ",CSMAINTAIN}
    {DOWN}
    {GETNUMBER "Enter the marginal tax rate (in percent): ",CSTAX}
    {DOWN}
    {GETNUMBER "Enter the company required rate of return (in percent): ",CSRROR}{DOWN}
    {GETLABEL "Hit <RETURN> key to go to the proposed situation section",JUNK}
    {GOTO}I21~      *--- The Proposed Situation Data ---*
    {GETLABEL "Hit <RETURN> key and enter the data for the new machine",JUNK}
    {GOTO}PSCOST~
    {GETNUMBER "Enter the cost of new machine: ",PSCOST}
    {DOWN}
    {GETNUMBER "Enter the shipping fee: ",PSFEE}
    {DOWN}
    {GETNUMBER "Enter the installation cost: ",PSINSTALL}
    {DOWN}
    {GETNUMBER "Enter the expected life of new machine: ",PSLIFE}
    {GOTO}PSSALVAGE~
    {GETNUMBER "Enter the expected salvage value of new machine: ",PSSALVAGE}
    {DOWN}
    {GETNUMBER "Enter the expected annual maintenance cost: ",PSMAINTAIN}
    {DOWN}
    {GETNUMBER "What's the exp. cost of defects caused by the new machine (per annum):",PSDEFECT}
    {GETLABEL "Hit the <RETURN> key to get the menu. ",JUNK}
O   {menubranch AX}

TEMP                      *--- Temporary Storage ---*

JUNK                      *--- Temporary Storage ---*

AX  Initial Cash Outlay  CashFlow Section  The Conclusion    QUIT
    The calculation of IThe calculation oThe Results (NPV,Quit the program.
    {GOTO}I41~           {GOTO}I61~         {GOTO}I81~        {PANELON}
    {BRANCH O}           {BRANCH O}         {BRANCH O}        {QUIT}

    *--- The Menu to see the RESULT ---*
```

Figure 12–3 Macro-Based Program Performing Capital Budgeting Analysis

Figure 12–3 (Cont.) Execution of the Macro-Based Capital Budgeting Program

```
P1: \x                                                              READY

      I    J        K        L        M        N        O        P
1  xxxxxxxxxxxxxxxxxxxxxxxxxxxxxxxxxxxxxxxxxxxxxxxxxxxxxxxxxxxxxxxxx
2              INPUT SECTION
3  xxxxxxxxxxxxxxxxxxxxxxxxxxxxxxxxxxxxxxxxxxxxxxxxxxxxxxxxxxxxxxxxx
4                 PART ONE:
5
6  Current Situation:
7      Salary one full-time worker ....................... $12,000 /per year
8      Overtime pay ...................................... $1,000 /per year
9      Fringe Benefits ................................... $2,000 /per year
10     Cost of defect .................................... $1,000 /per year
11     Original price of hand-operated machine .......... $20,000
12     Expected life ..................................... 20 years
13     Salvage value ..................................... $0
14     Age of the machine ................................ 5 years
15     Depreciation method ............................... Straight line
16     Current salvage value ............................. $5,000
17     Annual maintenance ................................ $1,500
18     Tax rate .......................................... 46.8%
19     Required rate of return ........................... 16.7%
20
01-Jan-89  12:35 PM
```

Figure 12–3 (Continued)

```
P21:                                                                READY

      I    J        K        L        M        N        O        P
21
22
23                       PART TWO:
24
25 Proposed Situation: Automated operation
26     Cost of machine ................................... $50,000
27     Shipping fee ...................................... $500
28     Installation cost ................................. $450
29     Expected economic life ............................ 20 years
30     Depreciation method ............................... Straight line
31     Salvage value after 10 years ..................... $0
32     Annual maintenance ................................ $350
33     Cost of defect .................................... $250 /per year
34
35
36
37
38
39
40
01-Jan-89  12:35 PM
```

Figure 12-3 (Continued)

```
P41: \x                                                          READY

        I    J      K      L        M       N       O        P
41  xxxxxxxxxxxxxxxxxxxxxxxxxxxxxxxxxxxxxxxxxxxxxxxxxxxxxxxxxxxxxxxxxxx
42                    OUTPUT SECTION
43  xxxxxxxxxxxxxxxxxxxxxxxxxxxxxxxxxxxxxxxxxxxxxxxxxxxxxxxxxxxxxxxxxxx
44
45
46                      Initial Outlay
47  Outflows
48      Cost of new machine .........................    $50,000
49      Shipping fee ................................       500
50      Installation cost ...........................       450
51      Increased taxes .............................    (4,600)
52  Inflows
53      Salvage value-old machine ...............   -    5,000
54                                                       -------
55      Net Initial Outlay ..........................    $41,350
56
57
58
59
60
01-Jan-89   12:36 PM
```

Figure 12-3 (Continued)

```
P61:                                                             READY

        I    J      K      L        M       N       O        P
61
62                                                    Non-cash
63  Calculation of Differential Cash Flows            flow profit  Cash Flow
64  Savings:
65      Reduced salary ..............................    $12,000   $12,000
66      Reduced overtime ............................      1,000     1,000
67      Reduced fringe benefits .....................      2,000     2,000
68      Reduced defects .............................        750       750
69  Costs:
70      Increased maintenance expenses ..............      (350)     (350)
71      Increased depreciation expenses .............    (1,548)
72                                                       -------   -------
73  Net savings before taxes ........................    $13,853   $15,400
74  Taxes ...........................................      6,372     6,372
75                                                       -------   -------
76  Net Cash Flow after taxes .......................              $9,028
77
78
79
80
01-Jan-89   12:36 PM
```

```
P81:                                                           READY

        I      J       K       L       M       N       O       P
81
82
83      Year   Cash Flow
84        0    ($41,350)              The Net Present Value (NPV) at
85        1     $9,028                     $1,170
86        2     $9,028                The Profitability Index (PI)
87        3     $9,028                     1.028
88        4     $9,028                The Internal Rate of Return (IRR)
89        5     $9,028                     17.47%
90        6     $9,028                The company's Required Rate of Return
91        7     $9,028                     16.70%
92        8     $9,028
93        9     $9,028                * CONCLUSION
94       10     $9,028                Accept the project
95
96
97   * This conclusion is based on the  NPV, PI, and IRR. The conditions
98     are NPV > 0, PI > 1.00, and IRR > Company Required Rate of Return
99     for the project to be accepted.
100
     01-Jan-89  12:36 PM
```

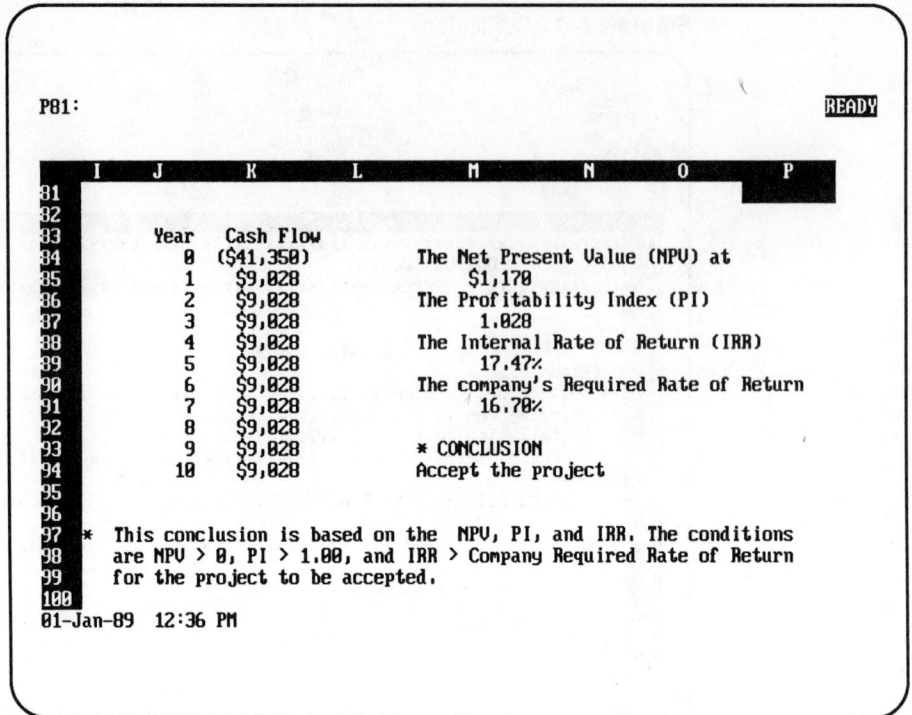

Figure 12–3 (Continued)

12-5 Accounting Applications

Preparing a balance sheet and an income statement are two of the most common tasks performed by any organization. Regardless of the size of the company, a balance sheet and an income statement are needed to determine its financial status. Balance sheets and income statements can be very long and complicated. However, they all follow the same format. We have developed a macro-based program to prepare these two important financial statements for you. This simple model should give you ideas for developing balance sheets and income statements. Figure 12–4 shows the documentation, the macro-based program, and the execution of this macro-based program.

12-6 The S-Curve

Forecasting, or projecting the future of total sales, total expenses, manpower planning, etc., is a common practice in the business world. In order to predict the future of a particular variable, some previous data is needed. Depending on the nature of the data (seasonal, trend, cyclical) and the time horizon for the forecast (short range, medium range, long range), different forecasting models can be chosen. As we discussed in Chapter 8, /Data Regression provides you with a tool for long-range forecasting. There are many forecasting tools, such as moving average, exponential smoothing, and multivariate forecast. Any of these models can be translated into Lotus in order to generate a forecast. As an example we have chosen the S-curve for such a translation.

```
****************************************************************************
                              DOCUMENTATION
****************************************************************************
THE PURPOSE OF THIS PROGRAM:
        This program will produce a balance sheet and an income statement
        after the user has entered the values for the different variables
        upon request.

INSTRUCTIONS:
    1. The macro for this program can be activated by pressing <ALT> & A
       keys simultaneously.

    2. The user will be asked to input the values while the program is
       executing.

    3. The first section will ask the inputs for the company's assets. The
       inputs are: CASH, ACCOUNTS RECEIVABLE, INVENTORY, LONG-TERM
       INVESTMENTS, PLANT & EQUIPMENT, and ACCUMULATED DEPRECIATION.

    4. The second section will ask for the company's liabilities and
       owners' equity. The inputs are: ACCOUNTS PAYABLE, TAXES PAYABLE,
       BONDS PAYABLE, COMMON STOCK, and RETAINED EARNINGS.

    5. The program will check the balance of the balance sheet. It
       will make sure that the TOTAL ASSETS will be equal to the TOTAL
       LIABILITIES and OWNERS' EQUITY.

    6. If the balance sheet is balanced, then it will go to the income
       statement. It will calculate the company's income. The inputs are:
       SALES, COST OF GOODS SOLD, SELLING EXPENSES, ADMINISTRATIVE
       EXPENSES, INTEREST EXPENSES, and CORPORATE TAX LEVEL.

    7. When you are done with the income statement, a menu will appear.
       Use the cursor keys to make your selection and hit <RETURN>.

    8. If you made any mistakes while entering the inputs, hit <CTRL>
       & <BREAK> simultaneously followed by <ESC>.  Repeat step
       1 to restart.

LIMITATIONS:
    1. The user may not change the format of the balance sheet and income
       statement because it is predefined.
```

Figure 12–4 Documentation for Macro-Based Balance Sheet and Income Statement

The S-curve model is a long-range forecasting model (two years or more). An S-curve model has a slow start, a rather steep growth, and a saturation point that comes after some period of time. The introduction of a new product, an information system life cycle, or the usefulness of a new machine all follow an S-curve model. There are several mathematical presentations of the S-curve model. The following formula is one way of showing this model:

$$Yt = e^{A+B/t}$$

where Yt is the S-curve estimate, e is the constant equal to 2.718, A is the equivalent of the intercept in the linear regression model, B is the equivalent of the slope in the linear regression model, and t is time.

Since the relationship between the independent variable (t) and the dependent variable (Y) is not linear, the classical least-squares method does not apply to this model. However, by taking the logarithm of both sides, we can convert this form to a linear one, as follows:

$$\text{Log}Yt = (\frac{A + B}{t}) \text{Log } e^e \quad (\text{Log } e^e = 1)$$

and if we replace $\frac{1}{t}$ by T, Log Yt by X_t we will have

```
\A   |GOTO|INPUT~|GOTO|CASH~              *--- The balance sheet input section ---*
     |GETNUMBER "Enter the cash amount: ",CASH||DOWN|
     |GETNUMBER "Enter the amount acc. receivable:",ACC.REC||DOWN|
     |GETNUMBER "Enter the amount on Inventory:",INV||GOTO|LT.INV~
     |GETNUMBER "Enter the amount of Long Term Investment:",LT.INV|
     |GOTO|PLANT~
     |GETNUMBER "Enter the amount of Plant & Equipment:",PLANT|
     |GOTO|DEPRE~
     |GETNUMBER "Enter the amount of Depreciation:",DEPRE||GOTO|TOT.AS.~
     /reOFF~
     |LET OFF,OFF+TOT.AS.|~
     |GETLABEL "Hit <RETURN> key to go to the LIABILITIES section",JUNK||PGDN|
     |GOTO|ACC.PAY~              *--- Liabilities & Owners' Equities Section ---*
     |GETNUMBER "Enter the amount of Account Payable:",ACC.PAY|
     |LET OFF,OFF-ACC.PAY|~
     |GOTO|TAX.PAY~
     |GETNUMBER "Enter the amount of Taxes Payable:",TAX.PAY|
     |LET OFF,OFF-TAX.PAY|~
     |GOTO|BONDS~
     |GETNUMBER "Enter the amount of Bonds Payables:",BONDS|
     |LET OFF,OFF-BONDS|~
     |GOTO|STOCK~
     |GETNUMBER "Enter the amount of Common Stock:",STOCK|
     |LET OFF,OFF-STOCK|~
     |GOTO|RET.EARN~
     |GETNUMBER "Enter the amount of Retained Earnings:",RET.EARN|
     |LET OFF,OFF-RET.EARN|~
     |IF (TOT.AS.-TOT.EQ)>0||BRANCH NO|
     |IF (TOT.EQ-TOT.AS.))>0||BRANCH NOT|
     |GETLABEL "Hit <RETURN> key to go to the income statement section",JUNK|
     |GOTO|INC~|GOTO|SALES~          *--- Income Statement Section ---*
     |GETNUMBER "Enter the amount Sales:",SALES||GOTO|COGS~
     |GETNUMBER "Enter the amount of Cost Of Goods Sold:",COGS|
     |GOTO|SELL.EXP~
     |GETNUMBER "Enter the amount of Selling Expenses:",SELL.EXP|
     |GOTO|AD.EXP.~
     |GETNUMBER "Enter the amount of Advertising Expenses:",AD.EXP.|
     |GOTO|INT.EXP~
     |GETNUMBER "Enter the amount of Interest Expenses:",INT.EXP|
     |GOTO|TAXLEVEL~
     |GETNUMBER "Enter the corporate tax level (in percent): ",TAXLEVEL|
     |GOTO|NI~
     |GETLABEL "Hit <RETURN> key to get the menu.",JUNK|
     |GETLABEL "Use the cursor keys to make your choice and hit <RETURN>.",JUNK|
O    |MENUBRANCH MENU|

MENUAssets           Liabilities         Income Statement    Quit
     View Total AsseView Liabilities & OView Income StatemenQuit the program
     |GOTO|INPUT~     |GOTO|SECOND~       |GOTO|INC~          |QUIT|
     |BRANCH O|       |BRANCH O|          |BRANCH O|

junk              *--- Temporary storage ---*

NO   |BEEP 5|
     |GETLABEL "TOTAL ASSETS is more than TOTAL LIABILITIES & OWNERS' EQUITIES. ",JUNK|
     |BRANCH \A|

NOT  |BEEP 5|
     |GETLABEL "TOTAL LIABILITIES & OWNERS' EQUITIES is more than TOTAL ASSETS. ",JUNK|
     |BRANCH \A|
```

Figure 12–4 (Continued) Macro-Based Program for Preparing a Balance Sheet and an Income Statement

$$Xt = A + BT$$

As we see, this has a linear form and we can apply the classical least-squares method in order to estimate the values for A and B (see the discussion of simple linear regression in Chapter 8).

We have developed a macro-based program which fits an S-curve to a series of data. Figure 12–5 shows the documentation, the macro-based program, and the execution of the program.

Figure 12–4 (Continued) Execution of Macro-Based Accounting Program

```
Q1: [W12]                                                          READY

      J   K   L       M       N       O       P       Q       R
1
2                        BALANCE SHEET
3    ======================================================================
4                           ASSETS                         19XX
5    CURRENT ASSETS:
6        CASH ...............................................  $1,600,800
7        ACCOUNTS RECEIVABLE ...............................   1,500,000
8        INVENTORY ........................................      900,000
9                                                            ------------
10           TOTAL CURRENT ASSETS .........................    4,000,800
11
12   LONG-TERM INVESTMENT ...............................     1,000,500
13   PLANT & EQUIPMENT .........................1,500,000
14   LESS: ACCUMULATED DEPRECIATION ..............   450,000
15                                                  ----------
16   NET PLANT & EQUIPMENT ..............................     1,050,000
17                                                            ------------
18   TOTAL ASSETS .......................................    $6,051,300
19                                                            ============
20
01-Jan-89  12:37 PM
```

Figure 12–4 (Continued)

```
Q21: [W12]                                                         READY

      J   K   L       M       N       O       P       Q       R
21
22                   LIABILITIES & STOCKHOLDERS' EQUITY
23   ======================================================================
24   CURRENT LIABILITIES
25       ACCOUNTS PAYABLE .................................  $1,500,000
26       TAXES PAYABLE ....................................     500,000
27                                                            ------------
28          TOTAL CURRENT LIABILITIES .....................   2,000,000
29   BONDS PAYABLE .......................................   1,000,900
30
31   STOCKHOLDERS' EQUITY
32       COMMON STOCK, $15.00 par value ..........1,500,000
33       RETAINED EARNINGS ........................   670,400
34                                                  ----------
35          TOTAL STOCKHOLDERS' EQUITY .....................   2,170,400
36                                                            ------------
37   TOTAL LIABILITIES & STOCKHOLDERS' EQUITY ..............  $6,051,300
38                                                            ============
39
40       This balance sheet is off by          $0
01-Jan-89  12:37 PM
```

Figure 12–4 (Continued)

```
Z1: [W13]                                                              READY

        S    T    U    U    W           X         Y           Z
     1                          INCOME STATEMENT
     2  ====================================================================
     3                                19XX
     4  SALES ..........................................    $2,800,500
     5  COST OF GOODS SOLD .............................     1,200,000
     6                                                      ----------
     7  GROSS MARGIN ...................................     1,600,500
     8  OPERATING EXPENSES
     9       SELLING EXPENSES ..................    580,000
    10       ADMINISTRATIVE EXPENSES ..........    600,000
    11                                            ----------
    12       TOTAL OPERATING EXPENSES ..........            1,180,000
    13                                                      ----------
    14  NET OPERATING INCOME  ..........................      420,500
    15  INTEREST EXPENSES ..............................       12,000
    16                                                      ----------
    17  NET INCOME BEFORE TAXES ........................      408,500
    18  INCOME TAXES AT .. 46% .........................      220,590
    19                                                      ============
    20  NET INCOME .....................................     $187,910
    01-Jan-89  12:37 PM
```

Figure 12–5 Documentation for the Macro-Based S-Curve Model

```
**********************************************************************
                          DOCUMENTATION
**********************************************************************
THE PURPOSE OF THIS PROGRAM:
     To calculate the S-curve model (2 years or more) for the long-range
     forecasting model.  It will calculate the slope and intercept point
     for the S-curve and draw the S-curve graph.

INSTRUCTIONS:
     1. The macro for this program can be activated by pressing <ALT> and Z
        keys simultaneously.

     2. You will be asked to input several variables and some other inputs
        while running the macro.

     3. The first input is how many sets of data the user wants to
        consider. Then it will ask the user to input the first independent
        variable followed by the first dependent variable. This will
        continue until the user has entered all the data.

     4. The next input will be the prediction data. The user will be asked
        if he/she wants to do any predicting; then the user has to input
        the value of independent variables.

     5. Finally, this program will draw the S-curve graph based on the
        calculated values.  The user will be asked if he/she wants the
        program to draw the S-curve graph.

     6. If you made any mistakes while entering the input, hit <CTRL>
        and <BREAK> simultaneously to stop the program.  Hit <ESC>
        and repeat step 1 to start all over again.

LIMITATIONS:
     1. To draw the graph, avoid overflowing, and make it easier to use,
        you should maximize the inputs to 17 sets of data.
```

```
\Z        |GOTO|INAREA~|PANELOFF|
          |GOTO|START~
          |GETNUMBER "How many sets of data to consider? ",DATA|~
          |FOR K,1,DATA,1,INPUT||BRANCH LOOP|

INPUT     /XNEnter the independent var (X): ~~
          |RIGHT|            *--- To enter the data  ---*
          /XNEnter the dependent var (Y): ~~
          |DOWN||LEFT|

DATA        10

K           11

LOOP      /RE|RIGHT||PGDN|~|GOTO|HEAD~/REWORKAREA~     *---  get ready for new calculation  ---*
          |GOTO|TOTAL~/MTOTAL~|END||UP||LEFT||DOWN||END||DOWN 3||RIGHT|~|GOTO|HEAD~|DOWN|
          /C|RIGHT 3|~|DOWN|.|LEFT 2||END||DOWN||RIGHT 5|~
          |GOTO|SUM(X2)~/RE~|GOTO|HEAD~|DOWN|
ONE       /RNCTEMP~~       *--- The accumulator macro for SUM(X2) ---*
          |GOTO|SUM(X2)~
          |IF TEMP>0||LET SUM(X2),SUM(X2)+TEMP|~
          |IF TEMP>0||ACCU|
          |IF TEMP>0||BRANCH ONE|
          /RNDTEMP~
          |GOTO|SUM(Y2)~/RE~|GOTO|HEAD2~
          |DOWN|
DUA       /RNCTEMP~~       *--- The accumulator macro for SUM(Y2) ---*
          |GOTO|SUM(Y2)~
          |IF TEMP>0||LET SUM(Y2),SUM(Y2)+TEMP|~
          |IF TEMP>0||ACCU|
          |IF TEMP>0||BRANCH DUA|
          /RNDTEMP~
          |GOTO|SUM(X2Y2)~/RE~|GOTO|HEAD3~
          |DOWN|
THREE     /RNCTEMP~~       *--- The accumulator macro for SUM(X2Y2) ---*
          |GOTO|SUM(X2Y2)~
          |IF TEMP>0||LET SUM(X2Y2),SUM(X2Y2)+TEMP|~
          |IF TEMP>0||ACCU|
          |IF TEMP>0||BRANCH THREE|
          /RNDTEMP~
          |GOTO|SUM(X2~2)~/RE~|GOTO|HEAD4~
          |DOWN|
FOUR      /RNCTEMP~~       *--- The accumulator macro for SUM(X2~2) ---*
          |GOTO|SUM(X2~2)~
          |IF TEMP>0||LET SUM(X2~2),SUM(X2~2)+TEMP|~
          |IF TEMP>0||ACCU|
          |IF TEMP>0||BRANCH FOUR|         *--- The Prediction Macro ---*
          /RNDTEMP~|GOTO|RESULT~|GOTO|NUM~|RECALC OUTPUT|~|PANELON|
          |GETLABEL "Do you want to do any prediction? (Y)es or (N)o: ",ANSWER||RECALC OUTPUT|~
          |IF ANSWER<>"y"||BRANCH DRAW|
          |IF ANSWER<>"Y"||BRANCH DRAW|
AGAIN     |GETNUMBER "The value of Independent Var: ",NUM||RECALC ANS|~
          |GETLABEL "Do you want to try another one (Y)es or (N)o ? ",ANSWER|
          |IF ANSWER="y"||BRANCH AGAIN|
          |IF ANSWER="Y"||BRANCH AGAIN|
DRAW      |GETLABEL "Do you want to draw the graph? (Yes) or (N)o: ",answer|
          |IF ANSWER<>"y"||quit|
          |IF ANSWER<>"Y"||quit|     *--- To draw the S-Curve graph  ---*
          |GOTO|AVAR~/GRGTLXX~A|DOWN|.|END||DOWN|~
          BTWO~OLAGIVEN VARS~
          LBTHE S-CURVE~
          FASQTXDEPENDENT VARS~
          TYINDEPENDENT VARS~QQ
          |GOTO|RESULT~
          |GETLABEL "Hit the <RET> & F10 key to see the graph ",ANSWER||PANELON|

ACCU      |GOTO|TEMP~      *--- The accumulator subroutine ---*
          /RNDTEMP~
          |DOWN|/RNCTEMP~~
          |RETURN|


ANSWER        *--- Temporary storage range  ---*
```

Figure 12–5 (Continued) Macro-Based Program for S-Curve Model

Figure 12–5 (Continued)

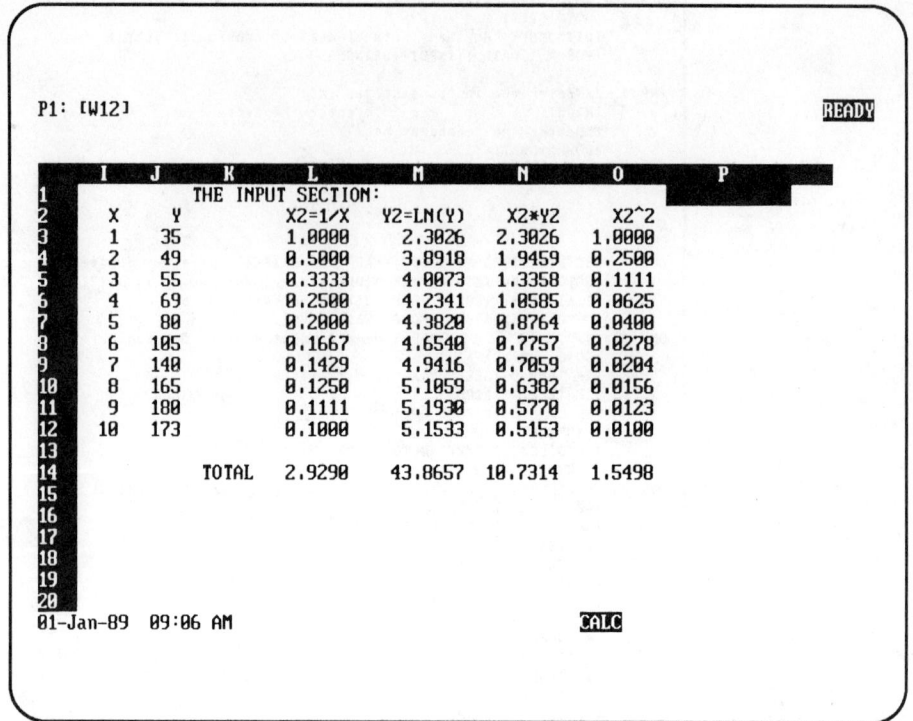

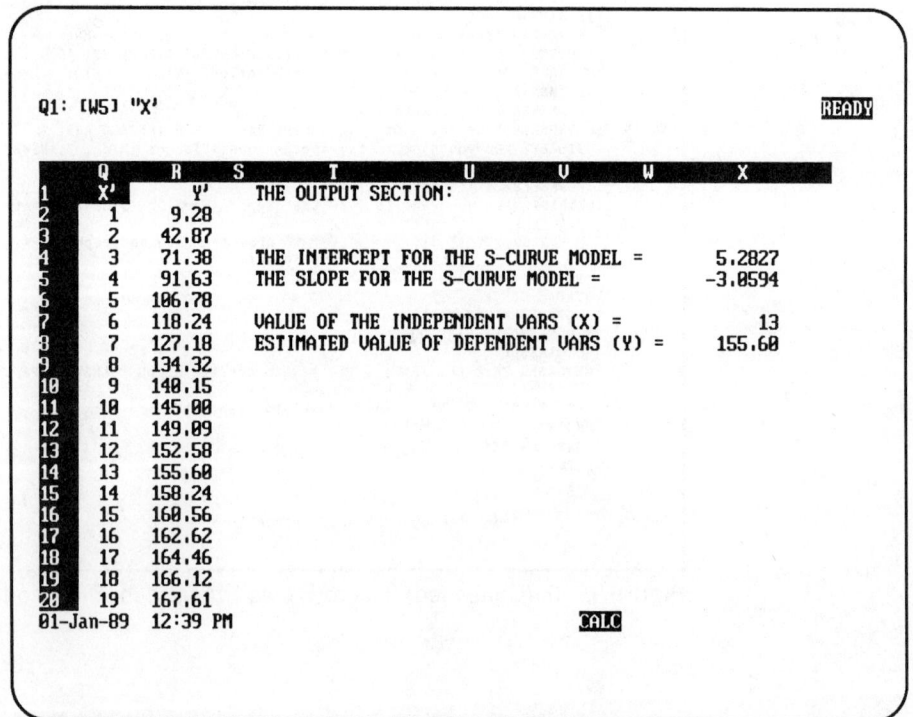

```
P1: [W12]                                                              READY

       I    J    K        L         M         N         O         P
1            THE INPUT SECTION:
2      X    Y          X2=1/X    Y2=LN(Y)    X2*Y2      X2^2
3      1    35         1.0000    2.3026     2.3026     1.0000
4      2    49         0.5000    3.8918     1.9459     0.2500
5      3    55         0.3333    4.0073     1.3358     0.1111
6      4    69         0.2500    4.2341     1.0585     0.0625
7      5    80         0.2000    4.3820     0.8764     0.0400
8      6    105        0.1667    4.6540     0.7757     0.0278
9      7    140        0.1429    4.9416     0.7059     0.0204
10     8    165        0.1250    5.1059     0.6382     0.0156
11     9    180        0.1111    5.1930     0.5770     0.0123
12     10   173        0.1000    5.1533     0.5153     0.0100
13
14          TOTAL      2.9290    43.8657   10.7314     1.5498
15
16
17
18
19
20
01-Jan-89  09:06 AM                                        CALC
```

Figure 12–5 (Continued)

```
Q1: [W5] "X'                                                           READY

       Q    R      S     T        U        V        W        X
1      X'   Y'           THE OUTPUT SECTION:
2      1    9.28
3      2    42.87
4      3    71.38        THE INTERCEPT FOR THE S-CURVE MODEL =      5.2827
5      4    91.63        THE SLOPE FOR THE S-CURVE MODEL =         -3.0594
6      5    106.78
7      6    118.24       VALUE OF THE INDEPENDENT VARS (X) =          13
8      7    127.18       ESTIMATED VALUE OF DEPENDENT VARS (Y) =   155.60
9      8    134.32
10     9    140.15
11     10   145.00
12     11   149.09
13     12   152.58
14     13   155.60
15     14   158.24
16     15   160.56
17     16   162.62
18     17   164.46
19     18   166.12
20     19   167.61
01-Jan-89  12:39 PM                                        CALC
```

Summary

In this chapter we provided five common business applications performed by Lotus. As you have seen, the number and types of applications handled by Lotus is theoretically unlimited. These applications can be solved directly using the Lotus worksheet or you can develop a series of macros to handle the particular situation. The advantage of using macros is the user friendliness of the process; you do not need to have any previous knowledge about Lotus and/or the application area. In the next chapter, we provide more diverse and complex applications of Lotus using macro commands.

Review Questions

1. Using the macro given in Figure 12-1, calculate the number of bouquets of flowers which should be ordered by Neighborhood Florists in order to minimize the undersupply and oversupply cost; given the following information:

   The cost of a bouquet of flowers is $15
   The sale price of a bouquet of flowers is $25
   The probability of past demands are:

Number of Bouquets of Flowers	Probability
20	.12
21	.18
22	.05
23	.25
24	.30
24	.10

2. Design a macro to calculate the return on investment of a portfolio. The macro must accept the net income and owner's equity from the keyboard and then generate the return on investment. The macro should provide an option for automatic retry.
3. Design a macro in order to calculate the current ratio. The current ratio is the ratio of current assets over current liabilities. The macro must be fully interactive.
4. Design an interactive macro to calculate the internal rate of return (IRR) of any given portfolio.
5. Design an interactive macro to calculate the monthly payment of an automobile purchased over any period with any interest rate.
6. Design an interactive macro to calculate the present value of any given portfolio with an any given interest rate.
7. Design an interactive macro using the regression model to generate a forecast for any given advertising budget. The model should use the data for the past six periods. As an example, you can use the following data:

Total Sales	Advertising
$200,000	$5,000
250,000	8,000
300,000	9,000
350,000	10,000
400,000	12,000

8. Design an interactive macro to generate a forecast using a simple three-period moving average. This means that the forecast for the next period is the average of the last three periods.

9. Design an interactive macro to generate the average of the total sales of the last 10 periods. The macro should tell us the maximum and minimum of these total sales. It should also generate a line graph, and a bar graph of the given data. Use a menu macro.

10. Modify the macro in Problem 9 to generate a forecast for the next period using simple regression.

11. Design a macro in order to accept 10 data points. The macro should generate the following statistics:

   • Average of the set

   • Standard deviation of the set

   • Maximum number in the set

   • Minimum number in the set

12. Design a word processing macro to accept a sentence, then do the following:

   1. Change the entire sentence to all capital letters.
   2. Change the entire sentence to all lowercase letters.
   3. Break the sentence into three smaller sentences, lined up.
   4. Extract the first three letters of the sentence.
   5. Extract the last three letters of the sentence.

13

Lotus Applications in Specific Disciplines/Part Two

13-1 Introduction

In this chapter we will introduce some varied applications of Lotus macros. These applications should expand and reinforce the versatility of Lotus macros for advanced users.

The materials presented in this chapter will illustrate the tremendous power and versatility of this amazing software. Try to be creative and generate your own applications!

Remember, these applications are by no means a comprehensive coverage of Lotus capabilities. These are only some of the more common applications.

To see the power of the macros presented in this chapter, load them from the diskettes provided and run them. *The listings provided here are only partial due to the space limitation.* You may be able to customize some of these macros for your specific needs.

13-2 Lotus for Home Use

There are many applications that can be done by Lotus for home use. Probably the most common use would be an automated telephone directory. You can use the Lotus worksheet to keep track of your friends' addresses, telephone numbers, birthdates, and so on.

Forgetting a friend's birthday can be embarrassing. You can keep track of your friends' birthdays in an address database, then ask Lotus to tell you all the birthdays in the next two weeks or so. Your manual directory, which has been erased so many times and is still missing some of your friends' recent addresses or phone numbers, is not needed any more. The design is very easy. Follow these steps:

Column A	First name
Column B	Last name
Column C	Street address
Column D	City
Column E	State
Column F	Zip code
Column G	Telephone number
Column H	Birthdate

Adding to or deleting from this database is no problem. Modification will also be an easy job. Sorting can be done and any specific values can be searched. You can add other friends to this database with no problem. Don't forget, there are 8,192 rows (records) and 256 columns (fields) available to you.

The default settings may not be adequate for this application. For example, some of the columns must be extended beyond 9 characters (e.g., /WCS).

When this database is designed, you may want to generate mailing labels for Christmas cards or for inviting all your friends to a party. (Think about the mailing list applications and see if you can do it.)

The following is the input/output of the macro we developed for this process.

Working Conditions: Completely interactive system with unlimited restarts.

Input:

Enter last name

Enter first name

Enter street address

Enter city

Enter state

Enter zip code

Enter date to recall (e.g., FEB-13)

Enter activity (birthday, anniversary, etc.)

More? Enter 1 for yes, 2 for no

Recall by name

Recall by date

Output:

Last name

First name

Street address

City

State

Zip code

Date to recall (e.g., FEB-13)

Activity

Figure 13–1 illustrates the listing of this macro.

Another home use could be a database for recipes. The rows would be for recipes, number 1 to number 8,192, and the columns would be for ingredients. Many inquiries can be answered by this database. You may want to list all the 1987 recipes, all the Chinese recipes, and so forth. To design a database refer to Chapters 7–8.

Lotus' financial functions can be used for home financial planning, paying a mortgage, planning for your children's college, education, retirement planning, and so on.

13-3 Accounting Applications

Any task in the accounting environment can be done by Lotus. However, you must remember that dedicated accounting packages may be more suitable for specific accounting and bookkeeping applications. We developed a series of macros that prepare a balance sheet and an income statement in Chapter 12. In this chapter, we would like to show you one very common accounting application — issuing a list of bad debts.

Let us say column A includes the purchase date, column B is the amount of purchase, column C is the payment, column D is the balance, and column E is today's date. You can perform a variety of analyses using this database. Let us say that if the balance is positive AND the difference between today's date and the purchase date is ≥45 days, issue a message or charge interest. Or you could say if the difference between purchase date and today's date is 30 days OR the balance is ≥5,000, issue a message.

As you remember from Chapter 7, AND, OR, and NOT analysis can be done in a Lotus database. Also, dates can be expressed in numbers, permitting you to do mathematical calculations with them.

The following is the input/output of the macro we developed for this process.

Figure 13–1 Home Use Example — Start-Up Menu

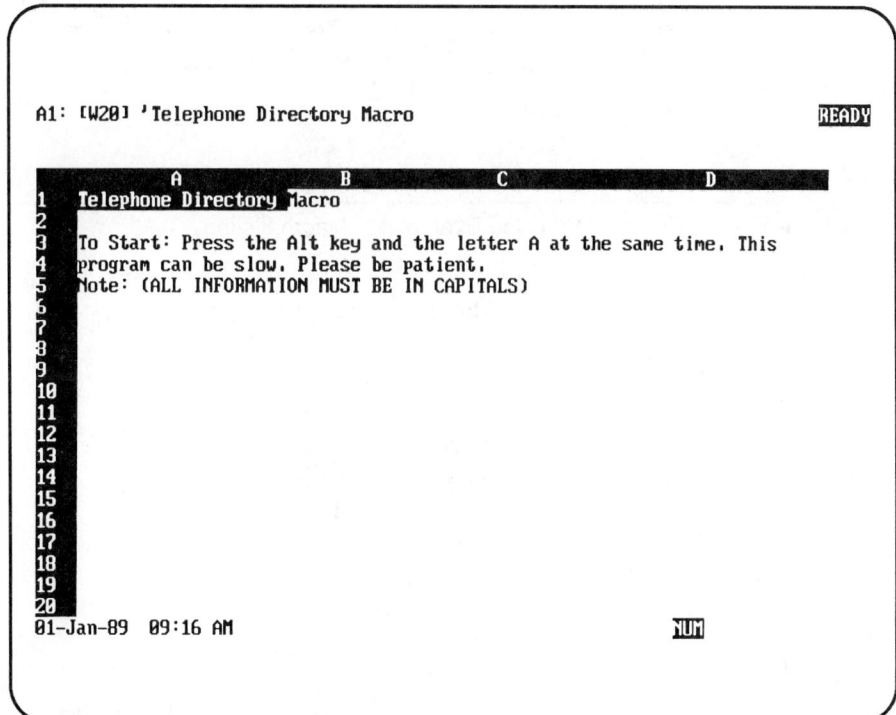

```
A1: [W20] 'Telephone Directory Macro                              READY


      ┌─────────A───────────B───────────C───────────D──────────┐
     1│Telephone Directory Macro
     2│
     3│To Start: Press the Alt key and the letter A at the same time. This
     4│program can be slow. Please be patient.
     5│Note: (ALL INFORMATION MUST BE IN CAPITALS)
     6│
     7│
     8│
     9│
    10│
    11│
    12│
    13│
    14│
    15│
    16│
    17│
    18│
    19│
    20│
      01-Jan-89  09:16 AM                              NUM
```

```
*-SET UP DATABASE FORMAT-*
\a
            {Goto}A4~Automated Telephone Directory~{down 2}
            Last Name~/Wcs20~{Right}
            First Name~/wcs11~{right}
            Street Address~/Wcs20~{Right}
            City~/Wcs15~{Right}
            State~/Wcs6~{Right}
            Zip Code{Right}
            Date~/Wcs6~{Right}
            Activity~/Wcs13~~
            ~
            {Goto}\A~{Down 25}/Rnc\O~~/rnc\B~~
            {down}/Rncmenu~~{up}/Rnc\C~{Esc}{Down 8}~~
            {down 8}/Rnc\C~~
            {down 14}/Rnc\D~~
            {down 13}/Rnc\F~~
            {down 11}/Rnc\G~~
            {down 10}/Rnc\E~~
            /Dqria6.H1000~G~
            {goto}a2~/re~{bigright}{bigright}
            {Branch \B}

            *-Set Up Function Menu-*
\b          {Windowsoff}{Menubranch Menu}
            Input                 Recall        Print              Quit
            Input Data            Recall Data   Print Data(Make sureReturn to Ready Status
            {Goto}\C~{Down}{Left}  {Branch \D} {Branch \E}         {home}{quit}
            /Rncloop~~
            {Branch \C}

            *-Input Data Loop-*
\c          {Goto}A2000~{End}{Up}{Down}/Rncinfo~~
            {Getlabel "Enter Last Name: ",Info}~/Rncinfo~{Right}~
            {Getlabel "Enter First Name: ",Info}~/Rncinfo~{Right}~
            {Getlabel "Enter Street Address: ",Info}~/Rncinfo~{Right}~
            {Getlabel "Enter City: ",Info}~/Rncinfo~{Right}~
            {Getlabel "Enter State(2 Characters i.e. CA.): ",Info}~/Rncinfo~{Right}~
            {Getlabel "Enter Zip Code: ",Info}~/Rncinfo~{Right}~
            {Getlabel "Enter Date To Recall (i.e. FEB-13): ",Info}~/Rncinfo~{Right}~
            {Getlabel "Enter Activity(Birthday, Anniversary,etc.): ",Info}~/Rncinfo~{Right}~
            /Rndinfo~
            {Down}{End}{Left}{Getnumber "More? Enter 1 For Yes, 2 For No : ",Loop}~
            {If (@Sum(Loop)=1)}{Branch \C}
            {goto}iv8192~{Branch \B}
```

Figure 13–1 (Continued) Home Use Example — Macro Listing

Working Conditions: Completely interactive system with unlimited restarts.

Input:

Add:

What is the purchase date (mm/dd/yy)?

What is the purchase amount?

What is the total payment to date?

Report: (report 1 and report2)

Printer, screen, or main menu

Output:

Report: (report 1 and report 2)

Purchase date

Amount of purchase

```
\D          *-Recall Data-*
            {Goto}A6~
            /C{End}{Right}~{End}{Right}{Right}{Right}~
            {End}{Right}{End}{Right}
            /Wcs20~{Right}/Wcs11~{Right}/Wcs20~{Right}/Wcs20~{Right}/Wcs6~{Right}
            /Dqoj6.Q6~Q~/Rncoutput~J6~
            {Goto}\D~{Down 7}/Rncmenu2~~~/Rnd\D~~~{Goto}Menu2~{Up}/Rnc\D~~~
            {gotO}iv8192~{Menubranch Menu2}
            Name                    Date
            Recall By Name          Recall by Date
            {Goto}\F~                {branch \g}
            {Branch \F}

/F          *-Extract By Name-*
            {Goto}\F~{Right 2}Last Name~{Down}/Rnccrit1~~
            {Getlabel "Last Name To Be Recalled: ",Crit1}~
            /Dqccrit1~C{Up}.{Down}~Q
            {Goto}Output~/Rej7.Q1000~{Down}No Record Found~
            /Dqeq~{Windowson}
            {Branch \B}

/G          *-Extract By Date-*
            {Goto}\G~{Right 2}Date~{Down}/Rnccrit2~~
            {Getlabel "Month To Be Recalled (i.e. APR.): ",Crit2}~
            /Dqccrit2~C{Up}.{Down}~Q
            {Edit}{Home}{Right 4}*{Del}~
            {Goto}Output~/Rej7.Q1000~{Down}No Record Found~
            /Dqeq~{Windowson}
            {Branch \B}

/E          *-Print Recalled Data-*
            {Goto}Output~/Ppcrr.{End}{Down}{Right 7}~
            Agpq{Goto}IV8192~{Branch \B}
```

Figure 13–1 (Continued)

Payment
Balance
Figure 13–2 illustrates the listing of this macro.

13-4 Tax Analysis

Lotus can be used effectively for calculating taxes. The design process is very easy. Let us say:

Row 4 includes a given taxpayer's wages
Row 5 includes interest income

Row 6 includes dividends
Row 7 includes other income
Row 11 includes adjustments such as moving expenses, medical bills, professional training, etc.
Row 12 includes all the other itemized deductions
Row 13 includes total exemption amount

You can make this as complicated as you like (for now this should show the point). Naturally the values included in these cells are different for different taxpayers. For example, a single person differs from a family with 18 children or a couple who have a lot of business expenses.

In the above example, the taxable income for a fictitious taxpayer would be (assuming everything is in row 1):

+A1+B1+C1+D1-E1-F1-G1*H1

The next step would be to build a tax table somewhere in the worksheet. And the final step would be to use — you guessed it — the Lookup Table (Horizontal or Vertical?). The Lookup Search will tell you, based on a particular taxable income, how much the tax is.

You can put in as much taxpayer data as you have room for. In theory you can have up to 8,192 taxpayers in your worksheet.

The following is the input/output of the macro we developed for this process.

Working Conditions: Completely interactive system with unlimited restarts.

Input:

Your name?
Your total wages for a given year?
Your interest income?
Your total dividend amount?
Your total amount of other income?
Your amount of other deductions?
Your exemptions?
Married or single (1=married, 0=single) status?

Output:

Wages
Interest income
Dividends
Other income
Total income
Adjustments
Other deductions
Total exemption amount
Total deductions
Taxable income
Tax owed
Report form or report database

Figure 13-3 illustrates the listing of this macro.

Figure 13–2 Accounting Application — Start-Up Menu

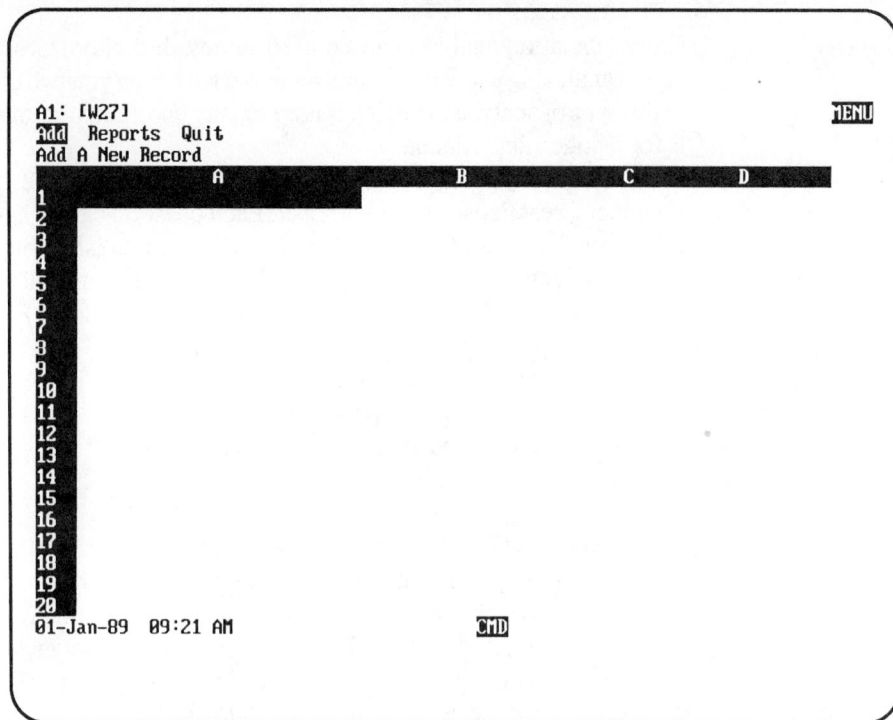

```
A1: [W27]                                                                    MENU
Add  Reports  Quit
Add A New Record
                    A                   B          C         D
1
2
3
4
5
6
7
8
9
10
11
12
13
14
15
16
17
18
19
20
01-Jan-89  09:21 AM                          CMD
```

Figure 13–2 (Continued) Accounting Application — Macro Listing

```
\0        {HOME}{PANELOFF}{WINDOWSOFF}{MENUBRANCH MENU}

MENU      Add                     Reports                 Quit
          Add A New Record        Display Credit Reports  Exit The Program
          {HOME}{PANELOFF}        {WINDOWSON}             {home}{quit}
          {GOTO}A42~/WIR~{HOME}   {MENUBRANCH REPORTS}
          {GETLABEL "What is the purchase date (MM/DD/YY)?",A42}
          {GETNUMBER "What is the purchase amount ?",B42}
          {GETNUMBER "What is the total payment to date?",C42}
          /RFD~A42~/RFD~E42~{let d42,b42-c42}
          {LET A42,@DATEVALUE(A42)}
          {LET E42,@Int(@NOW)}
          {LET F42,E42-A42}
          {BRANCH ab2}
          {GETNUMBER "What is the remaining balance?",D42}

REPORTS   Report 1                Report 2                Main Menu
          List Customers with PosiList Customers with OveReturn To The Main Menu
          /DQCCRITERION#1~EQ      /DQCCRITERION#2~EQ      {MENUBRANCH MENU}
          {GOTO}I41~              {GOTO}I41~
          {GETLABEL "Press The Ret{GETLABEL "Press The Return Key to Return To The Main Menu",Z1}~
          {BRANCH ab2}            {BRANCH ab2}
```

13-5 Cross-Tabulation Analysis

Cross-tabulation analysis can be used in any discipline. Cross-tabulation simply means analyzing a row by column data. We will show you two common applications of this type of analysis. The first is used for any questionnaire analysis and the second is for a police department.

Let us say you have designed a questionnaire with 52 questions regarding customers' reactions to a new product. Each question can be answered by choosing a number from one to seven: 1 means the least satisfaction, 7 means the most satisfaction, and 4 means average satisfaction. When you collect and store this data in your Lotus worksheet, a variety of analyses can be done. For example:

How many people answered 7?
How many people answered 1?
What is the standard deviation of each question?
What is the mean of each question?

You can use /Data Distribution in order to find out the distribution of each answer. You can also graph the data in almost any fashion you desire. When you are more comfortable with macros you may want to develop a macro-based program that analyzes any questionnaire and provides important statistics.

The second application is used by the Around-the-Corner Police Department. A portion of data collected recently is as follows:

Figure 13–3 Tax Analysis — Start-Up Menu

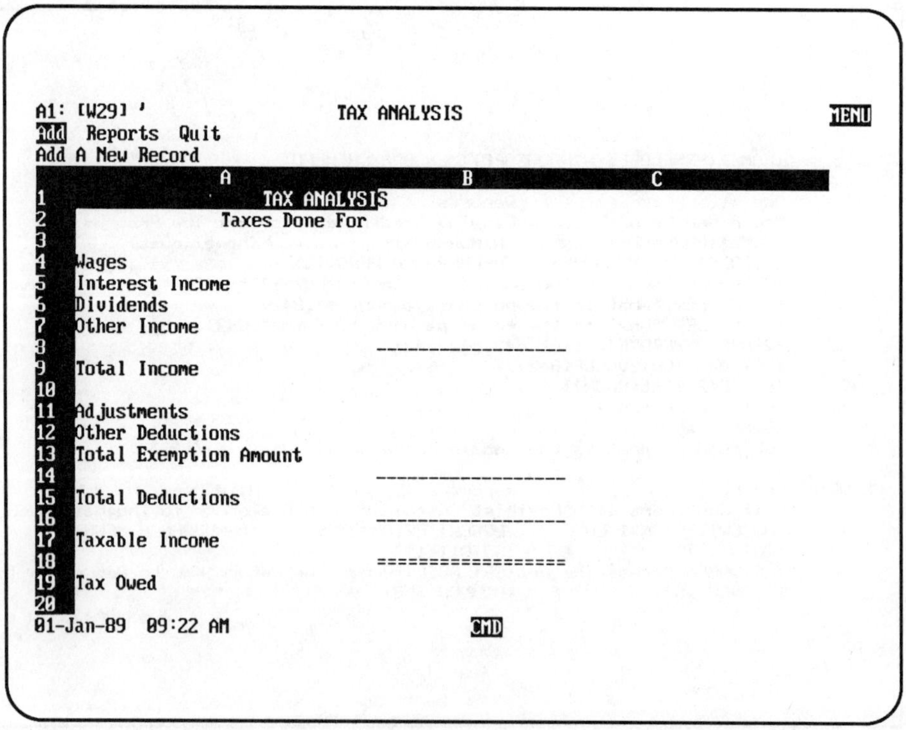

```
A1: [W29] '                    TAX ANALYSIS                              MENU
Add  Reports  Quit
Add A New Record
              A                         B                C
1                      TAX ANALYSIS
2                    Taxes Done For
3
4   Wages
5   Interest Income
6   Dividends
7   Other Income
8                                  -------------------
9   Total Income
10
11  Adjustments
12  Other Deductions
13  Total Exemption Amount
14                                 -------------------
15  Total Deductions
16                                 -------------------
17  Taxable Income
18                                 ===================
19  Tax Owed
20
01-Jan-89  09:22 AM                      CMD
```

	1985	1986	1987
Homicide	15	17	25
Robbery	21	29	32
Theft	91	107	99
Rape	17	13	18
Forgery	22	25	21
Assault	62	69	62
Burglary	73	85	81
Other	19	28	37

You can put this data in the worksheet and answer several interesting questions:

- What is the total number of crimes committed in each year?

- Which crime has the greatest growth rate for the past three years?

- Which crime occurred least often and which crime occurred most in each year?

- Generate a line graph on any of these crimes.

- Generate the percentage of each crime to the total number using a pie chart for each year.

- Generate a forecast for a future year based upon this data using /Data Regression for each crime.

The following is the input/output of the macro we developed for this process.

Figure 13–3 (Continued) Tax Analysis — Macro Listing

```
\0       {HOME}{MENUBRANCH MENU}~

MAIN MENUAdd                                          Reports              Quit
        Add A New Record                              Print Tax Reports    Exit The Program
        {HOME}{PANELOFF}~                             {MENUBRANCH REPORTS}  {CLEARFORM}~
        {CLEARFORM}~                                                        {home}{quit}
        {GETLABEL "What is your name? ",B2}~
        {GETNUMBER "What are your total wages for 1986? ",B4}~
        {GETNUMBER "What is your interest income? ",B5}~
        {GETNUMBER "What is your total dividend amount?",B6}~
        {GETNUMBER "What is your total amount of other income? ",b7}~
        {GETNUMBER "What is your total adjustments amount? ",b11}~
        {GETNUMBER "What is the amount of other deductions? ",b12}~
        {GETNUMBER "How many exemptions do you have? ",J2}~
        {GETNUMBER "Are you filing married or single? (1=married, 0=single)? ",J1}
        {LET B13,J2*1080}
        {LET b17,b4+b5+b6+b7-b11-b12-(j2*1080)}~
        {LET B9,@SUM(B4..B7)}
        {LET B15,@SUM(B11..B13)}
        {IF J1=0}{LET B19,@VLOOKUP(B17,bb3..bc54,1)}
        {IF J1=1}{LET B19,@VLOOKUP(B17,bf3..bg54,1)}
        {GOTO}A61~/WIR~{HOME}~
        {LET A61,B2}
        {LET B61,B4}
        {LET C61,B5}
        {LET D61,B6}
        {LET E61,B7}
        {LET F61,B9}
        {LET G61,B11}
        {LET H61,B12}
        {LET I61,B13}
        {LET J61,B15}
        {LET K61,B17}
        {LET L61,B19}
        {BRANCH aB1}
```

```
CLEARFORM -->        {BLANK B2}
                     {BLANK B4}
                     {BLANK B5}
                     {BLANK B6}
                     {BLANK B7}
                     {BLANK B9}
                     {BLANK B11}
                     {BLANK B12}
                     {BLANK B13}
                     {BLANK B15}
                     {BLANK B17}
                     {BLANK B19}
                     {RETURN}




REPORTS MENU ->      Form                     Database
                     Print this form          Print the entire database
                     {HOME}/PPRA1..C25~AGPQ   {GOTO}A60~
                     {BRANCH AB1}             /PPCRR.{END}{DOWN}{END}{RIGHT}~AGPQ
                                              {BRANCH aB1}
```

Figure 13–3 (Continued) A Sample Tax Table

Working Conditions: Completely interactive system with unlimited restarts.
Input:
For the years 1985, 1986, 1987 total number of homicides
For the years 1985, 1986, 1987 total number of robberies
For the years 1985, 1986, 1987 total number of thefts
For the years 1985, 1986, 1987 total number of rapes
For the years 1985, 1986, 1987 total number of forgeries
For the years 1985, 1986, 1987 total number of assaults
For the years 1985, 1986, 1987 total number of burglaries
For the years 1985, 1986, 1987 total number of other crimes
Enter the year for statistical crime projections or 0 to end program
Output:
Total, % change 1985-87 and % change 1986-87 for all crimes
Most prevalent crime for 1985, 86, and 87
Least prevalent crime for 1985, 86, and 87
Estimated crimes for projected year
Figure 13-4 illustrates the listing of this macro.

13-6 Examination Analysis

Examination analysis is another application of cross-tabulation. Imagine a teacher preparing final grades. The teacher has given five exams, seven homework assign-

Figure 13–4 Cross-Tabulation Analysis — Instructions

```
BB1: 'This program allows the user to input a number of crime statistics    READY

          BB       BC       BD       BE       BF       BG       BH       BI
 1   This program allows the user to input a number of crime statistics
 2   and will then perform various analyses on this information including
 3   predictive statistics for any year chosen.
 4
 5   Instructions:
 6   A sample database exists; you may add or alter information.
 7
 8   To begin, press the home key and that will place you near the database.
 9   Move the cursor and begin entering data.
10
11   Each crime must have a figure for each year.
12
13   Once you are sure that all the data is correct, press the Alt and A keys
14   at the same time. This screen will then reappear while the computer is
15   working. Please be patient. This program takes a few minutes. Once the
16   computer is done, a completed screen will appear.
17
18   Note: Predictive statistics employ simple linear regression utilizing
19   this formula: Y=A+BX or more specifically as used in the worksheet,
20   Dependent Variable = Constant + Independent Variable * X Coefficient.
01-Jan-89  09:23 AM
```

Figure 13–4 (Continued) A Sample Database

```
A1: [W10] 'Crime Statistics for Around-the-Corner P.D.                      READY

          A        B        C        D        E        F        G
 1   Crime Statistics for Around-the-Corner P.D.
 2
 3   Once all figures are correct,  press Alt and A keys at the same time.
 4
 5
 6                                                    % Change   % Change
 7   Crime       1985     1986     1987    Total   1985-1987  1986-1987
 8   Homicide      15       17       25
 9   Robbery       21       29       32
10   Theft         91      107       99
11   Rape          17       13       18
12   Forgery       22       25       21
13   Assault       62       69       62
14   Burglary      73       85       81
15   Other         19       28       37
16   TOTAL
17
18
19
20
01-Jan-89   09:25 AM
```

```
                *-Set Up Macro And Output Area-*
\a              {goto}bb1~
                {Indicate Macro}{Windowsoff}{Paneloff}
                {Goto}\A~{Down 6}/Rnc\B~~{Down 15}/Rnc\C~~{down 29}/rnc\d~~{branch \b}


\b              *-Perform standard statistics-*
                {Goto}Start~{end}{Down}{right}
                @Sum({Up}.{End}{Up}{Down})~
                /C~.{Right 2}~
                {Goto}Start~{Right 4}{Down}
                @Sum({Left 3}.{Right 2})~
                /C~.{Left}{End}{Down}{Right}~
                {Right}/Wcs11~
                ({Left 2}-{Left 4})~{Edit}/{Up}{Down}{Left 4}~
                /C~.{Left}{End}{Down}{Right}~
                {Right}/Wcs11~
                ({Left 3}-{Left 4})~{Edit}/{Up}{Down}{Left 4}~
                /C~.{Left}{End}{Down}{Right}~
                /Rfp~{Left}{End}{Down}~
                {branch \c}
\c              *-perform data base statistics-*
                {Goto}Start~{Right}/C.{Right 2}~{End}{Down}{Down 2}~
                /C.{Right 2}~{End}{Down}{Down 10}~
                {End}{Down}{Down 3}{Left}
                Largest{Right}Crime~/C~.{Right 2}~
                /C.{Right 2}~{Down 3}~{Down 3}{Left}
                Smallest~{Right}{End}{Down}{Down}
                @Dmax(A7..D15,1,B23..B24)~
                /C~.{Right 2}~/Rv{End}{Right}~~
                /Rff0~{End}{Right}~
                /Dqri{home}{Down 6}.{End}{Down}{Right 3}~0{Up 8}
                .{Down}~C{Up}.{Down}~Eq{Right}
                /Dqri{Home}{Down 6}.{End}{Down}{Right 3}~0{Up 8}
                .{Down}~C{Up}.{Down}~Eq{Right}
                /Dqri{Home}{Down 6}.{End}{Down}{Right 3}~0{Up 8}
                .{Down}~C{Up}.{Down}~Eq{Left 2}
                @Dmin(A7..D15,1,B23..B24)~
                /C~.{Right 2}~/Rv{End}{Right}~~
                /Rff0~{End}{Right}~
                /Dqri{Home}{Down 6}.{End}{Down}{Right 3}~0{Up 5}
```

Figure 13–4 (Continued) Cross-Tabulation Analysis — Macro Listing

ments, two presentations, and a grade for class participation. In this case you are dealing with a matrix of 15 columns and, let us say, 50 rows (50 students).

If this data is stored in a worksheet of 50 by 15, a variety of analyses can be done in a short period as follows:

- Total score of each student, e.g., @SUM

- Sorted list of students by their total score in descending order

- Distribution of grade, e.g., how many ≥ 90, ≥ 80, ≥ 70, ≥ 60, etc.

- Highest total score

- Lowest total score

- Mean, variance, and standard deviation of each exam

- A line graph of total scores of all students

- Best and worst performance in each of 15 cases of grading

- Comparing this year's average with the last three years, etc.

```
              /Dqri{Home}{Down 6}.{End}{Down}{Right 3}~0{Up 5}
              .{Down}~C{Up}.{Down}~Eq{Right}
              /Dqri{Home}{Down 6}.{End}{Down}{Right 3}~0{Up 5}
              .{Down}~C{Up}.{Down}~Eq{Right}
              /Dqri{Home}{Down 6}.{End}{Down}{Right 3}~0{Up 5}
              .{Down}~C{Up}.{Down}~Eq
              /Rlr{Left 2}{Up 9}~
              /re{up}{left 3}~
              {branch \d}

\d            *-Perform regression analysis-*
              {Goto}A5~{Windowson}{panelon}{Windowsoff}{Paneloff}
              {Getnumber "Enter Year For Statistical Crime Projections Or 0 To End Program: ",B1}
              {If B1=0}/Reb1~~{Indicate}{Home}{Quit}
              {Goto}Start~
              {End}{Down}{Right 5}{Down 2}
              Predicted Total Crime {Down}
              Current{down}
              1985{Down}
              1986{Down}
              1987{Down}
              Projected{down}
              (b1)
              ~/rv~~/reb1~~
              {End}{Up}{End}{Up}
              {Left 4}/Rv{Right 2}~~/Rt{Right 2}~
              {Right 5}{Down 4}~
              {Right 4}{Down 4}
              /Drrx.{Down 2}~Y{Right}.{End}{Down}~0{Right 2}~G~
              {Right}{End}{Down}{Down 2}
              ({Up 3}{Right 4})+{Left}*{Right 3}{Down 3}~
              /rv~~
              {up 4}{right}/re{down 9}{right 5}~
              {branch \d}
```

Figure 13–4 (Continued)

The following is the input/output of the macro we developed for this process:

Working Conditions: Completely interactive system with unlimited restarts.

Input:

Student

Exam number 1

Exam number 2

Exam number 3

Exam number 4

Exam number 5

Homework 1

Homework 2

Homework 3

Homework 4

Homework 5

Homework 6

Homework 7

Presentation 1

Presentation 2

Participation
Output:
Total score per student
Average score per student
Data distribution of scores in the range of 0-39
Data distribution of scores in the range of 40-49
Data distribution of scores in the range of 50-59
Data distribution of scores in the range of 60-69
Data distribution of scores in the range of 70-79
Data distribution of scores in the range of 80-89
Data distribution of scores in the range of 90-100
Statistics for all exams, homework, presentations, and participation to include mean, variance, standard deviation, best score, and worst score
Maximum of total score
Minimum of total score
Figure 13-5 illustrates the listing of this macro.

13-7 Banking Applications

Lotus has been utilized in the banking industry from the first day of its existence. Accounting and financial analyses are very common applications. Portfolio analysis and future investment analysis are also very common applications. What-if, goal-seeking, and sensitivity analyses using different interest rates can be done easily. We will show you a common application: a checking account report and how much to charge for the number of checks written.

Each bank has a different policy regarding checking accounts. Let us say Plaza Bank of Ocean City has established the following formula for its checking accounts:

Balance ≥$500 — No charge for writing checks
Balance ≥$300 and <$500 — 15 cents charge per check
Balance <$300 — $5 base charge and 12 cents per check

Your task is to calculate the charge for each customer. If you design a worksheet like the one below, you can do this calculation:

- Column A includes beginning balance

- Column B includes all the deposits

- Column C includes monthly total checks written

- Column D includes final balance (A+B-C)

- Column E includes number of checks

A simple comparison of column D against the above formula will tell you to which group a particular customer belongs. Then the charge can be calculated. Of course this analysis and database can be expanded to include more sophisticated analyses such as:

- The largest check written by a particular customer

- His/her average amount per check

- His/her smallest check

- Average balance of the customer per day

- Highest and lowest balance of a customer in a particular month, etc.

The following is the input/output of the macro we developed for this process.

Working Conditions: Completely interactive system with unlimited restarts.

Input:

Account name

Beginning balance

Deposits

Total deposits

Number of checks

Output:

Balance

Cost per charge

Base rate

Service charge

Final balance

Largest checking balance

Largest amount of checks written

Smallest checking balance

Figure 13–5 Examination Analysis — Instructions

```
BB1: 'This program allows the user to perform various analyses on a        READY

      BB    BC    BD    BE    BF    BG    BH    BI    BJ    BK
1    This program allows the user to perform various analyses on a
2    sample grading format. This format includes 5 exams, 7 homework
3    assignments, 2 presentations, and a grade for class participation.
4
5    Instructions:
6    A sample database exists; you may add or alter information.
7
8    To begin, press the home key and that will place you near the database.
9    Move the cursor and begin entering data.
10
11   There must be a response (even a 0) for each test for each student.
12
13   Once you are sure that all the data is correct, press the Alt and A keys
14   at the same time. This screen will then reappear while the computer is
15   working. Once the computer is done, a completed screen will appear.
16
17   At this point, you may use the program again.
18
19   Please be pateint as this program can take 5 minutes or more to
20   complete.
01-Jan-89  09:25 AM
```

Figure 13–5 (Continued) A Sample Grade Book

Examination Analysis
(Once information is correct, press the Alt and A keys,
at the same time, and the statistics will be generated.)

Student #	Exam 1	Exam 2	Exam 3	Exam 4	Exam 5	Hm Wk 1	Hm Wk 2	Hm Wk 3	Hm Wk 4	Hm Wk 5	Hm Wk 6	Hm Wk 7	Pres 1	Pres 2	Partici
1	85	67	89	92	76	92	77	65	79	62	75	98	65	92	89
2	96	74	78	92	92	65	83	72	95	97	78	95	79	84	92
3	72	87	93	62	62	90	98	78	87	95	80	91	75	66	66
4	60	67	88	83	61	99	95	81	93	76	88	99	89	71	99
5	76	61	60	68	94	72	96	96	92	73	79	92	75	70	89
6	85	95	95	64	65	75	87	80	80	95	64	72	78	75	88
7	68	93	61	68	86	65	90	88	89	98	87	61	71	67	87
8	77	61	92	78	70	79	75	91	67	96	60	64	65	71	97
9	98	74	76	100	62	72	80	63	77	90	75	78	91	98	85
10	77	65	80	65	72	98	63	79	100	63	89	96	67	67	93
11	98	98	86	89	90	100	90	100	99	97	90	84	99	87	87
12	73	65	77	64	76	69	80	90	96	84	69	61	63	66	94
13	62	74	88	73	78	61	69	76	94	86	74	80	67	62	87
14	84	67	81	71	71	80	75	90	97	65	75	66	96	90	92
15	63	78	67	87	63	75	65	76	67	67	61	59	67	66	66
16	86	62	72	83	96	72	79	97	91	63	65	92	89	79	89
17	96	73	91	95	99	67	74	86	63	81	99	99	92	63	92
18	53	69	21	61	64	66	66	69	55	55	29	67	69	70	70
19	85	79	67	70	83	79	93	75	99	78	71	90	84	80	93
20	62	79	93	99	93	84	62	95	72	90	76	67	69	92	88
21	85	74	82	66	98	86	67	86	73	96	80	78	60	61	87
22	75	78	87	65	95	63	60	77	61	95	87	68	66	92	90
23	90	90	82	93	99	92	100	85	95	71	98	100	95	100	99
24	62	94	61	79	63	100	89	90	65	74	78	85	72	96	85
25	88	66	75	74	73	86	71	97	93	94	84	72	94	95	92
26	68	80	96	75	65	77	81	62	64	95	96	74	73	87	91
27	99	86	100	95	100	89	92	88	92	73	97	98	100	72	95
28	68	95	87	66	99	67	98	95	93	68	76	80	66	91	88
29	94	96	77	79	94	63	98	66	64	89	87	62	82	86	88
30	80	83	78	85	85	99	68	69	64	94	97	84	90	93	92
31	75	73	93	85	93	72	63	68	70	73	80	66	65	68	85
32	77	69	67	65	62	88	93	77	71	78	84	67	77	82	87
33	90	74	70	87	97	94	96	98	78	96	67	85	62	76	94
34	87	85	77	73	72	64	88	72	98	67	63	75	69	76	87
35	95	73	87	96	76	99	94	60	92	84	69	96	79	72	86
36	98	96	60	68	97	90	60	83	63		97	91	66	80	96

```
                      *-Set Up Database And Perform Elementary Statistics-*
            \a        {Goto}Bb1~{Windowsoff}{Indicate Macro}{Paneloff}
                      {goto}Start~{bigright}{right 7}{down}
                      /re{right}{end}{down}~{goto}start~
                      {pgdn}{pgdn}{end}{down}{down}
                      /re{bigright}{bigright}{end}{down}.~
                      {goto}Start~{down}{end}{right}{right}
                      @sum({left}.{end}{left}{right})~{right}
                      @avg({left 2}.{end}{left}{right})~{left}
                      /c{right}~.{left}{end}{down}{right}~
                      {right}/rncavg~{end}{down}~
                      {goto}\a~
                      {down 20}/rnc\b~~
                      {down 6}/rnc\c~~
                      {down 24}/rnc\d~~
                      {down 8}/rnc\e~~
                      {down 22}/rnc\f~~
                      {down 10}/rnc\z~~
                      {branch \b}

            \b        *-Perform Sort-*
                      {goto}start~{Down}
                      /dsrd.{end}{down}{end}{right}~
                      p{end}{right}.{end}{down}~d~g
                      {branch \c}

            \c        *-Perform Distribution Analysis-*
                      {goto}start~{down}{end}{Down}{down 2}
                      Distribution of Grades(average of all scores){down 3}
                      50{down}
                      60{down}
                      70{down}
                      80{down}
                      90{down}
                      100{end}{up}
                      /rncbin~{end}{down}~
                      /dd{esc}
                      avg~
                      bin~
                      {goto}bin~/rndbin~
                      "40-49{down}
                      "50-59{down}
                      "60-69{down}
                      "70-79{down}
                      "80-89{down}
                      "90-100{down}
                      "0-39~
                      /m{right}~{end}{up}{up}~{down}
                      {branch \d}
```

Figure 13–5 Examination Analysis — Macro Listing

Total charge for service
Average service charge per check
Highest beginning balance
Lowest beginning balance
Figure 13-6 illustrates the listing of this macro.

13-8 Personnel Administration

Personnel departments of medium to large organizations are facing two application areas that can be handled by Lotus: affirmative action statistics and exam analysis.

```
\d      *-Perform data manipulation-*
        Highest Total Score{down}
        Lowest Total Score{up}{right 3}
        ({home}{down 6}{end}{right}{left}){down}
        ({home}{down 6}{end}{right}{left}{end}{down})~
        {UP}/rv{down}~~~
        {branch \e}

\e      *-Perform additional Statistics-*
        {goto}start~
        {right}/c.{end}{right}{left 2}~
        {down}{end}{Down}{down 15}~
        {down}{end}{Down}{down 15}{left}
        Statistics{down}
        Mean{down}
        Variance{down}
        Std. Dev.{down}
        Worst Score{down}
        Best Score{right}{up 4}
        @avg({pgup}{end}{up}{down}.{end}{down}){down}
        @sqrt(@std({pgup}{end}{up}{down}.{end}{down})){down}
        @std({pgup}{end}{up}{down}.{end}{down}){down}
        @dmin({pgup}{pgup}{end}{up}.{end}{down},0,{pgup}{pgup}{end}{up}.{end}{
        @dmax({pgup}{pgup}{end}{up}.{end}{down},0,{pgup}{pgup}{end}{up}.{end}{
        {up 4}
        /c{end}{down}~.{up}{end}{right}{down}~
        /rff0~{down 2}{end}{right}~
        {branch \f}

\f      *-Set up graph start-*
        {goto}start~{down}{end}{Down}{down 4}{right 2}
        To veiw a line graph of total scores,{down}
        press the Alt and the Z key{down}
        at the same time.{down}
        Once graph is shown, press any key to continue.~
        {up 3}/ru{down 3}~
        {left 2}
        {windowson}{panelon}{indicate}
        {quit}
        *-perform Graphics-*
        {windowsoff}{paneloff}
        /grga{home}{down 6}{end}{right}{left}.{end}{down}~
        otfTotal Scores~tyScores~txStudents~qvq
        {windowson}{panelon}{indicate}
        {quit}
```

Figure 13–5 (Continued)

For the affirmative action case you are usually dealing with a typical data table as follows:

- Column A includes   Employee name

- Column B includes   Sex

- Column C includes   Age

- Column D includes   Marital status

- Column E includes   Education

- Column F includes   Number of years of experience

- Column G includes   Race

Figure 13–6 Banking Application — Instructions

```
S1: 'This program allows the user to input an unlimited number of bank      READY

       S       T       U       V       W       X       Y       Z
 1  This program allows the user to input an unlimited number of bank
 2  account data and will then perform various analyses including
 3  determining an appropriate charge for checking and a final balance.
 4
 5
 6  Instructions:
 7  A sample database exists; you may add or alter any names or figures.
 8
 9  To begin, press the home key and that will place you near the database.
10  Move the cursor and begin entering data.
11
12  Each person must have a figure for the account name, beginning
13  balance, total of monthly checks and # of checks columns. All
14  other columns will be completed by the program.
15
16  Once you are sure that all the data is correct, press the Alt and A keys
17  at the same time. This screen will then reappear while the computer is
18  working. Once the computer is done, a completed screen will appear.
19
20  At this point, you may use the program again.
01-Jan-89  09:26 AM
```

Figure 13–6 (Continued) A Sample Database

```
A1: (D1) 'BANKING MACRO: (To start, press the Alt and A keys simultaneously READY

        A        B         C          D         E         F
 1  BANKING MACRO: (To start, press the Alt and A keys simultaneously)
 2  Checking rates:
 3  Balance greater than $500 = No charge.
 4  Balance greater than $300, less than $500 = $.15 per check.
 5  Balance less than $300 = $5.00 base charge & $.12 per check.
 6
 7                             Total of
 8  Account  Beginning        Monthly                         # of
 9  Name     Balance  Deposits  Checks         Balance       Checks
10  Nixon     $253.73    $852.18    $772.73                    38
11  Smith   $1,122.75  $1,000.60    $829.93                    27
12  Brown     $549.32    $907.99    $315.36                    27
13  Dixon   $1,051.19    $926.32    $472.09                    14
14  Roberts   $304.87  $1,004.04    $623.82                    22
15  Idol      $789.27    $724.89    $869.70                    21
16  Smythe    $462.22    $760.05    $922.26                    13
17  Orr       $177.30    $453.42    $812.20                    45
18  Kramer    $393.35    $847.34    $835.64                    24
19  Reid      $772.25    $425.46    $669.27                    49
20  Scott     $865.45    $796.41    $483.91                    26
01-Jan-89  09:27 AM
```

```
          *-Set Up Macro And Output Area-*
\a        {goto}s1~
          {Indicate Macro}{Windowsoff}{Paneloff}
          {Goto}Start~/Rfc2~.{End}{Down}{Right 10}~{Goto}L1~
          Statistics For Entire Account Data Base.{down}
          Largest Checking Balance ={Down}
          Most Amount Of Checks Written ={Down}
          Lowest Checking Balance = {Down}
          Total Charge For Service = {Down}
          Average Service Charge Per Check ={Down}
          Highest Beginning Balance ={Down}
          Lowest Beginning Balance ={Down}
          {Goto}\A~{Down 14}/Rnc\B~~~{Down 11}/Rnc\C~~~{Branch \B}~

          *-Figure Balance & Charge Rates-*
\b        {Indicate Macro}{Windowsoff}{Paneloff}
          {Goto}Start~{Right 4}{Down}
          ({Left 3}+{Left 2}-{Left})~
          /C~.{Left 4}{End}{Down}{Right 4}~
          {Goto}Start~
          {End}{Right}{Down}+{Left 5}-{Left}~
          /C~.{Left 5}{End}{Down}{Right 5}~
          {Left}+{Left}~{Edit}{Home}({End})+{Edit}{Left 2}*{Left 3}~
          /C~.{Right}{End}{Down}{Left}~
          {Left 3}/Rff0~.{End}{Down}~{Left}{End}{Down}{Down}.9~
\c        {Goto}Start~{End}{Right}{Down}{Left 3}
          {Left 2}/Rnca~~~{right 2}
          {If @Sum(A)>=500}0~/Rnda~~~{Down}{Branch \C}
          {If @Sum(A)>=300}.15~/Rnda~~~{Down}{Branch \C}
          {If @Sum(A)>=.9}{Goto}A~/Re~~~/Rnda~~~/Rncdata~~~{Goto}\C~{Down 8}~/Rnc\D~~~{Branch \
          {If @Sum(A)<=299}.12~{Right}5~{Left}/Rnda~~~{Down}{Branch \C}


          *-Data Base Sort-*
\d        {Goto}Start~/Rnddata~~~/Rncdata~{End}{Right}{End}{Down}~
          {Goto}P1~{down}/Wcs12~@Dmax(Data,9,J1..J2)~/Rfc~~~
          {Down}@Dmax(Data,5,J1..J2)~/Rff~~~
          {Down}@Dmin(Data,9,J1..J2)~/Rfc~~~
          {Down}@Dsum(Data,8,J1..J2)~/Rfc~~~
          {Down}({Up}/@Sum({Home}{Down 9}{Right 5}.{End}{Down}))~/Rfc~~~
          {Down}@Dmax(Data,1,J1..J2)~/Rfc~~~
          {Down}@Dmax(Data,1,J1..J2)~/Rfc~~~
          {Down}@Dmin(Data,1,J1..J2)~/Rfc~~~
          {Goto}\B~/Rnd\A~~~/Rnc\A~~~
          {Goto}L1~
          {Indicate}{Windowson}{Panelon}{Quit}
```

Figure 13-6 (Continued) Banking Application — Macro Listing

- Column H includes   Handicap status

- Column I includes   Veteran status

- Column J includes   Annual salary

   This data matrix can be of any size. Let us say you have 2,000 employees. Your matrix would then be 2,000 by 10. Numerous vital statistics can be generated as follows:

- Is the average salary of female employees and male employees the same?

- For the same age, which employee makes more money, male or female?

- Which ethnic group makes the highest salary?

- Which ethnic group makes the lowest salary?

- What is the mean salary for male employees?

- What is the mean salary for female employees?

- Plot a line graph of male employees' salary.

- Plot a line graph of female employees' salary.

- Data distribution of different ethnic groups.

- A pie chart of different ethnic groups.

- A pie chart for years of education of all the employees, etc.

You can go on and on, generating more statistics and expanding this database by including other data items.

The following is the input/output of the macro we developed for this process.

Working Conditions: Completely interactive system with unlimited restarts.

Input:

Employee number

Employee name

Sex

Age

Marital status

Education

Number of years experience

Race

Handicap status

Veteran status

Annual salary

Output:

Average salary for males

Average salary for females

Highest salary, lowest salary, and total number of Asian

Highest salary, lowest salary, and total number of Black

Highest salary, lowest salary, and total number of Hispanic

Highest salary, lowest salary, and total number of Other

Highest salary, lowest salary, and total number of White

View and/or save male/female line graph of salaries

View and/or save bar chart for ethnicity

View and/or save population pie chart

Figure 13-7 illustrates the listing of this macro.

The second common application for a personnel department is entrance test score analysis. Let us say you have a data matrix as follows:

Column A includes prospective employee age

Column B includes prospective employee high school GPA

Column C includes prospective employee SAT score

Column D includes prospective employee aptitude test score

Column E includes prospective employee years of experience

Using this database some very useful statistics can be generated as follows:

The highest and lowest of each test score

The youngest and oldest prospective employees

Is there any correlation between age and aptitude test?

Is there any correlation between the aptitude test and the SAT?

Is there any correlation between the high school GPA and the aptitude test?

To do the last three analyses you can use /Data Regression and look at the correlation coefficient (also review materials in Chapter 8, under simple linear regression).

The following is the input/output of the macro we developed for this process.

Working Conditions: Completely interactive system with unlimited restarts.

Input:

Name

Age

Experience

High school GPA

SAT score

APT score

Output:

Highest SAT scores

Lowest SAT scores

Figure 13–7 Personnel Administration — Instructions

```
BB1: 'This program allows the user to input a variety of personnel          READY


        BB      BC      BD      BE      BF      BG      BH        BI
1     This program allows the user to input a variety of personnel
2     information. The program will then perform various analyses on
3     this information and provide output.
4
5     Instructions:
6     A sample database exists; you may add or alter any information.
7
8     To begin, press the home key and that will place you near the database.
9     Move the cursor and begin entering data.
10    Each person must have information in every column.
11
12    Once you are sure that all the data is correct, press the Alt and A keys
13    at the same time. This screen will then reappear while the computer is
14    working. Once the computer is done, a statistics screen will appear.
15
16    At this point, you may use the program again.
17
18
19
20
01-Jan-89  09:27 AM
```

Highest APT scores
Lowest APT scores
Age and APT correlation
SAT and APT correlation
Figure 13–8 illustrates the listing of this macro.

13-9 Microeconomic Analysis

Lotus can be used to perform cost analysis, revenue analysis, production analysis, and so on. Here is a simple example. Let us say the cost equation of Productive Manufacturing Firm is estimated as $200 + 3Q + .015Q^2$ where Q is the number of units produced. Based on this equation, the average cost, average variable cost, and marginal cost can be estimated. Lotus can help you to generate a scenario regarding these different costs as follows:

Row 1 includes $200 + 3Q + .015Q^2$ (total cost)
Row 2 includes $(200 + 3Q + .015Q^2)/Q$ (average cost)
Row 3 includes $(200 + 3Q + .015Q^2 - 200)/Q$ (average variable cost)
Row 4 includes $\partial TC/\partial p = (3 + .030Q)$ (marginal cost)

Now you can input any value for Q (number of units produced) and Lotus will calculate total cost, average cost, average variable cost, and marginal cost.

Figure 13–7 (Continued) A Sample Database

```
A1: 'Personnel: (To begin, hold the Alt key down and then press the A key   READY


        A          B          C  D    E       F     G     H       I
1    Personnel: (To begin, hold the Alt key down and then press the A key
2              at the same time.)
3
4
5
6
7
8    Employee Employee                 Marital      # yrs       Handicap
9       #     Name        Sex Age Status  Ed.  Exp.  Race Status
10      499 NYLON, JOHN   M   30 M     BS     2 W          0
11      261 BROWN, TAMMY  F   44 M     HS    15 W          0
12      227 HUNTS, ROBBY  M   25 M     BS     1 O          0
13      363 PICKENS, GARY M   33 M     AA     6 W          0
14      465 CAGE, JOYCE   F   29 S     HS     8 B          0
15      329 NOMELY, PETE  M   42 M     BS    15 H          0
16      125 BAYLOR, GEARY M   43 M     MA    19 W          0
17       57 SCOTT, KELLY  M   31 S     MA     9 W          1
18      397 REID, STAN    M   29 S     BS     1 W          0
19      193 PENNICE, BILL M   59 M     HS    31 W          0
20       23 ADAMS, LYNDA  F   38 S     BS    12 B          0
01-Jan-89  09:28 AM
```

Also, you can conduct some interesting what-if, goal-seeking, and sensitivity analyses. The production equation can be a lot more complex than the one here. Just do the translation and leave the rest to Lotus.

Figure 13–7 (Continued) Personnel Administration — Macro Listing

```
                    #-set up macro and statistics legend
           \a       {Goto}Bb1~
                    {indicate Macro}{Windowsoff}{Paneloff}{goto}m1~
                    STATISTICAL TABLE {down 2}
                    Average Salary For Males ={down}
                    Average Salary For Females ={down 2}
                    Ethnicity Breakdown: {down}
                    {right 2}Highest{Right}Lowest{down}{left 3}
                    Group{right 2}Salary{right}Salary{right}Number{left 4}{down}
                    Asian{down}
                    Black{down}
                    Hispanic{down}
                    Other{down}
                    White~{GOTO}\A~{down 15}/rnc\b~~~{branch \b}

           \b       #-Do statistical Analysis-*
                    {goto}Start~/rncdata~{ESC}.{end}{right}{end}{down}~
                    {goto}r1~Race{down}a~{goto}R4~
                    @DMAX(A9..K25,10,R1..R2)~{RIGHT}
                    @DMIN(A9..K25,10,R1..R2)~{RIGHT}
                    @DCOUNT(A9..K25,10,R1..R2)~
                    {END}{LEFT}/RV{END}{RIGHT}~09~
                    {GOTO}R2~B~{GOTO}R4~
                    /RV{END}{RIGHT}~010~
                    {GOTO}R2~H~{GOTO}R4~
                    /RV{END}{RIGHT}~011~
                    {GOTO}R2~O~{GOTO}R4~
                    /RV{END}{RIGHT}~012~
                    {GOTO}R2~W~{GOTO}R4~
                    /RV{END}{RIGHT}~013~{goto}s1~
                    Sex{down}M~{goto}q3~
                    @davg(data,10,s1.s2)~/rv~~/rfc0~.{down 2}~
                    {goto}s2~F~{goto}q4~
                    @davg(data,10,s1.s2)~/rv~~/res1.s2~~
                    /RER1.T5~~{GOTO}09~/RFCO~.{RIGHT}{END}{DOWN}~{windowson}
                    {goto}m1~{windowsoff}{GOTO}\b~{down 22}/rnc\c~~~{branch \c}

           \c       #-set graph menu-*
                    {goto}\c~{down 2}/rncmenu~~~{UP}/RNC\D~~~
                    {menubranch menu}




Graphs                  View                          Exit
Line, Bar & Pie Graphs  When finished viewing press any key! Return to Ready Status
{goto}menu~            /gvq{windowsoff}{branch \d}    {goto}s1~/re.{Down 9}{end}{down}{right 2}~
{down 5}/rncgraph~~~                                  {goto}m1~{indicate}{quit}
{menubranch graph}
Male/Female Salary      Top Salary                    Ethnicity              Exit
Line Graph of Salaries  Bar Chart by Ethnicity        Population Pie Chart   Return to Main Menu
{goto}s1~              {goto}r9~/dfr9.r13~1~1~~~      {goto}r9~/dfr9.r13~1~1~~~ {branch \d}
Sex{down}M~{goto}s8~   {goto}o9~                      {goto}q9~
Salary                 /grga.{end}{down}~tbq~        /grga.{end}{down}~tpq~
~/dqridata~os8~cs1.s2~E {goto}r9~/gb.{end}{down}~q~  {goto}r9~/gb.{end}{down}~q~
q{goto}s8~/m~{right}~  {goto}m9~/gx.{end}{down}~     {goto}m9~/gx.{end}{down}~
{down}/dsrd.{end}{down}~ otfPersonnel Department~ts  otfPersonnel Department~ts
p.{end}{down}~a~g      Top Salary by Ethnicity~ty    Population by Ethnicity~qq
{goto}s2~F~            DOLLARS~QQ                     {branch \d}
/dqeq                  {branch \d}
{goto}t9~
/dsrd.{end}{down}~
p.{end}{down}~a~g{goto}s9~
/grga.{end}{down}~t1q~
{goto}t9~/gb.{end}{down}~
otfPersonnel Department~ts
Salary Male vs Female~la
Male~lb Female~ty
DOLLARS~QQ
{branch \d}
```

Figure 13–8 Personnel Administration Example 2 — Instructions

```
Q1: 'This program allows the user to input an unlimited number of names      READY

         Q         R        S         T        U        V        W        X
  1  This program allows the user to input an unlimited number of names
  2  and scores for high school GPA, ACT, and SAT scores. The program
  3  will then perform various analyses on this information and provide an
  4  output.
  5
  6  Instructions:
  7  A sample database exists; you may add or alter any names or scores.
  8
  9  To begin, press the home key and that will place you near the database.
 10  Move the cursor and begin entering data.
 11  Each person must have a score for every column.
 12
 13  Once you are sure that all the data is correct, press the Alt and A keys
 14  at the same time. This screen will then reappear while the computer is
 15  working. Once the computer is done, a statistics screen will appear.
 16
 17  At this point, you may use the program again.
 18
 19
 20
  01-Jan-89  09:29 AM
```

Figure 13–8 (Continued) A Sample Database

```
A1: 'APPLICANT RECORD                                                        READY

         A          B        C        D        E        F        G        H
  1  APPLICANT RECORD    (To begin, hold the Alt key down and then press the
  2                       A key at the same time.)
  3                                          TESTS
  4
  5  Name          Age     Exp.    HS GPA    SAT      APT
  6  Nilon          23      2      3.70     1100      87
  7  Nixon          28     15      3.00      900      72
  8  Johnson        33      1      3.60     1000      83
  9  Cooper         38      8      3.50      750      82
 10  Mchale         43     15      2.60      880      80
 11  Summers        48     19      3.90     1500      95
 12  Parrish        53      9      2.00      500      50
 13  Ainge          58      1      1.50      850      72
 14  Roberts        63     31      3.60      750      74
 15  Green          68     12      2.40      850      76
 16  Worthy         73     17      3.20      900      78
 17  Kite           78     18      3.40     1000      62
 18  Mathews        83      9      2.50      795      50
 19  Rambis         88     18      3.80      400      73
 20  Scott          93      4      4.00     1600      98
  01-Jan-89  09:29 AM
```

```
                        *-Data base and Statistical Table set up-*
        \A              {Goto}Q1~{Windowsoff}{Indicate Macro}{Paneloff}
                        {Goto}Start~
                        {Down}/Rncdatabase~{Esc}.{End}{Down}{End}{Right}~
                        {Home}{Bigright}
                        Statistical Table {Down 2}
                        Scores: {Down}
                        Sat {Down}
                        Highest ={Down}
                        Lowest ={Down 2}
                        Apt {Down}
                        Highest ={Down}
                        Lowest ={Down 2}
                        Correlations: {Down}
                        Age And Apt Test ={Down}
                        Apt And Sat  Tests={Down}
                        HS GPA And Apt Test =~
                        {Goto}\A~{Down 20}/Rnc\B~~
                        {Branch \B}

                        *-Perform Basic Statistical Manipulation-*
        \B              {Goto}Start~
                        /rncscope~{down}.{end}{down}{bigright}~
                        {Bigright}{Right 3}
                        @Dmax(scope,4,L1..L2){Down}
                        @Dmin(scope,4,L1..L2){Down 3}
                        @Dmax(scope,5,L1..L2){Down}
                        @Dmin(scope,5,L1..L2){Down 3}
                        {Goto}\B~{Down 11}/Rnc\C~~
                        /rndscope~
                        {Branch \C}
                        *-Set Up & Perform Regression Analysis-*
        \C              {Goto}\C~{Pgdn}/Rncoutput~~
                        {Goto}Start~{Down}
                        /Drrx{Right}.{End}{Down}~Y{Right 5}.{End}{Down}~
                        Ooutput~G~{Goto}Output~{Down 3}{Right 3}/Rncsquare~~
                        {Goto}Start~{Bigright}{Right 3}{Down 8}
                        '@Sqrt(Square)~
                        /C~.{Down 2}~{Edit}{Home}{Del}~/Rv~~
                        {Goto}Start~{Down}
                        /Drx{Esc}{Right 3}.{End}{Down}~G
                        {Goto}Start~{Bigright}{Right 3}{Down 9}
                        {Edit}{Home}{Del}~/Rv~~
                        {Goto}Start~{Down}
                        /Drx{Esc}{Left}.{End}{Down}~G
                        {Goto}Start~{Bigright}{Right 3}{Down 10}
                        {Edit}{Home}{Del}~/Rv~~
                        /Rff4~.{End}{Up}~{Left 3}{Up 12}
                        {Windowson}{Indicate}{Panelon}{Quit}
```

Figure 13–8 (Continued) Personnel Administration Example 2 — Macro Listing

The following is the input/output of the macro we developed for this process.

Working Conditions: Completely interactive system with unlimited restarts.
Input:
How many units were produced?
Output:
Total cost
Average cost
Average variable cost
Marginal cost

Figure 13-9 illustrates the listing of this macro.

13-10 Computerized Matching System

You can establish a fairly large database of all possible candidates for any selection purposes (up to 8,192). You can also include up to 256 attributes for each candidate (e.g., age, height, education, income, etc.). When the database is built, you can perform database and/or statistical analyses. You can do complicated searches with up to 32 fields with AND, OR, and NOT combinations. For example, you can develop your own dating service or any other search system (see Chapters 7–8).

The following is the input/output of the macro we developed for this process.

Working Conditions: Completely interactive system with unlimited restarts.

Input:

Enter last name, first name:

Enter phone number, (xxx) xxx-xxxx:

Enter sex (1 for male, 2 for female):

Enter age group:

1. 18-25
2. 26-35
3. 36-45
4. 46-55
5. 56 & above

Enter educational level:

1. High school
2. Some college
3. Bachelor's degree

Figure 13–9 Microeconomic Application — Start-Up Menu

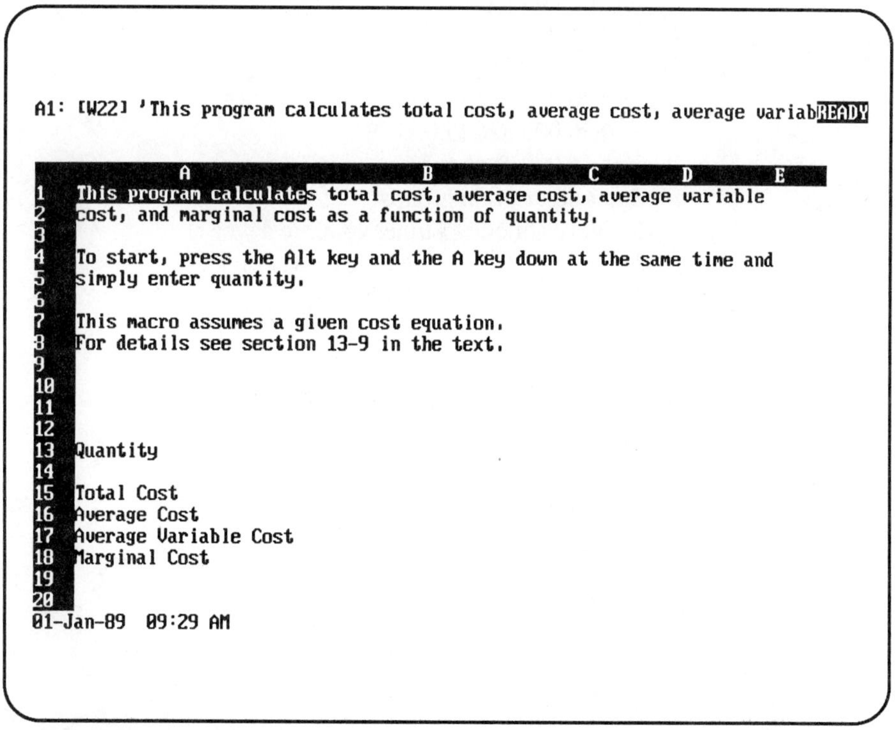

```
A1: [W22] 'This program calculates total cost, average cost, average variab READY


         A              B              C       D       E
1   This program calculates total cost, average cost, average variable
2   cost, and marginal cost as a function of quantity.
3
4   To start, press the Alt key and the A key down at the same time and
5   simply enter quantity.
6
7   This macro assumes a given cost equation.
8   For details see section 13-9 in the text.
9
10
11
12
13  Quantity
14
15  Total Cost
16  Average Cost
17  Average Variable Cost
18  Marginal Cost
19
20
01-Jan-89  09:29 AM
```

```
\a      {home}/reb13..b18~
        {goto}a13~
        {getnumber "What is the total quantity?     ",b13}
        {let b15,200+3*$b$13+.015*$b$13^2}
        {let b16,b15/$b$13}
        {let b17,(b15-200)/$b$13}
        {let b18,3+.03*$b$13}~
        {quit}
```

Figure 13–9 (Continued) Microeconimic Application — Macro Listing

4. Master's degree
5. Ph.D.
Enter income group:
1. $18,000 & below
2. $19,000 to $25,000
3. $26,000 to $35,000
4. $36,000 to $45,000
5. $46,000 & above
Enter description group:
1. Very athletic (5 times or more a week)
2. Athletic (3 or more times a week)
3. Average (weekend athlete)
4. Less active
5. Not active
Enter favorite activity for participation:
1. Sports
2. Crafts
3. Arts (music,dance)
4. Drama/speech
5. Hobbies (camping/fishing)
Enter favorite activity to attend:
1. Sports
2. Museums, historical sites
3. Arts (concerts, recitals)

4. Drama/special
5. Don't care to attend events
Enter (1) to start over or (2) to Quit
Output:
Name
Phone Number
Number
Figure 13-10 illustrates the listing of this macro.

13-11 World Population Analysis

It is a fact that the birth rate is higher than the death rate. This means that if nothing unexpected happens to reduce the world population, it will eventually explode. The following formula is used for predicting world population:

$$P = C*[1+(X-Y)]^N$$

where:

P = predicted level of future world population

C = current level of world population

X = birth rate

Figure 13–10 Computerized Matching System — Instructions

```
CC1: 'This program allows the user to input an unlimited number of names anREADY

         CC        CD        CE        CF        CG        CH        CI        CJ
1    This program allows the user to input an unlimited number of names and
2    personal characteristics into a population pool. The program will then
3    match the last entry with persons of similar characteristics.
4
5    Instructions:
6    This is an interactive macro that adds new data to the database as it
7    proceeds. Currently a sample database exists; you may use this
8    database as is or you may erase any or all of it. To begin erasing,
9    press the home key and that will place you near the database. Move the
10   cursor and begin erasing any data you choose. However:
11   Each person must have a score for every column.
12
13   Once you are sure that all the data is as you like or if you choose to
14   use the sample database, press the Alt and A keys at the same time.
15
16   You will now be asked questions; the answers to these questions will be
17   used for matching so please be as honest as possible with your
18   responses. Once the computer is done, the name and phone numbers of
19   similar persons will be provided. At this point, you may use the
20   program again.
01-Jan-89  09:31 AM
```

```
/A          *-setup instructions and format-*
            {goto}cc1~{indicate Macro}{windowsoff}{paneloff}
            {goto}start~{end}{down}{end}{down}{end}{up}{down}
            /rncname~~{right}
            /rncsex~~{right}
            /rncphone~~{right}
            /rncage~~{right}
            /rnced~~{right}
            /rncincome~~{right}
            /rncdes~~{right}
            /rncact1~~{right}
            /rncact2~~{right}
            {goto}ba1~/re{down 25}~{indicate Enter}{beep}{windowson}
            {getlabel "Please enter last name, first name: ",name}{beep}
            {getlabel "Please enter phone number xxx-xxxx: ",phone}{beep}
            {getnumber "Please enter sex (1 for male, 2 for female): ",sex}
            {windowsoff}{goto}ba1~/re{down 25}~{down}
            ^1. 18-25{down}
            ^2. 26-35{down}
            ^3. 36-45{down}
            ^4. 46-55{down}
            ^5. 56 & Above{DOWN}{windowson}{beep}{windowsoff}
            {getnumber " Enter age group: ",age}
            {windowsoff}{goto}ba1~/re{down 25}~{down}
            ^1. High school{down}
            ^2. Some college{down}
            ^3. Bachelor's degree{down}
            ^4. Master's degree{down}
            ^5. PH.D.~{down}{windowson}{beep}{windowsoff}
            {getnumber " Enter education level: ",ed}
            {windowsoff}{goto}ba1~/re{down 25}~{down}
            ^1. $18,000 & below{down}
            ^2. $19,000 to $25,000{down}
            ^3. $26,000 to $35,000{down}
            ^4. $36,000 to $45,000{down}
            ^5. $46,000 & Above{DOWN}{windowson}{beep}{windowsoff}
            {getnumber " Enter income group: ",income}
            {windowsoff}{goto}ba1~/re{down 25}~{down}
            ^1. Very athletic(5 times or more a week){down}
            ^2. Athletic(3 or more times a week) {down}
            ^3. Average(weekend althlete){down}
            ^4. Less active{down}
            ^5. Not active{DOWN}{windowson}{beep}{windowsoff}
            {getnumber " Enter description group: ",des}
            {windowsoff}{goto}ba1~/re{down 25}~{down}
            ^1. Sports{down}
            ^2. Crafts{down}
            ^3. Arts(music, dance){down}
            ^4. Drama/speech{down}
            ^5. Hobbies(camping, fishing){DOWN}{windowson}{beep}{windowsoff}
            {getnumber " Enter favorite activity for participation: ",ACT1}
            {windowsoff}{goto}ba1~/re{down 25}~{down}
            ^1. Sports{down}
            ^2. Museums, historical sites{down}
            ^3. Arts(concerts, recitals){down}
            ^4. Drama/speech{down}
            ^5. Don't care to attend events{DOWN}{windowson}{beep}{windowsoff}
            {getnumber " Enter favorite activity to attend: ",act2}
            {windowsoff}{goto}da1~/re{down 25}~{down}{WINDOWSON}{INDICATE}
            Thank you. In a few moments, you will receive the name and number of{DOWN}
            a person matched to your personal characteristics.~{windowsoff}
            {goto}\a~{end}{down}{down 4}/rnc\b~~{end}{down}{down 3}/rnc\c~~
            {goto}\c~{down 4}/rnc\d~~{branch \b}
```

Figure 13-10 (Continued) Computerized Matching System — Macro Listing

```
\b        *-set up data base and perform extractions-*
          {goto}start~
          {GOTO}START~/C.{END}{RIGHT}~{END}{DOWN}{DOWN 3}~
          {END}{DOWN}/C.{END}{RIGHT 2}~{DOWN 4}~
          {END}{DOWN}/C.{RIGHT 2}~{DOWN 3}~{DOWN 3}
          {RIGHT 2}/M~{LEFT}~{left 2}{UP 2}{RIGHT 2}/RE~~{LEFT}/RNCMF~~{RIGHT}~
          {up}{left 2}{edit}{home}{right}Your ~{DOWN}{RIGHT 2}
          /XI(@SUM(MF)=1)~2~
          /XI(@SUM(MF)=2)~1~
          /RNDMF~~/M~{LEFT}~{LEFT 2}{DOWN 2}
          {RIGHT 3}@COUNT({DOWN}{LEFT 3}.{END}{DOWN})~/RNCCOUNT~~
          {LEFT 3}/DQRO.{RIGHT}~C{RIGHT}{UP 3}.{DOWN}{END}{RIGHT}{END}{PIGHT}~I{HOME}
          {DOWN 4}.{END}{DOWN}{RIGHT 8}~EQ
          {if (@SUM(COUNT)>0)}~{branch \c}
          /DQC{LEFT}~EQ
          {if (@SUM(COUNT)>0)}~{branch \c}
          /DQC{LEFT}~EQ
          {if (@SUM(COUNT)>0)}~{branch \c}
          /DQC{LEFT}~EQ
          {if (@SUM(COUNT)>0)}~{branch \c}
          /DQC{LEFT}~EQ
          {if (@SUM(COUNT)>0)}~{branch \c}
          /DQC{LEFT}~EQ
          {if (@SUM(COUNT)>0)}~{branch \c}
          {GOTO}COUNT~{UP 3}{end}{left}/RE.{BIGRIGHT}{down 5}~ No matches available now;
               try again soon.~{BRANCH \d}


          *-re-run set-up and loop-
\C        /DQC~EQ{edit}{home}{right}Date's ~{down 15}
          {GOTO}COUNT~
          /rv~~{edit}{home}Number= ~
          {up 3}{left 2}/re.{bigright}{bigright}{right}{down}~
\D        {windowson}{windowsoff}{goto}start~
          {getnumber "Press Enter (1) to start over or (2) to quit: ",start}
          {if @sum(start)=2}{goto}start~Name~{end}{down}{down 20}{quit}
          {goto}start~{end}{down}{down 20}
          /ru~{windowson}{panelon}
          Please Wait~{right}
          {windowsoff}{paneloff}/rp~/re~~
          {goto}start~Name~{end}{down}{end}{down}/re{down 3}{end}{down}{bigright}{BIGRIGHT}~
          {goto}start~
          /rnd~~
          /rnd~~
          /rnd~~
          /rnd~~
          /rnd~~
          /rnd~~
          /rnd~~
          /rnd~~
          /rnd~~
          /rnd~~
          /rncstart~~
          /dqrq
          {branch \a}
          {quit}
```

Figure 13–10 (Continued)

Y = death rate

N = Number of years in the future

Put these values in a worksheet as follows:

Column A includes C (row 1)
Column B includes X (row 1)
Column C includes Y (row 1)
Column D includes N (row 1)
Column E includes A*(1-(B1-C1))^ D

Putting different values in cells A1, B1, C1, D1 you will see some horrifying numbers for the year 2500 and beyond. In 1976 the world population was approximately 4 billion, the birth rate was 2.5 percent, and the death rate was .9 percent. Use these numbers and put 13 for N. See what happens?

The following is the input/output of the macro we developed for the above process.

Working Conditions: Completely interactive system with unlimited restarts.
Input:
What is the current population?
What is the predicted birth rate?
What is the predicted death rate?
How many years in the future would you like to see?
Would you like a printout of this (Y or N)?
Would you like to run it again (Y or N)?
Output:
Current population; Birth rate; Death rate
Number of years in the future
World population in years =
Figure 13-11 illustrates the listing of this macro.

13-12 Calculation of Quadratic Roots

Quadratic equations have the following general formula:

$$Y \quad = \quad AX^2 + BX + C$$

$$X \quad = \quad \frac{-B \pm (B^2 - 4AC)^{1/2}}{2A} = \frac{-B \pm (B^2 - 4*A*C)^{1/2}}{2*A}$$

Let us use Lotus to calculate different values for X giving different values for A, B, and C. Build the following worksheet:

	A	B	C	D
(row 1)	10	12	2.70	$\dfrac{-B1+(B1\ ^2-4*A1*C1)^{1/2}}{(2*A1)}$

Figure 13–11 World Population Analysis — Start-Up Menu

```
A1: [W20] '                                                              READY
What is the current population?

             A              B    C                         D
1                         World Population Prediction
2
3   Current population
4   Birth rate
5   Death rate
6   Number of years in the future
7
8
9   World population in      years
10
11
12
13
14
15
16
17
18
19
20
01-Jan-89  09:31 AM                          CMD
```

Figure 13–11 (Continued) World Population Analysis — Macro Listing

```
{HOME}~
{BLANK D3..D6}~
{BLANK D9}~
{BLANK B9}~
{GETNUMBER "What is the current population? ",D3}~
{GETNUMBER "What is the predicted birth rate(In percent)? ",D4}~
{GETNUMBER "What is the predicted death rate?(In percent) ",D5}~
{GETNUMBER "How many years in the future would you like to see? ",D6}~
{LET D9,D3*(1+(D4-D5))^D6}~
{LET B9,D6}~
{GETLABEL "Would you like to run it again (Y or N)? ",I2}
{IF @UPPER(@LEFT(I2,1))="Y"}{branch \a}
{Home}{Quit}
```

We only translated the positive root, not the negative root (or the imaginary root). If you put in any valid values for A, B, and C, Lotus will tell you the value of X.

The following is the input/output of the macro we developed for this process.

Working Conditions: Completely interactive system with unlimited restarts.

Input:

Input A:

Input B:

Input C:

Care to repeat program (Y/N):

Output:

A=

B=

C=

X=

Figure 13-12 illustrates the listing of this macro.

13-13 Lotus as an Advanced Calculator

To illustrate the capabilities of Lotus as a full-featured programming language, we have chosen a vending machine problem to calculate the amount of change to be given to a customer.

The vending machine problem is a typical assignment in a programming course. Here we illustrate the power and flexibility of Lotus in such a setting.

Figure 13–12 Quadratic Roots — Start-Up Menu

```
A1: 'Quadratic Root Calculation                                    READY

         A       B       C       D       E       F       G       H
 1  Quadratic Root Calculation
 2
 3  To begin, press the Alt and A keys at the same time.
 4  This program translates the positive root only. Please respond to the
 5  prompts. If you put in any valid values for A, B, and C, this program
 6  will tell you how much X is.
 7  Note: B must be >= 2* @SQRT(A*C), if not there will be an error.
 8
 9         A       B       C       X
10
11
12
13
14
15
16
17
18
19
20
01-Jan-89  09:33 AM
```

The following is the input/output of the macro we developed for this process.

Working Conditions: Any U. S. currency up to $100.00.

Input:

Any of the following purchases:

$.35

$.50

$.75

$.45

$.55

$.65

$.98

$.89

$.50

Output:

Total payment

Total purchase price

Total change

Figure 13-13 illustrates the listing of this macro.

13-14 Lotus as a DSS Tool

To illustrate the power of Lotus 1-2-3 as a DSS tool, we have designed a final macro that performs what-if analysis, goal-seeking, different evaluations, and displays

Figure 13–12 Quadratic Roots — Macro Listing

```
       \a        *-Set-Up And Input-*
                 {Windowsoff}{Indicate Macro}{Paneloff}
                 {Home}
                 {Blank A10}
                 {Blank B10}
                 {Blank C10}
                 {Blank d10}
                 {Getnumber "Input A: ",A10}
                 {Getnumber "Input B: ",B10}
                 {Getnumber "Input C: ",c10}
                 {Goto}\a~{Down 14}~/Rnc\B~~{Down 7}/Rnc\C~~
                 {Branch \B}

       \b        *-Statistics-*
                 {Goto}D10~
                 /rff~.{left 3}~
                 (-B10+(B10^2-4*A10*C10)^0.5)/(2*A10)~
                 {home}{windowson}{windowsoff}
                 {Branch \C}

       \c        *-Return Loop-*
                 {Home}{Down}
                 /Rncinput~~
                 {Getlabel "Care to repeat program (Y/N): ",Input}
                 {If Input="Y"}{Blank Input}{Branch \A}
                 {Blank Input}
                 {Indicate}
                 {Home}{Quit}
```

```
A1: [W12]                                                            READY

        A          B       C D  E         F          G   HIJ
1                                !------------------------------!
2                                !       John's Vending Machine  !
3                                !------------------------------!
4
5                    ITEM
6       GOODIES       PRICE                MONEY SLOT              !-!
7                                                                 ! !
8       Fruit        $0.35                Place any U.S.          ! !
9       Candy        $0.50                currency up to          ! !
10      Sandwiches   $0.75                $100.00 in slot.        ! !
11      Chips        $0.45                You will receive        ! !
12      Soda         $0.55                change in highest       ! !
13      Diet soda    $0.65                denominations           ! !
14      Beer         $0.98                possible.               ! !
15      Wine         $0.89                                        !-!
16      Liquor       $1.50
17
18      Place cursor on item price for your selection, and press Alt
19      and A at the same time!
20
        01-Jan-89   09:35 AM
```

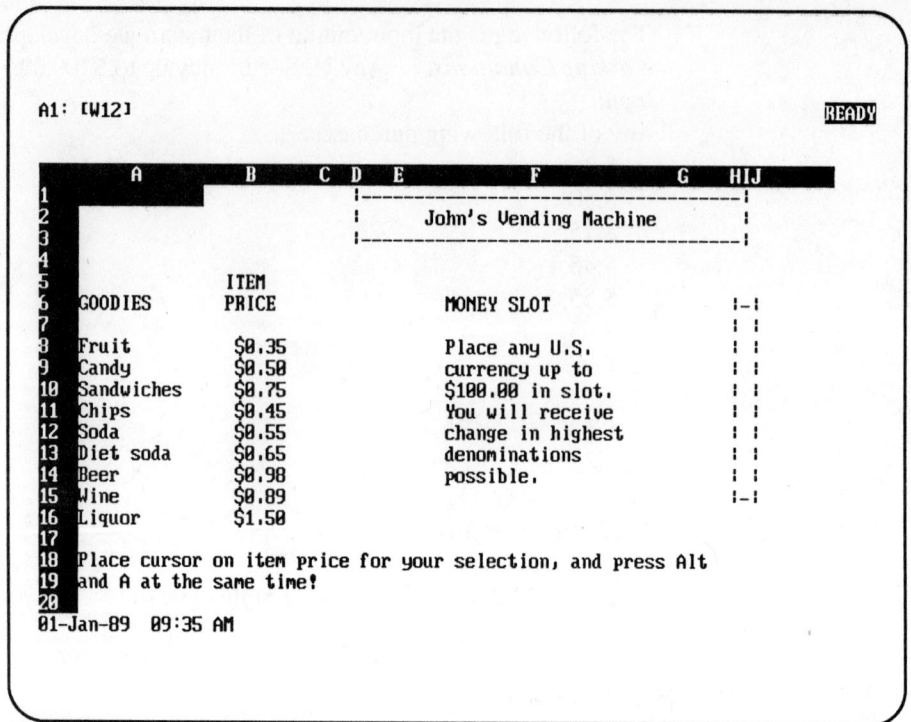

Figure 13–13 Lotus as an Advanced Calculator — Start-Up Menu

graphs on a database. Although this is a simple example, it clearly demonstrates the power of Lotus as a DSS tool.

The following is the input/output of the macro we developed for this process.

Working Conditions: A 10 by 10 database.

Input:

Input of a 10 by 10 matrix given by the user

Output:

Data manipulation:

    Evaluation of salespeople or products

    Goal-seeking analysis

    What-if analysis

    Graphic display

Figure 13-14 illustrates the listing of this macro.

Summary

In this chapter we presented over a dozen macros in different disciplines. This diverse collection should expand your knowledge of Lotus macros in many disciplines.

Try to be creative and extend the knowledge you have gained in this book to the discipline of your choice.

```
\c~g25~
{getnumber "Please enter amount you are paying (xxx.xxx): ",g24}~
{if (g26)<0}~/rnca~~{goto}h1~{?}{home}{goto}a~/rnda~{branch \c}
{if (g24)>100}~/rncb~{goto}BB1~{?}{home}{goto}b~/rndb~{branch \c}
{LET D20,     PLEASE WAIT}~/RUD20~
{indicate $$$$$$}{windowsoff}{paneloff}
{let k24,g26}~
{if k24>=50}~{goto}a1000~{end}{up}{down}1{right}50.00{right}bill~{let k25,50}~{let k26,k24-k25}~{let k24,k26}~
{if k24>=39.999}~{goto}a1000~{end}{up}{down}2{right}20.00{right}bills~{let k25,40}~{let k26,k24-k25}~{let k24,k26}~
{if k24>=19.999}~{goto}a1000~{end}{up}{down}1{right}20.00{right}bill~{let k25,20}~{let k26,k24-k25}~{let k24,k26}~
{if k24>=9.999}~{goto}a1000~{end}{up}{down}1{right}10.00{right}bill~{let k25,10}~{let k26,k24-k25}~{let k24,k26}~
{if k24>=4.999}~{goto}a1000~{end}{up}{down}1{right}5.00{right}bill~{let k25,5}~{let k26,k24-k25}~{let k24,k26}~
{if k24>=3.999}~{goto}a1000~{end}{up}{down}4{right}1.00{right}bills~{let k25,4}~{let k26,k24-k25}~{let k24,k26}~
{if k24>=2.999}~{goto}a1000~{end}{up}{down}3{right}1.00{right}bills~{let k25,3}~{let k26,k24-k25}~{let k24,k26}~
{if k24>=1.999}~{goto}a1000~{end}{up}{down}2{right}1.00{right}bills~{let k25,2}~{let k26,k24-k25}~{let k24,k26}~
{if k24>=.999}~{goto}a1000~{end}{up}{down}1{right}1.00{right}bill~{let k25,1}~{let k26,k24-k25}~{let k24,k26}~
{if k24>=.749}~{goto}a1000~{end}{up}{down}1{right}.50{right}coins~{let k25,.50}~{let k26,k24-k25}~{let k24,k26}~
{if k24>=.499}~{goto}a1000~{end}{up}{down}1{right}.50{right}coin~{let k25,.50}~{let k26,k24-k25}~{let k24,k26}~
{if k24>=.249}~{goto}a1000~{end}{up}{down}1{right}.25{right}coin~{let k25,.25}~{let k26,k24-k25}~{let k24,k26}~
{if k24>=.199}~{goto}a1000~{end}{up}{down}2{right}.10{right}coins~{let k25,.20}~{let k26,k24-k25}~{let k24,k26}~
{if k24>=.099}~{goto}a1000~{end}{up}{down}1{right}.10{right}coin~{let k25,.10}~{let k26,k24-k25}~{let k24,k26}~
{if k24>=.0499}~{goto}a1000~{end}{up}{down}1{right}.05{right}coin~{let k25,.05}~{let k26,k24-k25}~{let k24,k26}~
{if k24>=.0399}~{goto}a1000~{end}{up}{down}4{right}.01{right}coins~{let k25,.04}~{let k26,k24-k25}~{let k24,k26}~
{if k24>=.0299}~{goto}a1000~{end}{up}{down}3{right}.01{right}coins~{let k25,.03}~{let k26,k24-k25}~{let k24,k26}~
{if k24>=.0199}~{goto}a1000~{end}{up}{down}2{right}.01{right}coins~{let k25,.02}~{let k26,k24-k25}~{let k24,k26}~
{if k24>=.0099}~{goto}a1000~{end}{up}{down}1{right}.01{right}coin~{let k25,.01}~{let k26,k24-k25}~{let k24,k26}~
{blank k21,k26}~
{goto}e24~{{left 4}*{left 3}}~
{if b25=0}{goto}a21~{indicate}{quit}
/c~.{left 2}{end}{down}{right 2}~
{end}{down}{end}{up}{down})~
```

```
\b
{goto}a21~{indicate}{quit}
```

```
/rea24.e1000~
{BLANK D20}~
{home}{goto}b8~
```

Figure 13-13 (Continued) Lotus as an Advanced Calculator — Macro Listing

```
A3: [W11]                                                              READY

          A      B    C    D    E    F    G    H    I    J    K    L
 1                                 PRODUCTS
 2   SALESPEOPLE  1    2    3    4    5    6    7    8    9    10   TOTAL
 3
 4   Roberts    1000  100  100  100  100  100  100  100  100  100  1900
 5   Smith       100  100  100   10   36  100   29  300  100  100   975
 6   Jones       100  100  100  100  300  100  100  200  100  100  1300
 7   Baker       100   15  500  100  100  100  100  100  100  100  1315
 8   Brown       100  100  100  100  100  100   55  100  100  100   955
 9   Adam        100  100  100  100   45   50  100  100  100  100   895
10   Anderson     50  100  100  100  100  100  100  100  100  100   950
11   Donalds      50  100   20  100   57  100   28  100  100  100   755
12   Mcmahan     100  100  100  100  100  100  100  100  100  100  1000
13   Wild        100  100  100  100  100  100  100  100  100  100  1000
14
15      TOTAL   1800  915 1320  910 1038  950  812 1300 1000 1000 11045
16   ========================================================================
17            *****************************************************
18            ***    Use arrow keys [->] to input data.      ***
19            ***    Press [ENTER] when finished.            ***
20            *****************************************************
01-Jan-89   09:37 AM                                        CALC
```

Figure 13–14 Lotus as a DSS Tool — A Sample Database

```
\0          {PANELOFF}                                          \N      /RNLR~
            {BRANCH \SUB-MAIN}
                                                                \R      /FS~R~
\A          {PANELOFF}
            {BRANCH \SUB-MAIN}

\SUB-MAIN   {GOTO}BL500~
            {MENUBRANCH \MENU-MAIN}

\SUB-INPUT  /WGRA~
            /RUB4..K13~
            {PANELON}
            /RIA3..L15~
            {PANELOFF}
            /RPB4..K13~
            /WGRM~
            {MENUBRANCH \MENU-MAIN}

\SUB-GOAL   {WINDOWSOFF}
            {LET H05,L15}{LET H04,"Y"}
            {GOTO}A203~{GOTO}L215~{WINDOWSON}
            {GETNUMBER "ENTER THE TARGETED SALES TOTAL:    ",H05}
            {CALC}
            {MENUCALL \MENU-GOAL}
            {LET H04,"N"}
            {GOTO}BL500~{WINDOWSOFF}
            {MENUBRANCH \MENU-MAIN}

\SUB-WHAT   {WINDOWSOFF}
            /CA1..L15~A301..L315~
            {HOME}{DOWN 14}/WTH
            {GOTO}A304~{DOWN 2}
            /WWH{WINDOW}
            {DOWN 9}{WINDOW}
            /RUB304..K313~
            /WGRA~{CALC}
            {WINDOWSON}{PANELON}
            /RIA304..K313~
            /WGRM~
            {WINDOWSOFF}{PANELOFF}
            /RPB304..K313~/REA301..L315~
            /WWC/WTC
            {HOME}{DOWN 2}/WTH
            {GOTO}BL500~{WINDOWSON}{WINDOWSOFF}
            {MENUBRANCH \MENU-MAIN}
```

Figure 13–14 (Continued) Lotus as a DSS Tool — Macro Listing

```
\SUB-SP-EV   {LET H06,"S"} {CALC}
             {WINDOWSOFF} /WTC~
             {GOTO}A401~
             /RVA1..L15~~
             /DSDA404..L413~PL402~D~SA402~A~G
             /RUA402~{DOWN 3}
             {WINDOWSON} {GOTO}. {DOWN 2} {RIGHT 11} {WINDOWSOFF}
             ~/RPA402~/REA401..A415~
             {GOTO} {?} {ESC} {ESC} {ESC} {HOME} {DOWN 2} /WTH
             {GOTO}BL500~{WINDOWSON} {WINDOWSOFF}
             {MENUBRANCH \MENU-MAIN}

\SUB-PD-EV   {LET H06,"P"} {CALC}
             {WINDOWSOFF} /WTC~
             {GOTO}A401~
             /RVA1..L15~~
             /MA402..L402~A403~/MA415..L415~A414~
             /RTA403..L414~A421~
             /DSDA422..L431~PL421~D~SA421~A~G
             /RTA421..L431~A403~
             /MA403..L403~A402~/MA414..L414~A415~
             /RUF401~{RIGHT} {DOWN}
             {WINDOWSON} {GOTO}. {DOWN 13} {RIGHT 2} {WINDOWSOFF}
             ~/RPF401~
             {GOTO} {?} {ESC} {ESC} {ESC}
             /REA403..L415~/REA421..L432~
             {HOME} {DOWN 2} /WTH
             {GOTO}BL500~{WINDOWSON} {WINDOWSOFF}
             {MENUBRANCH \MENU-MAIN}

\SUB-SP-GR   /GNUSALESPEOPLE~Q
             {MENUBRANCH \MENU-MAIN}

     \SUB-PD-GR   /GNUPRODUCT~Q
                  {MENUBRANCH \MENU-MAIN}

     \SUB-QUIT    {CALC} /FS~R
                  {HOME} {QUIT}
```

Figure 13-14 (Continued)

Review Questions

1. Design a macro to retrieve a given database and generate a mailing label list. Your database may include six fields: first name, last name, street address, city, state, and zip code. Your macro should allow different sort options on the various fields.

2. Design a macro that balances a checkbook. You can use the following data: The beginning balance is $1,000.00. The bank pays 5 percent interest on the average balance at the first and end of the month. The macro should allow five withdrawals up to $500. Two deposits are allowed of any amount. If any withdrawal is above $500, the macro should issue a warning and ask for different data.

3. Using the following tax table, design a macro to tell how much tax must be paid by a prospective taxpayer.

Income	Tax
<$ 5,000	0
$ 7,000	200
$10,000	800
$12,000	1,800
$20,000	2,200
$30,000	3,500
$40,000	6,000
>$40,000	7,000

4. Design a macro that utilizes a summary of sales data, then generates selected statistics, a line graph, and a bar graph.

Region	Total Sales
Portland	200,000
Denver	150,000
Los Angeles	300,000
San Diego	240,000
Washington	320,000
Minneapolis	180,000
Las Vegas	100,000

The statistics should include the region with the highest sales, with the lowest sales, the average of total sales, and standard deviation of the given data. The macro should utilize the menu macro command and should include four options: statistics, line graph, bar graph, and quit.

5. Design a macro that utilizes a sample grade book and then generates a letter grade for all the students and the names of the students with the highest and lowest grades. Use the following convention for grading:

$$\geq 90 \rightarrow A$$
$$\geq 80 \rightarrow B$$
$$\geq 70 \rightarrow C$$
$$\geq 60 \rightarrow D$$
$$< 60 \rightarrow F$$

Sample Grade Book

Student Name	Test 1	Test 2	Test 3	Total Scores
Brown	80	70	90	
Campbell	100	90	80	
Lopez	90	60	70	
Jones	70	90	50	
Smith	60	70	60	
Grab	30	80	90	
Shank	90	80	65	
Stone	65	75	75	
Adam	70	50	90	
Kane	90	70	62	
Honnson	65	60	74	

Your macro should also generate a line graph of the total scores.

6. Design a macro that generates the future value of an IRA plan with three different interest rates and three payment periods. The following is sample data:

Interest Rate	Payment Period	Future Value of IRA
8%	20 years	
10%	23 years	
12%	80 years	

You can use either table manipulation or straight future-value analysis.

7. Using the macro given in Section 13-9 of the text, calculate the average cost, average variable cost, and marginal cost of the following cost equation:

500 +6Q + .01 Q2 (Q is the number of units produced)

8. Using the macro given in Section 13.11 of the text, calculate the world population in the year 2010 using the following data:

In 1989 the world population is 4.5 billion

Death rate — .8%

Birth rate — 2.6%

9. Using the macro given in Section 13.13, perform the following transaction:

Item chosen   = $.98

Money paid   = $15

How much is the change? What happens if you input $200?

10. Run the macro given in Section 13-14. What are the limitations of this macro as a DSS tool? How can it be improved?

Appendix A

Disk Operating System

A-1 Introduction

In this appendix we provide you with a quick review of the disk operating system for IBM PCs (PC-DOS) and PC compatibles (MS-DOS). This overview covers disk file creation, customizing your system, and manipulating your directory and gives a brief explanation of the EDLIN program, a simple line editor. We also provide you with over 80 of the most commonly used DOS commands. The appendix concludes with a brief review of the future of MS/PC DOS.

A-2 What is DOS?

In simple terms, DOS (Disk Operating System) is a collection of programs that enables you to interact with your computer. The following are some common uses:

- getting the system started

- housekeeping (e.g., creating a backup disk)

- housecleaning (e.g., changing or deleting files)

- customizing your PC (changing prompt, self-booting your system, etc.)

- simplifying system access for frequent and infrequent users

There are several versions of DOS available on the market. Some of these have a broader scope of application, e.g., CP/M, MS-DOS, PC-DOS, UNIX, and the like. Many software programs can be run by these operating systems. In addition, some special-purpose DOSs have been designed for particular microprocessor chips and brands of computers, for example, Apple DOS, TRS DOS, and so forth. Naturally, these operating systems run only the products for which they were designed.

Many advanced features, such as designing directories and subdirectories or linking of different programs, can be done by DOS. The information in this appendix applies specifically to MS-DOS or PC-DOS. You can always assume that between you and your application program (in this case, Lotus) there is a gate called DOS. To get to any application program you have to go through DOS.

A-3 Types of DOS Commands

To get your system started place the DOS disk in drive A and turn the computer on. Usually the system will ask you for the date and time. If you respond with the date and time in the proper format, the A> prompt will appear. Although you can bypass this step by hitting the **Return** key twice, it is a good practice to enter both date and time. If you save a program, the date and time will be saved in your program file. Then you will know which version of your program is the most recent. Figure A-1 shows this process.

The A> prompt means the disk operating system is activated in drive A. You can change the default drive by typing the drive specifier, A, B, or C, followed by a colon (e.g., B: or C:). Unless a hard disk is used to boot the system, the default drive is always A.

At this point you can access two types of DOS commands: external and internal. To execute any external command, you must have the DOS disk in your disk drive. An example of an external command is DISKCOPY. All the commands and files with the extension BAT, COM, or EXE are external.

To execute an internal command the DOS disk does not need to be in any of the drives. CLS, for example, is an internal command. At the A> prompt, you can type CLS to clear the screen.

A-4 File Specifications

Any disk file will have three distinct parts:

- drive name

- file name

- file extension

A drive name can be A:, B:, C:, etc. If you do not specify a drive name, the computer assumes the default drive has been selected.

```
Current date is Tue  1-01-1980
Enter new date (mm-dd-yy): 1-1-89
Current time is  0:01:24.36
Enter new time: 11:50


The IBM Personal Computer DOS
Version 3.00 (C)Copyright IBM Corp 1981, 1982, 1983, 1984

A>
```

Figure A–1 Getting the Sytsem Started

A file name can be up to eight characters long. It can include letters and digits. Do not use reserved words as file names, such as DISKCOPY or CON (console). Special characters such as @, %, or . can also be used but are not advisable.

The file extension is optional. If used, it can be up to three characters long. As with the file name, letters, digits, and special characters can be used.

It is imperative that you know which drive is the source drive and which is the target drive. The source drive is the one with the original program, the drive from which you transfer information. The target drive is the one to which the information is transferred. Mistaking these two drives can be dangerous.

It is a good practice to select file names that have some meaning. For example, Payroll, Credit, and Commission are some good names for business applications. Do not include any spaces in your file names or extension. Uppercase and lowercase are equivalent.

A-5 Wild Card Characters

Two characters have specific meaning to DOS One is the question mark (?) and the other is the asterisk (*). When the question mark is used, it replaces any character in that particular position. For example, when requesting a directory of DOS files, you may enter the following:

A>DIR AB?JACK

This will give you the following files:

ABAJACK

ABXJACK

ABBJACK

ABZJACK

ABCJACK, etc.

When the asterisk is used, it replaces any number of characters from that position on to the next specified character. For example:

A>DIR AB*.*

will list all the files that start with the letters AB. The rest of the name and extension are not considered. For example, A>DIR *.* will give you all the files with any name and any extension. A>DIR *.WK1 will give you all the files with the extension WK1.

These two wild cards can be very helpful for accessing specific sets of files. For example, COPY B: *.WK1 will copy all the worksheet files from the disk in drive B to the disk in drive A, assuming your current drive is A:.

A-6 Redirection and Piping

It is possible to direct the output of a command to a different device other than the standard selected by that command. For example, A>DIR>PRN will transfer the listing of your directory to the printer. A>DIR>Myfile will transfer the listing of your directory to a file called "Myfile".

Piping takes place when you combine two commands. For example, A>DIR ¦SORT will sort your directory alphabetically. A>DIR ¦SORT>Myfile will sort the directory and write the output into a file called "Myfile". Then, at the A> prompt, you can type TYPE Myfile and the computer will give you the sorted listing of your files.

Redirection can be in a left to right direction (as opposed to right to left) by using the < sign. For example, at the A prompt, if you type Program1 <input.ext, Program 1 receives its input from the input.ext file.

When you redirect to a file, the present contents of the file will be lost. If you would like to append to the file and not lose the present contents, use >>. For example, A>DIR>>Myfile will add the listing of the current directory to Myfile. Naturally, you can use << in the same manner as < without losing the contents of the file to the left of this sign.

A-7 Batch and Autoexec Files

Batch files or BAT files are disk files designed for a specific use. These files include a collection of DOS commands and other valid statement that will save operator time. The series of commands in the file is designed to run uninterrupted and is initiated by executing one command. A batch file can have any standard name but the extension must always be BAT. You can include any valid command or statement in your batch file. In theory, batch files can have any length.

To enter a command into a batch file, you must always hit the **Return** key after the specific command. To generate a batch file you can use EDLIN, the line editor available on DOS, or any word processing program. For simple files you can use a version of the copy command as follows:

A>COPY CON Myfile.BAT	(hit **Return**)
Command or statement	(hit **Return**)
Command or statement	(hit **Return**)
Command or statement	(hit **Return**)

To save a batch file press **Ctrl** and **Z** together (F6 function key) and hit the **Return** key. To execute a batch file all you need to do is to type the name of the file at the A> prompt.

We have designed a simple batch file as follows:

A> COPY CON HELLO.BAT	(hit **Return**)
DIR	(hit **Return**)
CLS	(hit **Return**)
BASICA	(hit **Return**)
	(hit **Ctrl + Z**) (press the **Ctrl** and **Z** keys together or press F6)

If you type HELLO at the A> prompt, you will see your directory, the screen will be cleared out, and BASICA will be loaded to RAM. The COPY CON generates an ASCII file (ASCII files are discussed in Appendix C.) To stop the execution of a batch file, press **Ctrl** and **Break** at the same time.

The major limitation with COPY CON is that you cannot edit a file that has been created. For editing you have to redo the entire file or use EDLIN or some other word processing or editor system. The EDLIN program is briefly explained in the next section.

If you call your file AUTOEXEC.BAT, it will be executed automatically as soon as the system is started. As a matter of fact, DOS always looks for this file first. This facility can be very helpful. You can design a menu, customize your system, and help other users unfamiliar with computers. Batch files in general are very helpful if you have to do a series of repetitive operations.

A-8 The EDLIN Program

As mentioned earlier, the COPY CON command will not allow you to perform any editing after the creation of a file. However, it is common to want to edit an existing file. Let us say you would like to add a few more commands to an existing file. You cannot edit a program generated by the COPY CON command. Since the EDLIN program is available on your DOS diskette (version 3.0 and above), it is a good idea to learn this simple and very effective program.

To start the EDLIN program, put your PC-DOS disk in drive A, put an empty formatted disk in drive B and type EDLIN B:Myfile. Txt. This command generates a permanent file. With EDLIN (the line editor program) you can do the following:

- create a file

- save a file

- update a file

- delete, edit, modify, insert lines to a file

- display an entire file or any portion of it

When you get the EDLIN started, the system will respond with the following messages:
New file
*

Type I for insert. At this point, you can type any line of information, up to 253 characters. EDLIN will generate line numbers for editing purposes only. These line numbers will not be part of the saved file.

To stop the EDLIN program and return to DOS you have two options, E and Q. If you wish to exit the editor and return to DOS, type E at the EDLIN prompt. If you wish to cancel the editing session, type Q. The system will respond "Abort Edit (Y/N)?" If you type Y the changes made during the editing session will not be saved. Table A-1 summarizes the EDLIN commands.

A-9 Directory and Subdirectory: Hard Disk Management

In order to effectively manage all the files in your secondary storage device (diskette and/or hard disk), you should establish a tree-structured directory. In this fashion, you will be able to organize groups of related files in separate directories. To access a particular file you have to define a path leading to it. Let us assume that Ocean City Manufacturing has stored all its files on a hard disk using a PC. The directory is structured as follows:

```
                                                        Product1

Root ——→ Division1 ——→ Manufacturing ——→ John ——→ Product2
  ↓                                          Bob        Product3

     ——→ Division2 ——→ Marketing ——→ Sales

                                      Advertising
```

Table A-1 EDLIN COMMANDS SUMMARY

EDLIN Myfile.ext	Create a new file called Myfile.ext
EDLIN oldfile.ext	Edit an existing file called oldfile.ext
C	Copy from one location to another
1,10,20C	Copy lines 1 through 10 to before line 20
D	Delete one or a series of lines
1,10D	Delete lines 1 through 10
50D	Delete line 50
I	Insert a line or a series of lines
5I	Insert text before line 5
L	List the entire file
1,10L	List lines 1 through 10
10L	List from line 10 to the end
M	Move a series of lines
1,10,50M	Move lines 1 through 10 to before line 50
R	Replace all occurrences of the first string in a given range with the second string
1,5?R old string F6 (Ctrl and Z) New String	Display the line where the old string occurs and ask the user if that line is correct. If the user answers yes, EDLIN goes to the next occurrence without changing the string. If the user answers No, the old string is replaced with the new string. EDLIN then continues to the next occurrence.
S	Search a given range to find a specified string
1,10SHappy	Search lines 1 through 10 for the string "Happy". If you would like to see all of the occurrences of a particular string use 1,10?SHappy and then follow the prompt
T	Merge a specified file into the current file being edited
10,T:B:Filename1.ext	Transfer Filename1.ext from drive B to the top of line 10 of the current file
W	Transfer lines from current file to disk. This command always writes starting from line 1
20W	Write the first 20 lines to disk
P	List 23 lines of the current file beginning with the current line
10,20P	List from line 10 to 20
E	End the EDLIN process and save the edited file
. or line number	Edit a line
6	Edit line 6. To move to a particular word, type the first letter of the word and hit F2. You can delete a character by using the **Del** key. After deleting process, hit F3. You can hit F5 to do additional editing to the altered line without changing the original line. Pressing **Return** will save the altered line. Pressing **Esc** or **Ctrl-Break** will cancel the changes you made to the line

This directory (called tree-structured) can help you access any of these files more effectively than a simple directory. For example, to list all the files under Product 1 from the root directory, you would have to type:

A:\Division 1\Manufacturing\John \Product 1

Figure A-2 displays this tree structure graphically.

The root directory always starts with a backslash (\). This directory is automatically generated when you format a diskette. The route to reach a particular file is called the path for that file. The above path for Product1 files is one example. The root directory in a single-sided diskette can hold up to 64 files, in a double-sided diskette up to 112. A high-density diskette can hold up to 224, and a hard disk up to 512 files.

Another type of directory is the subdirectory. A subdirectory is any directory under a primary directory. In other words, in the above example, the primary directory would be Division1, and all directories included in this directory, Manufacturing, John, and Product1, would be considered subdirectories. Subdirectory names follow the same format as file names. The extension is optional. Figure A-2 illustrates a directory structure more clearly.

The default directory is the directory at the start-up of th system. You can always change the current directory by using the CHDIR (CD) command. There is no limitation on the number of subdirectories. As we discussed earlier, the subdirectories are separated by a series of backslashes (\). The length of a directory path cannot exceed 63 characters. To create a directory, use the MKDIR (MD) command. To display the directory structure, use the TREE command. To remove a directory, use the RD command. However, the directory must be empty before it can be removed.

If you just installed a hard disk (fixed disk), you can transfer all DOS files into your hard disk and start your computer from the hard disk. To do so, you must use the FDISK program provided on your DOS disk. This program is menu driven and self-explanatory. For more information consult the chapter on preparing your fixed disk in the DOS manual. You should also remember that disk drives are identified by letters, A, B, C, and so on. For example, if you have two disk drives and two hard disks they are identified by the letters A through D. You can also have more than one operating system on your hard disk. The FDISK program allows you to do the following:

- create a DOS partition
- change a DOS partition
- display partition data
- delete an active partition

A-10 Important DOS Commands

In Table A-2 we have summarized most of the commonly used commands in DOS. An important point to remember is that PC-DOS/MS-DOS always work on the basis of from to, meaning the first drive is the source (from) and the second is the target (to).

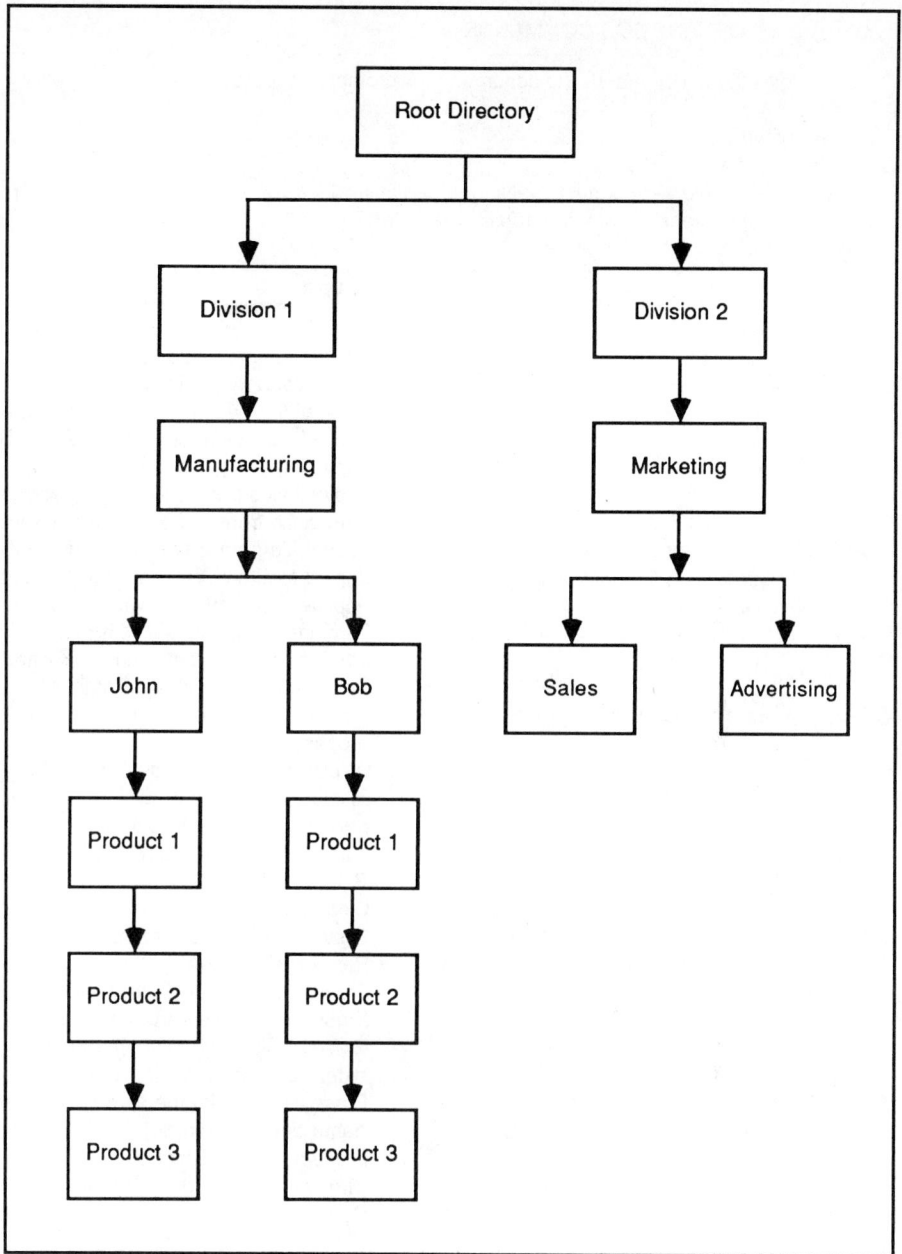

Figure A–2 Directory of Ocean City Manufacturing

To become more familiar with these commands you have to practice them. All you need is a DOS disk and an empty diskette. Remember that the FORMAT and DISKCOPY commands can be very dangerous!

The commands have been divided into two groups. Group 1 commands are used quite often. Group 2 is more advanced. Only users of advanced applications may have the opportunity to utilize commands in the second group. Following are brief descriptions of some of these commands.

Table A-2 IMPORTANT DOS COMMANDS

(To execute all these commands we assume the A prompt is apparent.)
A stands for A drive
B stands for B drive
C stands for C drive
D stands for any drive — you must specify the particular drive
ext stands for file extension (any three valid characters)
Filename can be any valid file name

	Group 1
BASICA SAMPLES	Load SAMPLES program from BASICA
COPY Filename.ext B:	Copy Filename. ext to B
COPY B:Filename.ext	Copy Filename.ext to A
COPY *.ext B:	Copy all files with the same ext from A to B
COPY B:*.ext	Copy all files with the same ext from B to A
COPY *.* B:	Copy all files from A to B
COPY B:*.*	Copy all files from B to A
COPY Filename1.ext Filename2.ext	Copy a file from A to A with a different name
COPY B:Filename1.ext B:Filename2.ext	Copy a file from B to B with a different name
COPY Filename1.ext B:Filename2.ext	Copy a file from A to B with a different name
COPY B:Filename1.ext Filename2.ext	Copy a file from B to A with a different name
COPY Filename1.ext+Filename2.ext Filename3.ext	Combine the first two files and make a third file in drive A
COPY *.WK1+*.PIC Total. WKS	Combine all files matching *.WK1 and then all files matching *.PIC into one file called Total. WKS
COPY Filename1.ext C:/V	Copy Filename1.ext from Drive A to C and verify the process
CHKDSK	Display free or unused space on diskette in default drive
CHKDSK B:	Display free space on diskette in drive B
COMP	Compare two disk files to determine if they are the same or if they are different, e.g., COMP A:TEXT.JOE B:TEXT.JACK
CLS	Clear screen
CTRL and ALT and DEL (three together)	System reset — reboot the system
DATE	Reset system date
DEL Filename.ext	Erase Filename.ext from drive A
DEL B:Filename.ext	Erase Filename.ext from drive B
DEL B:Filename.*	Erase all files with Filename as their name with any extension from drive B
DEL B:*.ext	Erase all files with the same extension from drive B (file name does not matter)
DEL C:*.*	Erase all files in Drive C
DIR	Directory of A (or default drive)
DIR B:	Directory of B
DIR/P	Display a complete directory of drive A with a pause before scrolling off the screen
DIR B:/P	Do the same thing as DIR/P for drive B
DIR/W	Display a wide directory of drive A
DIR B:/W	Display a wide directory of drive B
DIR ¦SORT	Display a sorted directory of drive A
DIR ¦MORE	Display one screen at a time
DIR ¦SORT/R MORE	Sort directory in descending order and display one screen at a time
DIR B:¦ SORT	Display a sorted directory of drive B
DISKCOPY A: B:	Copy a diskette in drive A to a diskette in drive B
DISKCOMP	Compare two diskettes track-by-track, sector-for-sector to determine if their contents are identical, e.g., DISKCOMP A: B:

Group 1

ERASE Filename.ext	Erase Filename.ext on A
ERASE B:Filename.ext	Erase Filename.ext on B
ERASE *.ext	Erase all files with same extension (ext) on A
ERASE B:*.ext	Erase all files with same extension (ext) on B
FORMAT	Erase and format a diskette in default drive
FORMAT B:	Erase and format a diskette in drive B
FORMAT/V	Format a diskette with a volume label in default drive
FORMAT B:/V	Format a diskette with a volume label in drive B
FORMAT B:/S	Format a diskette with DOS in drive B. This procedure will put IBMBIO.COM, IBMDOS.COM, and COMMAND.COM on this diskette. This disk can be used to boot the system
FORMAT D:/1	Format a diskette for single-side use
FORMAT D:/8	Format an eight sector per track diskette
FORMAT D:/4	Format a double-sided diskette in a high-capacity drive
FORMAT D:/B	Format for eight sectors and leave space for the systems files. These files include IBMBIO.COM and IBMDOS.COM and can be copied later
LABEL	Create, change, or delete a volume label for a disk, e.g., LABEL C:ACCOUNT
RENAME Filename1.ext Filename2.ext	Rename a file Filename1.ext to Filename2.ext on A
RENAME B:Filename1.ext B:Filename2.ext	Rename a file on B from Filename1.ext to Filename2.ext
SHIFT and PrtSc key (together)	Print a copy of the screen
TYPE Filename.ext	Display content of Filename.ext on A
TYPE B:Filename.ext	Display content of Filename.ext on B
TYPE Myfile.ext>PRN	Redirect the output of command TYPE to a file called Myfile.ext
TIME	Reset system time

Group 2

ASSIGN	Tell DOS to use a different disk drive from the one specified by a program or command, e.g., ASSIGN A=C
ATTRIB +R	Make a file read-only. ATTRIB +R Myfile.ext sets Myfile.ext a read-only file
ATTRIB -R	Make a file read or write accessible
BACKUP	Back up files from a fixed (hard) disk or diskette onto a diskette or another fixed disk, e.g., BACKUP A: B:
BUFFERS	Allow the user to specify the number of disk buffers that DOS will allocate in the memory when the system is started, e.g., BUFFERS=10. Default is 2 for IBM PC; 3 for IBM AT. Maximum is 99
CHDIR (DC)	Change the current directory or display the current directory path, e.g., CD\ changes the current directory of drive A to its root directory
ECHO ON	Display the execution of DOS commands in a batch file
ECHO OFF	Do not allow DOS commands to be displayed when a batch file is being executed
ECHO DOS IS EASY	Display the text DOS IS EASY on the monitor when executing a batch tile
FILES	Tell DOS how many files can be used at one time, e.g., FILES=12. Default is 8 and maximum is 255
FIND	Display all lines from a given file(s) that contain a given string
	/V Display all lines not containing the desired string
	/N Display the relative line number of each candidate line
	/C Display the total of occurrences of desired string

Group 2

B>DIR A: FIND/V "BOB"	Display the name of all files in drive A that do not contain string "BOB"
B>FIND/N"BOB"A:Myfile.ext	Locate and count all occurrences of string "BOB" in Myfile.ext
MKDIR (MD)	Create a subdirectory on a disk, e.g., MKDIR C: CLIENTS; MD C: CLIENTS
PATH	Instruct DOS to search a specified directory for a program that cannot be found in the current directory, e.g., PATH C: \Jack \Sales
PAUSE	Suspend the program and wait for the user to see the message
PROMPT	Customize the DOS system prompt, e.g., PROMPT Hello changes the system prompt to Hello, PROMPT Pq changes the prompt to display the current directory, PROMPT changes the system prompt back to the default
RECOVER	Recover a disk or a file with defective sectors, e.g., RECOVER Myfile
RMDIR (RD)	Remove a subdirectory from a disk, e.g., RMDIR C:CPA or RD C:CPA. Directory must be empty before you can remove it
SORT	Sort in ascending order
SORT/R	Sort in descending order
SORT/+n	Sort by one of the five directory parameters:
	n=1 by file name (default value)
	n=10 by file extension
	n=14 by file size
	n=24 by date that file was created
	n=34 by time that file was created
SYS	Put a copy of operating system files IBMDOS.COM and IBMBIO.COM on the specified diskette or fixed disk, e.g., SYS B:
TREE	Display the structure of the current directory
TREE/F	Display the structure and the files in the subdirectory
VER	Display the DOS version number on the screen, e.g., VER
VERIFY	Check the data just written to a disk to be sure the data has been correctly recorded and then display whether the data has been checked, e.g.,
	VERIFY ON set verify on
	VERIFY OFF set verify off
	VERIFY show verify status
VOL	Display the volume label of a disk, if the label exists, e.g., VOL B:

When you type DIR, the single dot (.) and double dot (..) tell you that you are not in the root directory. The single dot refers to the current directory and the double dot refers to the directory immediately above the current directory.

When you refer to a file which is not in the current directory, you must either make that directory current by using the CD command or specify the path to that directory; for example, path =\A: JACK Marketing. When a path is specified, the computer will search for data in the current directory plus all directories specified in the path.

The COPY command is used for copying one or a series of individual files. The source and target drive can be any drive.

The CHKDSK command is used in order to find out about any free space on a particular diskette.

CLS is used to clear the screen. This is an example of a DOS internal command. This command can be used in BASIC as well as in DOS.

DEL or ERASE is used to delete a disk file. Remember, to delete a disk file you must always use the file name and the file extension.

DIR is used to display the directory of your system. The drive identified can be A:, B:, C:, etc.

DISKCOPY is used to duplicate a diskette. Remember, when you use this command, the target diskette does not need to be formatted. DISKCOPY formats the target diskette while it is doing the copying.

DISKCOMP and COMP are used for comparing two diskettes and comparing two files, respectively. If the two diskettes and/or two files are not identical you receive an error message.

FORMAT is used to format, or prepare, a diskette. If for any reason the diskette is damaged, you will receive an error message.

FORMAT/V is used for putting a volume label on a diskette. The label name can be any combination of characters up to 11, including a space. This is a nice feature to have for internal identification of diskettes. For example, volume labels may be total sales, total cost, etc.

The RENAME command is used to change a file name to a different file name.

The TYPE command will give you a listing of the contents of a file in DOS.

To implement the majority of DOS commands, just type the command, then follow the system prompt.

A-11 Future of MS/PC DOS

The newer versions of DOS have added new capabilities and have also fixed some of the previous bugs. Most recently, a new version of DOS (under several names such as Future DOS, New DOS, Advanced DOS 1.0, DOS 5, ADOS) has attracted much attention in the microcomputer community.

The new version of DOS has gained popularity by the support of Intel 80286 and 80386 microprocessors. The new DOS has claimed several specific goals:

- Expanded memory, beyond the traditional 640K

- Multitasking

- Multiprocessing

- Upward compatibility

- Ease of use or user-friendliness

Memory expansion is essential in order to access more sophisticated software. Also, to improve the user-friendliness, the system may have to use DOS shells, spelling checkers, electronic mail, notepads, pull-down windows, and so on. All these require enhanced and expanded memory.

Multitasking and multiprocessing will add a new dimension to the microcomputer environment. This feature allows a user to run more than one task or more than one program at the same time. This feature should assist a PC user to perform more sophisticated operations.

The multiprocessing (networking) feature enables more than one user to access the same application program. This feature makes a PC more cost effective. However, a multiprocessing system may run slower than single-tasking systems and may cause compatibility problems.

Upward compatibility allows PC users to upgrade to better and more powerful operating systems without losing what they already have.

User-friendliness is of significant importance to PC users. A typical user often does not have much experience with computers. The easier the system to use, the more attractive it is to the user. User friendliness can be improved by DOS shells or through graphic interface, such as Apple's Macintosh. IBM has developed Top View, and Microsoft has a graphic interface called Windows. To include these features in DOS, the PC must have expanded memory.

Several versions of the new IBM PC called Personal System 2 (PS/2) have already entered the market. Other vendors have also introduced PS/2 compatibles. PS/2 performs multitasking, utilizes the 16-megabyte address space of the 80286 microprocessor, and works with a DOS-compatible environment. At the same time, OS/2 addresses one gigabyte of virtual memory. The new operating system also includes many new features for programmers and application developers.

The new microprocessors, 286, 386, and possibly 486, can benefit immensely from the new DOS. DOS users should remember that AT&Ts Unix Operating System may be a major competitor to MS-DOS. However, at the present time, it is too complex for novice computer users.

Summary

In this appendix we have provided a brief discussion of the disk operating system, DOS, as the starting point for using any application program. We discussed, batch and AUTOEXEC files for more convenient system operations and disk file creation by using COPY CON or EDLIN. Table A-2 provided you with two sets of DOS commands. Group 1 consists of some of the most commonly used commands, while group 2 commands are used for some of the more advanced applications. Knowledge of these commands should prove very helpful for more effective use of your PC.

Review Questions

1. What is DOS?
2. How many different types of DOS do we have?
3.* Which DOS is used for the IBM PC? For its clones/compatibles?
4.* What is the difference between external and internal DOS commands?
5. How many different DOS prompts do we have?
6.* What is the purpose of the date and time prompts?
7. How do you bypass the date and time prompts?
8. Can you customize your DOS prompt? If yes, how?
9.* What is the difference between DISKCOPY and COPY *.*?
10. When you use DISKCOPY, do you need to format your diskette first?

11. What is a batch file?
12. What are some of the uses of a batch file?
13. How do you design a batch file?
14. What is an AUTOEXEC file?
15. What are some of the uses of an AUTOEXEC file?
16. How many different ways can you use the DIR command?
17. How do you rescue a file from a damaged disk?
18. How do you stop the execution of a batch file?
19. Get your system started. Format a blank disk, then copy three files from the DOS disk to this disk.
20. Copy your DOS disk to any empty disk.
21. Using wild card *, get a listing of all files with the BAT extension.
22. Sort your directory and direct the result to a file called Sfile. Now, using your printer, generate a printed copy of this file.
23. Sort your directory by file extension in descending order.
24.* Generate a batch file that will do the following:

Change directory from A to B:

Change directory back to A:

Generate a wide directory

Erase the screen

25. Generate a directory that includes three subdirectories as follows:

Worksheet

Graph

Print

Copy three files in each subdirectory.
26. Generate any batch file once with COPY CON and once with the EDLIN program. What are the advantages of the EDLIN program?

Misconceptions and Solutions

M — If you want to transfer the content of one diskette to another, you can use either DISKCOPY or COPY *.*. However, DISKCOPY will first erase the content of the second diskette, then copy the first diskette to the second one.

S — Use COPY *.*, if you want to keep the content of the second diskette.

M — You turn the computer on, and you may see an unfamiliar message, such as OK Prompt instead of the A> Prompt. Your computer has booted the cassette BASIC from ROM.

S – You either forgot to put the DOS disk in drive A or you inserted your disk from the wrong direction! Insert the DOS disk into drive A and reboot the system.

M – You issue a DOS command and the error message says BAD COMMAND.

S – Most probably you have issued an external DOS command without having the DOS disk in one of the drives. Insert the DOS disk into the right drive and issue the appropriate command again.

Appendix B

Installing Lotus

B-1 Introduction

In this appendix, we will explain how you can tailor Lotus to your particular system. This procedure is needed if you just purchased Lotus or if you made some changes in your existing equipment. You do the installation only once. Installation simply means tailoring Lotus to different hardware. If you do not install Lotus your program will still run, but you won't be able to use your printer or generate any graphs. This appendix should answer questions regarding tailoring the Lotus program to different systems.

B-2 Why Is Installation Needed?

Since Lotus has been designed to work on many different systems, you must tailor this program to your specific hardware. Installation is needed for three different components:

Monitor Which monitor are you planning to use (color, black and white, monochrome with Hercules graphics card, etc.)?

Printer Is it a standard dot matrix printer, letter quality, or a printer with 132 characters?

Secondary Storage (data disk) Which drive will be used for storing data and programs generated by Lotus, drive B or drive C (hard disk)?

B-3 Getting Ready for Installation: Two-Disk Systems

Lotus Release 2 comes with six disks:

System Disk
Backup System Disk
A View of 1-2-3 Disk
PrintGraph Disk
Utility Disk
Install Library Disk

The System disk includes everything you need except instructions for printing graphs. This information is stored on the PrintGraph disk. Before you do the installation, it is advisable to make a backup copy of all disks and do the installation with the copies. In case of damage to any of the master disks, you will have a copy of it. Remember, you cannot copy the system disk since it is copy protected. Lotus has provided you with a backup copy of this disk. To make backup copies of the other four disks, follow these steps:

1. Prepare four empty disks. To do so, put the DOS disk in drive A, put an empty disk in drive B, type FORMAT B:, and press the **Return** key. Do this for all four disks. (For more information on formatting, see Appendix A.)
2. Now you have to make a copy of the Install Library, Utility, PrintGraph, and A View of 1-2-3 disks. To do this, put the DOS disk in drive A. At the A> prompt pull DOS out and put one of the four disks in drive A. Put one of the formatted disks in drive B, type COPY *.* B:, and press the **Return** key. Follow these steps for the other three disks. You now have a backup copy of all five disks. You could use the DISKCOPY command for making a backup copy as well; however, Lotus recommends that you use COPY instead of DISKCOPY.
3. The next step is to copy COMMAND.COM to these six disks. If you do not do this, you will get the following error message:
    Insert Disk with COMMAND.COM in Drive A and strike any key when ready.
    Copying this command to your disks helps you get back to DOS when you are exiting 1-2-3 or the Lotus Access System. To copy COMMAND.COM to the six disks, put DOS in drive A, put any of the six disks in drive B, type Copy COMMAND.COM B:, and press the **Return** key. Follow these steps for the other five disks.

B-4 Getting Ready for Installation: Hard Disk Systems

The steps just discussed are used for a two-disk system. If you have a system with hard disks (drive C) and one floppy drive (drive A), follow these steps:
You have to copy all five Lotus disks onto your hard disk. To get Lotus started, you need either your system disk or its backup. This is only for getting started; you can pull it out later and continue working with Lotus.

1. If drive C is not the default drive, make it the default drive by typing C: and pressing the **Return** key.

2. Create a subdirectory to hold 1-2-3 programs. Type MD 123 (see Appendix A for more information on subdirectories).
3. Make this subdirectory the current directory by typing CD 123.
4. Now copy all five Lotus disks onto drive C by putting one of the five disks in drive A and typing COPYA:*.*. Do this for the other four disks.

Now you are ready to go to the Install program.

B-5 Installing the Drivers

To tailor Lotus to your particular system, you have to transfer a series of drivers to Lotus disks. Drivers are simply a series of programs that monitor and run the hardware. To run the Install program, you must know the specifications of your hardware. To get the procedure started, put the DOS disk in drive A and boot the system. At the A> prompt, pull the DOS disk out, put the Utility disk into drive A, and type INSTALL. This procedure is for a two-disk drive system. For hard disk systems you first have to change the current directory to the subdirectory containing the Lotus programs (CD C:\123) and at the C prompt type INSTALL. In any event, you will be given a screen describing the procedure. Press the **Return** key and the program will ask you to remove the Utility disk and put the Install Library disk in drive A. Do this and press the **Return** key. Now it asks you to put the System disk in drive A and press the **Return** key. The Install menu will appear. You will be given four options:

First-Time Installation
Change Selected Equipment
Advanced Options
Exit Install Program

If you just purchased Lotus, choose First-Time Installation. Change Selected Equipment is used if you must change one of your components. Advanced Options allows you to do certain things that you can't do elsewhere in the Install program; for example, adding new drivers to the library, modifying the current drivers set, or changing the collating sequence (for sorting, the number to come first or the number to be last). The last option is used to exit the menu. The rest of the procedure basically means following a series of menus. If you follow these menus carefully, you should not have any problem installing the Lotus program for any system that Lotus supports.

Driver programs must be installed on the System disk, A View of Lotus, and PrintGraph. You can do these one by one, replacing the System disk with the next disk.

B-6 Defining Default Settings for Secondary Storage and Printer

You can change and/or maintain the default settings of your secondary storage (drive B or C) and the printer. The /Worksheet Global Default Printer command will tell you the default settings of your printer. This includes:

Interface   Auto-LF   Left   Right   Top   Bottom   Pg-Length   Wait
Setup   Name

Any of these settings can be changed and restored in the future by issuing /Worksheet Global Default Update.

/Worksheet Global Default Directory will tell you the current directory or the current secondary storage. These settings can be changed and maintained permanently by issuing /Worksheet Global Default Update.

If you encounter any problems, consult *123 Getting Started*. This brief manual explains these steps in detail.

Summary

In this appendix, we have provided you with some guidelines regarding tailoring Lotus to your system. Since Lotus has been designed to work on several systems, customization is needed. If you don't install Lotus, your 1-2-3 program will still run but you won't be able to generate graphs or use your printer. We gave a quick review of the Utility and Install Library programs. These two programs provide you with the information needed for the installation of 1-2-3 and its companion programs.

Review Questions

1. Why must Lotus be installed?
2. If you do not install Lotus, which part of the program may not work?
3.* Which disk among the six disks cannot be copied and why?
4.* How do you make a backup copy of the PrintGraph disk?
5. Why must COMMAND.COM be copied to all the Lotus disks?
6. How do you copy PrintGraph to a hard disk?
7. What is a directory? A subdirectory?
8. How do you make a directory the current directory?
9. On which disk is the Install program?
10.* How do you get the installation procedure started?
11. What are drivers?
12. How many driver sets can you have?
13.* What is the default driver name for 1-2-3?

Appendix C

File Transfer Between Lotus and Other Software

C-1 Introduction

In this appendix we will provide you with some guidelines for importing and exporting files to and from Lotus. This facility enables you to utilize the best features of each software package. Also, by importing other files, you should be able to save time and frustration by not duplicating the same data file. Lotus provides several facilities for data transfer. The Translate utility provided by Release 2 is an excellent program that makes the task of file transfer a very easy job. In this appendix, we will talk about these facilities. We will also talk about the /File Import and /Data Parse commands.

C-2 Why File Transfer?

There are several reasons for using file transfer facilities. File transfer simply means the transfer of a file generated by one applications software program to another. There are three reasons for such a task:

1. Utilizing a facility of one software package which is not available in another; for example, transferring a Lotus spreadsheet to a report generated by a word processing program. There are several benefits to this process, e.g., factual and comprehensive reports by integrating worksheet analysis into your WordStar report.

2. Utilizing the enhanced power available for the same basic tasks performed by two applications software programs. For example, since the database operations performed by Lotus are much faster than dBASE III Plus, you want to bring a dBASE file into a Lotus worksheet for processing.

3. Converting data files from earlier applications software programs to more recent versions. This is a very common practice. Consider converting VisiCalc files into Lotus files. Without data transfer facilities you would have to enter all the data again, a time-consuming and tedious task.

C-3 What Is an ASCII File?

ASCII (American Standard Code for Information Interchange) is a data format generated and accepted by many applications software packages.

An ASCII file, or simply a "print image" file, is a file in standard keyboard characters. To verify whether a file is ASCII or not is very simple. At the A> prompt in DOS, enter "TYPE filename.extension". If a file is listed in standard keyboard characters, it is ASCII; otherwise it is not. For example, Lotus files generated by the /Print File command (files with the PRN extension) are ASCII files. VisiCalc generates all its files in ASCII, as do WordStar, WordPerfect, dBASE II and III, and BASICA (sequential files).

C-4 Lotus Facilities for File Transfer

Lotus Release 2 provides several facilities that make the job of file transfer a relatively easy task. These tools include the Lotus Translate utility program, /File Import command, /Data Parse command, /Print File Options Other Unformatted command, and Lotus macros related to sequential ASCII files.

In the next few pages we will explain techniques for accessing these facilities and provide you with several examples. The goal of this section is to help you to better understand these powerful features provided by Lotus.

C-5 Lotus Translate Utility Program

When you access the Lotus Access System, one of the options provided is Translate. When you select this option, Lotus asks you to insert the utility disk. Another way to load the utility disk is through DOS. At the A> prompt, type TRANS and press the **Return** key (assuming the utility disk is in drive A).

This utility gives you nine options from which you can translate data:

1-2-3, Release 1A

1-2-3, Release 2

dBASE II

dBASE III

DIF (Data Interchange Format), a well-known ASCII file)

Jazz

SYMPHONY, Release 1.0

SYMPHONY, Release 1.1

VisiCalc

You may select any of these options and press the **Return** key. To exit the Translate utility, press the **Escape** key. Should you require assistance you can press F1 for on-line help. As an example, if 1-2-3 Release 2 is chosen, after you press the **Return** key, the Translate utility gives you the following options:

1-2-3, Release 1A

1-2-3, Release 2

SYMPHONY, Release 1.0

SYMPHONY, Release 1.1

You can translate files from any of the above nine options to any of the four options. If you select 1-2-3, Release 2, you will be given a series of instructions. Continue to press Escape. Insert the diskette that includes the desired files. Move the cursor to the file you would like to translate. We chose the file in Figure C–1. The menu will indicate that the source file with the WK1 extension will be changed to a file with the DBF extension (database file). If you correctly follow the sequence specified, the final message will be "Translation Successful". Now if you look at the directory of the diskette, you will see that the file you just translated has DBF (database file) as an extension.

Remember, if you do not follow the right sequence, you will receive an error message. You must follow the instructions provided by the Translate utility exactly.

After translation this is a dBASE file and you can perform any operation with it using all the dBASE commands.

C-6 Using the File Import and /Data Parse Commands

To demonstrate how the /File Import and /Data Parse commands work, we will walk through an example. We used /Print File to write the worksheet in Figure C–2 to a new file (Figure C–3). this file is now an ASCII file with a PRN extension. (The / Print File command was discussed in Chapter 3).

Now we want to bring this file back to the worksheet. When you issue /File Import, Lotus gives you two options: text or numbers. We chose the text option (if the numbers option is chosen, only numeric values will be transferred).

If you move the cursor, you will see that each line of the ASCII file has been entered into one cell. For example, Cell A2 contains FIRST NAME AGE SEX OCCUPATION INCOME. Naturally, this file cannot be manipulated by Lotus spreadsheet commands. We have to use the /Data Parse command in order to parse the data. Parsing splits the long labels into a series of data items or labels.

The procedure for using this very powerful command is straightforward. Move the cursor to the left corner of the first row, which contains the first data item. Now invoke the /Data Parse command. You will be given the following options:

Format-Line   Input-Column   Output-Range   Reset   Go   Quit

Figure C–1 An Example of a Lotus Workheet File Translated into a dBASE III File

```
A1: [W12] 'FIRST NAME                                                    READY

         A           B              C   D   E                F            G
1   FIRST NAME   LAST NAME        AGE  SEX OCCUPATION      INCOME
2   Randy        Alexander         36   M  Professor       $40,000
3   Fay          Alexander         30   F  Mayor           $30,000
4   Adam         Alexander         31   M  Engineer        $30,000
5   Andrea       Byan              36   F  Teacher         $31,000
6   Moe          Byan              40   M  Officer         $40,000
7   Bob          Adam              32   M  Engineer        $72,000
8   Anna         Adam               4   F  Unemployed      $11,000
9   Vicki        Adam               9   F  Unemployed      $12,000
10  Paula        Bobby             55   F  Housewife       $20,000
11  Jack         Jones             69   M  Artist          $19,000
12  Mary         Fishler           30   F  Interpreter     $19,000
13  Sue          Hayword           22   F  Student         $18,000
14  Tammy        Smith             29   F  Student         $18,000
15  Jacky        Brown             72   F  Engineer        $52,000
16  Lora         Jones             30   F  Nurse           $31,000
17
18
19
20
01-Jan-89  01:15 PM
```

Figure C–2 A Sample Worksheet

```
A1: [W12]                                                               READY

         A           B    C    D              E           F      G
1                   MY FIRST DATABASE
2   FIRST NAME      AGE  SEX OCCUPATION      INCOME
3   Randy            36   M  Professor       $40,000
4   Fay              30   F  Mayor           $30,000
5   Adam             31   M  Engineer        $30,000
6   Andrea           36   F  Teacher         $31,000
7   Moe              40   M  Officer         $40,000
8   Bob              32   M  Engineer        $72,000
9
10
11
12
13
14
15
16
17
18
19
20
01-Jan-89  01:15 PM
```

A10: [W12]   READY

	A	B	C	D	E	F	G
1		MY FIRST DATABASE					
2							
3	FIRST NAME	LAST NAME	AGE	SEX	OCCUPATION	INCOME	
4	Randy	Alexander	36	M	Professor	$40,000	
5	Fay	Alexander	30	F	Mayor	$30,000	
6	Adam	Alexander	31	M	Engineer	$30,000	
7	Andrea	Byan	36	F	Teacher	$31,000	
8	Moe	Byan	40	M	Officer	$40,000	
9	Bob	Adam	32	M	Engineer	$72,000	
10							
11							
12							
13							
14							
15							
16							
17							
18							
19							
20							

01-Jan-89 01:16 PM

Figure C–3 Sample File Retrieved by File Import

The Format-Line command will provide you with a pattern or patterns for splitting up the numbers or labels. You can change it or take it as is. There are two options: Create or Edit. Choose the Create option. You will see a format line starting with four asterisks (four spaces), L (for labels), 10 asterisks, and V (for value), etc.

Besides the L and V options, there is option D for Date, T for Time, S to Skip the corresponding characters in the input line, > to continue the field, and * for characters that are undefined but belong to the current block.

The Input-Column specifies the range to be parsed. In our example, the range is A2..A10.

Output-Range is the left corner of the block for the parsed data. We specified All.

Reset will cancel the previous settings, and Go will execute the /Data Parse command.

Remember, in this example we have used two format lines; one for database fields FIRST NAME, AGE, SEX, OCCUPATION, and INCOME, and the other for database records. The result of this /Data Parse operation is in cells A12..E18. As you see, the currency format is lost. But all the data was split and you will be able to use this database for any Lotus operation. Figure C–4 shows the result.

Remember that there are other commands provided by Lotus to split a long label. For example, string functions (@Left, @Mid, @Right) can be used to extract substrings from whole strings. The /Range Justify command can split a long label into several shorter ones. The /Data Parse command is more flexible and easier to use than the other commands.

Lotus macros for sequential file processing can provide you with some extra features for file handling between Lotus and other standard ASCII files (see Ch. 10).

```
A1: '                    MY FIRST DATABASE                          READY

        A       B      C      D             E        F      G      H
 1                   MY FIRST DATABASE
 2   ****L>>>>*L>>>***L>>**L>>*L>>>>>>>>>>******L>>>>>
 3      FIRST NAME    AGE  SEX OCCUPATION      INCOME
 4   ****L>>>**********U>***L**L>>>>>>>>*******U>>>>>
 5      Randy         36   M   Professor      $40,000
 6      Fay           30   F   Mayor          $30,000
 7      Adam          31   M   Engineer       $30,000
 8      Andrea        36   F   Teacher        $31,000
 9      Moe           40   M   Officer        $40,000
10      Bob           32   M   Engineer       $72,000
11
12   FIRST    NAME    AGE      SEX      OCCUPATIOINCOME
13   Randy            36 M     Professor    40000
14   Fay              30 F     Mayor        30000
15   Adam             31 M     Engineer     30000
16   Andrea           36 F     Teacher      31000
17   Moe              40 M     Officer      40000
18   Bob              32 M     Engineer     72000
19
20
01-Jan-89  01:16 PM
```

Figure C–4 An Original Database and the Parsed Version

C-7 File Transfer between Lotus and Word Processing Programs

As mentioned earlier, the /Print File command generates an ASCII file with the PRN extension. This file can be exported to a variety of programs that accept ASCII files. WordStar, WordPerfect, and Volkswriter are three such programs. To make the ASCII file generated by /Print File a more suitable candidate for use in other software programs, consider the following steps:

- Word processing programs accept up to a certain number of columns as a full line (e.g., 40, 80, etc.). Set the right margin to the maximum number accepted by your word processing program.

- Set the right margin to max and all the other margins top, bottom, left, to 0.

- By using /Print File Options Other Unformatted eliminate headers, footers, and other spacing in the files.

To bring a file from a word processor that generates ASCII files into your Lotus worksheet you must use /File Import Text. The file will be entered to the Lotus worksheet from the present position of the cursor one line per cell from top to bottom, left to right, e.g., cell A1, A2, etc.

If there are unwanted characters in the imported file, by using the F2 function key you can edit the file and change it to the desired format. If you would like to split long labels, you must use the /Data Parse command.

C-8 Lotus and BASICA Sequential Files

BASICA can generate ASCII files in several ways. The following program is one that can be used to generate a sequential ASCII file. The resulting file can easily be imported to a Lotus worksheet by using the /File Import command.

```
10    REM TO CREATE ASCII FILE CALLED STUREC
20    OPEN "STUREC" FOR OUTPUT AS #1
30    FOR I=1 TO 3
40        READ A$,B$,C
50        WRITE #1,A$,B$,C
60    NEXT I
70    CLOSE
80    DATA SUSAN SHAY, BUSINESS,3.85
90    DATA KIM BROWN,COMPUTER,2.60
100   DATA ED STRONG,MATH,4.00
110   END
```

In order to see the contents of the ASCII file STUREC, follow these instructions:

```
RUN                (program will run)
SYSTEM             (change from BASICA to SYSTEM mode)
A > TYPE STUREC
"SUSAN SHAY", "BUSINESS",   3.85
"KIM BROWN", "COMPUTER",  2.60
"ED STRONG", "MATH",         4.00
```

Also, if a file is saved under SAVE"Filename.BAS",A command, this file is saved in ASCII format.

BASICA can read an ASCII file by using the LINE INPUT #1 command. For example, you can read an ASCII file line by line into a one-dimensional array in a BASICA program.

The following routine reads a Lotus ASCII file (PRN file) into array X$(100):

```
10    DIM X$(100)
20    OPEN "Myfile.PRN" FOR INPUT AS #1
30    J=1
40    WHILE NOT EOF(1)
```

```
50          LINE INPUT #1, X$(J)

60          J=J+1

70     WEND
```

The following routine prints the contents of array X$:

```
FOR I=1 to J

PRINT "X$(I)=",X$(I)

NEXT I
```

Every line of the ASCII file in Figure C–5 has been entered into one of the X$ array's cell.

Figure C-5 is a listing of a Lotus ASCII file generated by /Print File. Figure C–6 is a BASICA program listing and the contents of Array X$.

If you would like to enter each data item to a cell instead of the entire line, the ASCII file must be comma-delimited. To make a file coma-delimited, one option is to use the @STRING function as illustrated in Figure C–7.

As discussed in Chapter 10, Lotus macros for sequential file processing enable you to read from and write to an ASCII file.

Figure C–5 Myfile.PRN — An ASCII File Example

```
A1:                                                                    READY

        A         B         C         D      E    F         G         H
 1
 2
 3
 4
 5
 6
 7
 8
 9      Randy     Alexander      36   M   Professor   $40,000
10      Fay       Alexander      30   F   Mayor       $30,000
11      Adam      Alexander      31   M   Engineer    $30,000
12      Andrea    Byan           36   F   Teacher     $31,000
13
14
15
16
17
18
19
20
01-Jan-89   09:11 AM
```

```
Ok
LIST
10 DIM X$(100)
20 OPEN "MYFILE.PRN" FOR INPUT AS #1
30 J=1
40 WHILE NOT EOF(1)
50     LINE INPUT #1,X$(J)
60     J=J+1
70     PRINT X$(J)
80 WEND
90 END
Ok
RUN


Randy       Alexander      36   M   Professor      $40,000
Fay         Alexander      30   F   Mayor          $30,000
Adam        Alexander      31   M   Engineer       $30,000
Andrea      Byan           36   F   Teacher        $31,000
```

Figure C–6 Program Listing and Output of the BASIC Program
Reading an ASCII FILE

C-9 File Transfer and R:BASE 5000

R:BASE 5000, a powerful database management system, is also capable of file
export and import to and from a number of popular software programs including
Lotus 1-2-3. Through a utility program called the FileGateway, R:BASE 5000 can
import from the following software:

dBASE

Lotus 1-2-3

Symphony

PFS:FILE

DIF files from VisiCalc

SYLK files from Multiplan

ASCII files from a majority of micro and mainframe computers

For more specific information, consult the R:BASE Series 5000 user's manual,
Chapter 13, "The FileGateway Contents."

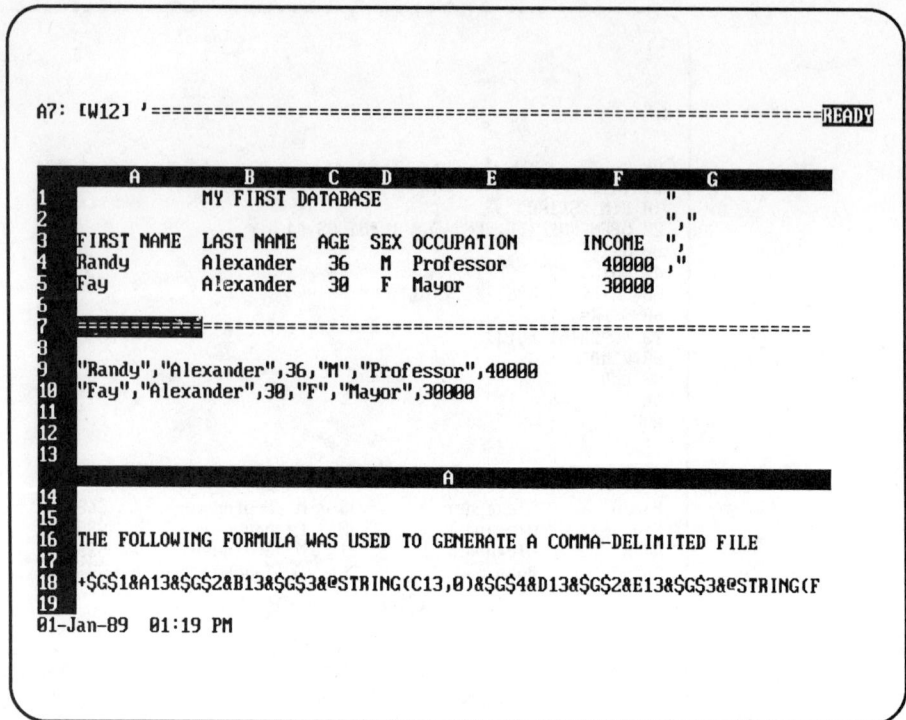

Figure C-7 Generating a Comma Delimited File

Summary

In this appendix, we have provided a review of Lotus facilities for file transfer between programs. The Translate utility can assist you in transferring files between versions of Lotus, dBASE, DIF, Jazz, VisiCalc, and Symphony. Also, by using the /File Import command, you should be able to import any ASCII file to your worksheet. The /Data Parse command will enable you to parse (split up) long labels into a series of labels and values. Be aware that other commands and facilities for file handling are available in Lotus. These include Lotus macros for sequential files, string functions, and /Print File for generating ASCII files. We also provided guidelines for import/export to and from other software including word processors, BASICA, and R-BASE 5000.

Review Questions

1. Why is file transfer needed?
2.* What are the requirements for any file transfer?
3. How do you get the Translate utility started?
4.* What application software packages can directly benefit from the Translate utility?
5.* How do you ask for help in the Translate utility?
6. How do you exit the Translate utility?
7. When a file is translated from Lotus to dBASE, what is actually changed?

8.* How do you generate an ASCII file using Lotus?

9. How do you verify if a file is an ASCII file?

10. How do you load an ASCII file into the Lotus worksheet?

11. What is the major function of the /Data Parse command?

12.* Why is parsing needed?

13. Are there other methods of data parsing besides using the /Data Parse command?

14. What are the options available under the /Data Parse command?

15.* What is the function of Reset in the /Data Parse menu?

16. How many format lines are needed for a typical database?

17. Choose one of the worksheets in any of the chapters of this book and convert this worksheet into a dBASE III file. How will you know if your translation is successful?

18. Using the /Print File command, generate an ASCII file.

19. Using /Data Parse, split a long label into four shorter labels.

20. Generate a comma-delimited file in Lotus.

21. Export a Lotus ASCII file into a BASICA program.

Misconceptions and Solutions

M – When you translate, if you generate a file with the same name as one of the existing files on your directory, this new file will overwrite the old file regardless of differences in size.

S – Check your directory first, then do the translation.

M – The translate utility is constrained by the limitations of the program. For example, if you are translating from dBASE to Lotus, your dBASE file cannot have more than 8,192 records.

S – Break the large databases into a series of smaller ones, then do the transfer.

M – Translation between dBASE and Lotus may produce incorrect decimal places.

S – In the 1-2-3 worksheet, use Format options besides the General default option and specify as many decimal places as needed. When the dBASE file is generated, you will have the same number of decimal places.

M – Field names and numbers moved from 1-2-3 to dBASE may cause errors.

S – Your database in the 1-2-3 worksheet must follow the same rules that apply to field names in dBASE, e.g., 1 to 10 characters long, include only letters of the alphabet, use digits 0-9, and start with a letter of the alphabet. Also, from Release 2.0/2.01 to dBASE III Plus you cannot have more than 128 fields.

M – If you use /File Import Numbers to import an ASCII file to your Lotus worksheet, you may generate undesired results.

S– Check the spacing in the incoming file. There must be at least one space between each field or, if your data is nonnumeric, these must be enclosed in double quotation marks and separated by commas. Usually /File Import Text is safer than /File Import Numbers.

Appendix D

Add–On Products

D-1 Introduction

In this appendix we will explain the SIDEWAYS program. This software is extremely useful for printing wide worksheets. We will also discuss some add-on products, all by the Lotus Development Corporation. This diverse range of products gives you an opportunity to analyze and utilize your worksheet in many different dimensions. They make it more user-friendly and let you export and import data to and from other computers, interface with mainframe computers, and generate diverse types of graphics.

D-2 SIDEWAYS

In Chapter 3 we explained different methods for generating reports using Lotus. In that chapter we explained one method for printing wide spreadsheets by using the Set-up option and generating compressed reports. However, the compressed option will not solve all the problems related to a wide worksheet. It only allows up to 132 characters. What about spreadsheets wider than 132 characters? SIDEWAYS, by Funk Software, Inc., Cambridge, Mass., will solve the problem of printing wide spreadsheets.
SIDEWAYS:

- Rotates your spreadsheet by 90 degrees.

- Prints any ASCII text file.

- Prints right through the perforation of your printer paper if necessary.

- Controls type sizes.

- Controls margins.

- Controls spacing between characters.

- Controls spacing between lines.

- Controls print density.

SIDEWAYS is compatible with popular spreadsheet programs such as Lotus 1-2-3, Symphony, VisiCalc, Multiplan, SuperCalc, and numerous word processors and text editors.

SIDEWAYS comes with one diskette which includes three programs:

SIDEWAYS.COM — This is the program itself.

INSTALL.EXE — This program allows SIDEWAYS to be configured to different printers.

SAMPLE.PRN — A sample spreadsheet.

D-3 Before Using SIDEWAYS

Before starting the SIDEWAYS program, you must generate a print file by using the /Print File command (/PF). The following specific instructions should be followed:

- Use the unformatted option. It is possible to use the formatted option; however, it is easier to generate reports this way. This is done by issuing /PFOOU (Print File Options Other Unformatted).

- Set the right margin to the highest possible number or higher than the number of character columns in your worksheet.

- Set the left margin to 0.

- Issue Quit to return to the previous menu (/PFOQ).

- Issue /PFR (Range) to specify the desired range of the report.

- Issue Align to reset the Lotus internal line counter (/PFA).

- Issue Go to write the worksheet onto the diskette (/PFG).

- Issue the Quit command to complete the writing process.

Now you can exit from Lotus and get SIDEWAYS started.

D-4 Preparing SIDEWAYS

If you just purchased the SIDEWAYS program, you may have to configure the program for your specific printer. The process is easy and straightforward. At the A>

prompt, insert the SIDEWAYS diskette in drive A and type INSTALL. At this point the program asks you about the type of printer that you have.

You can run this program as many times as you wish. Also, it is a good idea to make a backup copy of the SIDEWAYS program in case of damage to the original diskette. To do so, use the DOS Copy command and copy SIDEWAYS to a formatted disk. (For information on formatting and copying, see Appendix A.) Now you can store the original diskette in a safe place and use the copy for your daily operations.

D-5 Getting In and Getting Out of SIDEWAYS

After generating an ASCII file by using the Lotus /PF command, exit from Lotus. At the A> prompt insert the SIDEWAYS disk in drive A and type SIDEWAYS. Figure D–1 displays the SIDEWAYS menu. (We will explain this menu step by step in the next section.) This menu shows the default settings. You may change any of these settings to suit your specific needs. To exit from SIDEWAYS, press the F10 function key. This will return you to DOS.

You can use either the up or down arrow in order to move the cursor around. You may also enter any new values and press the **Return** key. The **Backspace** key deletes the last character entered and the **Escape** key deletes the entire entry line. The rest of the fields are toggle fields. Their contents may be changed by pressing the space bar.

You may type the name and extension of your desired ASCII file in order to bring it to the SIDEWAYS program. If you are not using the default drive you must also identify the drive name. You may also see all the file names by typing the drive name, e.g., B:, and then using the right arrow ($\rightarrow$) to sequentially display all the files on a particular drive. Once the program is started, the following message is displayed:

Strike "P" to stop printing

If you do strike "P", your printer will stop printing as soon as the current character column is finished.

D-6 Options Available on the SIDEWAYS Menu

As Figure D–1 shows, the following options are available on the SIDEWAYS menu:

1.   Print Select allows you to direct the output to any parallel or serial printer. This is a toggle field; it only toggles between printer ports you actually have.
2.   Vertical Form Size determines the distance between perforations on your printer paper. Default is 11 inches.
3.   Horizontal Form Size determines printer paper width. It toggles between 8 and 13 inches.
4.   Double Strike can be On or Off. If it is on, each line will be printed twice to generate higher density.
5.   Character Font allows you to choose type sizes from Tiny to Extra Large.
6.   Character Spacing determines the distance between successive character columns. The number of characters per inch is displayed at the right of the menu.

Figure D–1 SIDEWAYS Menu

```
                    S I D E W A Y S   Version 2.11              Ser#4067046
                       (C) Funk Software, Inc. 1982                  EPS

                                                Printer select: LPT1:

Vertical form size (inches):   11.00
Horizontal form size (inches):  8.00

Double strike:                  OFF
Character font:              NORMAL           5 x 15 dot matrix

Character spacing (dots):         1          12.00 characters per inch
Line spacing (dots):              3           6.66 lines per inch

Left margin (inches):          0.00
Max printing width (inches):   0.00          65535 characters per line

Top margin (inches):           0.00
Printing length (inches):      0.00             53 lines per page

Enter name of print file: scurve.prn         Starting page:  1
                                             Glue lines:      0

"  and "" to move from field to field
    "F1" to save current options
    "F10" to exit from program
```

7. Line Spacing determines the distance between successive lines. The number of lines per inch is displayed at the right of the menu.

8. Left and Top Margins determine the amount of space from left and top of a printed page.

9. Printing Length determines the number of lines printed on a page. Remember, printing length plus top margin may not exceed horizontal page size. This number is displayed at the right of the menu. You may set this length to 0.

10. Maximum Printing Width determines the maximum number of characters per SIDEWAYS line. Leave this value at 0. The nonzero value will tell SIDE-WAYS where to wrap around a line.

11. Starting Page allows you to choose the beginning of your report. Default is page 1. You can start at any page.

12. Glue Lines allows you to electronically glue two worksheets together. You only need to use glue lines if the width of your spreadsheet exceeds the maximum allowable print width of your worksheet. In the case of Lotus and Symphony, the maximum length is 240; Multiplan is either 512 or 165. If this is not the case, set it to 0. Different versions of Lotus use different glue lines. For your specific version consult the SIDEWAYS manual.

You can save the current settings of your SIDEWAYS disk by pressing the F1 key. If you don't save the current settings, SIDEWAYS will always read the default settings from its SIDEWAYS.DFT file.

D-7 An Example

Figure D–2 was generated by using the SIDEWAYS program. We first generated an ASCII unformatted file by using the /PF command. Figure D-2 was generated using the default settings. This is Figure 3-2 from Chapter 3. In this figure the worksheet is not too wide; we just wanted to show the process.

D-8 Lotus HAL

Lotus HAL is an add-on product to 1-2-3 by Lotus Development Corporation. The following are some of the key characteristics of this software:

• Allows freeformat user/system interface. For example, instead of entering commands and formulas, you can type, "Total all columns" or "Graph June to August."

• Increases productivity by both experienced as well as inexperienced users.

• Allows you to "undo" your last command — even a dangerous command such as /Worksheet Erase.

• Allows linkages between different worksheets and different cells.

• Simplifies and speeds up spreadsheet, database, and graphic tasks by entering commands using simple English phrases.

Figure D–2 An Example of a Report Generated by SIDEWAYS

```
                       OCEAN CITY TOURIST ATTRACTION
                     (1986-87 Figures in thousands of dollars)

                                  Spring      Summer      Fall      Winter

Current Assets
  Cash                           $36,249     $42,495    $58,761    $72,300
  Accounts Receivable             26,700      23,821     22,545     22,768
  Inventory                        8,000       7,625      9,025      8,475
                                 -------     -------    -------    -------
Total Current Assets              70,949      73,941     90,331    103,543

Fixed Assets
Property, Plant and Equipment
  Land                            49,121      48,700     45,600     40,410
  Building                        82,212      82,212     79,100     78,275
  Leasehold Improvements          22,400      18,506     17,900     20,145
  Equipment                        8,364       8,544      9,106      9,364
  Gross P, P and E               162,097     157,962    151,706    148,194
  Accumulated Depreciation       (48,814)    (37,600)   (36,945)   (29,725)
                                 -------     -------    -------    -------
Net P, P and E                   113,283     120,362    114,761    118,469

Other Assets                         545         489        513        606
                                 -------     -------    -------    -------
Total Fixed Assets               113,828     120,851    115,274    119,075

Total Assets                    $184,777    $194,792   $205,605   $222,618
                                 =======     =======    =======    =======

Current Liabilities
  Accounts Payable                34,522      37,819     33,245     31,009
  Notes Payable                   10,000      11,321      7,369      8,655
  Income Tax Payable               4,500       4,789      5,802      6,134
                                 -------     -------    -------    -------
Total Current Liabilities         49,022      53,929     46,416     45,798

Noncurrent Liabilities
  Long Term Debt                  52,242      48,700     46,345     40,300
                                 -------     -------    -------    -------
Total Liabilities                101,264     102,629     92,761     86,098

Stockholders' Equity
  Common Stock                     2,555       2,644      2,750      2,936
  Retained Earnings               80,958      89,519    110,094    133,584
                                 -------     -------    -------    -------
Total Stockholders' Equity        83,513      92,163    112,844    136,520

Total Liabilities and Equity    $184,777    $194,792   $205,605   $222,618
                                 =======     =======    =======    =======
```

- Allows sharing files with other users, including those who don't use Lotus HAL.

System Requirements

- 1-2-3 Release 1A, Release 2, or Release 2.01 (5.25 inch or 3.5 inch).
- Two disk drives, DOS 2.0 to 3.3, minimum of 512K RAM.

D-9 Lotus Freelance Plus

Freelance Plus by Lotus Development Corporation offers complete graphics capabilities:

- Allows importing data from 1-2-3 or Symphony files.
- Generates many different graphs and charts including maps, pie charts, organization charts, flow charts, etc.
- Generates word charts, slides, report covers, and diagrams with words.
- Includes over 500 symbols for different chartings.
- Allows mouse or digitizing tablet interface.

System Requirements

- IBM PC, XT, or AT (min. of 384K RAM); IBM PS/2 Models 30, 50, and 60; IBM 3270 (640 RAM).
- Hercules Graphics Card, IBM Color Card, IBM Enhanced Graphics Adapter, or IBM Video Graphics Array.

It also works with diverse plotters and printers, as well as diverse input devices. The output options can be paper, transparencies, or 35mm slides.

D-10 Lotus Graphwriter II

This software by Lotus Development Corporation generates 24 different chart formats including Gantt, bubble, pie, grouped bar, XY, scatter, and so on. Some of the other unique features include:

- Automatically updates charts when spreadsheet changes.
- Allows printing up to 100 charts by issuing single command from DOS.
- Allows you to position more than one chart on a page.
- Uses familiar Lotus menus.
- Allows diverse file input including 1-2-3, Symphony, ASCII, DIF, and dBASE files.

System Requirements

• IBM PC, XT, AT, or certified compatible with 512K RAM and a hard disk. PS/2 models 30, 50 or 60. It works with diverse plotters and printers.

D-11 Lotus Manuscript

Lotus Manuscript by Lotus Development Corporation provides full-feature word processing on the worksheet data. You can import a Lotus worksheet into Manuscript as a table, then perform different operations. For example, you can change the appearance of the worksheet by making the titles boldface, rearranging rows or columns, and so on. You can also import graphs from 1-2-3 into Manuscript. The following are specific characteristics of Lotus Manuscript:

• Organize your thoughts with the built-in, integrated outlines.

• Combine text and graphics on the same page.

• Create columns, tables, and borders.

• Format the entire document with one set of instructions, or format portions individually.

• Include graphics and tables from Freelance Plus and 1-2-3.

• Merge data and standard text to create form letters.

• Create an index and table of contents automatically.

• Change typefaces and point sizes.

• Find spelling typing errors quickly and easily.

• Highlight changes in different versions of a document.

• Produce high-quality documents on a wide variety of printers, from dot matrix to laser.

• Create documents up to 800 pages long.

System Requirements

IBM PC, XT, AT, PS/2, and several IBM compatibles. It interfaces with several printers and scanners including Apple Laserwriter; Epson LQ-800, 1000, 1500; H-P Laser Jet, and others.

D-12 Lotus Metro

Lotus Metro by Lotus Development Corporation provides desktop accessories. It is both a desktop organizer and a macro processor. It is compatible with Lotus 1-2-3, Symphony, and many other programs. Some of the key characteristics of this software include:

- *Calculator*. Full business calculator with memory, constant financial functions, and exponential display.

- *Phone book*. Dials phone numbers and produces mailing labels.

- *Appointment book*. Maintains daily, weekly, and monthly calendars. Reminds you of appointments with an audible alarm.

- *List manager*. Maintains to-do lists and tracks tasks and projects.

- *DOS file manager*. Organizes data and program files and simplifies DOS functions.

- *Clipboard*. Allows you to clip and paste data between Metro accessories, 1-2-3, Symphony, and many other programs.

- *Editor*. Allows you to create and edit memos and spreadsheet reports without leaving 1-2-3 or Symphony. Also works with other software.

- *Notepad*. Allows you to record ideas, memoranda, and notes without leaving your main program.

- *Watch*. Multiple stopwatches time up to 100 different events at the same time. Includes an audible alarm.

- *Special characters*. Displays ASCII characters and their codes.

- *Kaleidoscope*. Customizes the accessory display for color monitors.

- *Configuration*. Allows you to build your own product, combining just the functions you want to use.

- *Macros*. This single Metro function gives you more power than many programs that provide macros only.

System Requirements

IBM PC, XT, AT, and many PC compatibles; minimum of 80K of RAM; DOS 2.0 or higher.

D-13 Lotus Report Writer

Lotus Report Writer by Lotus Development Corporation generates diverse reports from 1-2-3 or Symphony database files. It also generates mailing labels. Some of the features of this program include:

- Produces row-oriented, columnar, and free-form reports.

- Generates preprinted forms and mailing labels.

- Sorts fields on up to four levels, in ascending or descending order.

- Specifies bold, underline, and italic printing for selected portions.

- Adds multiline headers and footers.

- Performs calculations such as total, subtotal, average, count, minimum, and maximum.

- Creates an unlimited number of reports from one database.

- Stores and recalls formats for fast, convenient updating of periodic reports.

System Requirements

Any worksheet from Lotus 1-2-3 or Symphony; IBM PC, XT, AT, and several other compatibles; 256K of RAM and two disk drives; DOS 2.0 and above.

D-14 Other Add-On Products

Lotus Express by Lotus Development Corporation for MCI Mail provides a full-featured electronic mail facility. It reads mail, manages mail, and sends or receives Telex messages. It is compatible with Lotus 1-2-3, and Symphony, and many other software products.

The Application Connection (T-A-C) by Lotus Development Corporation provides a connecting facility between PC and mainframe computers. Using this software mainframe, data can be brought to the 1-2-3 worksheet for further analysis and the result can be sent back.

Lotus Measure by Lotus Development Corporation moves data from measurement hardware directly into 1-2-3 or Symphony in real time for immediate retrieval, storage, and analysis. The result is enhanced efficiency by not having to retype data.

Lotus One Source Database by Lotus Development Corporation provides financial information from diverse sources. It can be accessed from 1-2-3 without leaving it. It provides daily and weekly updates on available financial information.

Lotus Signal by Lotus Development Corporation provides a constant flow of information on market changes in real time. Signal delivers prices directly into your Lotus 1-2-3 or Symphony spreadsheets. You do not need to enter data again.

Summary

This appendix explained the SIDEWAYS program for printing wide worksheets. Using this program eliminates the frustration facing the users of wide worksheets by printing right through the perforation of the paper. We also briefly introduced other products by Lotus Development Corporation that work with Lotus 1-2-3 as well as other software. These products can significantly improve your worksheet. You can customize your worksheet, generate numerous types of graphs, produce reports, and send reports over telephone lines.

Review Questions

1.* What is the function of the SIDEWAYS program?
2. If you don't have access to a program such as SIDEWAYS, what are other options for printing wide worksheets?

3.   How do you get SIDEWAYS started?
4.   What is available on the SIDEWAYS disk?
5.   What types of files can be utilized by the SIDEWAYS program?
6.   Using Lotus, how do you generate a file for the SIDEWAYS program?
7.   Why should you generate an unformatted file for the SIDEWAYS program?
8.*   How do you exit the SIDEWAYS program?
9.   What are some of the limitations of the SIDEWAYS program?
10.   What are the glue lines on the SIDEWAYS program?
11.   Using SIDEWAYS, generate a report.
12.* What are the uses of HAL?
13.   What product gives you enhanced graphics?
14.   What are the differences between Graphwriter II and Freelance Plus?
15.   What are the applications of Lotus Manuscript?
16.   Which program is used for desktop publishing?
17.   Which program is used for office management? For appointment calendars?
18.   Which program is used for word-processing purposes?
19.   What are some of the other programs introduced in this chapter?
20.* What other software is compatible with Lotus 1-2-3?

Appendix E

Differences between Release 2.0/2.01 and Release IA

Lotus Release 2.0/2.01 includes a series of enhanced features not available in the earlier releases of this package. These enhancements include new security features, memory management, additional worksheet and range commands, new functions and a number of new macro commands that complement the macro commands available in Release 1A and make Lotus a full-featured programming language.

Memory management gives you complete freedom to utilize a worksheet in any style. For example, a data item in cell A1 or cell A2000 will occupy the same amount of memory. However, in Release 1A, the active area is important. In the above example the active area would be the entire rectangle of A1..A2000. This means you will run out of memory very fast.

Release 2.0/2.01 implements security features by allowing you to have a password for a file. You can also use the /Range Protect or /Worksheet Global Protection commands.

In Release 2.0/2.01 you can access DOS from the 1-2-3 spreadsheet by using the /System command from the main menu. This release also enables you to export or import files between 1-2-3 Release 1A or 2, dBASE II, dBASE III, DIF, Jazz, SYMPHONY Release 1.0 and 1.10, and VisiCalc. We discussed this facility in Appendix C.

For those who are still using Release 1A or who are interested in knowing some of the differences between Release 2.0/2.01 and Release 1A, we have provided Table E-1. This table should assist you in quickly discovering all the features available in Release 2.0/2.01 but not in Release 1A.

In some cases the commands are different but perform the same task; this table also highlights such cases. For easy reference to these new features, we refer you to the section of this book where a particular feature was first presented. This should save you a lot of time in discovering the new enhancements in Lotus.

Table E-1 Release 2.0/2.01 and Release 1A Comparison

FEATURE	RELEASE 2.0/2.01	SECTION NUMBER	RELEASE 1A
	GENERAL INFORMATION		
Worksheet size	256 columns by 8,192 rows	1-4	256 by 2,048
The entire package	System disk	B-3	System disk
	Backup system disk		Backup system disk
	Utility		Utility disk
	PrintGraph		PrintGraph
	A View of Lotus		Tutorial disk
	Install library		
Alt & F1	available	1-21	not available
	WORKSHEET COMMANDS		
/Worksheet Global Protection	available	2-9	not available
/Worksheet Global Default Other	Currency available	2-10	not available
International	Date available		not available
	Time available		not available
/Worksheet Global Zero	available	2-11	not available
/Worksheet Column Hide	available	2-14	not available
/Worksheet Column Display	available	2-14	not available
/Worksheet Status	available	2-18	not available
/Worksheet Page	available	2-19	not available
	RANGE COMMANDS		
/Range Unprotect or Protect	available	2-20	not available
/Range Name Table	available	2-23	not available
/Range Transpose	available	2-26	not available
/Range Value	available	2-27	not available
/Range Format Hidden	available	2-42	not available
File Extension	WK1 (worksheet)	2-47	WKS (worksheet)
	FUNCTIONS		
@ATAN2 (A,B)	available	4-4-5	not available
@CTERM	available	4-5-6	not available
@TERM	available	4-5-7	not available
@SLN	available	4-5-9	not available
@SYD	available	4-5-10	not available

FEATURE	RELEASE 2.0/2.01	SECTION NUMBER	RELEASE 1A
@DDB	available	4-5-11	not available
@ISNUMBER	available	4-7-5	not available
@ISSTRING	available	4-7-6	not available
@CHAR	available	4-8-1	not available
@CODE	available	4-8-2	not available
@CLEAN	available	4-8-3	not available
@EXACT	available	4-8-4	not available
@FIND	available	4-8-5	not available
@LEFT	available	4-8-6	not available
@LENGTH	available	4-8-7	not available
@LOWER	available	4-8-8	not available
@MID	available	4-8-9	not available
@N	available	4-8-10	not available
@PROPER	available	4-8-11	not available
@REPEAT	available	4-8-12	not available
@REPLACE	available	4-8-13	not available
@RIGHT	available	4-8-14	not available
@S	available	4-8-15	not available
@STRING	available	4-8-16	not available
@TRIM	available	4-8-17	not available
@UPPER	available	4-8-18	not available
@VALUE	available	4-8-19	not available
@DATE	available	4-9-1	not available
@DATEVALUE	available	4-9-2	not available
@NOW	available	4-9-6	not available
@TIME	available	4-9-7	not available
@TIMEVALUE	available	4-9-8	not available
@HOUR	available	4-9-9	not available
@MINUTE	available	4-9-10	not available
@SECOND	available	4-9-11	not available
@@	available	4-10-1	not available
@CELL	available	4-10-2	not available
@HLOOKUP	available for both numeric and nonnumeric search	4-10-11	available for numeric search only
@INDEX	available	4-10-8	not available
@VLOOKUP	available for both numeric and nonnumeric search	4-10-11	numeric search only
@CELLPOINTER	available	4-10-3	not available
@COLS	available	4-10-5	not available
@ROWS	available	4-10-10	not available

GRAPHICS

| Exploding a pie chart | available | 5-8 | not available |

PRINTGRAPH

Availability of several interfaces for DOS Device

FEATURE	RELEASE 2.0/2.01	SECTION NUMBER	RELEASE 1A
LPT1	available	6-6	not available
LPT2	available	6-6	not available
LPT3	available	6-6	not available
LPT4	available	6-6	not available
Choosing font option	available	6-7	not available

DATABASE

/Data Matrix			not available
Invert	available	8-9	not available
Multiply	available	8-10	not available
/Data Regression	available	8-12	not available

MACRO COMMANDS

BIGLEFT	available	9-3	not available
BIGRIGHT	available	9-3	not available
Multiple action (e.g., DOWN 6 or UP 2)	available	9-3	not available
BLANK	available	10-5-1	not available
LET	available	10-5-2	not available
CONTENTS	available	10-5-3	not available
PUT	available	10-5-4	not available
RECALC	available	10-5-5	not available
RECALCCOL	available	10-5-5	not available
BRANCH	available	10-6-1	/XG
DEFINE	available	10-6-2	not available
DISPATCH	available	10-6-3	not available
FOR and FORBREAK	available	10-6-4	not available
IF	available	10-6-5	/XI
QUIT	available	10-6-5	/XQ
ONERROR	available	10-6-5	not available
RESTART	available	10-6-6	not available
RETURN	available	10-6-7	/XR
SUBR-Name	available	10-6-7	/XC Name
BREAKOFF	available	10-7-2	not available
WAIT	available	10-7-3	not available
GET	available	10-7-4	not available
GETLABEL	available	10-7-5	/XL
GETNUMBER	available	10-7-5	/XN
LOOK	available	10-7-6	not available
MENUBRANCH	available	10-7-7	/XM
BEEP	available	10-8-1	not available
INDICATE	available	10-8-2	not available
PANELOFF	available	10-8-3	not available
PANELON	available	10-8-3	not available
WINDOWSOFF	available	10-8-4	not available
WINDOWSON	available	10-8-4	not available
CLOSE	available	10-9-1	not available
FILESIZE	available	10-9-2	not available

FEATURE	RELEASE 2.0/2.01	SECTION NUMBER	RELEASE 1A
GETPOS	available	10-9-3	not available
READ	available	10-9-5	not available
READLN	available	10-9-6	not available
SETPOS	available	10-9-7	not available
WRITE	available	10-9-8	not available
WRITELN	available	10-9-9	not available

Appendix F

Lotus International Character Set

Lotus uses the Lotus International Character Set (LICS) for displaying, transmitting, printing, and storing characters. These 256 characters are represented by numbers 0 through 255. Numbers 0 through 32 represent control characters (**Ctrl** + a letter); 32 through 127 represent ASCII codes; and 128 through 255 represent international characters.

The *compose sequence* is a series of keystrokes used to enter a character that is not on the keyboard. To do this, press **Alt**, then the desired compose sequence.

For printers and monitors that cannot directly represent all LICS characters, there are fallback presentations. These are listed in Table F-1. Table F-1 has been adopted from Lotus Development Corporation, 1987, used with permission.

LICS Code	Character	Description	Compose Sequence	Fallback Monitor Presentation	Fallback Printer Presentation
0	Control @				
1	Control A				
2	Control B				
3	Control C				
4	Control D		*(Note: Character codes 0 through 31 are not LICS codes.)*		
5	Control E				
6	Control F				
7	Control G				
8	Control H				
9	Control I				
10	Control J	Line feed			

LICS Code	Character	Description	Compose Sequence	Fallback Monitor Presentation	Fallback Printer Presentation
11	Control K				
12	Control L	Form feed			
13	Control M	Return			
14	Control N				
15	Control O				
16	Control P				
17	Control Q				
18	Control R				
19	Control S				
20	Control T				
21	Control U				
22	Control V				
23	Control W				
24	Control X				
25	Control Y				
26	Control Z				
27	[Escape]				
28	FS				
29	GS				
30	RS				
31	US				
32	(Space)				
33	!				
34	"				
35	#		+ +		
36	$				
37	%				
38	&				
39	'	Apostrophe			
40	(				
41	)				
42	*				
43	+				
44	,				
45	-				
46	.				
47	/				
48	0				
49	1				
50	2				
51	3				
52	4				
53	5				
54	6				
55	7				
56	8				
57	9				
58	:				
59	;				
60	<				
61	=				
62	>				
63	?				
64	@		a a A A		
65	A				
66	B				
67	C				

LICS Code	Character	Description	Compose Sequence	Fallback Monitor Presentation	Fallback Printer Presentation
68	D				
69	E				
70	F				
71	G				
72	H				
73	I				
74	J				
75	K				
76	L				
77	M				
78	N				
79	O				
80	P				
81	Q				
82	R				
83	S				
84	T				
85	U				
86	V				
87	W				
88	X				
89	Y				
90	Z				
91	[		(	(	
92	\		/	/	
93	]		)	)	
94	^		v	v	
95	_				
96	`				
97	a				
98	b				
99	c				
100	d				
101	e				
102	f				
103	g				
104	h				
105	i				
106	j				
107	k				
108	l				
109	m				
110	n				
111	o				
112	p				
113	q				
114	r				
115	s				
116	t				
117	u				
118	v				
119	w				
120	x				
121	y				
122	z				
123	{		(-		
124	¦		^/		

LICS Code	Character	Description	Compose Sequence	Fallback Monitor Presentation	Fallback Printer Presentation
125	}		) -		
126	~	Tilde	- -		
127	DEL				
128	`	Uppercase grave	* ` space		
129	´	Uppercase acute	* ´ space		
130	^	Uppercase circumflex	* ^ space		
131	¨	Uppercase umlaut	* " space	"	"
132	~	Uppercase tilde	* ~ space		
133					
134					
135			*Do not type* `*`. *It indicates that*		
136			*compose sequence is order-sensitive.*		
137					
138					
139					
140					
141					
142					
143					
144	`	Lowercase grave	* space `		
145	´	Lowercase acute	* space ´		
146	^	Lowercase circumflex	* space ^		
147	¨	Lowercase umlaut	* space "	"	"
148	~	Lowercase tilde	space ~		
149	ı	Lowercase i without dot	i space		
150	_	Ordinal indicator	_ space		
151	▲	Begin attribute (display only)	b a		
152	▼	End attribute (display only)	e a		
153	■	Unknown character (display only)			
154	·	Hard space (display only)	space space		
155	←	Merge character (display only)	m g		
156					
157	►	Tab character			
158					
159					
160	ƒ	Dutch Guilder	f f		f
161	¡	Inverted exclamation mark	! !		i
162	¢	Cent sign	c¦ C¦ c/ C/		c⟨BS⟩¦
163	£	Pound sign	L= l= L- l-		L⟨BS⟩=
164	„	Low opening double quotes	" "	"	"
165	¥	Yen sign	Y= y= Y- y-		Y⟨BS⟩=
166	Pts	Pesetas sign	* P T pt Pt		Pt
167	§	Section sign	S O so S0 s0		Sc
168	¤	General currency sign	X O xo X0 x0		O⟨BS⟩=
169	©	Copyright sign	C O co C0 c0	c	(c)
170	ª	Feminine Ordinal	a_ A_		a⟨BS⟩_
171	«	Angle quotation mark left	< <		< <
172	Δ	Delta	d d D D		D
173	π	Pi	* P I pi Pi		pi
174	≥	Greater-than-or-equals	* > =		> =
175	÷	Divide sign	: -		/
176	°	Degree sign	^ 0		o(superscripted, if possible)
177	±	Plus/minus sign	+ -		+⟨BS⟩_
178	²	Superscript 2	^ 2		2 (superscripted, if possible)
179	³	Superscript 3	^ 3	3	3 (superscripted, if possible)
180	„	Low closing double quotes	" v	"	"
181	µ	Micro sign	* / u		u

LICS Code	Character	Description	Compose Sequence	Fallback Monitor Presentation	Fallback Printer Presentation
182	¶	Paragraph sign	! p ! P		Pr
183	·	Middle dot	^ ·		·(superscripted, if possible)
184	™	Trademark sign	* TM Tm tm	T	TM
185	¹	Superscript 1	^ 1	1	1 (superscripted, if possible)
186	º	Masculine ordinal	o _ O _		o⟨BS⟩
187	»	Angle Quotation mark right	> >		> >
188	¼	Fraction one quarter	* 1 4		1/4
189	½	Fraction one half	* 1 2		1/2
190	≤	Less-than-or-equals	* = <		= <
191	¿	Inverted question mark	? ?		?
192	À	Uppercase A with grave	A `	A	A
193	Á	Uppercase A with acute	A ´	A	A
194	Â	Uppercase A with circumflex	A ^	A	A
195	Ã	Uppercase A with tilde	A ~	A	A
196	Ä	Uppercase A with umlaut	A "		A
197	Å	Uppercase A with ring	A *		A
198	Æ	Uppercase A with ligature	* A E		AE
199	Ç	Uppercase C with cedilla	C ,		C ⟨BS⟩ ,
200	È	Uppercase E with grave	E `	E	E
201	É	Uppercase E with acute	E ´		E
202	Ê	Uppercase E with circumflex	E ^	E	E
203	Ë	Uppercase E with umlaut	E "	E	E
204	Ì	Uppercase I with grave	I `	I	I
205	Í	Uppercase I with acute	I ´	I	I
206	Î	Uppercase I with circumflex	I ^	I	I
207	Ï	Uppercase I with umlaut	I "	I	I
208	Ð	Uppercase eth (Icelandic)	D –	D	D ⟨BS⟩ –
209	Ñ	Uppercase N with tilde	N ~		N
210	Ò	Uppercase O with grave	O `	O	O
211	Ó	Uppercase O with acute	O ´	O	O
212	Ô	Uppercase O with circumflex	O ^	O	O
213	Õ	Uppercase O with tilde	O ~	O	O
214	Ö	Uppercase O with umlaut	O "		O
215	Œ	Uppercase OE diphthong	* O E	O	OE
216	Ø	Uppercase O with slash	O /		O ⟨BS⟩ /
217	Ù	Uppercase U with grave	U `	U	U
218	Ú	Uppercase U with acute	U ´	U	U
219	Û	Uppercase U with circumflex	U ^	U	U
220	Ü	Uppercase u with umlaut	U "		U
221	Ÿ	Uppercase Y with umlaut	Y "	Y	Y
222	Þ	Uppercase thorn (Icelandic)	P –	P	P ⟨BS⟩
223	ß	Lowercase German sharp s	s s		ss
224	à	Lowercase a with grave	a `		a ⟨BS⟩ `
225	á	Lowercase a with acute	a ´		a ⟨BS⟩ ´
226	â	Lowercase a with circumflex	a ^		a ⟨BS⟩ ^
227	ã	Lowercase a with tilde	a ~	a	a ⟨BS⟩ ~
228	ä	Lowercase u with umlaut	a "		a ⟨BS⟩ "
229	å	Lowercase a with ring	a *		a
230	æ	Lowercase ae with ligature	a e		ae
231	ç	Lowercase c with cedilla	c ,		c ⟨BS⟩ ,
232	è	Lowercase e with grave	e `		e ⟨BS⟩ `
233	é	Lowercase e with acute	e ´		e ⟨BS⟩ ´
234	ê	Lowercase e with circumflex	e ^		e ⟨BS⟩ ^
235	ë	Lowercase e with umlaut	e "		e ⟨BS⟩ "
236	ì	Lowercase i with grave	i `		i ⟨BS⟩ `
237	í	Lowercase i with acute	i ´		i ⟨BS⟩ ´
238	î	Lowercase i with circumflex	i ^		i ⟨BS⟩ ^

LICS Code	Character	Description	Compose Sequence	Fallback Monitor Presentation	Fallback Printer Presentation
239	ï	Lowercase i with umlaut	i "		i ⟨BS⟩ ¨
240	ð	Lowercase eth (Icelandic)	d –	d	d ⟨BS⟩ -
241	ñ	Lowercase n with tilde	n ˜		n ⟨BS⟩ ˜
242	ò	Lowercase o with grave	o `		o ⟨BS⟩ `
243	ó	Lowercase o with acute	o ´		o ⟨BS⟩ ´
244	ô	Lowercase o with circumflex	o ˆ		o ⟨BS⟩ ˆ
245	õ	Lowercase o with tilde	o ˜	o	o ⟨BS⟩ ˜
246	ö	Lowercase o with umlaut	o "		o ⟨BS⟩ ¨
247	œ	Lowercase oe with diphthong	o e	o	oe
248	ø	Lowercase o with slash	o /	o	o ⟨BS⟩ /
249	ù	Lowercase u with grave	u `		u ⟨BS⟩ `
250	ú	Lowercase u with acute	u ´		u ⟨BS⟩ ´
251	û	Lowercase u with circumflex	u ˆ		u ⟨BS⟩ ˆ
252	ü	Lowercase u with umlaut	u "		u ⟨BS⟩ ¨
253	ÿ	Lowercase y with umlaut	y "		y ⟨BS⟩ ¨
254	þ	Lowercase thorn (Icelandic)	p –	p	p ⟨BS⟩
255					

Answers to the Selected Review Questions

Chapter 1

1. VisiCalc, SuperCalc, ProCalc, and Context MBA. (Context MBA was introduced approximately at the same time as Lotus.)

8. 1) Lotus for forecasting that integrates database, spreadsheet, and graphic capabilities.

   2) Lotus for financial analysis whic, again, utilizes and integrates the three components of Lotus.

16. There are four types of indicators: mode, status, time, and date.

23. What-if with a break-even model. What is the break-even point if the selling price is decreased by 2%?

   What-if with the interest rate in a mortgage model. What is the monthly payment if the interest rate is decreased by 1%?

   What-if with an advertising model. What is the estimated total sales if the advertising budget is increased by 7%?

25. A1*A2/A3 = 6.666666

   (A1+A2)/A3 = 1

   A1/A2/A3 = 0.166666

Chapter 2

3. Nine characters.

10. Range Names cannot be longer than 14 characters.

16. There are nine format options: Fixed, Scientific, Currency, Comma, +/-, Percent, Date, Time, and Text.

19. Five.
24. Three.
32. With the /File Text option a formula can be transferred in its original form.
36. No. Yes.

Chapter 3

2. At the A> prompt type TYPE Filename.PRN. This will give you a listing of your file on the monitor. Transfer this to the printer.
6. The at sign (@).
9. No. /Worksheet Page may not override this command if the number of lines specified by /Print, Printer, options, Pg-Length is less than the number of lines covered by /Worksheet Page.
10. To print the exact characters, formulas, date, and so forth in a worksheet or a range.
14. Out of 66 lines per page, only 56 lines are available for use.
16. First use /Worksheet Global Default Printer. Change whatever you would like to change, then use /Worksheet Global Default Update.

Chapter 4

4. No.
6. No.
11. In the @NPV function the cashflows don't need to be equal. In the @PV function all the cashflows must be equal.
16. Seven.
22. @Cell function.
27. 167.29.
33. $1,573.40.
35. @AVG = 81.375   @STD = 72.15770
     @COUNT = 8   @SUM = 651
     @MAX = 220   @VAR = 5,206.734
     @MIN = 1.

Chapter 5

3. One limitation is that you can only use six data ranges. Another limitation is the variety (only five types); a third limitation is that the graphs are only two-dimensional.
4. In an XY graph there must be two sets of data, one for the X-axis and the other for the Y-axis; one of these two data ranges must be X. There is no such limitation in a line graph.
6. The X range is used for labeling the X-axis. It is also used as one of the data ranges in an XY graph and for labeling the pieces of a pie chart.
8. Yes. Your worksheet will have extension WK1; your graph will have extension PIC.
9. No.
11. There is no limit.
13. Two types: horizontal and vertical.
16. The Scale option gives you the opportunity to override the automatic scaling

done by Lotus. This means you can tell Lotus how to fit your data on the X and Y axes.

18. Legends are used to make your graph more understandable. They will tell you, for example, which symbol belongs to which data.

Chapter 6

3. It depends on how you got to the PrintGraph program in the first place. If you got to it from DOS, you will return to DOS. If you got to the program from the Lotus Access System, you will return to the Lotus Access System when you exit.

5. Yes. Press F10.

7. You cannot. You have to go to the worksheet and retrieve the worksheet file, do all your changes there, save it by using /Graph Save, then go to PrintGraph and print the new graph.

12. Yes. Otherwise you will create an ellipse instead of a circle.

16. Minimum is 110 and maximum is 19,200.

18. Action, Pause, Yes makes PrintGraph pause between printing.

Chapter 7

4. Use /Worksheet Delete Row, then specify the row address.

10. The primary key is the first field chosen to sort and the secondary key is the second field chosen to sort. There are no other differences between these two keys.

12. You can search with single criterion, double criteria, OR search, AND serach, multiple criteria, or with wild cards.

15. The Xtract option extracts all the records that meet a particular criteria. The Unique option will extract only the records that have at least one field different from the others.

16. Up to 32 fields.

Chapter 8

5. It stops when the range is filled or the stop value has been reached.

8. No.

11. This will show up at the end of Frequency. For example, 1 means there was one data item that was not included in the bin range.

15. Yes, if the number of columns of the first matrix is equal to the number of rows of the second matrix; otherwise, no.

17. The right-hand side array is the right side of all the equations. For example, in

$$X1 + X2 \quad = \quad 10$$
$$X1 - X2 \quad = \quad 15$$

10 and 15 are the right-hand side array.

18. This command does not provide important statistical measures such as a t-test, Durbin-Watson test, and so on.

Chapter 9

4. Press the **Alt** key and the name of the macro at the same time.

6.   The zero macro will be executed automatically as soon as the worksheet, including this macro, is loaded.
9.   It can be very useful for designing menus and helping non computer experts with easy system access.
13.   The CMD indicator means a macro is being executed.
15.   Press **Ctrl** and **Break** together.
16.   Up to 240.

Chapter 10

3.   No. Some advanced commands do not need arguments; for example, QUIT, RETURN, RESTART, etc.
4.   There are four types of arguments: address or location, numeric value, condition, and string.
7.   /Range Erase.
11.   The macro will not be executed.
12.   No.
16.   Otherwise, Lotus will always choose the first item in the menu.
20.   Three. Read, Write, and Modify.

Chapter 11

4.   Two types: external and internal.
7.   Logical errors.
11.   Because this methodology advocates programming techniques that are easier to develop and maintain. Also, this methodology increases a programmer's productivity.
13.   Random numbers are used for investigation of a random process. For example, in an inspection of a shipment of goods, we must decide to accept or reject the goods. We may take a random sample and, based upon this sample, make a decision.
17.   A subroutine within another subroutine is called a nested subroutine. There are many uses of such a subroutine. For example, a subroutine calculating the net pay may call another subroutine for tax calculation.
18.   If a macro is designed for depreciation calculation, the user does not need to know detailed operations about Lotus to use this function.

Chapter 12

Similar questions have been solved in the chapter.

Chapter 13

Similar questions have been solved in the chapter.

Appendix A

3.   PC DOS for the IBM PC and MS DOS for its clone.
4.   To execute DOS external commands a DOS disk *must* be in one of the drives; internal commands can be executed if the A> prompt is on the screen.

6. Date and Time are used to document files. This means if you save a file it will also save the time and date of the storage.

9. DISKCOPY erases and then copies the source disk to the target disk. Copy will not erase the target disk.

24. At the A> prompt type the following:

COPY CON Mybatch. BAT	(RETURN)
B:	(RETURN)
A:	(RETURN)
DIR/W	(RETURN)
CLS	(RETURN)

(Ctrl and Z to save it)

To execute this batch file, at the A> prompt type Mybatch.

Appendix B

3. The System disk cannot be copied because it is copy-protected.

4. Put DOS in drive A, type DISKCOPY A: B: and press Return. Then follow the prompt.

10. At the A> prompt put the Utility disk into drive A and type INSTALL. Then follow the prompt.

13. It is 123.

Appendix C

2. The file to be transferred must be compatible to the file structure of the destination system. For example, if a system only accepts an ASCII file, your file must be in ASCII format before the transfer can take place.

4. dBASE II and III, VisiCalc, Symphony, DIF, and Jazz.

5. Press the F1 key.

8. You have to use /Print File.

13. It is used to split long labels into a series of shorter ones.

16. Reset will cancel the previous setting. This means, for example, that all your data ranges will be erased.

Appendix D

1. The SIDEWAYS is used to print wide worksheets.

8. Press **F10**.

12. HAL can enhance the operation of Lotus 1-2-3 by providing a more flexible interface, simplifying and speeding up Lotus operations, et cetera.

20. Any software that generates ASCII files is compatible with Lotus. There are numerous software packages of this type on the market.

Index

Lotus Command Menu

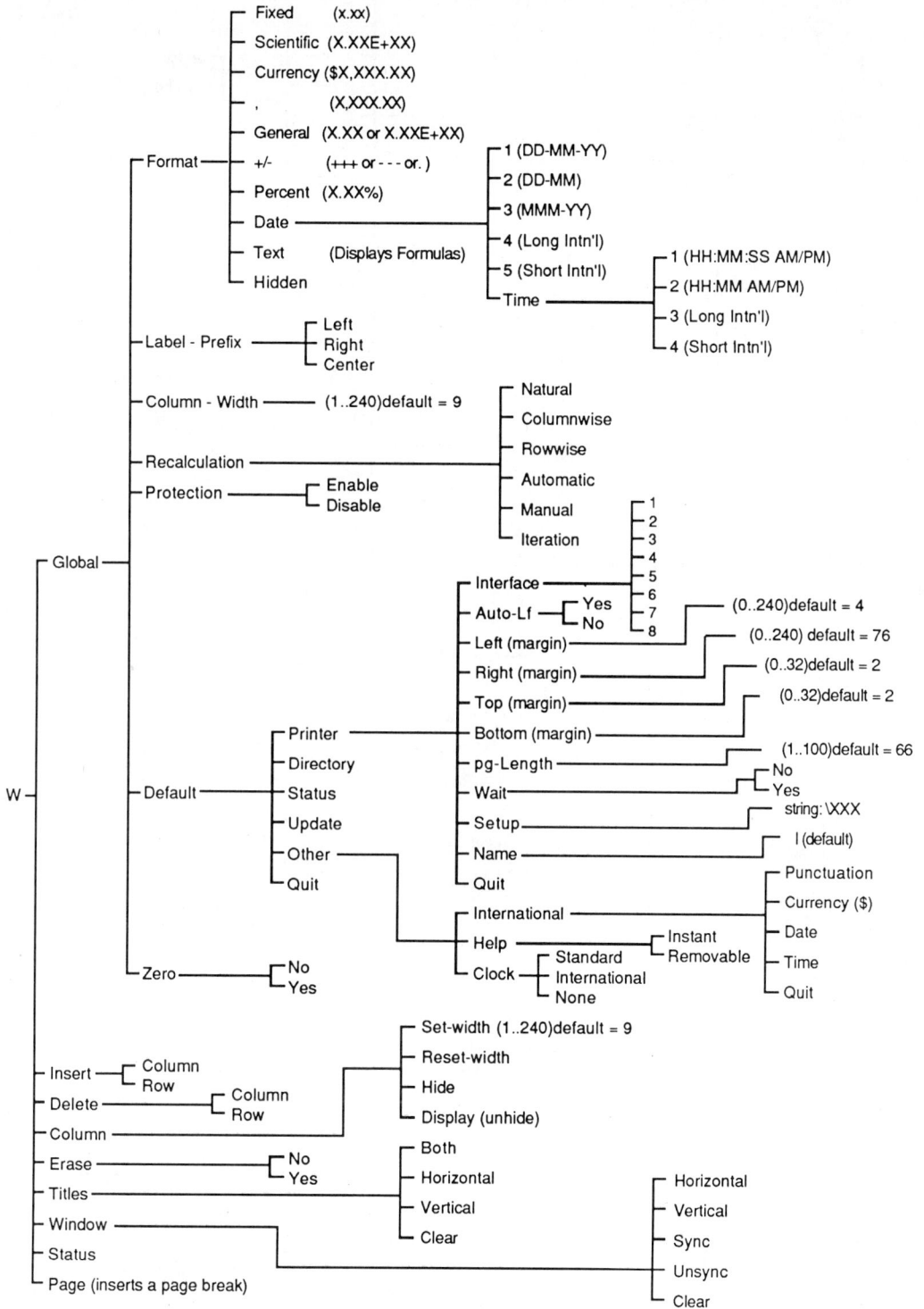

W
- Global
  - Format
    - Fixed (x.xx)
    - Scientific (X.XXE+XX)
    - Currency ($X,XXX.XX)
    - , (X,XXX.XX)
    - General (X.XX or X.XXE+XX)
    - +/- (+++ or - - - or .)
    - Percent (X.XX%)
    - Date
      - 1 (DD-MM-YY)
      - 2 (DD-MM)
      - 3 (MMM-YY)
      - 4 (Long Intn'l)
      - 5 (Short Intn'l)
      - Time
        - 1 (HH:MM:SS AM/PM)
        - 2 (HH:MM AM/PM)
        - 3 (Long Intn'l)
        - 4 (Short Intn'l)
    - Text (Displays Formulas)
    - Hidden
  - Label - Prefix
    - Left
    - Right
    - Center
  - Column - Width — (1..240)default = 9
  - Recalculation
    - Natural
    - Columnwise
    - Rowwise
    - Automatic
    - Manual
    - Iteration
      - 1
      - 2
      - 3
      - 4
      - 5
      - 6
      - 7
      - 8
  - Protection
    - Enable
    - Disable
- Default
  - Printer
    - Interface
    - Auto-Lf
      - Yes
      - No
    - Left (margin) — (0..240)default = 4
    - Right (margin) — (0..240) default = 76
    - Top (margin) — (0..32)default = 2
    - Bottom (margin) — (0..32)default = 2
    - pg-Length — (1..100)default = 66
    - Wait
      - No
      - Yes
    - Setup — string: \XXX
    - Name — I (default)
    - Quit
  - Directory
  - Status
  - Update
  - Other
    - International
      - Punctuation
      - Currency ($)
      - Date
      - Time
      - Quit
    - Help
      - Instant
      - Removable
    - Clock
      - Standard
      - International
      - None
  - Quit
- Zero
  - No
  - Yes
- Insert
  - Column
  - Row
- Delete
  - Column
  - Row
- Column
  - Set-width (1..240)default = 9
  - Reset-width
  - Hide
  - Display (unhide)
- Erase
  - No
  - Yes
- Titles
  - Both
  - Horizontal
  - Vertical
  - Clear
- Window
  - Horizontal
  - Vertical
  - Sync
  - Unsync
  - Clear
- Status
- Page (inserts a page break)

/G

- **Type**
  - Line
  - Bar
  - XY
  - Stacked-Bar
  - Pie
- **X**
- **A**
- **B**
- **C**
- **D**
- **E**
- **F**
- **Reset**
- **View**
- **Save**
- **Options**
  - Legend
    - A
    - B
    - C
    - D
    - E
    - F
  - Format
    - Graph
    - X
    - A
    - B
    - C
    - D
    - E
    - F
    - Quit
      - Graph
      - X
      - A
      - B
      - C
      - D
      - E
      - F
      - Quit
        - Lines
        - Symbols
        - Both
        - Neither
  - Titles
    - First
    - Second
    - X-Axis
    - Y-Axis
  - Grid
    - Horizontal
    - Vertical
    - Both
    - Clear
  - Scale
    - Y Scale
    - X Scale
      - Automatic
      - Manual
      - Lower
      - Upper
      - Format (see/w Global Format)
      - Indicator
      - Quit
    - Skip (1..8192)default = 1
  - Color
  - B & W
  - Data-Labels
    - A
    - B
    - C
    - D
    - E
    - F
    - Quit
  - Quit
- **Name**
  - Use
  - Create
  - Delete
  - Reset
- **Quit**

/D

- **Fill**
- **Table**
  - 1
  - 2
  - Reset
- **Sort**
  - Data-Range
  - Primary-Key
  - Secondary-Key
  - Reset
  - Go
  - Quit
- **Query**
  - Input
  - Criterion
  - Output
  - Find
  - Extract
  - Unique
  - Delete
    - Cancel
    - Delete
  - Reset
  - Quit
- **Distribution**
- **Matrix**
  - Invert
  - Multiply
- **Regression**
  - X- Range
  - Y- Range
  - Output Range
  - Intercept
    - Compute
    - Zero
  - Reset
  - Go
  - Quit
- **Parse**
  - Format-Line
    - Create
    - Edit
  - Input Column
  - Output Range
  - Reset
  - Go
  - Quit

/S

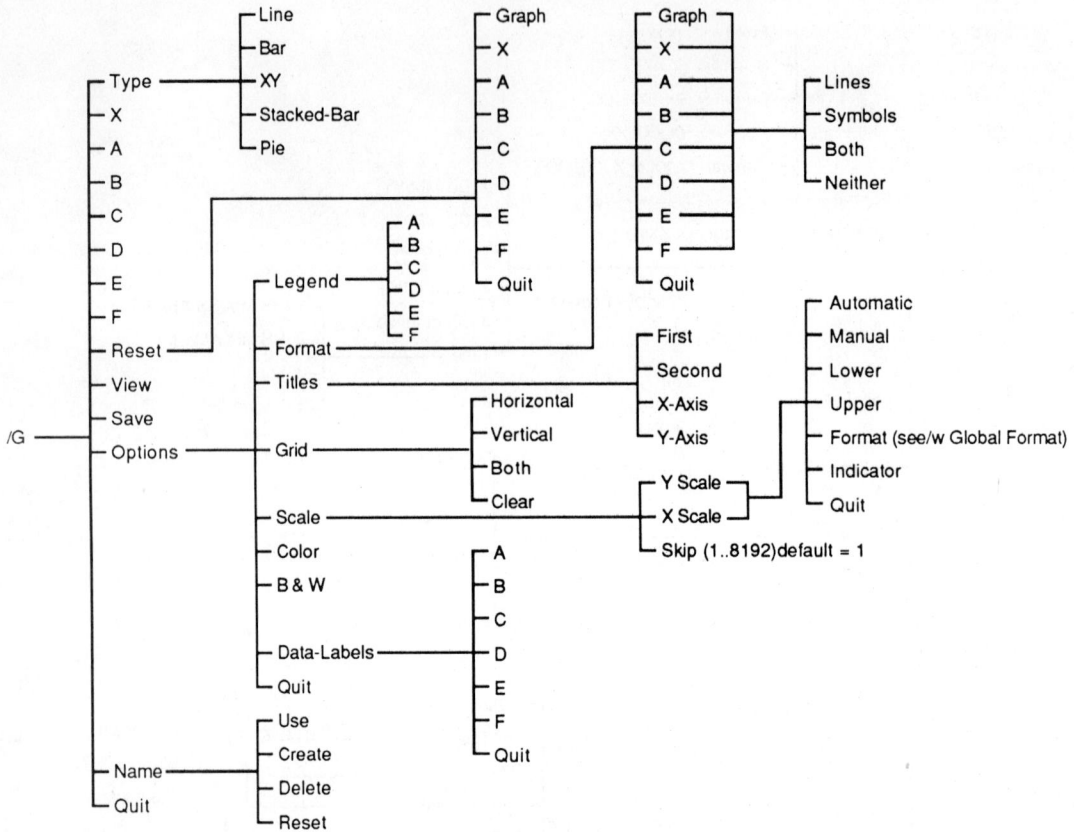

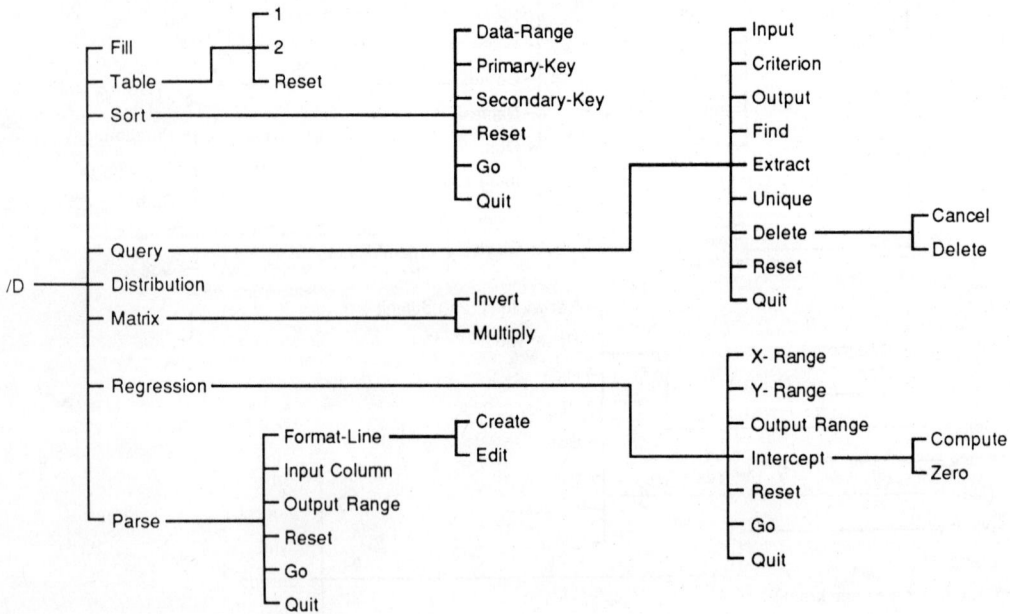

Invoke the DOS Command Interpreter

/Q

- No   Do not end 1-2-3 session
- Yes   End 1-2-3 session

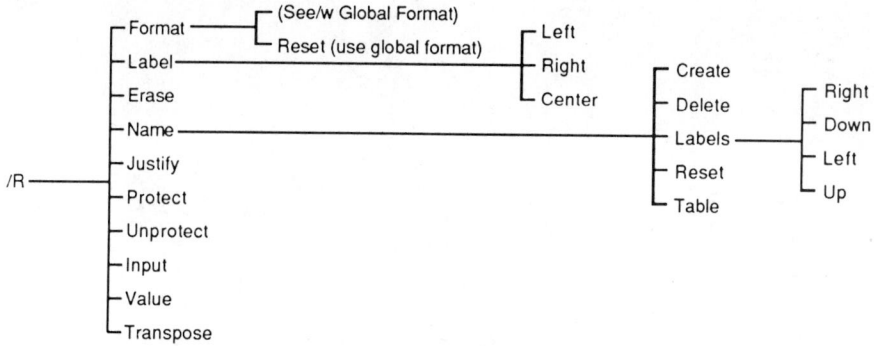

```
/R ─┬─ Format ──┬─ (See/w Global Format)
    │           └─ Reset (use global format)
    ├─ Label ──────┬─ Left
    │              ├─ Right
    │              └─ Center
    ├─ Erase                      ┌─ Create
    ├─ Name ──────────────────────┼─ Delete
    │                             ├─ Labels ──┬─ Right
    ├─ Justify                    ├─ Reset    ├─ Down
    ├─ Protect                    └─ Table    ├─ Left
    ├─ Unprotect                              └─ Up
    ├─ Input
    ├─ Value
    └─ Transpose

/C ─────── Enter range to copy FROM , Enter range to copy TO

/M ─────── Enter range to move FROM , Enter range to move TO

/F ─┬─ Retrieve          ┌─ Copy ──────┬─ Entire file
    ├─ Save              ├─ Add ───────┴─ Named/Specific-Range
    ├─ Combine ──────────┴─ Subtract
    ├─ Extract ──┬─ Formulas
    ├─ Erase     └─ Values            ┌─ Worksheet
    ├─ List ─────────────────────────┼─ Print
    ├─ Import ──┬─ Text              ├─ Graph
    └─ Directory └─ Numbers          └─ Other

/P ─┬─ Printer ─┬─ Range
    └─ File ────┤                  ┌─ Header                ┌─ Left (0..240)default = 4
               ├─ Line            ├─ Footer                ├─ Right (0..240)default = 76
               ├─ Page            ├─ Margins ──────────────┼─ Top (0..32)default = 2
               ├─ Options ────────┼─ Border ──────┐        └─ Bottom (0..32)default = 2
               ├─ Clear           ├─ Setup        ├─ Columns
               ├─ Align           ├─ Pg-Length    └─ Rows              ┌─ As-Displayed
               ├─ Go              ├─ Other ───────┬─ (1..100)default = 66 ├─ Cell-Formula
               └─ Quit            └─ Quit (Return to Print Menu)        ├─ Formatted
                                  ┌─ All                                └─ Unformatted
                                  ├─ Range
                                  ├─ Borders
                                  └─ Format
```

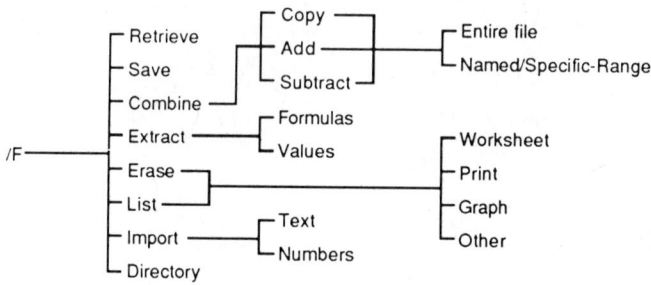

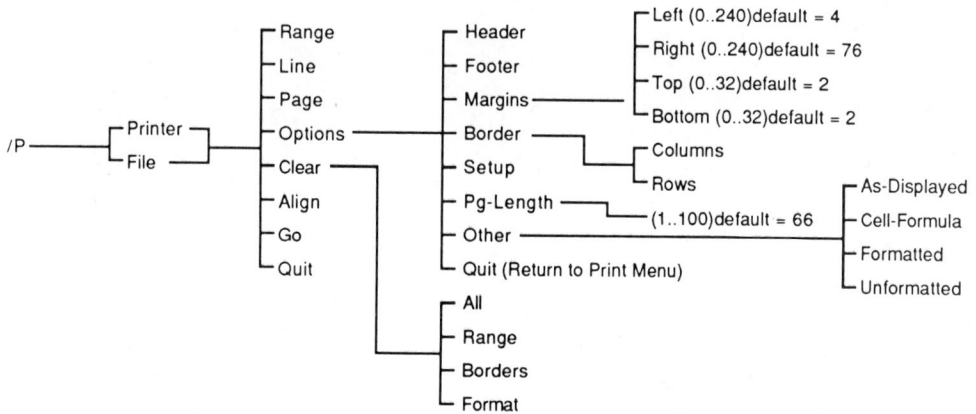